Property of York Mills C.I. English Department		
Name	Class	Year

P9-AOP-582

336-01

ELEMENTS OF
English 11

Douglas Hilker

Sue Harper

Peter J. Smith

Harcourt Canada

Toronto Orlando San Diego London Sydney

Copyright © Harcourt Canada Ltd.

All rights reserved. No part of this publication may be reproduced or transmitted in any form or by any means, electronic or mechanical, including photocopy, recording or any information storage and retrieval system, without permission in writing from the publisher. Reproducing passages from this book without such written permission is an infringement of copyright law.

Requests for permission to photocopy any part of this work should be sent to: Schools Licensing Office, CANCOPY, 1 Yonge Street, Suite 1900, Toronto, ON, M5E 1E5. Fax: (416) 868-1621. All other inquiries should be directed to the publisher.

Every reasonable effort has been made to acquire permission for copyright material used in this text, and to acknowledge such indebtedness accurately. Any errors or omissions called to the publisher's attention will be corrected in future printings.

Canadian Cataloguing in Publication Data

Hilker, Douglas
  Elements of English 11

Includes index.
ISBN 0-7747-1492-1

1. Readers (Secondary). 2. English language – Problems, exercises, etc.
I. Harper, Sue, 1952- . II. Smith, Peter J., 1943- . III. Title.

PE1121.H5384 2001   428.6   C00-932870-X

AUTHORS

Douglas Hilker
Writing Team Leader for the Ontario Curriculum Policy Document for English and Lead Developer for the Ontario Secondary School Grade 10 Literacy Test

Sue Harper
Former Head of English, John Fraser Secondary School, Mississauga, ON, and Developer for the Ontario Secondary School Grade 10 Literacy Test

Peter J. Smith
Education Consultant, Writer for the Ontario Curriculum Policy Document for English, Grades 11 and 12, and General Editor of *The Harcourt Writer's Handbook*

REVIEWERS

The authors and publisher gratefully acknowledge these reviewers for their contribution to the development of this project:

Vicky Armanios, Harbord Collegiate Institute, Toronto District School Board, Toronto, ON
Nancy Lutke Browne, Pinetree Secondary School, Coquitlam School District #43, Coquitlam, BC
Mike Budd, Program Department, Greater Essex County District School Board, Windsor, ON
Cathy Costello, York Region District School Board, Aurora, ON
Sandy Dobec, Ottawa Carleton Catholic District School Board, Ottawa, ON
Noeline Laccetti, St. Martin Secondary School, Dufferin-Peel Catholic District School Board, Mississauga, ON
Rocky Landon, Keewaytinook Internet High School and Limestone District School Board, Kingston, ON
Tim Lee, Marshall McLuhan Catholic High School, Toronto Catholic District School Board, Toronto, ON
John Liandzi, Ernest Manning Senior High, Calgary School District 19, Calgary, AB
Sue McIlveen, Cardinal Newman Catholic Secondary School, Hamilton-Wentworth Catholic District School Board, Stoney Creek, ON
Doris McWhorter, Limestone District School Board, Kingston, ON
Phil Midgely, Pauline Johnson Collegiate and Vocational School, Grand Erie District School Board, Brantford, ON
Murray Richardson, Waterdown High School, Hamilton-Wentworth District School Board, Waterdown, ON
Edmund Tell, Resurrection Catholic Secondary School, Waterloo Catholic District School Board, Kitchener, ON
Kristine van Leenen, Strathcona Senior High, Edmonton School District 7, Edmonton, AB

Editorial Project Manager: Ian Nussbaum
Developmental Editor: Su Mei Ku
Senior Production Editor: Karin Fediw
Copy Editors: Dianne Broad, James Leahy
Production Coordinator: Jon Pressick
Photo Research: Mary Rose MacLachlan

Permissions Editor: Cindy Howard
Cover Design: Sharon Foster Design
Interior Design/Page Composition: Sharon Foster Design
Cover Photographs: Andre Gallant/Image Bank
Cover Illustration: Alex Murchison/Three in a Box Inc.
Printing and Binding: Friesens

∞ Printed in Canada on acid-free paper
1 2 3 4 5   05 04 03 02 01

CONTENTS

UNIT 2   LITERATURE

 **UNIT 3**   MEDIA STUDIES

 **UNIT 4**   THE REFERENCE SHELF

Section One: The English Language

ALTERNATIVE GROUPINGS OF THE SELECTIONS

GENRES

AUTHORS

According to Country of Origin
or Cultural Background

THEMES

War

The World of School

Sports

Welcome to *Elements of English 11*. The purpose of this book is to help you develop the literacy, critical thinking, and communication skills that you will need to pursue your postsecondary educational and career goals. The reading selections cover a wide range of historical and contemporary texts, both literary and informational. The writing activities are similarly wide-ranging, including academic, informational, and creative writing for a variety of purposes and audiences. As well, there are selections and activities to increase your knowledge about language and media and how to use them effectively.

What Is Expected of You

By this point in your education, there is an expectation that you have already acquired a substantial range of academic attitudes, knowledge, and skills, including the following:

- Commitment: You are seriously committed to academic progress and success.
- Persistence: When faced with a challenge, you accept it and find ways to make progress and accomplish the task.
- Equity: You recognize, accept, and respect the diverse communities that contribute to the success and prosperity of Canadian society.
- Research: You know how to access information from a variety of print and electronic sources and make accurate, well-documented notes when doing research.

- Technology: You understand and use computer applications that assist you to do research, organize information, revise and edit your written work, and enhance your written and oral presentations.
- Writing process: You understand the stages of the writing process and use them appropriately to write effectively for a range of purposes and audiences.

What You Can Expect of This Textbook

Unit I Introduction reviews key literacy concepts and skills from earlier grades and introduces you to those that are the focus for this grade. As you work through the reading selections and activities in this unit, you will be able to identify your strengths and weaknesses and set goals for achieving success this year.

Unit II Literature introduces you to a variety of authors from Canada and around the world. The thematically arranged reading selections and activities help you explore the role of language and communication in society ("Ultimate Discourse"), the impact of science and technology in the modern world ("The Real and the Virtual"), perspectives on social and cultural issues ("To Set Our House in Order"), average and not-so-average individuals ("The Average"), the choices individuals make in their daily lives ("The Road Not Taken"), and the meaning of life ("I Let the World Spin On").

Unit III Media Studies focuses on issues raised by the ubiquitous presence of media in today's society.

The Reference Shelf and Glossary

provide you with information, rules, and tips for understanding and using language in a variety of contexts correctly, creatively, and effectively. Glossary items appear in bold the first time they are used in any set of activities.

Icons appear in the Before and After Reading activities and indicate language/grammar activities (⬛▶), independent study activities (📖), and media activities (⚛). The media icon does not appear in the Media Studies unit because most activities in this unit are, by nature, media-related.

Tracking Your Progress

Although the activities in this text will provide you with opportunities to develop, demonstrate, and master a wide variety of language and literacy skills, it is important for you to understand the specific learning expectations you will be required to meet throughout the year. Ask your teacher for the curriculum expectations you will be evaluated on and how you will be required to demonstrate the knowledge and skills described in those expectations.

Your teacher's ongoing assessment of your performances in class and on assignments, projects, tests, and exams will provide you with valuable information on your academic progress. However, you will want to track your own progress toward meeting the course expectations. Some ways you can monitor your progress are as follows:

- Keep a record of your tests and assignments and the feedback you receive on them.
- Keep an up-to-date portfolio of your own work (which will be a helpful source of information when you apply for postsecondary studies) with written reflections on your strengths and weaknesses, clearly articulated goals for future progress, and specific study strategies and work habits you will employ to achieve them.
- Work with peers regularly, recording their feedback on your drafts or rehearsals and using it to improve your work before submitting it for evaluation.
- Create a reading log that tracks the types of texts you have read and what you have read about in both assigned and personally selected readings.
- Keep a response journal in which you record reactions to selections read, presentations heard or made, activities done in class, and results of tests or exams.
- Make a personal word list of new words with their definitions.
- Create a tracking sheet of personal spelling, grammar, or usage errors that you can refer to when doing homework or studying for tests and exams.

We hope you enjoy the book and extend our best wishes as you use it to increase your knowledge and develop your skills.

Doug Hilker
Sue Harper
Peter Smith

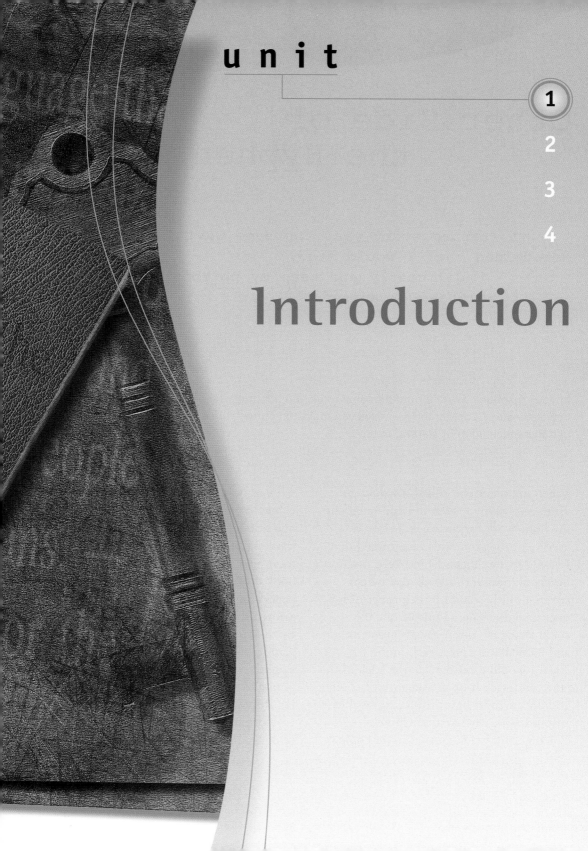

unit

1
2
3
4

Introduction

Other Side of the Hyphen

LYNN TEO

"I started every year the same way:
determined that I would study
diligently and keep my notebook
neat and organised."

BEFORE READING

In your notebook, write a brief personal reflection about starting a new school year or new semester. Consider the promises you make to yourself, the newness of everything, and the anticipation of starting fresh.

When my name was called, I would go up to receive my reader, my duo-tang, and my homework for the week. I started every year the same way: determined that I would study diligently and keep my notebook neat and organised. I would ceremoniously stand up the prongs of my new crisp duo-tang (a purple one if I could swing it), insert my assignments, and meticulously press each prong flat. Then I would carefully lick the back of the label, and stick it on as straight as I could and, in the most beautiful hand possible, I would write my name in Chinese: "Chǎng Ling." (Of course I never could

write as beautifully as I wanted to. The characters would always look unbalanced: one side bigger than the other, strokes too long or too short.) Then I would open my reader and press the centre of the book down with my fingers. Off the pages would rise the smell of those newly printed readers I would smell every year. By this time the teacher would have begun reading. My friends and I hushed our English conversation to repeat after her, phrase by phrase, the story of a Taiwanese family going to the supermarket.

Now, looking at my older brother's set of duo-tangs and readers neatly lined up,

I imagine he also shared a similar ritual in his class at the beginning of each Chinese school year. Year after year, the duo-tangs are still crisp; the assignments inside completed with hardly an error and with beautiful characters all written in mechanical pencil. His readers still look new. I always wanted to be like that.

All signs of my efforts from the beginning of each year are gone. Mayhem surrounds the first week's assignments, which are still neatly attached in each duo-tang. The labels, so neatly stuck on, are missing or partially torn off. The duo-tangs are doodle-ridden and badly dog-eared. Most of the assignments are gone now. Those remaining are loosely tossed in. Chinese characters are mixed in with English notes between my two friends and me whining about the teacher and gossiping about our classmates. Some years are completely missing a duo-tang altogether.

Notebook after notebook, I'm saddened by the years of laziness and apathy and resentment that quickly shadowed my spurt of enthusiasm I had each September. Besides that first day, I passed through most of those Saturday mornings watching the clock, living for noontime when the hand held bell would ring through the halls, and I would run out to meet my parents. Proudly, they'd take us out for lunch at the local noodle house. My mother would order me broad rice noodles with fish balls while my father would ask Owen about his quiz.

Eight years of Chinese school and still those words remain locked doors leading into parts within me I long to find the keys to.

after READING

UNDERSTANDING THE TEXT

1. After rereading your own reflection from "Before Reading," briefly record experiences you have had in common with the writer.

2. Create a **graphic organizer** that captures the main and supporting ideas in this **essay**. As a class, compare your findings.

3. In your notebook, explain the meaning of the title of this **personal essay**.

4. With a partner, examine the **tone** in the first paragraph and the third paragraph. Identify the differences in tone between the two paragraphs, and explain how the writer's **diction**, sentence structures, and use of **antithesis** create the difference in tone. Compare your notes with those of another pair or discuss your findings as a class.

5. In your notebook, explain the difference between the uses of the two sets of parentheses in the first paragraph. (See The Reference Shelf, page 413.)

6. Make a list of the transition words and phrases Lynn Teo uses throughout her essay to unify her writing. (See The Reference Shelf, page 445.)

EXPLORING IDEAS AND IMPLICATIONS

7. Using the content of your "Before Reading" reflection and "Other Side of the Hyphen" as a model, write a personal essay on starting a new school year or semester. Focus on making a distinct change in tone using organization, diction, and sentence structures. With a partner, revise and edit your essay in preparation for submission.

MAKING CONNECTIONS

8. a) Read "The Interview" (pages 71–72). In a small group, discuss the pressures "hyphenated Canadian" students (e.g., French-Canadians, Japanese-Canadians, Italian-Canadians) face that others may not. Use print, electronic, and human resources to enhance your discussion. Write a script in which your group explores one of these pressures.

   b) Pair up with another group to revise your work. Pay close attention to the following: avoiding stereotypes; capturing the **voice** of the **characters**; portraying a realistic situation; maintaining a strong beginning, middle, and end.

   c) Revise, rehearse, and perform your script for the class. ■

E.J. Pratt's "Erosion"

```
"... the forces of nature ...
        have an amazing power ... that is
    even more awesome and devastating
            when it affects human life."
```

BEFORE READING

With a partner, look at the title of the **poem**. Create a **graphic organizer** to record your associations with this word. Be prepared to present your ideas to the class.

The following poem by E.J. Pratt is based on an experience that Pratt had as a boy. He had accompanied his father, a Methodist minister, who had gone to tell a fisherman's wife that her husband and two remaining sons were lost at sea.

Erosion

E.J. PRATT

It took the sea a thousand years,
A thousand years to trace
The granite features of this cliff,
In crag and scarp and base.

It took the sea an hour one night,   5
An hour of storm to place
The sculpture of these granite seams
Upon a woman's face.

Poetic Techniques and Theme in the Poem "Erosion"
(A Student Essay)

STEPHANIE POLANSKY

Introduction:
- poem's theme

- statement of thesis for the essay

Body:
1st paragraph
- parallel structure

The short and powerful poem "Erosion" by E.J. Pratt expresses the theme that the forces of nature represented by the sea have an amazing power to shape the world's geographical features, but that this power is even more awesome and devastating when it affects human life. Pratt emphasizes the power of the sea against nature and humanity through the use of parallel structure, repetition, and effective diction.

The way in which the poet has constructed his poem helps the reader to understand the destructive forces of the sea in carving out the landscape and in affecting human life. The poem consists of two four-line stanzas which are constructed parallel to each other. In addition, the only rhymes in the poem, in lines 2, 4, 6, and 8, emphasize the parallel structure ("trace," "base," "place," "face"), tying the two stanzas together. If we were to write the two stanzas side by side, this parallelism would immediately become obvious. The first two lines of each stanza tell the length of time it took the sea to produce its effect. The last two lines of each stanza describe its effect. This parallel structure sets up a clear contrast between the two situations. The sea takes a thousand years to carve the face of a cliff, but it takes only an hour one night to change the features of a woman by sculpting seams or deep lines in her features. Human beings seem to be more easily affected by the forces of nature, much less able to withstand the devastating effects of the sea.

 Repetition is also used effectively in the poem. In such a short poem, we might not expect to see words or phrases repeated, but Pratt has used repetition to reinforce his description of the awesome power of the sea. In the second line of each stanza, the poet repeats the words from the first line which describe the length of time:

> It took the sea a thousand years,
> A thousand years to trace ... (lines 1 and 2)

> It took the sea an hour one night,
> An hour of storm to place ... (lines 5 and 6)

This repetition emphasizes the power of the sea and also draws our attention to the contrast between the two stanzas. The sea is able to cause changes in humanity far more quickly than it can alter geographical features. Another example of repetition occurs in the use of the word "granite." In the first stanza, "granite" is used in a literal sense to describe the stone of the cliff; in the second stanza it is used figuratively to describe the permanence of the seams etched by the sea on the woman's face. Once again, the repetition has reinforced the idea that the powers of nature can have a swift, destructive, and lasting effect on human beings.

 A third technique used to emphasize the theme is the poet's diction or choice of words. It is interesting to note that the word "granite" (mentioned above) is used as an adjective rather than as a noun describing a very hard and permanent stone. Using the word as an adjective to describe the face of the cliff emphasizes the power of the sea, since granite is harder to wear away than softer stones such as shale or limestone. In using the word to describe the seams on the woman's face, the poet suggests the permanence of the effects

- explanation and examples

- with references to the thesis

2nd paragraph
- repetition

- examples and discussion

- with references to the thesis

3rd paragraph
- poetic diction

- examples
  and
  analysis

of the sea upon the woman. Since granite is also frequently used for gravestones, the word contains a connotation appropriate for the tragic situation in the second stanza. Other words such as "features" (line 3), "sculpture" (line 7), and "face" (line 8) are terms which could describe both the cliff and the woman, reminding us of the parallels and contrasts between the two stanzas. The word "features" can be used to describe physical features or geographical features as well as human facial features. We can refer to the face of a cliff and to the face of a human being. The word "sculpture" is most often associated with carving in stone, and we might have expected the poet to use it in the first stanza to describe the way in which the sea has sculpted or carved the cliff. Instead, Pratt has chosen to use the word in the second stanza to describe the way in which the sea has changed the face of the woman. It might also suggest that the sea, as a sculptor, has done its work deliberately, and with some degree of joy. A sculptor demonstrates talent and control over the stone by carving and changing it. So too, the sea may be demonstrating control over human beings by "sculpting" or permanently changing them. The use of the simple verbs "trace" and "place" seems to suggest the relative ease with which the sea is able to bring about its destructive effects. Perhaps the most effective word chosen by Pratt is "Erosion" for the title. Most readers think of the word as it is used in geography or geology, to describe the slow process of wearing away the landscape over long periods of time. The use of the term "erosion" to describe the effects of nature on the life of a human being is unusual, and the short period of time in which the changes occur in human beings helps to emphasize the contrast and the defencelessness of humans against nature's power.

- with clear
  reference to
  the thesis

Conclusion:
- summary of
  ideas
- with clear
  reference to
  the thesis

This eight-line poem is a good example of the economy of poetic expression. It demonstrates the effects of poetic techniques such as parallel structure, repetition, and the power and beauty of language in describing the awesome forces of nature and their effects on the world around us. Pratt has been able to show the vulnerability of human nature when confronted with the strength of natural forces such as the power of the sea.

after READING

UNDERSTANDING THE TEXT

1. **a)** In your own words, using the background information and the poem itself, **summarize** what Pratt is saying in this poem.

   b) In a small group, come to a **consensus** about whether or not reading the poem without the background would have led you to the same conclusions about its meaning. Be prepared to present your group's viewpoint to the class for discussion.

2. **a)** Identify the rhythm pattern and **rhyme scheme** of the poem. (See The Reference Shelf, pages 423–425.)

   b) The poem maintains a solemn **voice** throughout. In a series of paragraphs, discuss the techniques Pratt uses in his poem to achieve this solemnity.

3. With a partner, examine Pratt's use of the following devices to enhance the **theme** of his poem: **antithesis**, **imagery**, **connotation**. Discuss your observations with the class.

4. Create an outline of Stephanie Polansky's **essay**. Compare your outline with those of your classmates.

5. Examine the writer's use of commas in the second paragraph. Referring to each sentence in which a comma appears, justify its use.

EXPLORING IDEAS AND IMPLICATIONS

6. **a)** In a small group, examine the rough drafts of Pratt's poem. Hypothesize the thought processes that went through the poet's mind as he redrafted his work. Support your hypothesis with direct reference to the drafts and the final product.

   b) Be prepared to present your hypothesis to the class. As a class, vote on the hypothesis that is best presented and validated.

   c) In your notebook, write a paragraph on what we can learn by seeing a poet's writing process.

MAKING CONNECTIONS

7. **a)** Using print and/or electronic sources, research events in Canada's recent history that demonstrate nature's power over humankind. Using the details of one of these events, write your own poem demonstrating nature's power over humans.

   b) With a different partner for each stage, take your poem through the stages of the writing process. Be sure each partner gives written feedback at each stage. ■

What's in This Toothpaste?

"... chalk, water, paint, seaweed, antifreeze, paraffin oil, detergent, peppermint, formaldehyde and fluoride."

BEFORE READING

Canadian law requires food manufacturers to list all ingredients in the food on the package. As a class, discuss the importance and value of this law.

Introduction

Into the bathroom goes our male resident, and after the most pressing need is satisfied it's time to brush the teeth. The tube of toothpaste is squeezed, its pinched metal seams are splayed, pressure waves are generated inside, and the paste begins to flow. But <u>what's in this toothpaste</u>, so carefully being extruded out?

Statement of topic

First ingredient (water)

<u>Water mostly</u>, 30 to 45 per cent in most brands: ordinary, everyday, simple tap water. It's there because people like to have a big gob of toothpaste to spread on the brush, and water is the cheapest stuff there is when it comes to making big gobs. Dripping a bit from the tap onto your brush would cost virtually nothing; whipped in with the rest of the toothpaste the manufacturers can sell it at a neat and accountant-pleasing price. Toothpaste manufacture is a very lucrative occupation.

Second ingredient (chalk)

<u>Second</u> to water in quantity is <u>chalk</u>: exactly the same material that schoolteachers use to write on blackboards. It is collected from the crushed remains of long-dead ocean creatures. In the Cretaceous seas [from the age of dinosaurs], chalk particles served as part of the wickedly sharp outer skeleton that these creatures had to wrap around themselves to keep from getting chomped by all the slightly larger other ocean creatures they met. Their massed graves are our present chalk deposits.

The individual <u>chalk particles</u>—the size of the smallest mud particles in your garden—have kept their toughness over the eons, and now on the toothbrush they'll need it. The enamel outer coating of the tooth they'll have to face is the hardest substance in the body—tougher than skull, or bone, or nail. Only the chalk particles in toothpaste can successfully grind into the teeth during brushing, ripping off the surface layers like an abrading wheel grinding down a boulder in a quarry.

Description

The craters, slashes, and channels that the chalk tears into the teeth will also remove a certain amount of built-up yellow in the carnage, and it is for that <u>polishing function</u> that it's there. A certain amount of unduly enlarged extra-abrasive chalk fragments tear such cavernous pits into the teeth that future decay bacteria will be able to bunker down there and thrive; the quality control people find it almost impossible to screen out these errant super-chalk pieces, and government regulations allow them to stay in.

What it does

In case even the gouging doesn't get all the yellow off, <u>another substance</u> is worked into the toothpaste cream. This is <u>titanium dioxide</u>. It comes in tiny spheres, and it's the stuff bobbing around in white wall paint to make it come out white. Splashed around onto your teeth during the brushing, it coats much of the yellow that remains. Being water soluble it leaks off in the next few hours and is swallowed, but at least for the quick glance up in the mirror after finishing it will make the user think his or her teeth are truly white. Some manufacturers add optical whitening dyes—the stuff more commonly found in washing machine bleach—to make extra sure that glance in the mirror shows reassuring white.

Third ingredient (titanium dioxide)

What it does

<u>These ingredients alone</u> would not make a very attractive concoction. They would stick in the tube like a sloppy white plastic lump, hard to squeeze out as well as revolting to the touch. Few consumers would savour rubbing in a mixture of water, ground-up blackboard chalk and the whitener from latex paint first thing in the morning. To get around that finicky distaste the manufacturers have mixed in a host of <u>other goodies</u>.

Need for other ingredients

To keep the glop from drying out, a mixture including <u>glycerine glycol</u>—related to the most common car antifreeze ingredient—is whipped in with the chalk and water, and to give *that* concoction a bit of substance (all we really have so far is wet coloured chalk) a large helping is added of gummy molecules from the <u>seaweed</u> *Chondrus crispus*. This seaweed ooze spreads in among the chalk,

Three more ingredients

paint and antifreeze, then stretches itself in all directions to hold the whole mass together. A bit of <u>paraffin oil</u> (the fuel that flickers in camping lamps) is pumped in with it to help the moss ooze keep the whole substance smooth.

Two more to come

With the glycol, ooze and paraffin we're almost there. Only <u>two major chemicals are left</u> to make the refreshing, cleansing substance we know as toothpaste. The ingredients so far are fine for cleaning, but they wouldn't make much of the satisfying foam we have come to expect in the morning brushing.

Next ingredient (detergent)

To remedy that, every toothpaste on the market has a big dollop of <u>detergent</u> added too. You've seen the suds detergent will make in a washing machine. The same substance added here will duplicate that inside the mouth. It's not particularly necessary, but it sells.

The only problem is that by itself this ingredient tastes, well, too like detergent. It's horribly bitter and harsh. The chalk put in toothpaste is pretty foul-tasting too for that matter. It's to get around that gustatory discomfort that the manufacturers put in the ingredient they tout perhaps the most of all. This is the <u>flavouring</u>, and it has to be strong. Double rectified peppermint oil is used—a flavourer so powerful that chemists know better than to sniff it in the raw state in the laboratory. Menthol crystals and saccharin or other sugar simulators are added to complete the camouflage operation.

Next ingredient (flavouring)

<u>Is that it? Chalk, water, paint, seaweed, antifreeze, paraffin oil, detergent and peppermint?</u> Not quite. A mix like that would be irresistible to the hundreds of thousands of individual bacteria lying on the surface of even an immaculately cleaned bathroom sink. They would get in, float in the water bubbles, ingest the ooze and paraffin, maybe even spray out enzymes to break down the chalk. The result would be an uninviting mess. The way manufacturers avoid that final obstacle is by putting something in to kill the bacteria. Something good and strong is needed, something that will zap any accidentally intrudant bacteria into oblivion. And that something is <u>formaldehyde</u>—the disinfectant used in anatomy labs.

Final ingredient (formaldehyde as a disinfectant)
Conclusion

<u>So</u> it's chalk, water, paint, seaweed, antifreeze, paraffin oil, detergent, peppermint, formaldehyde and fluoride (which can go some way towards preserving children's teeth)—that's the usual mixture raised to the mouth on the toothbrush for a fresh morning's clean. If it sounds too unfortunate, take heart. Studies show that brushing with <u>just plain water will often do as good a job</u>.

after READING

UNDERSTANDING THE TEXT

1. As a class, discuss your reaction to the **essay**. Explain whether or not knowing the ingredients of a product affects your attitude toward the product.

2. In your notebook, write one sentence that states the **thesis** of this essay. Below it, write a paragraph explaining why the writer would not state the thesis as directly as it is stated in your sentence. Compare your response with that of a classmate.

3. The first sentence of the second paragraph is not a complete sentence. Give a reason why you think this is acceptable or unacceptable in an essay like this.

4. Make a list of 10 technical or scientific words in this essay. Make a second list of colloquial words in this essay. In your notebook, explain why and assess how well the writer has combined technical and nontechnical vocabulary.

5. Identify the probable purpose and **audience** of this essay. In your notebook, write a short **report** explaining how the content, organization, vocabulary, and sentence structure are appropriate to the purpose and audience you identified.

EXPLORING IDEAS AND IMPLICATIONS

6. a) Recall your discussion in the "Before Reading" activity. Write an **opinion essay** on whether you think manufacturers of nonfood products should be required to list the ingredients of their products on the packaging.

   b) Exchange your work with a partner. Comment on your partner's **diction**, **tone**, and use of evidence for support.

   c) Revise your work using your partner's feedback, and prepare it for submission.

7. With a small group, create an advertisement for toothpaste where an ingredient is the focus of the advertisement. Be prepared to share and explain your ad to the class.

MAKING CONNECTIONS

8. Select another short essay in this textbook, photocopy it, and annotate each paragraph in a manner similar to the annotations beside each paragraph of this essay. Write a brief assessment of the essay based on your annotations. ■

"Grandmother" and Esther's Comments

"... her grandmother was her biggest cheering squad—
an ordinary woman who proved extraordinary."

BEFORE READING

As life expectancy in our society gets longer, more young people today can get to know their grandparents and even great-grandparents. List at least three benefits and three challenges that result from these intergenerational relationships. With a partner, discuss your lists and determine whether or not the benefits outweigh the challenges for the two of you.

Grandmother

PAT KERTZMAN

"You'll go far, girl, I know it," Grandmother coached
my lofty dreams, starved for belief in their remotest
possibility. Already I imagined myself philosopher,
already I was secretly in love with words.

She did her daily dance of alchemy, from earth's tender   5
eruptions to simmering pot, trekking back and forth
garden to kitchen to bed in housedress and slippers,
tending the urgencies of home.

That particular wisdom of blood and bone.

Wasn't she the smart one after all, a remedy for each   10
calamity, poison oak to heartache? And wasn't she

the bright one after all, who burned every book
in the house one winter to keep the fire stoked?

Simple woman, small pond, you might think   15
in your educated way. Yet the silent circles
reverberating out and out and beyond sight
anywhere in this world and into the next

With one small stone are made.

Esther's Comments

ESTHER LEIPER-JEFFERSON

Grandmother by Pat Kertzman ... returns
to the loving side of inter-generational
experience. The girl in the poem, evidently
a woman now looking back, is the recipi-
ent of devoted love; her grandmother was
her biggest cheering squad—an ordinary
woman who proved extraordinary.

This fact is emphasized by the persona
telling the story cautioning, "Simple
woman, small pond, you might think."
Not that Grandmother is a college professor or a career woman in the sense that
today's woman thinks of a career. Nor is
Grandmother a fashion model: she wears
a housedress and slippers, and her daily
round is between garden, kitchen, and bed.
Perhaps she *is* educated after all, having
possessed enough books to burn—by
necessity—in a harsh long-back winter.
Isn't she "the bright one after all," always
knowing what to do and how to comfort,
without complaining?

Her daily round does not take her or
her granddaughter very far physically—
and yet she has opened vistas and new

worlds to the child. She may not be
healthy, either. Even going from "earth's
tender eruptions to simmering pot" is
described as a "trek." Perhaps she is infirm.
Going to bed may involve catnaps as well
as her nighttime sleep.

Notice how deftly Kertzman brings
out such details and implied ramifications:
far more succinctly than my trying to
write *about* how she achieves the poem's
power. Grandmother may or may not have
a high IQ; may not have been formally
educated—but she has the wisdom of age,
and the kind of enthusiasm that could
be described as childlike herself. Surely
her granddaughter—like the child with
the moon, pony, and a father's loving
commitment—will be successful throughout life; will be ready in turn to nurture
a new generation.

The poem's closing image is both
simple and profound. All of us have seen
ripples spread as a stone sinks, and have
been amazed or intrigued at the cause-
and-effect of a simple action moving

outward in concentric circles long after the cause seems gone. So Grandmother will die—but the impact she has made on the "small pond" that is her granddaughter will not disappear. Hopefully, the old lady's gift will be passed on.

after READING

UNDERSTANDING THE TEXT

1. In a single sentence, sum up the **narrator**'s memory or attitude toward her grandmother.

2. In a paragraph or two, explain the contrast developed in the poem between the grandmother's "particular wisdom" (**stanza** 3) and the reader's "educated way" (stanza 5).

3. Write an explanation of how the life of a "simple" person like the narrator's grandmother reverberates "out and out and beyond sight."

4. Select one of Esther's observations that helped you better understand and/or appreciate the poem. Write a paragraph in your notebook explaining your choice.

5. With a partner, discuss the effectiveness of the single-line sentence fragment: "That particular wisdom of blood and bone." Be prepared to present your ideas to the class.

EXPLORING IDEAS AND IMPLICATIONS

6. The "small pond" in stanza 5 refers to the age-old debate about whether it is better to be a big frog in a small pond or a small frog in a big pond. Write a **personal essay** explaining whether you think you can make your best contribution to the world in a small or a large **context**.

MAKING CONNECTIONS

7. Look up the term "prose poem" in a dictionary of literary or poetic terminology. (See also The Reference Shelf, page 424.) Find another prose poem in a book of poetry. Write your own comments on the poem using "Esther's Comments" on "Grandmother" as a model. ■

The Life and Work of Aphra Behn

"... Behn's groundbreaking literary career
was characterized by remarkable
productivity."

BEFORE READING

1. Read the **biography** below. With your classmates, discuss the advantages and disadvantages of learning about a writer's life before reading the writer's work.

2. The **poem** by Aphra Behn is entitled "Love Armed." Draw a mind map of ideas you associate with each of the title's words separately and then together.

A Biography of Aphra Behn (1640–1689)

While little is known of Aphra Behn's early life, much is known about her incredible career as a spy, a world traveller, and as England's first professional woman writer. At a young age she travelled to the South American colony of Surinam. Among her adventures there, she is said to have participated in a slave revolt, an experience that left a lasting influence on her and proved to be major influence on her writing. On her return to England in 1664, Behn married a certain Mr. Behn, about whom little is known except that he was a London merchant of Dutch descent who died the year following their marriage, possibly of the plague.

Widowed at 25, "Mrs. Behn," as she referred to herself, was in search of a means to support herself. In 1666, Behn became a spy for King Charles II, a rare position for someone, as she herself said, "with my sex, or in my years." However, her career as a spy was short-lived as she was grossly underpaid for her duties and found herself, in 1668, in a London debtor's prison.

It was in prison that Behn began to write in earnest, taking an unprecedented leap: writing for pay. In 1670, her first play, *The Forc'd Marriage*, was performed at London's Lincoln Inn Fields. Behn wrote upwards of 15 plays, including *The Rover* (1677), *The Roundheads* (1681), and *The City Heiress* (1682). However, later in her career, Behn found that her opportunities as a playwright diminished because of turmoil in the London theatre.

Still possessing the passion to write, and the need to support herself, Behn began writing prose fiction, including *Oroonoko* (1688), which was based on her experiences in Surinam. Not only was *Oroonoko* seen as a breakthrough for women writers, it was at the forefront of a newly developing literary genre: the novel.

Behn was also a prolific poet, publishing her collected poems in 1684. As a poet Behn posed the question, "What has poor woman done that she must be / Debarred from … sacred poetry?" demanding the freedom to assert "my masculine part, the poet in me"—a direct barb at her critics. While their male counterparts were given extraordinary poetic licence, female poets were expected to keep their desires to themselves. Behn's critics considered poems such as "Love Armed" scandalous.

Virginia Woolf, in *A Room of One's Own*, said of Behn that "All women together ought to let flowers fall upon the tomb of Aphra Behn, for it was she who earned them the right to speak their minds." And that she did, not only writing scandalously about the nature of female desire, but publicly satirizing politicians of her time. Behn, as England's first professional woman writer, was buried in Westminster Abbey, a place reserved for royalty, politicians, and writers of high merit.

Love Armed

APHRA BEHN

Love in fantastic triumph sat
Whilst bleeding hearts around him flowed,
For whom fresh pains he did create
And strange tyrannic power he showed.

From thy bright eyes he took the fires   5
Which round about in sport he hurled,
But 'twas from mine he took desires
Enough t'undo the amorous world.

From me he took his sighs and tears,
From thee his pride and cruelty;   10
From me his languishments and fears.
And every killing dart from thee.

Thus thou and I the God have armed
And set him up a deity;
But my poor heart alone is harmed,   15
Whilst thine the victor is, and free.

after READING

UNDERSTANDING THE TEXT

1. a) In your own words, **summarize** the poem.
   b) In a small group, discuss your understanding of the poem and come to a **consensus** on the poet's **theme**. Be prepared to present your group's choice of theme using evidence from the poem.

2. a) Compare the words used to describe what Eros took from the **narrator** and what he took from her lover.
   b) Explain how these words support the idea stated in the last two lines of the poem.

3. The poet writes in the first person **point of view** using "you" instead of "he" or "she" when referring to the lover. With a partner, describe the effect this (**narrative**) design has on the **tone** of the poem and on the reader. Discuss your conclusions with the class.

4. Write a **thesis** based on your opinion of the title "Love Armed." In a short **literary essay**, support your opinion with references to the poem.

EXPLORING IDEAS AND IMPLICATIONS

5. Look back to the mind map you created in the "Before Reading" activity. In your notebook, describe how thinking about the title helped or hindered your reading of the poem.

6. With a partner, look up the **etymology** of the following words: "fantastic," "triumph," "languishments." In your notebook, write a short explanation of how the evolved meanings of these words could change the meaning of the poem.

7. Write a reply, either in poetic or **prose** form, to the narrator in "Love Armed" from her lover's point of view. With a partner, revise and edit your work. Read your revised work to the class or post your final drafts.

MAKING CONNECTIONS

8. a) Using print and/or electronic sources, research the Greek myth of Eros (Cupid) and images of Eros as he has been depicted in art over the centuries (Bronzino, Caravaggio, Bernini). Find information from these sources that helps you better understand "Love Armed." Take notes, being sure to record accurate bibliographic information. (See The Reference Shelf, pages 431–433.)

   b) Use your notes to write a short **informational essay** on Eros and the importance of knowing his history when studying this poem. ■

What I Have Lived For

BERTRAND RUSSELL

"Three passions, like great winds, have blown me
hither and thither, on a wayward course ..."

BEFORE READING

Make a list of things you would like to accomplish in your life. Look over the list and decide which accomplishments are primarily for yourself and which are for others.

Three passions, simple but overwhelmingly strong, have governed my life: the longing for love, the search for knowledge, and unbearable pity for the suffering of mankind. These passions, like great winds, have blown me hither and thither, on a wayward course, over a deep ocean of anguish, reaching to the very verge of despair.

I have sought love, first, because it brings ecstasy—ecstasy so sweet that I would often have sacrificed all the rest of life for a few hours of this joy. I have sought it, next, because it relieves loneliness—that terrible loneliness in which one shivering consciousness looks over the rim of the world into the cold unfathomable lifeless abyss. I have sought it, finally, because in the union of love I have seen, in a mystic miniature, the prefiguring vision of the heaven that saints and poets have imagined. This is what I sought, and though it might seem too good for human life, this is what—at last—I have found.

With equal passion I have sought knowledge. I have wished to understand the hearts of men. I have wished to know why the stars shine. And I have tried to apprehend the Pythagorean power by which number holds sway above the flux. A little of this, but not much, I have achieved.

Love and knowledge, so far as they were possible, led upward toward the heavens. But always pity brought me back to earth. Echoes of cries of pain reverberate in my heart. Children in famine, victims tortured by oppressors, helpless old people a hated burden to their sons, and the whole world of loneliness, poverty, and pain makes a mockery of what human life should be. I long to alleviate the evil, but I cannot, and I too suffer.

This has been my life. I have found it worth living, and would gladly live it again if the chance were offered me.

after READING

UNDERSTANDING THE TEXT

1. In your notebook, summarize the main ideas in this **essay**. Compare your **summary** with a partner.

2. Analyze carefully the organization of the essay. Record, in point form, the purpose or function of each paragraph. Identify the transitional words or phrases that link the paragraphs to each other and to the **thesis** of the essay. (See The Reference Shelf, page 430.) Write a few sentences about the order Russell uses to outline his points or arguments. Be prepared to discuss your ideas with the class.

EXPLORING IDEAS AND IMPLICATIONS

3. In a small group, discuss which of Russell's "passions" is most important. If there is disagreement between at least two groups in the class, conduct a class discussion to reach a **consensus**.

4. Consult a short **biography** of Bertrand Russell in a reference text or on the Internet. Take notes and prepare a short oral **report** evaluating whether his own observations on his accomplishments are valid.

5. a) Using the list that you made for the "Before Reading" activity, write a well-organized short essay discussing three things you would like to accomplish in your life.

   b) After completing your first draft, have a partner read it to check the clarity of expression, the organization, and the links between paragraphs and thesis. Revise and edit your essay to produce a final draft for submission.

MAKING CONNECTIONS

6. Read "If I Can Stop One Heart from Breaking" by Emily Dickinson (page 315). Make notes outlining similarities and differences in the ideas expressed by Russell and by Dickinson. Share your observations with a small group. ■

About Effie

TIMOTHY FINDLEY

"It looked like a ghost ... and then it looked like a great big grey overcoat."

BEFORE READING

In your notebook, describe a person who influenced your life for a brief period of time and then moved away (or you might have moved away).

I don't know how to begin about Effie, but I've got to because I think you ought to know about her. Maybe you'll meet her one day, and then you'll be glad I told you about this. If I didn't, then maybe you wouldn't know what to do.

I don't remember her last name, but that isn't important. The main thing is to watch out for her. Not many people have the name Effie, so if you meet one, take a good look, because it might be her. She hasn't got red hair or anything, or a spot on her face or a bent nose or any of those things, but the way you'll know her is this: she'll look at you as if she thought you were someone she was waiting for, and it will probably scare you. It did me. And then if she lets on that her name is Effie, it's her.

The first time I saw her, she saw me first. I'll tell you.

I came home from school one day, and it was springtime, so I had to put my coat in the cellar stairway because it was all wet. There was a terrific thunderstorm going on and I was on my way upstairs to look at it. But after I put my coat away I thought I'd go into the kitchen, which was right there, and get a glass of milk and a piece of bread. Then I could have them while I was watching.

I went in, and there was a shout.

Maybe it was a scream, I don't know. But somebody sure made a noise and it scared the daylights out of me.

Right then I didn't know what it was. It looked like a ghost, you know, and then it looked like a great big grey overcoat, and it sort of fell at me.

But it was Effie.

Of course, I didn't know her name then, or who she was or anything, but I figured out that she must be the new maid that my mother told me to watch out for because she was coming that day. And it was.

It was then that she gave me that look I told you about—the look that said "Are you the one I'm waiting for"—and then she sat down and started to cry.

It wasn't very flattering to have someone look at you and then burst into tears, exactly. I mean it doesn't make you want to go up and ask them what's the matter with them or anything. But I thought right then that I had to anyway, because I felt as though maybe I'd really let her down by turning out to be just me and everything. You know, I thought maybe she thought it was Lochinvar or someone. I'd seen maids break up like that before, when they didn't like Toronto and wanted to go home. They just sat around just waiting all the time for some guy on a horse.

I soon found out that I was wrong, though.

Effie was waiting all right, but not the way most women do. She knew all about him, this man she wanted—just when he'd come and what it would be like, all that stuff. But the man she was waiting for certainly didn't sound like any man I'd ever heard of.

She just called him "him," and sometimes it was even "they," as if there were a thousand of them or something.

That first afternoon, for instance, when I went up to her and asked her what was wrong, she sort of blew her nose and said: "I'm sorry, I thought you were him." Then she looked out of the window beside her and shook her head. "But you weren't. I'm sorry."

I couldn't figure out whether she meant "I'm sorry I scared you" or "I'm sorry you weren't this man I was expecting." But I guess it didn't matter because she really meant it, whichever way it was. I liked that. I didn't know anybody who went around saying they were sorry as though they meant it, and it made a big change. So I got my glass of milk and piece of bread and sat down with her.

"Would you like some tea? I'll make some," she said.

"I'm not allowed to drink tea, but I could have some in my milk. I'm allowed that. My mother calls it Cambridge tea."

"Cambric—" She stood up.

"I thought it was Cambridge. I thought my mother said Cambridge tea."

"No, cambric. Cambridge is a school," she said.

Then she smiled. Boy, that was certainly some smile. And it was then she told me her name and where she came from. Howardstown.

I'd seen it once—it was all rocks and chimney stacks and smoke. I saw it from the train and it didn't exactly make you want to go out and live there. Howardstown had that sort of feeling that seems to say "I wish everyone would go away and leave me alone for a change." So you can see what I mean. And that's where Effie came from. So knowing that, you could tell why she preferred to come to Toronto to wait for this man she was expecting.

About that. I had to ask her but I didn't know how. I mean when somebody flings themselves at you like that, how do you go about asking them why? You can't say "Gee, you sure did behave sort of peculiar just then." You can see what I mean. It would just be rude.

So I sat there drinking my milk; and while she waited for the kettle to boil, she came over and sat down beside me at the table.

"Do you like the rain?" she asked me.

"Sometimes."

"Like today? Like now?"

"Sometimes."

She gave up on that and said: "When does your brother come in?" instead.

"Bud? Oh, he doesn't come in till it's time to eat. He plays football."

"In the rain?"

"No, I guess not. I don't know, then. Maybe he's over at Teddy Hartley's. He goes over there sometimes."

"Oh." She didn't know about Teddy Hartley and Bud being such great friends.

I began to wonder if when Bud came in she'd leap at him too. I had a picture of Bud's face when she scared him. The trouble was that he'd probably start right out with his fists. He was like that. If you surprised him or anything, he just started swinging. With his eyes closed—he didn't care who you were. Sometimes you can really get hurt that way. Surprising Bud.

When I thought of that, I thought maybe I should warn her. But I couldn't figure out how to say that, either. It was the same sort of thing. I thought of saying, "By the way, if my brother comes in, don't go leaping out at *him*—or *else*!" But before I could, the kettle boiled.

Effie got up and put some of the hot water into the teapot. "Always warm the pot," she said, "first. Then pour it out and put in the tea leaves. Like this. Then you pour the boiling water over them—see? Or else you don't get any flavour. Remember that."

I do. My first lesson in how to make tea. She came back and sat down.

"Now it has to steep." I remember that, too.

She folded her hands.

Her hair was black and it was tied in a big knot at the back. She had brown eyes that sort of squinted and she had a smell like marmalade. Orange marmalade. And she looked out of the window.

Then she said that the tea had steeped itself for long enough and was ready. She filled my glass because I'd drunk all my milk. I hoped my mother wouldn't come in and see me.

Effie said: "Your mother told me I could have a cup of tea every afternoon at four o'clock. It's four-fifteen now." And she poured her own cup.

I got back to what I wanted to know.

"That sure is some thunderstorm out there," I said.

"Yes." She went very dreamy. "That's why I thought you were him."

"Who?" I certainly would have made a terrific spy. Why, you wouldn't have known I really cared at all, the way I asked that.

"Him."

"Who's that?"

"There has to be thunder, or he won't come."

"Why is that? Is he afraid you'll hear him or something?" I let myself get sarcastic like that because I thought it was time I got to the bottom of things.

"On a cloud," she whispered. "A big black cloud. That's a rule."

All those other men always come on horses—white horses. Not Effie's. A big black cloud. I felt pretty strange when she came out with that one. It sort of scared me.

"Will he take you away?"

"Of course he will. That's why he's coming. That's why I'm waiting."

"Do you wait for him all the time?"

"Oh no. Not always. Only when it rains. Then I get prepared."

I looked around, but there weren't any suitcases or anything. I wondered what she meant by "prepared."

"That's why I thought you were him. There had just been a pretty big thunder and there was lightning and then you were there. I even thought I heard music."

"Maybe my mother has the radio on."

I listened, but she didn't.

"Did you hear anything?" she asked.

"You mean like music?"

"Yes."

"No, I didn't think so. I can't remember, maybe I did—"

"You *did*!" She leapt up. I got scared again. "Did you, did you? Tell me if you did. Tell me. Did you hear it? The music? Did you hear it?"

"I don't know."

"Oh, but you said ..."

Then she sat down and it looked like she might cry again.

"Do you want Howardstown?" I asked. I had to say something.

But she said: "No, thank you."

"Wouldn't you like to go back?"

"No, thank you."

"I was there once. It was pretty."

I lied again, but I thought maybe I had to for her sake. Then I lied again.

"I was there in the summertime. We spent our whole summer holiday there because we liked it so much. Don't you want to go back?"

"No————thank you."

That long line there is where she blew her nose.

"Don't you want to see those nice rocks and everything? I liked those."

Then I thought of something. I thought I had it.

"Effie?"

"Yes?"

"Doesn't it rain there?"

"In Howardstown?"

"Yes."

"Of course it does."

"But does it thunder?"

"Of course it does."

"And lightning?"

"Certainly."

"Oh."

I guess it wasn't such a brilliant idea after all. So I thought again.

"Did he say he'd meet you here—I mean in Toronto?"

That at least made her laugh, which was something. It was nice when she laughed.

"Of course not. Don't be silly. Why, if I went to Timbuctoo he'd just as soon find me there. Or in Madagascar even. I don't have to wait around in any old Toronto."

"Oh."

I was trying to think where that was. Madagascar.

"Besides, it's not just me he's after."

That really got me. I thought he *was* after Effie.

Then she looked at me and all of a sudden I felt it. That it wasn't just some knight in shining armour she had in mind. Or some crazy man on a black cloud, either. No, sir. Whoever he was, he surely was coming. You could tell that just from the way she looked.

Then she said: "Some day when I know you better, I'll tell you. Right now it's four-thirty."

And she put her cup into the sink and washed it. And my glass and the plate from my bread and butter. She ran the water over them and she sang a song.

And it rained and it rained and it rained.

But there was no more thunder.

That was over.

The next time it was the middle of the night. About two weeks later.

There was another of those storms. I didn't wake up at first, but then there was a crash of thunder that really did shake my bed. I mean it. I nearly fell out, even.

I called out in a whisper to Bud, but he was asleep. I forgot to tell you we sleep in the same room. Anyway, I knew I didn't *have* to be afraid, so it didn't matter that he didn't wake up. Thunder doesn't scare me when you can look at it—I even like watching it—but when it's night-time and everyone is asleep but you, then you begin to wonder if it really is just thunder. And sometimes you begin to think that maybe somebody will come and grab you when you can't hear them because of the noise. I wondered if that was what Effie meant.

"Thunder and lightning and music," she'd said. It was like that. If there was ever thunder and lighting and music, then he'd come.

I began to get scared. There was thunder all right, and there was lightning, but there wasn't any music.

Then there was.

I didn't exactly think I'd sit around to make sure. I thought I'd better tell my mother.

Thunder and lighting and music. Yes, there certainly was music all right. It was faint, but it was there. Maybe I'd better warn Effie too, I thought. Mother first, and then Effie.

I went into the hallway. My mother's door was open, and she was lying there only covered with the sheet because it was so hot. She was asleep, though. The street lamp shone through the window and I can remember the metal smell of the screens. They smelt sort of electric.

"Mother."

She sort of moved.

"Hey, Mother."

I was very quiet, but I had to wake her up. I could hear that music even more now.

"Neil?"

She rolled over towards me and took my hand. I could tell she really didn't want to wake up. Maybe she'd been dreaming. Our dad was away.

"I'm sorry, but I had to."

"Are you sick?"

"No."

"Then what is it?"

"Can I get in with you?"

"All right. Pull the cover up. That's right."

We lay there and heard the rain.

"Now tell me about it. Can't you sleep?"

"No." I didn't know whether to begin. "Mother, has Effie ever talked to you?"

"What about?"

"I don't know. But she said to me that if there was rain, and if there was thunder, and if there was lightning, then maybe something would happen."

"The end of the world?" Mother laughed very quietly.

"No, I don't mean that. Some man."

"A man? What do you mean?"

"Well, she said if there was thunder and lightning and everything, to watch out for music. Because if there was music too, then he'd come."

"*Who'd* come, dear?"

"This *man*. This man she's waiting for."

"Well, if she's waiting for him, then it's all right."

I guess she didn't take it very seriously.

"Besides," she said, "there isn't any music."

"Yes there is."

"There is?"

She sounded serious *now* all right.

"Yes, I heard it. That's why I woke you up. I thought maybe we'd better tell her so she could be ready."

"Ready? Does she ... does she really know who he is?"

"Well, she seemed to. She never said his name or anything. She just said that—"

"And you heard it? The music, you really heard it?"

"Yes."

"Now don't joke with me, Neil. This may be very serious."

"Spit. Honestly, I really heard it."

"Where from?"

"I don't know. I just heard it."

My mother got out of bed.

All this time the thunder was getting louder and the lightning was like daylight.

"Well, we'll wake her up and ask her what it's all about. Is Bud awake?"

"No."

"Leave him, then."

She tried to turn on the lights, but they didn't work. (That always happened two or three times a year in those big storms. Toronto never worked when you needed it to.) So we went into the hall in the dark.

Effie's room was at the top of the stairs. Very small, but it was the only one we had for her. It used to be mine. It had a sloping ceiling.

We knocked on her door.

No answer.

It was pitch black. Effie always pulled the blinds. My mother went over and opened them and a bit of light came in. And then we saw that she wasn't there. Her bed was all slept in and everything, but she wasn't there.

My mother let out a yell. Very quiet, but it was certainly a yell.

We didn't know what to do.

We went out into the hall again.

"Shall I get Bud?" I asked.

"No. No, not yet." She was trying to get calm. Very calm. And then she was all right.

"Maybe we'd better go and look downstairs. We can get some candles from the dining room."

We started down the staircase. Halfway down we heard the music again.

Very low it was. No words or anything, just the tune. It didn't seem to come from anywhere in particular—it was just there.

We stood still and listened. If we hadn't been so scared, it would have been pretty. I mean it was a good tune. One that you could hum.

My mother caught my hand and we started down again.

"Dining room," she whispered.

The dining room was down the hall, and beyond it there was a sun room, all glass windows, and in the summertime, screens.

We got into the dining room all right, and from there the music was louder.

Then we saw her.

She was in the sun room, watching from the windows. All her black hair fell down her back. When there was lightning she stood up, and when there wasn't she sat down. All the time she sort of rocked to and fro to the sound of the music.

She was crying—but she had that wonderful smile.

Just once, when the music stopped, she said something. I don't know what it was because she said it too quietly for me to hear. And the reason she said it when the music stopped was because *she* was the

music. *She* was. It was Effie singing.

My mother and I didn't bother her, though. She looked so happy there—even with the tears down her face—and as my mother said, "It doesn't hurt people to sing once in a while. Even at night."

So we went back to bed and my mother said would I like to sleep with her, and I said yes. We got in and we thought about Effie downstairs.

"Do you know?"

"No. Do you?"

"No."

Then later on—I think it was about three months later—Effie came to my mother and said she'd been called away.

"Where to, dear?" my mother asked her.

"Just away," said Effie, like a princess. "And so I've got to go."

My mother didn't ask her because Effie had been such a good person in the house, and Mother knew that if she had to go away then she had to, and it was honest. You never had to think about that with Effie—she always told the truth and everything had a reason. Even if you didn't get to know what it was.

We certainly hated to see her leave us. Even Bud was sad about it, and he was never much good with maids. He used to be too shy with them.

Before she left, she gave me a set of toy animals, little ones—a pig and a cow and a horse and four sheep—all in a box. She knew that I had this toy farm.

And for Bud she had a box of toy soldiers. Only they were very peaceful soldiers, just standing at ease, and there was a little sentrybox too, for them to go into when it rained.

She gave my mother a hankie with an M on it because my mother's name is Margaret. It was real linen and she still has it.

The day she left, she was having a cup of tea just before she went to get on the streetcar and I found her in the kitchen just like the first time. I had some flowers for her. Little ones, that she could carry without them getting in the way.

And she looked at them and said: "That's his favourite colour." (They were purple.) And she thanked me.

So I asked her right then and there.

"Tell me who he is."

She smiled and winked at me.

"That's a secret."

"But is he real? Will he really come for you some time? Please tell me."

Then she did this wonderful thing. She got down on her knees and put her arms around me and her head against me. I remember looking down at her hair underneath her hat.

And she said: "Don't worry about me." Then she got up.

"Now it's time to go. Thank you for the flowers."

She picked up her suitcase and went in to say goodbye to my mother.

"Do you want Neil to take you to the streetcar?"

"No, thank you, Mrs. Cable. I'll be all right. It's such a lovely day."

I think we both knew what she meant.

I didn't watch her go. Not at first. But then I ran out to see her before she turned the corner. Then she did—and was gone.

Effie.

So you can see what I mean. It still worries me. And that's why I want you to be sure—to be *sure* to recognize her when you see her. She'll look at you, just like she did at me that first day in the kitchen, as though you were someone she was looking for. But if she does, don't be scared. This man, I don't know who he is, but if it's Effie he wants, then he's all right.

after READING

UNDERSTANDING THE TEXT

1. This **story** is ambiguous and can be interpreted in a variety of ways. Discuss with a partner your ideas about the mysterious behaviour of Effie. Find evidence in the story to back up your opinions. Compare your conclusions with those of another pair of students and try to reach a **consensus**.

2. Reread the story and find examples of the **narrator** talking (or writing) directly to the reader. Discuss with a partner the effectiveness of this **narrative** technique used in the story, and record your conclusions in your notebook.

EXPLORING IDEAS AND IMPLICATIONS

3. a) Imagine that Effie has written a letter to the young boy a year or two after her departure. What would she have to say about the mysterious, unidentified man? about the young boy? Write the body of the letter from Effie.
   b) Have a partner read your letter and comment on how well you have captured the **character** of Effie and the mystery of the story.
   c) Revise your letter based on your partner's comments.

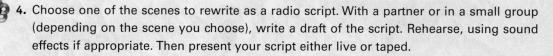

4. Choose one of the scenes to rewrite as a radio script. With a partner or in a small group (depending on the scene you choose), write a draft of the script. Rehearse, using sound effects if appropriate. Then present your script either live or taped.

MAKING CONNECTIONS

5. Read the story "To Set Our House in Order" (page 138). One of the adults in the story who relates to Vanessa and gives her information is her mother's sister, Aunt Edna. In your notebook, compare the influences of Effie and Aunt Edna on the young narrators of the stories. ■

To Everything There Is a Season

ALISTAIR MACLEOD

"... I am not so much surprised as touched by a pang
of loss at being here on the adult side of the world."

BEFORE READING

Describe a time of the year when it is important for you and your family to be together.
Be prepared to present your choice to the class.

*I am speaking here of a time when I was
eleven and lived with my family on our
small farm on the west coast of Cape Breton.
My family had been there for a long, long
time and so it seemed had I. And much of
that time seems like the proverbial yesterday.
Yet when I speak on this Christmas 1977,
I am not sure how much I speak with the
voice of that time or how much in the voice
of what I have since become. And I am not
sure how many liberties I may be taking
with the boy I think I was. For Christmas is
a time of both past and present and often the
two are imperfectly blended. As we step into
its nowness we often look behind.*

We have been waiting now, it seems,
forever. Actually, it has been most
intense since Hallowe'en when the first
snow fell upon us as we moved like muffled
mummers upon darkened country roads.

The large flakes were soft and new then
and almost generous, and the earth to
which they fell was still warm and as yet
unfrozen. They fell in silence into the
puddles and into the sea where they
disappeared at the moment of contact.
They disappeared, too, upon touching
the heated redness of our necks and hands
or the faces of those who did not wear
masks. We carried our pillowcases from
house to house, knocking on doors to
become silhouettes in the light thrown
out from kitchens (white pillowcases
held out by whitened forms). The snow
fell between us and the doors and was
transformed in shimmering golden beams.
When we turned to leave, it fell upon
our footprints, and as the night wore on
obliterated them and all the records of
our movements. In the morning everything was soft and still and November
had come upon us.

My brother Kenneth, who is two and a half, is unsure of his last Christmas. It is Hallowe'en that looms largest in his memory as an exceptional time of being up late in magic darkness and falling snow. "Who are you going to dress up as at Christmas?" he asks. "I think I'll be a snowman." All of us laugh at that and tell him Santa Claus will find him if he is good and that he need not dress up at all. We go about our appointed tasks waiting for it to happen.

I am troubled myself about the nature of Santa Claus and I am trying to hang on to him in any way that I can. It is true that at my age I no longer *really* believe in him, yet I have hoped in all his possibilities as fiercely as I can; much in the same way, I think, that the drowning man waves desperately to the lights of the passing ship on the high sea's darkness. For without him, as without the man's ship, it seems our fragile lives would be so much more desperate.

My mother has been fairly tolerant of my attempted perpetuation. Perhaps because she has encountered it before. Once I overheard her speaking about my sister Anne to one of her neighbours. "I thought Anne would *believe* forever," she said. "I practically had to tell her." I have somehow always wished I had not heard her say that as I seek sanctuary and reinforcement even in an ignorance I know I dare not trust.

Kenneth, however, believes with an unadulterated fervour, and so do Bruce and Barry, who are six-year-old twins. Beyond me there is Anne who is thirteen and Mary who is fifteen, both of whom seem to be leaving childhood at an alarming rate. My mother has told us that she was already married when she was seventeen, which is only two years older than Mary is now. That, too, seems strange to contemplate and perhaps childhood is shorter for some than it is for others. I think of this sometimes in the evenings when we have finished our chores and the supper dishes have been cleared away and we are supposed to be doing our homework. I glance sideways at my mother, who is always knitting or mending, and at my father, who mostly sits by the stove coughing quietly with his handkerchief at his mouth. He has "not been well" for over two years and has difficulty breathing whenever he moves at more than the slowest pace. He is most sympathetic of all concerning my extended hopes, and says we should hang on to the good things in our lives as long as we are able. As I look at him out of the corner of my eye, it does not seem that he has many of them left. He is old, we think, at forty-two.

Yet Christmas, in spite of all the doubts of our different ages, is a fine and splendid time, and now as we pass the midpoint of December our expectations are heightened by the increasing coldness that has settled down upon us. The ocean is flat and calm and along the coast, in the scooped-out coves, has turned to an icy slush. The brook that flows past our house is almost totally frozen and there is only a small channel of rushing water that flows openly at its very centre. When we let the cattle out to drink, we chop holes with the axe at the brook's edge so that they can drink without venturing onto the ice.

The sheep move in and out of their lean-to shelter, restlessly stamping their feet or huddling together in tightly packed groups. A conspiracy of wool against the cold. The hens perch high on their roosts with their feathers fluffed out about them, hardly feeling it worthwhile to descend to the floor for their few scant kernels of grain. The pig, who has little time before his butchering, squeals his displeasure to the cold and with his snout tosses his wooden trough high in the icy air. The splendid young horse paws the planking of his stall and gnaws the wooden cribwork of his manger.

We have put a protective barricade of spruce boughs about our kitchen door and banked our house with additional boughs and billows of eel grass. Still, the pail of water we leave standing in the porch is solid in the morning and has to be broken with the hammer. The clothes my mother hangs on the line are frozen almost instantly and sway and creak from their suspending clothespins like sections of dismantled robots: the stiff-legged rasping trousers and the shirts and sweaters with unyielding arms outstretched. In the morning we race from our frigid upstairs bedrooms to finish dressing around the kitchen stove.

We would extend our coldness half a continent away to the Great Lakes of Ontario so that it might hasten the Christmas coming of my oldest brother, Neil. He is nineteen and employed on the "lake boats," the long flat carriers of grain and iron ore whose season ends any day after December 10, depending on the ice conditions. We wish it to be cold, cold on the Great Lakes of Ontario, so that he may come home to us as soon as possible. Already his cartons have arrived. They come from different places: Cobourg, Toronto, St. Catharines, Welland, Windsor, Sarnia, Sault Ste. Marie. Places that we, with the exception of my father, have never been. We locate them excitedly on the map, tracing their outlines with eager fingers. The cartons bear the lettering of Canada Steamship Lines, and are bound with rope knotted intricately in the fashion of sailors. My mother says they contain his "clothes" and we are not allowed to open them.

For us it is impossible to know the time or manner of his coming. If the lakes freeze early, he may come by train because it is cheaper. If the lakes stay open until December 20, he will have to fly because his time will be more precious than his money. He will hitchhike the last sixty or hundred miles from either station or airport. On our part, we can do nothing but listen with straining ears to radio reports of distant ice formations. His coming seems to depend on so many factors which are out there far beyond us and over which we lack control.

The days go by in fevered slowness until finally on the morning of December 23 the strange car rolls into our yard. My mother touches her hand to her lips and whispers "Thank God." My father gets up unsteadily from his chair to look through the window. Their longed-for son and our golden older brother is here at last. He is here with his reddish hair and beard and we can hear his hearty laugh. He will be happy and strong and confident for us all.

There are three other young men with him who look much the same as he. They, too, are from the boats and are trying to get home to Newfoundland. They must still drive a hundred miles to reach the ferry at North Sydney. The car seems very old. They purchased it in Thorold for two hundred dollars because they were too late to make any reservations, and they have driven steadily since they began. In northern New Brunswick their windshield wipers failed, but instead of stopping they tied lengths of cord to the wipers' arms and passed them through the front window vents. Since that time, in whatever precipitation, one of them has pulled the cords back and forth to make the wipers function. This information falls tiredly but excitedly from their lips and we greedily gather it in. My father pours them drinks of rum and my mother takes out her mincemeat and the fruitcakes she has been carefully hoarding. We lean on the furniture or look from the safety of sheltered doorways. We would like to hug our brother but are too shy with strangers present. In the kitchen's warmth, the young men begin to nod and doze, their heads dropping suddenly to their chests. They nudge each other with their feet in an attempt to keep awake. They will not stay and rest because they have come so far and tomorrow is Christmas Eve and stretches of mountains and water still lie between them and those they love. After they leave we pounce upon our brother physically and verbally. He laughs and shouts and lifts us over his head and swings us in his muscular arms. Yet in spite of his happiness he seems surprised at the appearance of his father, whom he has not seen since March. My father merely smiles at him, while my mother bites her lip.

Now that he is here there is a great flurry of activity. We have left everything we could until the time he might be with us. Eagerly I show him the fir tree on the hill which I have been watching for months and marvel at how easily he fells it and carries it down the hill. We fall over one another in the excitement of decoration.

He promises that on Christmas Eve he will take us to church in the sleigh behind the splendid horse that until his coming we are all afraid to handle. And on the afternoon of Christmas Eve he shoes the horse, lifting each hoof and rasping it fine and hammering the cherry-red horseshoes into shape upon the anvil. Later he drops them hissingly into the steaming tub of water. My father sits beside him on an overturned pail and tells him what to do. Sometimes we argue with our father, but our brother does everything he says.

That night, bundled in hay and voluminous coats, and with heated stones at our feet, we start upon our journey. Our parents and Kenneth remain at home, but all the rest of us go. Before we leave we feed the cattle and sheep and even the pig all that they can possibly eat, so that they will be contented on Christmas Eve. Our parents wave to us from the doorway. We go four miles across the mountain road. It is a primitive logging trail and there will be no cars or other vehicles upon it. At first the horse is wild with excitement and lack of exercise and my brother has to stand at the front of the sleigh and lean backwards on the reins. Later he settles down to a trot and still later to a walk as the mountain rises before him. We sing all the Christmas songs we know and watch for the rabbits and foxes scudding across the open patches of snow and listen to the drumming of partridge wings. We are never cold.

When we descend to the country church we tie the horse in a grove of trees where he will be sheltered and not frightened by the many cars. We put a blanket over him and give him oats. At the church door the neighbours shake hands with my brother. "Hello, Neil," they say. "How is your father?"

"Oh," he says, just "Oh."

The church is very beautiful at night with its festooned branches and glowing candles and the booming, joyous sounds that come from the choir loft. We go through the service as if we are mesmerized.

On the way home, although the stones have cooled, we remain happy and warm. We listen to the creak of the leather harness and the hiss of runners on the snow and begin to think of the potentiality of presents. When we are about a mile from home the horse senses his destination and breaks into a trot and then into a confident lope. My brother lets him go and we move across the winter landscape like figures freed from a Christmas card. The snow from the horse's hooves falls about our heads like the whiteness of the stars.

After we have stabled the horse we talk with our parents and eat the meal our mother has prepared. And then I am sleepy and it is time for the younger children to be in bed. But tonight my father says to me, "We would like you to stay up with us a while," and so I stay quietly with the older members of my family.

When all is silent upstairs Neil brings in the cartons that contain his "clothes" and begins to open them. He unties the intricate knots quickly, their whorls falling away before his agile fingers. The boxes are filled with gifts neatly wrapped and bearing tags. The ones for my younger brothers say "from Santa Claus" but mine are not among them any more, as I know with certainty they will never be again. Yet I am not so much surprised as touched by a pang of loss at being here on the adult side of the world. It is as if I have suddenly moved into another room and heard a door click lastingly behind me. I am jabbed by my own small wound.

But then I look at those before me. I look at my parents drawn together before the Christmas tree. My mother has her hand upon my father's shoulder and he is holding his ever-present handkerchief. I look at my sisters, who have crossed this threshold ahead of me and now each day journey farther from the lives they knew as girls. I look at my magic older brother who has come to us this Christmas from half a continent away, bringing everything he has and is. All of them are captured in the tableau of their care.

"Every man moves on," says my father quietly, and I think he speaks of Santa Claus, "but there is no need to grieve. He leaves good things behind."

after READING

THINKING AND UNDERSTANDING

1. With a partner, read the second paragraph ("We have been waiting...") of this **story** aloud. Select two or three words that describe the **mood** created in the paragraph. Be prepared to explain why you selected the words you did to describe the mood.

2. Explain how any three details in this story reveal important information about the feelings and relationships of the **characters** in the story.

3. Give one reason why there are few cases of direct speech in this story.

4. Time is important in this story. State one important idea about time that is presented in this story and explain how it is developed.

5. Although this story is a **memoir** of his youth, the **narrator** tells it in the present tense. Explain how this fact provides an extra level of meaning to the last paragraph of the story.

EXPLORING IDEAS AND IMPLICATIONS

6. With a partner, find out more about Cape Breton Island in a Canadian encyclopedia or on the Internet. Explain to the class how knowledge about Cape Breton Island helps the reader to understand better one or two details presented in the story.

7. **Debate** the following resolution: Be It Resolved that Commercialization Has Ruined the True Meaning of Santa Claus (or Christmas). (See The Reference Shelf, pages 455–458.) Research may be necessary to help you prepare your arguments.

MAKING CONNECTIONS

8. **a)** As an independent study, research the life and work of MacLeod. Make notes, being sure to record accurate bibliographic information. (See The Reference Shelf, pages 431–433.) Consider how knowing background information about MacLeod helps you to better understand the story.

   b) Find and read another story written by Alastair MacLeod. Compare and contrast it with "To Everything There Is a Season."

   c) Present your findings to the class. Consider using visuals and sound to enhance your presentation. ■

Getting Carried Away With Shoes

ALYSE FRAMPTON

"... the Bata Shoe Museum celebrates footwear
and shoemaking not as a footnote to fashion
but as a window on human history."

BEFORE READING

1. As a class, make a list of what our own old shoes can tell us about our past.

2. In your notebook, write about whether or not it is important that you own brand-name shoes.

Clad in a designer suit and a silk scarf, Sonja Bata looks like she shops in the exclusive boutiques of Toronto's Bloor Street, not on icebound islands in the Arctic or in the dusty market towns of Tibet. But Bata, businesswoman, philanthropist and founder of North America's largest shoe museum, will go just about anywhere to get what she wants.

In 1992 she travelled by single-engine plane to the Arctic community of Grise Fiord on Ellesmere Island, one of the most remote places on earth. "I'd heard of an elderly Inuit woman there who was known for making bearded sealskin boots, or *kamiks*, the traditional way," says Bata.

"Of course, I wanted to commission a pair for our collection."

Bata found the old woman without difficulty. "She kept completely silent while her daughter translated my proposal," Bata recalls. "Then all at once she started to roar with laughter. Finally the old lady wiped her eyes and spoke. The daughter translated: 'My mother says that chewing the sealskin is very hard. Therefore her price to make the boots is a new set of teeth!'"

The woman may have been joking, but the bargain wouldn't have been unusual among the many that Bata has struck during more than 50 years of amassing the superb collection now housed in the

Toronto museum that bears her name. Opened in 1995, the Bata Shoe Museum celebrates footwear and shoemaking not as a footnote to fashion but as a window on human history. Its collection includes such treasures as woven funerary shoes from a royal tomb in ancient Thebes, 15th-century German foot armour and crowd-pleasers like Madonna's hot-pink platform pumps.

Explaining how she came to acquire nearly 10,000 shoes and related artifacts that span 4,500 years, Bata says simply, "I married a shoe man." Her husband is the international shoe manufacturer and retailer Thomas Bata. The Batas, for generations the village cobblers of Zlin, Czechoslovakia, had made their fortune by mechanizing their country's shoe industry and becoming a world supplier of footwear. In 1939, as the Nazis advanced across Europe, Thomas Bata immigrated to Canada and began anew.

When the couple wed in 1946, Sonja was studying architecture in her native Switzerland. It wasn't long, however, before she was helping to rebuild the family business. On visits to company plants around the world, she applied her interest in design to product development and to adapting traditional footwear for mass production.

Realizing that local styles were losing ground to Western ones, Bata began gathering shoes to preserve the heritage they represented. When the collection overflowed the archives of the Bata company's Toronto headquarters, she decided to create a museum.

Designed by Canadian architect Raymond Moriyama, the three-storey, $12-million museum is a striking structure often likened to a shoe box with its lid ajar.... [T]he museum's founder is greeting visitors behind a shoe-shaped reception desk. "People arrive thinking, 'What kind of wacky place is this, a footwear hall of fame?' " Bata breaks into a wide grin. "They leave saying shoes are more interesting than they ever dreamed possible. That's my mission."

The first crude foot wrappings were probably improvised from bark and other plant materials. Actual evidence of early foot apparel came with the 1991 discovery of a virtually intact 5,300-year-old human now known as the Iceman. Complementing a finely designed coat of animal skins and fur, the man's ingenious leather shoes had an upper flap sewn onto a bottom sole, with a socklike, net liner to hold grasses for insulation, and laces made of grass rope.

Shoemaking is one of the oldest crafts in the world. In virtually every early civilization, skilled craftsmen used hand tools and techniques that were to remain essentially unchanged for thousands of years. Shoes themselves, however, have undergone countless changes. They have been used not only for work, sport and play but also to display status and even express religious beliefs. In ancient Egypt, Greece and Rome, shoes were an established symbol of rank, worn mainly by the rich and powerful. In the Yoruba culture of Nigeria, royal status was indicated by the quantity of beads and patterns on boots.

In the 14th century, shoes with comically long, pointed toes were all the rage. Although the style seems more appropriate to a court jester than a gentleman, the fashion was no laughing matter and ultimately forced King Edward III of England to put his foot down. In 1363 an edict was issued decreeing a 15-centimetre toe for commoners, a 30-centimetre toe for gentlemen and a 60-centimetre toe for nobility.

For most of history, fashionable footwear was the preserve of the well-to-do. Others thought themselves lucky to own a single sturdy pair of work shoes. All that changed when shoemaking was mechanized in the 19th century, displacing handwrought shoes with cheaper, factory-made products.

No longer defined by the narrow tastes of a ruling elite, today's footwear fashions are driven by popular and street culture. Through highly paid product endorsements, celebrity athletes like Donovan Bailey and Michael Jordan have helped push the mania for designer athletic shoes that has gripped North America since the 1970s.

Meanwhile, handcrafted shoes have come full circle and are now a luxury reserved for royalty and their ilk. Arab oil princesses were kept in rhinestone-studded sandals by craftsmen at the Rayne company in London until it folded in 1992, while Prince Charles is shod by British shoemakers at John Lobb Limited.

The Bata Shoe Museum explores all these themes with a deliberately playful touch, says former curator Jonathan Walford, who [in 1998] left to launch his own consulting business. A charming guide to the collection, he takes the inherent humour in his former job very seriously. "It seems to be part of our culture that footwear is seen as necessary but somehow frivolous," he says. "That paradox is what the museum plays on."

In fact, the museum has gained international attention for its sometimes irreverent treatment of an offbeat subject. Its rich and varied educational program covers topics that range from shoe and foot fetishism to the role of shoe prints in crime detection. For the past two years [1997 to 1999], museum staff created a display about shoes and horticulture for a local flower show. Among the items shown were Dutch wooden clogs with flat bottoms to tamp the earth for tulip planting, and from Japan, a 20-centimetre-high stilted shoe worn to pick pears.

One group of sixth graders is visiting the museum as part of a social studies project. "Show me your shoes and I'll tell you who you are," Walford proclaims. A red high heel is the tip-off for an aristocrat's shoe, the guide tells the children; in late 17th-century France, such shoes were worn only at the court of Louis XIV. In fact, the term "well-heeled" originated from the upper-class fashion of high-heeled footwear. The elite of late-Renaissance

Europe favoured elevated shoes that gave them a literal leg up on their social inferiors while protecting their feet from the muck of the street.

Platform shoes, which came into vogue around 1600 and were worn by both men and women, had initially been adopted by wealthy Venetians. The style in its most exaggerated form made the wearer, who often needed the assistance of two servants to maintain balance, appear as much as two feet taller. The elite scorned the style as it filtered down to the lesser classes, and last to wear it in Venice were street prostitutes, who wanted to stand head and shoulders above the competition.

An exquisitely embroidered silk slipper represents an extreme example of foot mutilation perpetrated in the name of beauty. Just eight to 15 centimetres long, such slippers once covered a woman's foot crippled by the Chinese custom of foot binding. Initiated in the royal courts of the 10th century, the painful procedure was finally banned in 1911. The resulting "lotus" feet looked like tiny hooves and almost immobilized a woman. A symbol of high status, they were also considered powerfully erotic.

Also compelling is an ivory sandal from India that belonged to a follower of the Jain religion, a main tenet of which is avoiding the destruction of life. Its sole rests on a thin-sided, five-centimetre-high hollow platform that helps its wearer avoid crushing insects underfoot.

The collection also includes a pair of cowboy boots, donated by Robert Redford, that owes more to Hollywood than the Old West. The dandyish stacked heel, pointed toe and decorative stitchery were inspired by Spanish equestrian leather gear: A boot with a tapered toe slid easily into the stirrup, and the raised heel helped it stay there. The style made its way from Spain to Mexico and from there to the United States, where it was popularized by Tom Mix westerns during the 1920s.

An installation called Star Turns is the museum's biggest crowd-pleaser. A glitzy array of celebrity footwear is displayed onstage under a flashing marquee, behind which a screen shows footage about the original owners. Here, a pair of low-heeled black pumps worn by Indian Prime Minister Indira Gandhi shares the spotlight with Marilyn Monroe's saucy red stilettos. Here, too, are Elton John's outrageous rhinestone-studded platforms, rivalled in popularity by a fuchsia pump made for Diana, Princess of Wales.

"All About Shoes," the museum's main exhibition, is complemented by installations in three smaller galleries with more specialized themes. The bearded sealskin *kamiks* that drew Sonja Bata to Ellesmere Island, for example, were destined for the Indigenous Gallery, which has showcased the collection's 500 traditional handmade boots gathered from across the Arctic Circle. "Even the Inuit who've seen the boots here are amazed," says Walford.

Although the museum will continue to collect shoes and related objects from around the world, Bata's aim is to make it a centre of footwear scholarship, with an emphasis on Native American and circumpolar footwear. "Preserving footwear helps enlarge our knowledge of a disappearing way of life," she says.

The museum's most recent exhibition, "Paduka: Feet and Footwear in the Indian Tradition," has special meaning for Bata. It was during her early travels in India and Pakistan as the young wife of a shoe magnate that her fascination with traditional footwear took root.

Some of her first acquisitions were proudly displayed in her Toronto home. "Other people put porcelain bowls on their shelves," Bata recalls. "Mine were filled with Indian *paduka*—ivory and silver platform sandals with superbly shaped knobs that fit between the wearer's toes. To my eye, nothing could be more beautiful."

For a second, the footwear museum founder sounds faintly abashed. "I'm afraid I just get carried away with shoes."

—*Originally published July 2000*

UNDERSTANDING THE TEXT

1. Record your initial reactions to the Bizarro cartoon. Compare your reactions with those of another student. Try to explain why your reactions are similar or different.

2. Humour often depends on hyperbole. (See The Reference Shelf, page 423.) Explain how Dan Piraro has used visual and rhetorical hyperbole in his cartoon to increase the humorous effect.

3. List five of the most interesting facts that you learned about shoes from "Getting Carried Away with Shoes." Compare your list with those of two other students, looking at the similarities and differences among your lists and discussing the reasons for your choices.

4. a) Explain how the opening descriptions of Sonja Bata used in the first two paragraphs help engage the reader.
   b) The writer uses an anecdote in the third paragraph. What does this anecdote add to the article?

5. a) Reread the article and cluster ideas from the article under appropriate subheadings. Compare your headings with the rest of the class and come to a **consensus** on a list of subheadings.
   b) Using these subheadings, create an outline that the writer might have made before she wrote her article.

 6. With a partner, write one sentence from the article that demonstrates each of the following: adjective phrase, adjective clause.

EXPLORING IDEAS AND IMPLICATIONS

7. a) In a paragraph, **summarize** the social comment Dan Piraro is making about modern Western society. Refer specifically to the cartoon in your explanation.
   b) In a second paragraph, agree or disagree with Piraro's commentary and explain your **point of view** with examples from your experiences.

MAKING CONNECTIONS

8. Read either "The Branding of Learning" (pages 379–382) or "As You Can See from My Brand Name Clothing, I Am NOT Poor" (pages 384–385). In a short, well-constructed **essay**, show how the Bizarro cartoon illustrates society's obsession with consumerism. ■

What Do I Remember of the Evacuation?

JOY KOGAWA

BEFORE READING

1. In your notebooks, respond to the following two statements:
   - We remember only the good times from our childhood.
   - Parents should not protect children from hard times.

2. As a class, discuss your knowledge of the evacuation of Japanese Canadians in Canada during the Second World War.

What do I remember of the evacuation?
I remember my father telling Tim and me
About the mountains and the train
And the excitement of going on a trip.
What do I remember of the evacuation?   5
I remember my mother weeping
A blanket around me and my
Pretending to fall asleep so she would be happy
Though I was so excited I couldn't sleep
(I hear there were people herded   10
Into Hastings Park like cattle.
Families were made to move in two hours
Abandoning everything, leaving pets
And possessions at gun point.
I hear families were broken up   15
Men were forced to work. I heard
It whispered late at night
That there was suffering) and
I missed my dolls.

What do I remember of the evacuation?   20
I remember Miss Foster and Miss Tucker
Who still live in Vancouver
And who did what they could
And loved the children who gave me
A puzzle to play with on the train.   25
And I remember the mountains and I was
Six years old and I swear I saw a giant
Gulliver of Gulliver's Travels scanning the horizon
And when I told my mother she believed it too
And I remember how careful my parents were   30
Not to bruise us with bitterness
And I remember the puzzled look of Lorraine L
Who said "Don't insult me" when I
Proudly wrote my name in Japanese
And Tim flew the Union Jack   35
When the war was over but Lorraine
And her friends spat on us anyway
And I prayed to the God who loves
All the children in his sight
That I might be white.   40

after READING

UNDERSTANDING THE TEXT

1. **a)** Reread the **poem**, making a list of information Kogawa assumes readers know about
   the evacuation.
   b) Write down questions you still have about the evacuation as a result of reading the
   poem, and using print and/or electronic sources, find answers to your questions.
2. In a small group, using specific references to words and phrases in the poem, show how
   the **tone** of the narration changes from the beginning to the end of the poem. Explain how
   this helps establish the poem's **theme**. Be prepared to compare your conclusions with
   those of other members of the class.

3. Nine lines in the poem are contained within parentheses. (See The Reference Shelf, page 413.) Explain Kogawa's use of this device in light of the theme of the poem.

4. With a partner, examine the structure of the poem. Together, write an explanation of how each of the following enhances the meaning of the poem: free verse, absence of **stanzas**, line divisions, lines containing one or two words. (See The Reference Shelf, pages 423–427.)

EXPLORING IDEAS AND IMPLICATIONS

5. a) In a small group, create a choral reading of this poem. Use your voices in a variety of ways. Include music, sound effects, and visuals to enhance your presentation. (See The Reference Shelf, pages 460–461.)

 b) As a class, create a feedback form for these presentations. Assess the performance of one other group, discussing your assessment with the presenting group.

6. Research the steps the Canadian government has taken to compensate Japanese Canadians sent to internment camps during the war. In a **persuasive essay**, argue for or against these actions. Have a partner comment on your work, focusing specifically on the main idea, use of organizational patterns to develop that idea, and use of transitions. (See The Reference Shelf, pages 441–443.) Revise and edit your writing.

MAKING CONNECTIONS

7. Read Alistair MacLeod's "To Everything There Is a Season" (pages 32–36). Create a **thesis** and write an **essay** comparing and contrasting the growing up experiences described in "What Do I Remember of the Evacuation?" and MacLeod's **story**. Take the essay through the writing process in preparation for submission. ■

My Canada

TOMSON HIGHWAY

"My eyes lit up, my heart gave a heave,
        and I felt a pang of homesickness
    so acute I actually almost hurt."

BEFORE READING

In a small group, brainstorm characteristics on which a designation of "Number One Country in the World" should be based. Be prepared to discuss your ideas with the class.

Three summers back, a friend and I were being hurtled by bus through the heart of Australia, the desert flashing pink and red before our disbelieving eyes. It never seemed to end, this desert, so flat, so dry. For days, we saw kangaroos hopping off into the distance across the parched earth. The landscape was very unlike ours—scrub growth with some exotic species of cactuses, no lakes, no rivers, just sand and rock and sand and rock for ever. Beautiful in its own special way, haunting even—what the surface of the moon must look like, I thought to myself as I sat there in the dusk in that almost empty bus.

I turned my head to look out of the front of the bus and was suddenly taken completely by surprise. Screaming out at me in great black lettering were the words "Canada Number One Country in the World." My eyes lit up, my heart gave a heave, and I felt a pang of homesickness so acute I actually almost hurt. I was so excited that it was all I could do to keep myself from leaping out of my seat and grabbing the newspaper from its owner.

As I learned within minutes (I did indeed beg to borrow the paper from the Dutchman who was reading it), this pronouncement was based on information collected by the United Nations from studies comparing standards of living for every nation in the world. Some people may have doubted the finding (what about Switzerland, Denmark, Sweden and even Australia or New Zealand?), but I didn't, not for an instant.

Where else in the world can you travel by bus, automobile or train (and the odd ferry) for 10, 12 or 14 days straight and see a landscape that changes so dramatically, so spectacularly. The Newfoundland coast with its white foam and roar; the red sand beaches of Prince Edward Island; the graceful curves and slopes of Cape Breton's Cabot Trail; the rolling dairy land of south shore Quebec; the peerless, uncountable maple-bordered lakes of Ontario; the haunting north shore of Lake Superior; the wheat fields of Manitoba and Saskatchewan; the ranch land of Alberta; the mountain ranges, valleys and lush rainforests of the West Coast. The list could go on for 10 pages, and still only cover the southern section of the country, a sliver of land compared with the North, whose immensity is almost unimaginable.

Have you ever seen the barrens of Nunavut? Have you ever laid eyes on northern bodies of freshwater vaster than some inland seas, titans like Great Bear and Great Slave Lakes? Have you ever seen the icebergs and whales of Hudson Bay, the gold sand eskers of northern Saskatchewan, northern Manitoba's rivers, rapids, water-falls and 10,000 lakes, all with water so clean you can dip your hand over the side of your canoe and drink it? Have you ever had the privilege of getting off a plane on a January day at a remote settlement in the Yukon and having the air hit your lungs with a wallop so sharp you gasp quite audi-bly—air so clean, so crisp you swear you see it sparkle pastel pink, purple and blue in the midmorning light?

It has been six years in a row now that the United Nations has designated Canada the number one country in which to live. We are so fortunate. We are water wealthy and forest rich. Minerals, fertile land, wild animals, plant life, the rhythm of four

distinct, undeniable seasons, the North—we have it all.

Of course Canada has its problems. We'd like to lower our crime rate, but it is under relative control, and the fact is, we live in a safe country. We struggle with our health-care system, trying to find a balance between universality and afford-ability. But no person in this country is denied medical care for lack of money, no child need go without a vaccination. Oh yes, we have our concerns, but in the global scheme of things we are so well off. Have you ever stopped to look at the oranges and apples piled high as mountains in supermarkets from Sicamous, B.C., to Twillingate, Nfld.? Have you paused to think about the choice of meat, fish, vegetables, cheese, bread, cereals, cookies, chips, dips and pop we have? Or even about the number of banks, clothing stores and restaurants?

And think of our history. For the greater part, the pain and violence, tragedy, horror and evil that have scarred for ever the history of too many countries are largely absent from our past. There's no denying we've had our trials and times of shame, but dark though they may have been, they pale by comparison with events that have shaped many other nations.

Our cities, too, are gems. Take Toronto, where I have chosen to live. My adopted city never fails to thrill me with its racial, linguistic, cultural—not to mention lifestyle—diversity. On any ordinary day on the city's streets and subway, in stores and restaurants, I can hear the muted ebb and flow—the sweet chorus—of 20 differ-ent tongues. At any time of day, I can feast on food from six different continents, from Greek souvlakia to Thai mango salad, from Italian prosciutto to French bouillabaisse, from Ecuadorian empanada to Jamaican jerk chicken, from Indian lamb curry to Chinese lobster in ginger and green onion (with a side order of greens in oyster sauce). Indeed, one could probably eat in restaurants every week for a year and never have to eat of the same cuisine twice.

And do all these people get along? Well, they all live in a situation of relative harmony, cooperation and peace. They certainly aren't terrorizing, torturing and massacring one another. They're not igniting pubs, cars and schools with explosives that blind, cripple and maim. And they're not killing children with machetes, cleavers and axes. Dislike—rancour—may exist in pockets here and there, but not, I believe, hatred on the scale of such blistering intensity that we see elsewhere. Is Canada a successful experiment in racial harmony and peaceful coexistence? Yes, I would say so, proudly.

Much as I often love and admire the countries I visit and their people, I can't help but notice when I go abroad that most people in France look French, most in Italy, Italian. In Sweden they look Swedish and in Japan they look Japanese. Beautiful, absolutely beautiful. But where's the variety? I ask myself. Where's the mix, the spice, the funk?

Well, it's here, right here in Canada—my Canada. When I, as an aboriginal citizen of this country, find myself thinking about all the people we've received into this homeland of mine, this beautiful country, when I think of the millions of people we've given safe haven to, following agony, terror, hunger and great sadness in their own home countries, well, my little Cree heart just puffs up with pride. And I walk the streets of Toronto, the streets of Canada, the streets of my home, feeling tall as a maple.

after READING

1. a) Create a two-column chart. In one column, list Highway's arguments that convince you that Canada is the best place. In the other, list those arguments that do not convince you.

   b) Within a small group appoint a leader to organize your discussion. Have group members discuss their reactions to the **essay** and why they feel the way they do. As each member of the group speaks, jot down the arguments made so you can build on or disagree with specific points when it is your turn to speak.

   c) Have one member of the group **summarize** the points made within the group for the class.

2. a) Explain how the construction of the second sentence in paragraph 4 complements the ideas in that paragraph.

   b) Explain how Highway's series of questions create the main idea in paragraph 5.

3. List the problems Highway acknowledges Canada has. In your notebook, describe the impact this information has on the effectiveness of his argument.

EXPLORING IDEAS AND IMPLICATIONS

4. In a small group, create a 30-second television advertisement designed to convince the International Olympic Committee to hold the next summer or winter Olympic games in Canada. Use the content of Tomson Highway's essay as your starting point. Design a **storyboard** or a shooting script for the advertisement and present the ad to the class using both visual and audio aids. Be prepared to explain your design and production choices.

MAKING CONNECTIONS

5. Read the poem "Unnatural Causes" by Lillian Allen (pages 151–153). With a partner, create a **dialogue** between Allen and Highway based on the ideas in their writing in which they discuss their views of Canada. Revise and rehearse your dialogue before you present it. ■

Excerpt From the Novel
Green Grass, Running Water

THOMAS KING

"Americans are independent … Canadians are dependent."

BEFORE READING

From a dictionary or companion to Canadian literature, make notes on the following people: Susanna Moodie, Pauline Johnson, Archibald Belaney, John Richardson. Be prepared to discuss your findings with the class.

In this excerpt from Thomas King's humorous novel about five Blackfoot Indians living in Alberta, Latisha, the manager of the Dead Dog Café, knows that something is different about the four tourists (who just happened to share their names with four long-dead Canadian authors) who have just entered her diner, but she's not quite sure what it is.

The second wave of tourists arrived just before five. Latisha got off the stool and took a deep breath. Dinner was the toughest shift. At lunch, everyone was still energetic, looking forward to what lay ahead. After five, tourists tended to sag, get grouchy. Food was never quite right. Service was always too slow. The adventure of the day had floated away, and all they had to look forward to was a strange bed in a strange motel.

"Bus in," Latisha shouted into the kitchen.

"What flavor?" Billy shouted back.

The bottom half of the bus was crusted with dirt, as if it had spent part of the morning wallowing in a mud hole. Latisha couldn't see the license plates.

Billy leaned around the doorway. "Not Canadian, I hope."

As the people got off the bus, Latisha could see that they all had name tags neatly pasted to their chests. They filed off the bus in an orderly line and stood in front of the restaurant and waited until

they were all together. Then, in unison, they walked two abreast to the front door, each couple keeping pace with the couple in front of them.

"Canadian," Latisha shouted.

Early on in their marriage, George began to point out what he said he perceived to be the essential differences between Canadians and Americans.

"Americans are independent," George told her one day. "Canadians are dependent."

Latisha told him she didn't think that he could make such a sweeping statement, that those kinds of generalizations were almost always false.

"It's all observation, Country," George continued. "Empirical evidence. In sociological terms, the United States is an independent sovereign nation and Canada is a domestic dependent nation. Put fifty Canadians in a room with one American, and the American will be in charge in no time."

George didn't say it with any pride, particularly. It was, for him, a statement of fact, an unassailable truth, a matter akin to genetics or instinct.

"Americans are adventurous," George declared. "Canadians are conservative. Look at western expansion and the frontier experience. Lewis and Clark were Americans."

What about Samuel de Champlain and Jacques Cartier? Latisha had asked.

"Europeans." George laughed, and then he gave her a hug. "Don't take it personally, Country."

The woman at the near table held up her hand and waited. Her name tag said "P. Johnson."

Latisha took four menus with her. "Good evening."

"Yes, it is," said the woman. "And your name is?"

"Latisha."

"That's a lovely name," said the other woman, whose name tag said "S. Moodie."

"My name is Sue and this is my good friend Polly."

The two men nodded as Latisha passed out the menus. They smiled and stuck out their chests so Latisha could read their tags: "A. Belaney" and "J. Richardson."

"Could you tell us what the special is?" asked Polly.

"Everything smells so wonderful," said Sue.

"Old Agency Puppy Stew."

"And how much is it?"

"Six ninety-five."

Polly looked at Sue and the two men. "Archie? John?" Both men nodded. "Excellent. We'll all have the special."

"Four specials."

"Does the special come with a vegetable?" asked Archie.

"Vegetables are in the stew," said Latisha.

"And bread?" asked John.

"Bread comes with it."

"I don't suppose dessert is included," said Sue.

"Ice cream or Puppy Chow. Coffee comes with it too."

"Wonderful," said Polly. "We'll all take the special."

"Four specials," said Latisha, holding her tongue between her teeth.

It hadn't bothered Latisha at first. But as George made these comparisons a trademark of his conversations, Latisha became annoyed, then frustrated, and then angry. After a while, she began to lay in wait for him.

"All the great military men in North America," George began, "were Americans. Look at George Washington, Andrew Jackson, George Armstrong Custer, Dwight D. Eisenhower."

"What about Montcalm?"

"He was French, and he got beat by an American."

"Wolfe was British."

"Almost the same thing."

"What about Louis Riel? What about Red River and Batoche?"

"Didn't they hang him?"

"Billy Bishop!" Latisha almost shouted the name.

George put his arms around her and kissed her forehead. "You're right, Country," he said. "There's always the exception."

"With the exception of Archie," said Sue, "we're all Canadians. Most of us are from Toronto. Archie is from England, but he's been here for so long, he thinks he's Canadian, too."

"It's nice to meet you."

"None of us," said Polly, looking pleased, "is American."

"We're on an adventure," said Sue.

"We're roughing it," said Archie.

"The last motel was as rough as I want it," said John, and Polly and Archie and Sue laughed, though not loud enough to disturb the other people at the other tables.

"Well, there's lots to see around here."

"What we really want to see," said Archie, "are the Indians."

"Mostly Blackfoot around here," said Latisha. "Cree are a little farther north."

Sue reached over and put her hand on Polly's arm. "Polly here is part Indian. She's a writer, too. Maybe you've read one of her books?"

Latisha shook her head. "I'm sorry, I don't think I know them."

"It's all right, dear," said Polly. "Not many people do."

It was a stupid game, but Latisha had to will herself not to play it. The baby helped. After Christian was born, Latisha had little time for George's nonsense. It was a stage, she told herself. But if anything, George's comparisons became even more absurd. The United States had more doctors, more lawyers, more writers, more motels, more highways, more universities, more large cities, and had fought in more wars than Canada.

Americans were modern, poised to take advantage of the future, to move ahead. Canadians were traditionalists, stuck in the past and unwilling to take chances. Americans liked adventure and challenge. Canadians liked order and guarantees.

"When a cop pulls a Canadian over for speeding on an open road with no other car in sight, the Canadian is happy. I've even seen them thank the cop for being so alert. What else can I say?"

In the end, simple avoidance proved to be the easiest course, and whenever George started to warm up, Latisha would take Christian into the bedroom and nurse him.

There, in the warm darkness, she would stroke her son's head and whisper ferociously over and over again until it became a chant, a mantra, "You are a Canadian. You are a Canadian. You are a Canadian."

Latisha shook hands with Polly and Sue and Archie and John as they left the restaurant. None of them bought menus. Latisha got the trolley from the kitchen and began clearing the dishes off the tables.

"Thank God they're not all Canadians," said Billy.

"You sound like George," said Latisha.

"And how many specials did we serve?"

Latisha laughed. "Okay, so they all had the special."

"Twenty-six specials. Baaaaaa," said Billy. "It was like feeding cheap sheep. Oh, Cynthia said that that guy called again."

"He leave a message?"

"Nope."

Latisha began clearing the tables. She was finishing up when she saw it. Sitting on a chair under a napkin. For a moment she thought someone had forgotten it, and she tried to remember who had been sitting at the table.

The Shagganappi.

Under the book was a twenty-dollar tip.

after READING

UNDERSTANDING THE TEXT

1. In your notebook, write your initial reaction to this excerpt. Explain your reactions with specific references to the excerpt.

2. a) Explain the humour in the description of the tourists in paragraph 6.
   b) Make a list of words from the paragraph that sustain the humour.

3. Referring to the notes you made in "Before Reading," show how a knowledge of these four **characters** allows readers to share the "in joke" the writer is making for his **audience**.

4. Explain the importance of the final two lines to the meaning of this excerpt. Discuss your conclusions with the class.

EXPLORING IDEAS AND IMPLICATIONS

5. a) Using print and/or electronic sources, locate information on one Canadian hero and research the heroic acts of that person. As part of your investigation, focus on the challenges he or she faced and consider his or her independent and adventurous nature.
   b) Prepare an oral presentation on the hero you researched. Work with a partner or small group to practise voice projection, pacing, gestures, body language, and the use of visual aids and/or technology.
   c) During presentations, take notes on each of the Canadian heroes and be prepared to ask probing questions at the end of each presentation.

MAKING CONNECTIONS

6. Read several **short stories** by Thomas King. In a **persuasive essay** referring to at least two of these stories, argue for or against his use of stereotypes to create humour.

7. a) Individually, watch a Canadian and American news broadcast and read Canadian and American news coverage of the same event. Compare the way the same story is covered in each country. List the similarities and the differences.
   b) Would you be able to tell the origin of the report just from reading or seeing it? If so, explain the differences in the Canadian and American approaches; if not, explain why not.
   c) Write a **report** on your conclusions and prepare a presentation of your ideas to the class. ■

el·e·ment [EL-uh-n...
any one of the more
which all other things
atoms of only one kind a
down into any simpler su
oxygen, and hydrogen are co
nature. **2.** one of the basic parts
teresting characters and exciti
ments of a good story. **3.** the m
or setting: Fish can live only i
ment, which is water. **4. the elem
of nature, such as wind, rain, and

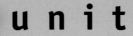

unit

1
2
3
4

Literature

The Clerk of Oxenford

GEOFFREY CHAUCER

BEFORE READING

With a partner, discuss and make notes on the contemporary **images** (from films, literature, or television) of a university student struggling to finance her or his studies.

A Clerk[1] ther was of Oxenford also	1. Clerk= cleric, student
That unto logyk hadde longe ygo.	
As leene was his hors as is a rake,	
And he nas nat right fat, I undertake,	
But looked holwe, and therto sobrely. 5	
Ful thredbare was his overeste courtepy[2];	2. overeste courtepy= outer short coat
For he hadde geten hym yet no benefice,	
Ne was so worldly for to have office.[3]	3. office= paid employment
For hym was levere[4] have at his beddes heed	4. levere= rather
Twenty bookes, clad in black or reed, 10	
Of Aristotle and his philosophie,	
Than robes riche, or fithele,[5] or gay sautrie.[6]	5. fithele= fiddle
But al be that he was a philosophre,	6. sautrie= psalter or psaltery, a stringed instrument
Yet hadde he but litel gold in cofre;	
But al that he myghte of his freendes hente,[7] 15	7. hente= get
On bookes and on lernynge he it spente,	
And bisily gan for the soules preye	
Of hem that yaf hym wherwith to scoleye.	
Of studie took he moost cure and moost heede.	
Noght o word spak he moore than was neede, 20	
And that was seyd in forme and reverence,	
And short and quyk and ful of hy sentence;	
Sownynge[8] in moral vertu was his speche,	8. Sownynge in= tending towards
And gladly wolde he lerne and gladly teche.	

after READING

1. As a class, take turns reading a few lines of the **poem** aloud. Stop after each reading to discuss what you think the lines mean. After reading the entire poem, in your notebook, **summarize** what it is about.

2. List details from the poem that provide the reader with a description of the physical appearance of the clerk and also an understanding of his character.

3. Imagine that you have just met this student from fourteenth-century England. Write an e-mail note to a friend telling your impressions of him. Be sure to include details that help to describe him as an "admirable, likeable **character**" or as "someone I wouldn't want to associate with."

4. Examine the poem's use of poetic techniques such as **rhyme scheme**, rhythm, **simile**, and deliberate understatement. (See The Reference Shelf, pages 423–427.) In your notebook, explain the effectiveness of these techniques in adding to the meaning of the poem.

EXPLORING IDEAS AND IMPLICATIONS

5. **a)** Geoffrey Chaucer wrote *The Canterbury Tales* in the 1380s. Consult The Reference Shelf (pages 396–397) to review information about the English language in the Middle English period.

   b) In a group, discuss the techniques you used to understand the language of the poem. Assess the importance of the **context** in which words occur; the phonetic clues from the sound of the words; your awareness of root words and prefixes and suffixes; your knowledge of other words in English, French, or German that are formed from similar root words.

MAKING CONNECTIONS

6. With a partner, use print and/or electronic sources to research the life and times of Geoffrey Chaucer. Make notes on at least three interesting pieces of information you find. Be prepared to present your findings to the class.

7. Read "Which Is Better: College or University?" (pages 224–226) and "Leaving" (pages 228–233). Based on your discussion and notes from "Before Reading," write a news report comparing the challenges of modern students with those of Chaucer's time. With a partner, revise and edit your essay in preparation for submission. ■

How Does a Word Get into the Dictionary?

MERRIAM-WEBSTER

"Change and variation are as natural in language
as they are in other areas of human life ..."

BEFORE READING

As a class, brainstorm the various kinds of information that can be found in a dictionary. Determine the reasons why most students in your class consult a dictionary most frequently.

"How does a word get into the dictionary?" That's one of the questions Merriam-Webster editors are most often asked.

The answer is simple: usage.

To decide which words to include in the dictionary and to determine what they mean, Merriam-Webster editors study the language to determine which words people use most often and how they use them.

Each day most Merriam-Webster editors devote an hour or two to reading books, newspapers, magazines, electronic publications—in fact a cross-section of all kinds of published materials; in our office this activity is called "reading and marking." The editors are looking for new words, new meanings of existing words, evidence of variant spellings or inflected forms—in short, anything that might help in deciding if a word belongs in the dictionary, understanding what it means, and determining typical usage. Any word of interest is marked, along with surrounding context that offers insight into its form and use.

The marked passages are then input into a computer system and stored both in machine-readable form and on 3" x 5" slips of paper to create *citations*.

Each citation has the following elements:
1. the word itself
2. an example of the word used in context
3. bibliographic information about the source from which the word and example were taken

Merriam-Webster's citation files, which were begun in the 1880s, now contain nearly 15 million examples of words used in context and cover all aspects of the English vocabulary. Citations are also available to editors in a searchable text database (linguists call it a *corpus*) that includes 50,000,000 words drawn from a great variety of sources.

How does a word make the jump from the citation file to the dictionary?

The process begins with dictionary editors reviewing groups of citations. Definers start by looking at citations covering a relatively small segment of the alphabet—for example *gri-* to *gro-*—along with the entries from the dictionary being reedited that are included within that alphabetical section. It is the definer's job to determine which existing entries can remain essentially unchanged, which entries need to be revised, which entries can be dropped, and which new entries should be added. In each case, the definer decides on the best course of action by reading through the citations and using the evidence in them to adjust entries or create new ones.

Before a new word can be added to the dictionary, it must have enough citations to show that it is widely used. But having a lot of citations is not enough; in fact, a large number of citations might even make a word more difficult to define, because many citations show too little about the meaning of a word to be helpful. A word may be rejected for entry into a general dictionary if all of its citations come from a single source or if they are all from highly specialized publications that reflect the jargon of experts within a single field.

To be included in a Merriam-Webster dictionary, a word must be used in a substantial number of citations that come from a wide range of publications over a considerable period of time. Specifically, the word must have enough citations to allow accurate judgments about its establishment, currency, and meaning.

The number and range of citations needed to add a word to the dictionary varies. In rare cases, a word jumps onto the scene and is both instantly prevalent and likely to last, as was the case in the 1980s with *AIDS*. In such a situation, the editors determine that the word has become firmly established in a relatively short time and should be entered in the dictionary, even though its citations may not span the wide range of years exhibited by other words.

The size and type of dictionary also affect how many citations a word needs to gain admission. Because an abridged dictionary, such as *Merriam-Webster's Collegiate Dictionary, Tenth Edition*, has fairly limited space, only the most commonly used words can be entered; to get into that type of dictionary, a word must be supported by a significant number of citations. But a large unabridged dictionary, such as *Webster's Third New International Dictionary*, has room for many more words, so terms with fewer citations can still be included.

Change and variation are as natural in language as they are in other areas of human life and Merriam-Webster reference works must reflect that fact. By relying on citational evidence, we hope to keep our publications grounded in the details of current usage so they can calmly and dispassionately offer information about modern English. That way, our references can speak with *authority*, without being *authoritarian*.

after READING

UNDERSTANDING THE TEXT

1. Write a short **report** explaining the role of citations in helping the Merriam-Webster company decide whether to include a word in a dictionary and which dictionary to include it in.

EXPLORING IDEAS AND IMPLICATIONS

2. With a partner, brainstorm a list of new words that may or may not have found their way into a dictionary. Consult several print and on-line dictionaries to see if you can find the words.

3. Research the jobs involved in publishing a new or revised edition of a dictionary. Write a paragraph explaining which job you think would be the most interesting and challenging.

4. In a small group, research the earliest dictionaries ever developed for English words. (See also The Reference Shelf, page 400.) Prepare an oral report on your findings. Use visual and technological aids to present your report.

MAKING CONNECTIONS

5. Considering what is said about electronic publishing in "In Praise of the Printed Word" (pages 109–112), write a report for the Merriam-Webster company explaining why it should adopt a policy of publishing dictionaries only in books, only electronically, or in both formats.

Or

Prepare a sales talk in which you try to convince potential customers to buy dictionaries in print, electronic, or both formats. After completing a draft of your sales talk, read it to a small group of your classmates for revision suggestions. Revise and edit your work before presenting it to the class. ■

Authors' Ideas on Literature

"Fiction gives counsel ... It distributes the suffering. It says we must compose ourselves in our stories in order to exist."

BEFORE READING

In a small group, brainstorm and record ideas about the importance of fiction or poetry to contemporary society. Be prepared to present your ideas.

The following pages contain a speech made by American novelist William Faulkner when he was awarded the Nobel Prize in 1950, and an essay by E.L. Doctorow, written in 1986.

The Nobel Prize Speech

WILLIAM FAULKNER

I feel that this award was not made to me as a man, but to my work—a life's work in the agony and sweat of the human spirit, not for glory and least of all for profit, but to create out of the materials of the human spirit something which did not exist before. So this award is only mine in trust. It will not be difficult to find a dedication for the money part of it commensurate with the purpose and significance of its origin. But I would like to do the same with the acclaim too, by using this moment as a pinnacle from which I might be listened to by the young men and women already dedicated to the same anguish and travail, among whom is already that one who will some day stand here where I am standing.

Our tragedy today is a general and universal physical fear so long sustained by now that we can even bear it. There are no longer problems of the spirit. There is only the question: When will I be blown up? Because of this, the young man or woman writing today has forgotten the problems of the human heart in conflict with itself which alone can make good writing because only that is worth writing about, worth the agony and the sweat.

He must learn them again. He must teach himself that the basest of all things is to be afraid; and, teaching himself that, forget it forever, leaving no room in his workshop for anything but the old verities and truths of the heart, the old universal truths lacking which any story is ephemeral and doomed—love and honor and pity and pride and compassion and sacrifice. Until he does so, he labors under a curse. He writes not of love but of lust, of defeats in which nobody loses anything of value, of victories without hope and, worst of all, without pity or compassion. His griefs grieve on no universal bones, leaving no scars. He writes not of the heart but of the glands.

Until he relearns these things, he will write as though he stood among and watched the end of man. I decline to accept the end of man. It is easy enough to say that man is immortal simply because he will endure: that when the last ding-dong of doom has clanged and faded from the last worthless rock hanging tideless in the last red and dying evening, that even then there will still be one more sound: that of his puny inexhaustible voice, still talking. I refuse to accept this. I believe that man will not merely endure: he will prevail. He is immortal, not because he alone among creatures has an inexhaustible voice, but because he has a soul, a spirit capable of compassion and sacrifice and endurance. The poet's, the writer's, duty is to write about these things. It is his privilege to help man endure by lifting his heart, by reminding him of the courage and honor and hope and pride and com-passion and pity and sacrifice which have been the glory of his past. The poet's voice need not merely be the record of man, it can be one of the props, the pillars to help him endure and prevail.

Ultimate Discourse

E.L. DOCTOROW

When I was a boy everyone in my family was a good storyteller, my mother and father, my brother, my aunts and uncles and grandparents; all of them were people to whom interesting things seemed to hap-pen. The events they spoke of were a daily, ordinary sort, but when narrated or acted out they took on great importance and excitement as I listened.

Of course, when you bring love to the person you are listening to, the story has to be interesting, and in one sense the task of a professional writer who publishes books is to overcome the terrible loss of not being someone the reader knows and loves.

But apart from that, the people whose stories I heard as a child must have had a very firm view of themselves in the world.

They must have been strong enough as presences in their own minds to trust that people would listen to them when they spoke.

I know now that everyone in the world tells stories. Relatively few people are given to mathematics or physics, but narrative seems to be within everyone's grasp, perhaps because it comes of the nature of language itself.

The moment you have nouns and verbs and prepositions, the moment you have subjects and objects, you have stories.

For the longest time there would have been nothing but stories, and no sharper distinction between what was real and what was made up than between what was spoken and what was sung. Religious arousal and scientific discourse, simple urgent communication and poetry, all burned together in the intense perception of a metaphor—that, for instance, the sun was a god's chariot driven across the heavens.

Stories were as important to survival as a spear or a hoe. They were the memory of the knowledge of the dead. They gave counsel. They connected the visible to the invisible. They distributed the suffering so that it could be borne.

In our era, even as we separate the functions of language, knowing when we speak scientifically we are not speaking poetically, and when we speak theologically we are not speaking the way we do to each other in our houses, and even as our surveys demand statistics, and our courts demand evidence, and our hypotheses demand proof—our minds are still structured for storytelling.

What we call fiction is the ancient way of knowing, the total discourse that antedates all the special vocabularies of modern intelligence.

The professional writer of fiction is a conservative who cherishes the ultimate structures of the human mind. He cultivates within himself the universal disposition to think in terms of conflict and its resolution, and in terms of character undergoing events, and of the outcome of events being not at all sure, and therefore suspenseful— the whole thing done, moreover, from a confidence of narrative that is grounded in our brains as surely as the innate talent to construe the world grammatically.

The fiction writer, looking around him, understands the homage a modern up-to-date world of nonfiction specialists pays to his craft—even as it isolates him and tells him he is a liar. Newsweeklies present the events of the world as installments in a serial melodrama. Weather reports on television are constructed with exact attention to conflict (high-pressure areas clashing with low), suspense (the climax of tomorrow's prediction coming after the commercial), and the consistency of voice (the personality of the weathercaster). The marketing and advertising of product-facts is unquestionably a fictional enterprise. As is every government's representations of its activities. And modern psychology, with its concepts of *sublimation, repression, identity crisis, complex,* and so on, proposes the interchangeable parts for the stories of all of us; in this sense it is the industrialization of storytelling.

But nothing is as good at fiction as fiction. It is the most ancient way of knowing but also the most modern, managing when it's done right to burn all the functions of language back together into powerful fused revelation. Because it is total discourse it is ultimate discourse. It excludes nothing. It will express from the depth and range of its sources truths that no sermon or experiment or news report can begin to apprehend. It will tell you without shame what people do with their bodies and think with their minds. It will deal evenhandedly with their microbes or their intuitions. It will know their nightmares and blinding moments of moral crisis. You will experience love, if it so chooses, or starvation or drowning or dropping through space or holding a hot pistol in your hand with the police pounding on the door. This is the way it is, it will say, this is what it feels like.

Fiction is democratic, it reasserts the authority of the single mind to make and remake the world. By its independence from all institutions, from the family to the government, and with no responsibility to defend their hypocrisy or murderousness, it is a valuable resource and instrument of survival.

Fiction gives counsel. It connects the present with the past, and the visible with the invisible. It distributes the suffering. It says we must compose ourselves in our stories in order to exist. It says if we don't do it, someone else will do it for us.

after READING

UNDERSTANDING THE TEXT

1. a) From the first paragraph of Faulkner's **speech**, locate and record in your notebook two sets of words that emphasize the idea that writing is not easy work.
   b) List suggestions Faulkner makes in the second paragraph about appropriate subjects for literature.
   c) **Summarize** Faulkner's statements from the third paragraph about the duties and responsibilities of poets and writers.

2. a) With a partner, discuss what historical event in the years before the speech might have led Faulkner to state: "There are no longer problems of the spirit. There is only the question: When will I be blown up?"
   b) Discuss how knowledge of the social and historical values of the period in which a text is written can influence our interpretation of the text. In your notebook, summarize the main points from the discussion.

3. In your notebook, explain your reaction to Faulkner's use of male pronouns in his speech. (See The Reference Shelf, page 403.) Be prepared to discuss your thoughts with the class.

4. Write brief **definitions** for the words "antedates," "innate," and "sublimation" as they are used in context in Doctorow's **essay**. Compare your definitions with those of a classmate. Discuss how knowledge of root words, prefixes, and suffixes helped you to understand these words. (See The Reference Shelf, page 411.) If necessary, use a dictionary to verify or correct your definitions.

5. a) As a class, discuss the following statements from Doctorow's essay:
   - "The moment you have nouns and verbs and prepositions, the moment you have subjects and objects, you have stories." (page 65)
   - "... a confidence of narrative that is grounded in our brains as surely as the innate talent to construe the world grammatically." (page 65)

   b) In your notebook, record the main ideas raised during the discussion.

EXPLORING IDEAS AND IMPLICATIONS

6. Using two columns, one for each writer, record statements made by each about writing and fiction that seem to correspond to each other. Reread the texts carefully and record any statements that appear to disagree. Share your findings and the reasons for your choices with a partner. After discussion, revise or correct your chart where necessary.

7. As an independent study, use the school library and/or the Internet to research the published works of William Faulkner and E.L. Doctorow. (See The Reference Shelf, pages 429–431.) Make notes on the forms of writing and the topics covered by each author, then write a brief comparison/contrast essay about the two writers. Revise and edit your draft, focusing on the organization and the use of transition words.

MAKING CONNECTIONS

8. Read "Hey, It's Not as if I'm a Serial Killer" (pages 386–387). With a small group, discuss the comments in this essay about public relations in the light of Doctorow's statement: "The marketing and advertising of product-facts is unquestionably a fictional enterprise. As is every government's representations of its activities." Then choose one member of the group to present the group's observations to the class. ■

Writers Don't Have to Explain

SUSAN SWAN

"I am part of the worldwide diaspora of ideas.
I will write on any subject that interests me."

BEFORE READING

In groups of three or four, recall Canadian novels, **stories**, **poems**, or **plays** that you have read recently. Discuss whether being a "Canadian" writer places any special responsibilities on these authors.

What are the writer's obligations as a citizen? And what does the writer's conscience mean for Canadian writers? I was born in 1945, the year *Two Solitudes* was published in Canada. It was written by my former creative writing teacher, the late Canadian novelist Hugh MacLennan, several years after he was rejected by a U.S. publisher for an earlier novel.

The U.S. publisher wrote about that early work of MacLennan ... "There is something indefinably wrong in this book. We don't know who he is and the author's presence, at least invisibly, must be implicit in the book. He does not write like an American and he does not write like an Englishman. Who is he?"

It was then MacLennan said he realized that he was stuck with Canada, that

"Canada was a country unknown even to itself, but as drama depends on recognitions, it would be very necessary for a time to labour very hard to create an authentic background. The results were my three novels."

By the time my first novel appeared in 1983, Canadian writers had gone on to form The Writers' Union of Canada and successfully lobby for political issues that affected them as storytellers and citizens. When I attended my first Writers' Union meeting in the early 1980s, it was made clear to me that as a writer I had duties, not only to the world around me, but to my own literary community.

The writer as citizen was a busy cultural worker whose job was selling Canadian literature to Canadian citizens. In 1984,

I wrote an essay asking Canadian bookstores to stop selling Canadian books in the Canadiana section at the back of the store.

"Our writers are not a specialty taste like haggis or tripe ..." I fumed. "Why can't we take it for granted that our works of fiction and biography are the artichokes, the sushi, the pistachio nuts of modern writing the world is waiting to enjoy?"

Of course, I sometimes felt resentful about sacrificing precious writing time, but, nevertheless, I also felt as if I were doing something valuable for my culture. I was helping to create an infrastructure that allowed good writing to be written and read. Because not all books are good books; great books grow out of a literary tradition that has been cultivated by a society, the way a crocus will flower in the midst of a compost heap. Michael Ondaatje and numerous others like Cordelia Strube and Andre Alexis sprung up from a small press now called Coach House Books.

You need a community where writing matters or there will be few good writers. So even though I sometimes felt rebellious, I also felt a sense of purpose beyond the demands of my own literary career with its pressures to sell enough copies of my next novel here and abroad in order to keep my various publishers interested.

In those years, I accepted the fact that the writer's conscience was inextricably bound not only to literature but to the duties of citizenship and literary community.

Today, I'd like to argue that it was not only MacLennan but all Canadian writers whose conscience has called Canada into being, moving us through both their literature and their literary activism into a stage where the international success of authors like Alice Munro, Carol Shields, Robertson Davies, Michael Ondaatje and Margaret Atwood have made it possible for writers here to write about anything they want without the obligation to explain where they're coming from.

In this new international phase of Canadian literary success, it's now possible to see stories not only from famous native playwrights but writers from backgrounds from all over the world. I recently heard about a reading series that calls itself The New Internationalism: Canadian Writers from Everywhere!

The vastly differing racial backgrounds of the students in my creative writing seminars at York University are beginning to be reflected in spring and fall lists of Canadian publishers. Canadian writers have travelled from a bipolar tradition of anglo and francophone writers to an international tribe of multiple perspectives, and their stories have won foreign literary prizes and found readers all over the world. It is now acceptable for a Canadian writer to say: "I am part of the worldwide diaspora of ideas. I will write on any subject that interests me."

Novels and short stories have given us a vision of ourselves where no vision existed before. Now as Canadian culture matures, the role of writers may be to act as life-giving voices in a global marketplace— voices that help to ward off the threat of silence and domination from governments and multinational corporations.

A beautifully written description of a field or a city street is a way to preserve that field or street—a way often more persuasive than any political lobby.

Canadian writers, who come from a country highly skilled in the field of communications with a long tradition of social compassion, are ideally suited to be leading voices for freedom in the next millennium.

after READING

UNDERSTANDING THE TEXT

1. In your notebook, **summarize** the main arguments made by Susan Swan in this selection.

2. Write a paragraph explaining whether you agree with Swan's comments about the responsibilities or consciences of Canadian authors. Compare your paragraph with that of a classmate.

3. In a small group, discuss the meaning of the title in relation to the selection. Assess whether the title is an effective one.

4. This is an excerpt from a lecture delivered at York University in Toronto. Examine the text to locate any characteristics that would identify this as a **speech**. Discuss your findings as a class.

EXPLORING IDEAS AND IMPLICATIONS

5. As an independent study assignment, choose one of the authors (including Susan Swan) mentioned in the speech. (See The Reference Shelf, pages 429–431.) Using a variety of print and electronic sources, research the time period and the literary works of the author. Use your research notes to prepare an oral report to the class.

MAKING CONNECTIONS

6. Read "Authors' Ideas on Literature" (pages 63–66). In a small group, discuss whether Swan's ideas about a writer's responsibility are similar to (or different from) those expressed by Faulkner and Doctorow. Summarize the ideas from your discussion. ■

The Interview

UMA PARAMESWARAN

BEFORE READING

As a class, make a list of skills that are essential for a successful job **interview**.

Wanted, a bilingual office supervisor,
The ad had said, but the four mouths
    that spoke at her
Made no reference to bilingual or
    supervisory skills.
Marketing, said the Walrus, tell us
How you would market product X.   5
And she, adeptly riffling through cards
in filing cabinets stored back of her
    memory
told him how, step by neat correct step.

And then there was a pause.
Her clear brown eyes surveyed theirs   10
That studiously looked down at graffiti
They had scribbled on their pads.

Then Grendel's Mother reared her head
And said:
Our corporation is funded entirely
    by taxpayers   15
but we take pride in running a tight ship
Like the rest of the megacartels.
Toe the line, as we say, toe the line.
The sidekick to her right nodded
    admiringly.

You do see the need, yes? he said
    earnestly   20
As Mother G. boomed forth again:
Now, about those placards you wear
from time to time, would you be, hm,
wearing them if we take you in?

And she answered with even keel: 25
All my placards, buttons, pins
Always say the same thing—Equality.
I wear one all the time,
And I would wish that all of woman born
Would wear one too, with me.   30

And four silent hisses breathed
Yes, that's the problem.
Placards, buttons, pins,
Yes, that's why we cannot hire you.
And she answered their unspoken fears.   35
I *am* your problem.
In me the bodies of those you've stepped
    over in your
    race to the ivory tower;
In me the voices of those you've silenced
    in your climb
    to brutal power;   40

In me the sweat and tears of those you
    have drugged
    into helpless trance
In your Urizenic plans for perpetual
    dominance.

I am your *problem*, she said,
But only because you brand me as
    such—   45
A problem to be swept under the rug.
I have been there, she said,
Under the rug with dustmice
That once were human beings:
once-girls pawed by your friends,
    crude, ruddy;   50
older women joked at by your drinking
    buddies;
secretaries silenced by your veiled
    threats of firing;
workers baited by your carrot powers
    of hiring.

I am your problem, she said,
But I am your *answer* too.   55
For I have been there under the rug
And I really do know
    how it can be cleaned
Without undue hurt to your ego.

I am with them, she said,   60
I in them as they in me,
Words and voices muted in helpless grief,
Words and voices shared in agony,
Words and voices that will ring again
    and again
Even though you shoot down my friends
    and me,   65
Words and voices that will echo and
    resound
For our time that is yet to come.

The Walrus, Grendel's mother and
    sidekicks doodled on.
NEXT, they said. Let's call in the next.

after READING

THINKING AND UNDERSTANDING

1. With a partner, identify the **theme** of this **poem**.

2. In your notebook, **summarize** the arguments the interviewers make against the interviewee and the arguments the interviewee makes for herself.

3. In your notebook, explain how the poet's repetition reinforces the meaning of this poem.

4. **a)** Referring specifically to word choice, describe the **voice** in this poem.
   b) Support or refute the following in a short **essay**: "The voice in this poem is effective in transmitting the poet's message." Work with a partner to revise and edit your essay in preparation for submission.

EXPLORING IDEAS AND IMPLICATIONS

5. In a paragraph, explain the references to Grendel, Urizen, and the Walrus. In a second paragraph, explain what they add to the meaning and impact of the poem.

6. Find or devise a **definition** for "megacartel" (line 17). Choose additional words from the poem to show the **narrator**'s disrespect for "big business."

7. In a small group, discuss the following question: Can a person be totally honest in an interview? Be prepared to present your conclusions to the class.

MAKING CONNECTIONS

8. **a)** Human rights are protected in an interview. Using print and/or electronic resources, research the "rules" interviewers must follow in order to conduct a fair interview.
   b) Research, as well, how a person is able to lodge a human rights complaint against a company for unfair interviewing. Compare your findings with those of your peers. ■

Can the Inuit Keep Their Voice?

STEPHANIE NOLEN

"Inuktitut is a soft, rolling,
mouthful-of-shiny-marbles language."

BEFORE READING

1. In a small group, discuss what you know about languages that have become extinct or have been assimilated into other languages. Refer to the information about the Anglo-Saxon language in The Reference Shelf (pages 394–396).

2. With a partner, research information about the establishment of Nunavut, Canada's newest territory. Be prepared to share your findings with the class.

IQALUIT, NUNAVUT—

"Aaksurulauqsimajjaajunniirasugittailigitsi," Josie Kusugak said.

We were talking about land claims and that's what he told me. It means "do not think things are going to be easy after that," after the last of the treaties are signed. Except in Inuktitut, Kusugak's native language, that's all one word.

Go ahead and try that: Just let it roll off your tongue. I did. I got to the fifth A and gave up. Kusugak had the grace to laugh only a little.

In Kusugak's mouth, on the other hand, Inuktitut is a soft, rolling, mouthful-of-shiny-marbles language. You hear it in the headquarters of the Inuit Taparitsat of Canada, the umbrella political organization for Inuit, of which Kusugak is president.

And you hear it all over Canada's newest territory, spoken by old people in the hospital waiting room, and by moms alarmed at the price of bananas at the Northern store, and by teenagers on the basketball courts, still packed at 2 a.m. in the season of midnight sun.

Inuktitut, in sharp contrast to most other aboriginal languages, is alive and well. It's an official language of the year-old territorial government, newspapers are published in it and, crucially, children learn in Inuktitut for the first three years of school. But a new threat is looming at the edges of Nunavut's snowy borders: The Internet is coming, and not much happens on the Internet in Inuktitut.

Less than a century ago, 60 aboriginal languages were spoken in Canada. Eight of those have since disappeared entirely, while only four (Cree, Ojibway, Dakota and Inuktitut) are spoken widely enough that they are likely to survive the next few generations. Six languages have fewer than 10 known speakers. In 1951, 87 per cent of aboriginal people reported their native language as their mother tongue; by 1996, half of native adults and 71 per cent of children had never spoken an aboriginal language, according to the Assembly of First Nations.

Inuktitut has survived in large part because of the geographic isolation of the Inuit. Contact with non-aboriginal people was limited, until only 30 years ago, almost entirely to missionaries and traders with the Hudson's Bay Company. And while the capital city has a population split between Inuit and white, most other communities are still more than 90 per cent Inuit.

Enter the Internet. Connectivity is being heralded as a godsend for Nunavut, where fewer than 25,000 people are spread over two million square kilometres. Less than 20 per cent of households have home computers, compared with a national average of 50 per cent—however, the government has an ambitious plan to wire its remote communities in the next few years.

Inuktitut is an oral language. It had no written form until the arrival of missionaries in the north. Today, Inuktitut is written both in transliterated Roman orthography and in a system of syllabics developed by an Anglican missionary, Sir Edmund Peck, in 1894, based on Pittman shorthand. But both systems—and the complex grammatical structure of Inuktitut—create a wealth of problems for computer programmers.

There is a standardized Inuktitut transliteration, but not everyone knows it, or uses it. There are only three computer fonts for Inuktitut syllabics. Anything written in syllabics must be in Unicode, an international standard accepted by major computer manufacturers as a way to represent all written languages unambiguously. It uses two bytes to represent one character, and can represent 65,000 unique glyphs. That means you can write a little in English, a few words in Arabic, a bit in Japanese and not have the coding clash. However, only computers made in the last two years use it.

Then, there is the issue of grammar. English works with a word, a space, a word; in Inuktitut, all the characters needed to express an idea are joined together. In addition to suffixes and prefixes, the language has infixes, denoting tense or gender or quantity, which go in the middle of a word—which words are another matter.

The language reflects traditional Inuit culture. For example, there are no words for "come to my place" in Inuktitut because nobody lived by themselves, Mr. Kusugak noted. There are "an incredible number of words for war" in English, he said, while Inuktitut only has one, which means to fight. He marveled at the range of words for sex in English; there is just one in his language. And love—"In Inuktitut, it doesn't make a difference if it's 'I love you' or 'I pity you' or 'I cherish you.' If it's your girlfriend or your daughter or your wife, it's all the same."

New words have to be invented; a computer, for example, is called qaritaujaq, which means "brainlike."

The only books available in Inuktitut, other than the Bible, are for children. So imagine the software situation: programming an oral language with a variety of dialects, two writing systems, "words" that can easily run to 40 characters, and others for which there may be a dozen English definitions.

One of the success stories for Inuktitut on-line, oddly enough, is a project dedicated to preserving the language.

A few years ago, in preparation for the creation of the territory, bureaucrats at what would become the Ministry of Culture, Language, Elders and Youth began work on a technical dictionary—but it quickly became clear that it wasn't just tech terms that needed translating. There was medical and legal terminology, and more traditional words to define. The small word list grew into a project called the Inuktitut Living Dictionary, one that would be searchable and universally available (to anyone with Internet access), unlike the existing 20-odd paper dictionaries of Inuktitut-English.

Working with an Ottawa firm called Multilingual E-data Solutions, the ministry developed an open-source dictionary (http://www.livingdictionary.com) where people can search in English, French and

Inuktitut, and also submit their own definitions, which are moderated and updated accordingly by a linguist.

The project is now three years old but still a work in progress—and sometimes Carmen Levi, deputy minister for CLEY, and her staff, have to pick up the phone and track down some old people in remote communities, and ask "Hey, what's that mean?"

Ms. Levi, 48, learned to read syllabics in order to memorize the Bible; she went to school, in English, at age six, when the first schools were opened. Her mastery of English, though, came when she was shipped south as a child of 10 to a Toronto sanitorium after she caught tuberculosis.

Inuktitut had started to die during her lifetime, she said, the most complex and specific words fading first. "We used to learn those words by doing things but because we weren't doing those things, we weren't using those words and we lost them," she said; Inuit children were in schools instead of on the land hunting with their elders. "The more complicated words I'm learning now."

Today there are many young people with a good grasp of the language but not the fluency to work in it at the government level, she said. But children coming out of Grade 4 can write comfortably in syllabics, and she expects that to improve as Inuktitut classes are added to the middle and high school curricula.

But Sandra Inutiq, a young civil servant passionate about language, wonders if this is enough. English, she said, is a lazy language; its structure lends itself more easily to hasty communication, and that, combined with the proliferation of southern pop culture in the North, means you hear English more and more.

The Nunavut government has a goal of 85 per cent Inuit staff but it is far from filled, due to a shortage of qualified aboriginal people. Ms. Inutiq, for example, is the only Inuuk in her division and so works almost totally in English. She does, however, sometimes e-mail colleagues in Inuktitut, typing in transliterated Roman orthography. She thinks that with less emphasis on syllabics, more people would write in Inuktitut, noting that the syllabics were imposed recently and the simpler Roman letters are therefore just as good.

And while the living dictionary is working well, that won't be enough to carry Inuktitut into the Web.

"If Inuktitut is going to survive as a working language, it will have to be able to do more than word processing," said Michael Roberts, president of Nortext Inc., which publishes the Nunatsiaq News and developed Nunacom, the first Inuktitut font. You can't yet sort alphabetically in it, he noted, or do accounting, or run a database, functions crucial to the running of a government.

Mr. Kusugak acknowledges that English increasingly permeates the North. "The exposure of English is incredible—even if you're out on the land and not hearing the language, if you turn on the radio it's in English, and any pop can or instruction sheet is in English."

But he isn't worried about Inuktitut. "One of the things I really like about our short history of being exposed to English is that it [made us aware], in learning about other aboriginal peoples, that when you lose your language, you feel the real loss and try to retrieve it," Mr. Kusugak said. "And for a lot of them it's very late. So we have learned an awful lot from their mistakes. This generation is the one that says we have to keep the language—as much as we have to know French and English."

Want to try writing in Inuktitut? Go to the Web site:
www.halfmoon.org/inuit.html#tryit

INUKTITUT: WHAT ALL QABLUNAAT SHOULD KNOW

Every syllable ends in a vowel sound, unless there are two consecutive consonants, in which case the syllable is split between the two consonants. So "Inuktitut" is pronounced "Ee-nook-tee-toot."

R and K sounds are released in the back of the throat, in an enunciation closer to French than English. And pronunciation is key: the strength of staccato on a K sound determines, for example, whether a word means "woman" or "ship"—"you've got to be sure you're talking about the Blessed Virgin Mary and not some boat," notes Josie Kusugak.

There are a range of dialects in Inuktitut, but the same basic language is spoken by the Inuvialuit in the Northwest Territories and the aboriginal population of Greenland. Mr. Kusugak compared the difference to Liverpool, Newfoundland and Texas versions of English. "When I heard [IRA prisoner] Bobby Sands on the radio when he was elected to Parliament, I didn't understand a word he said and apparently it was English," he said.

And what about the old gag about the Inuit having dozens of words for snow? Mr. Kusugak sighs. "I imagine people in the Sahara get those kinds of jokes about sand," he said. At a language conference, he and his colleagues once came up with 46 different words for snow without even trying. "It is necessary when you're living in the environment and two snow flakes make a difference, then you have to respond to that," he said. The words for snow refer to the type of snow used to build an *igluvigak* (a snow house), snow to track in and snow to travel on. "Snow just happens to be very prevalent [for us]."

—Originally published July 25, 2000

after READING

1. In your notebook, make a list of the reasons given in this **article** for the survival of the Inuktitut language up to the present day and for the disappearance of other aboriginal languages.

2. List three or four statistics used by the writer to illustrate her arguments about aboriginal languages.

3. In your notebook, **summarize** the writer's statements about the difficulties of adapting the Inuktitut language to computers or summarize the information in the article that communicates an optimistic view that the Inuktitut language may survive.

4. From information provided in the article, make brief notes about the differences between English and Inuktitut under the following headings: how words or ideas are grouped or separated; how number, gender, or tense is indicated; how new words are developed.

EXPLORING IDEAS AND IMPLICATIONS

5. With a partner, discuss what this article teaches us about the relationship between language and culture. Include specific examples from the article in your discussion. Make a point-form summary of the ideas in your notebook.

6. Find and record details in the article that seem to contradict stereotyped ideas about the Inuit. In a small group, discuss your findings. Include in your discussion the dangers of stereotyping, the relationship between stereotyping and racism, and the importance of knowledge and awareness in helping to combat stereotyping and racism.

MAKING CONNECTIONS

7. Visit the two Web sites mentioned in the article to discover more about Inuktitut. Try using the computer to write in Inuktitut. Locate and record the meaning of the word "qablunaat." In your notebook, record two or three pieces of new information that you discovered at the Web sites, and bring them to class for discussion. ■

Those Anthropologists

LENORE KEESHIG-TOBIAS

BEFORE READING

Consult university calendars (or **interview** students at university) to learn about the type of topics covered in anthropology and sociology courses.

Or

Using print and/or electronic sources, investigate the types of research conducted by anthropologists and sociologists.

Those anthropologists,
sociologists and
historians who
poke at our bones,
our social systems   5
and past events
try to tell us
who we are.

When we don't read
their book   10
they think we are
rejecting
our heritage.

So, they feel
sorry for us   15
and write
more books
for themselves.

after READING

UNDERSTANDING THE TEXT

1. In your notebook, explain what the poet suggests that anthropologists, sociologists, and historians do. Compare the poet's views with what you found in the Before Reading activity.

2. With a partner, discuss who is being referred to by the poet's use of "our" and "we." Record your conclusion in your notebook.

3. Describe the poet's **tone** in the final **stanza**. Compare your response with that of a partner and defend your choice by referring to the language in the **poem**.

EXPLORING IDEAS AND IMPLICATIONS

4. Review the characteristics of free verse. (See The Reference Shelf, page 423.) With a partner, discuss the advantages and disadvantages of the poet's use of the free verse form to express the ideas in this **poem**. Make notes to **summarize** your discussion.

5. In a small group, collect several poems by First Nations poets. Put together a "sound collage" that conveys Aboriginal issues by piecing together important lines from these poems. Present your sound collage to the class.

MAKING CONNECTIONS

6. a) Read "The Grand Academy of Lagado" (pages 91–94). Use a **graphic organizer** to outline in point-form notes the similarities and differences between Swift's description of the scientific experiments and Lenore Keeshig-Tobias's description of the work of anthropologists and historians.

   b) Using your notes, write a draft of a **satiric** description of an imaginary project that might be conducted by the anthropologists or sociologists. With a partner, revise your draft to include specific details and to maintain a consistent tone. Rewrite and edit your satiric description for publication. ■

To Keep the Memory of So Worthy a Friend

ETHEL WILSON

"Reade him, therefore; and againe, and againe."

BEFORE READING

1. In your notebook, make a list of all the **plays** by William Shakespeare that you have read or seen in performance, on film, video, television, or in **adaptations**. Compare your list with that of a peer.

2. Only about half of Shakespeare's plays were published in his lifetime. Discuss with another student your thoughts about the impact on our cultural and artistic heritage if the other half of his writings had been lost.

One of the advantages of being lame is that one can sit and think without the shame of being lazy and with no apology to anyone. And so I often think and think about the two actors Henry Condell and John Heminge, and I can never get to the end of the wonder of what they did and what they do in the world today, even though not even their dust remains— unless it was wiped off a London window-sill this morning. Scholars know about them, of course, even amateur scholars like myself; but one is inclined to take them for granted, like the unicorn, and that is not fair to such great and humble men.

The last time but one that my husband and I were in London, we said, "We will not go home without finding the place where Condell and Heminge were buried." But London began to exercise her manifold arts, and we went home without trying to find the church of St. Mary the Virgin Aldermanbury.

Next time we arrived from Portugal on a Tuesday night in May, and on Wednesday morning we hailed a taxi, looked at the taxi driver, said "St. Mary the Virgin Aldermanbury," and experienced at once a feeling of disquiet.

The mind of the London taxi driver is a wonderful organism. His taxi is an extension of himself. He needs only a word to start him off, taxi and all, by devious routes to any place, however obscure, in the London area. Twice only I have found him not knowing: once when I wanted to go to Great Turnstile (there is, of course, no turnstile; Great Turnstile has other fame), and now when we wanted to go to St. Mary the Virgin Aldermanbury, and the expression of not knowing came on the taxi driver's face. "Down in the City, beyond the bombed part behind St. Paul's," we said, and he nodded.

Down in the City he stopped. "Well, 'ere we are," he said pleasantly, and indicated the little church of St. Mary Aldermary. We did not blame him although this was not what we wanted. St. Mary Aldermary would not do, but we got out. I leaned against St. Mary Aldermary, which Stow said "… is elder than any church of St. Marie in the Citie," and my husband went up a side street. I saw him in conversation with a policeman and a taxi driver. Another policeman joined me, a very nice man, but he did not know where St. Mary the Virgin Aldermanbury might be. He wanted to know if I would mind telling him why we wanted to go there, and also where I came from. As I could not begin telling him about the burial place of Condell and Heminge and what they had done and why they were important to me, I continued to lean against St. Mary Aldermary and said that I came from British Columbia, which interested him very much. When we were well into the climate of British Columbia my husband arrived in another taxi and I had to leave the policeman.

The new taxi driver was young and keen and anxious to find this place that he did not know. We drove up Love Lane and past Little Love Lane and past the Roman Wall and past the empty air of St. Alphege, and Cripplegate, with all the bombed area on one side, and gutted walls, and now large blocks of buildings arising (incongruous) on the other side, and found ourselves in Little Love Lane again and then went down Love Lane once more. After doing this kind of thing for some time we saw a dark wall of survival and on it the words carved in stone, grimly decipherable, St. Mary the Virgin Aldermanbury. I experienced that spring at the heart which is so rare. There was no entrance available on that side, so we rounded the corner and stopped at a small garden that was enclosed—except for the paved entrance—by a railing, and we found what we came to seek.

All that can be seen of St. Mary the Virgin Aldermanbury is gutted walls, and windows that have a fey look, as though invisible glass segments remain. This must be because of the illogical effects of blast or because spiders have spun their webs; but it is probably mainly blast, not spiders. The small church is from the fifteenth century, but Sir Christopher Wren rebuilt it in the seventeenth.

Across the rough road a large new building rises, an uninvited handsome stranger in uniform. Behind, lies bombed area, like craters of the moon. You enter the small neat garden on which the gutted church wall abuts. The path is of ancient paving stones. Two green trees survive and flourish, giving a prettiness and humanity to the bombed scene. On the left, beside a wall, is a long jumbled pile of stone. Will it ever be used? The ancient stones were part of the destroyed church. There are some benches in the small, unlikely garden, and naturally one sits (no one else is there) and becomes lost in speculation and in admiration and in gratitude.

For this was the place where the two men worshipped and were buried, where their wives were buried, and their children were baptized and married and buried—the two authentic friends who, after the death of their fellow actor William Shakespeare, collected his works, and so those works remain to us. That is what John Heminge and Henry Condell did for Shakespeare and for themselves and for posterity, and then—a few years later—they died, and were buried here in St. Mary the Virgin Aldermanbury, the church of their parish, and their life here was over; and now we are here, and soon we shall be gone, and others will listen to Shakespeare and read him, and will owe these men a great and unpayable debt.

Here are the first names on the list of twenty-six actors of Richard Burbage's company of players which Condell and Heminge have placed at the beginning of the First Folio. The introduction and the plays themselves display the irrelevance of spelling that later assumed, and now assumes, a static importance.

Thus they list:

THE NAMES OF
THE PRINCIPALL ACTORS
IN ALL THESE PLAYES
William Shakespeare
Richard Burbadge
John Hemmings
...
Henry Condell
...

Condell is eighth on the list.

Then come the plays, arranged according to the considered decision of Heminge and Condell as Comedies, Histories, Tragedies, instead of chronologically, to the manifold pleasant despairs of literary scholars and historians.

One does not need to be a scholar, or not a scholar, to sit on a bench in this small garden and feel the immediacy of Henry Condell and John Heminge of this parish. Three hundred years go by very easily. In spite of footnotes, quartos, contexts, interpretations, inconsistencies, arguments, and psychology (a new invention, Sirs), scholars are human and would not be impervious to this place.

Sitting there, I needed to know what these two men of Burbage's company of players looked like, and what their daily and nightly friend and fellow actor Shakespeare looked like. (I remembered that Burbage, Heminge, and Condell were the three actor-friends who were mentioned in friendship in Shakespeare's will.) I needed to know what clothes they wore, and when they spoke would I understand them plainly? They worked with him, and acted with him, sat and ate with him, and drank with him. They played in his plays, and after his death they sat down and with infinite labour they with their intimate knowledge compiled the First Folio of his plays.

Sitting there in the small neat garden of St. Mary the Virgin Aldermanbury where these two men feel near at hand, one does not embark on argument. The men, the plays, are there, so clear; but for a moment one marvels that men and women of these distant days take trouble to ignore the fact of the two men (fellow actors with Shakespeare) who collected the plays. These two men lived here, and died, and were buried here; the people of these distant latter days take great trouble to think up theories based on fancy or irresponsible choice; they choose to attribute the plays to anyone except "our so worthy Friend and Fellow, Shakespeare"; they turn away from those two solid men, Condell and Heminge, of this parish, as if they have never heard their names—and perhaps they have not—and pursue their fantasy.

Now let us read the words on a small plaque near the ground, and also the words graven on the sides of a pedestal in the centre of the garden. (Garden? It is an innocent plot of green, hardly a garden.) Upon the pedestal is a bust of Shakespeare. It is not authentic. It rather resembles the bust in Westminster Abbey, which is not authentic either, or the Chandos portrait. As the Christ of Renaissance and pre-Renaissance art became a visual Christ for generations of people, so this is the visual and symbolic Shakespeare; no assertions are made, and no harm is done.

Here, then, are the words we read on the ground plaque:

ST. MARY THE VIRGIN
ALDERMANBURY
NOTICE
This pleasant garden full of memories of Shakespeare, and his friends, Heminge and Condell, wardens of this church, is open to all who need rest and quiet. Gratitude is due to American friends who helped to restore the garden to its present condition, and co-operation in keeping it fresh and tidy will be much appreciated.

Here follow some of the words graven on the sides of the pedestal:

JOHN HEMINGE
lived in this Parish upwards of forty-two years and in which he was married. He had fourteen children thirteen of whom were baptized, four buried and one married here. He was buried here October 12, 1630. His wife was also buried here.

HENRY CONDELL
lived in this Parish upwards of thirty years. He had nine children eight of whom were baptized here and six buried. He was buried here December 29, 1627. His wife was also buried here.

The date of the First Folio being 1623, Heminge and Condell did not long survive the completion of their work.

The second side of the pedestal bears these words:

The fame of Shakespeare rests on his incomparable Dramas. There is no evidence that he ever intended to publish them and his premature death in 1616 made this the interest of no one else. Heminge and Condell had been co-partners with him in the Globe Theatre Southwark and from the accumulated Plays there of thirty-five years with Great Labour selected them. No men then living were so competent having acted with him in them for many years and well knowing his manuscripts. They were Published in 1623 in Folio thus giving away their Private Rights therein. What they did was priceless, for the whole of his manuscripts with almost all those of the Drama of the Period have perished.

Below the graven face we read from the title and introduction to the First Folio of the plays, as inscribed by the compilers:

Mr. William Shakespeares Comedies, Histories, Tragedies. Published according to the True Originall Copies.

And then from the first Introduction to the First Folio, addressed:

To the most noble and incomparable paire of brethren, William, Earle of Pembroke, etc., and Philip, Earle of Montgomery, etc.
[That "etc." holds a rare vitality.]
We have but collected them and done an office to the dead ... without ambition either of selfe-profit or fame, only to keep the memory of so worthy a Friend, & Fellow alive, as was our SHAKESPEARE ...

JOHN HEMINGE
HENRY CONDELL

Then following a passage from Heminge and Condell's second Introduction to the First Folio, which is addressed to us all, under the heading

TO THE GREAT VARIETY OF READERS

It had bene a thing, we confesse, worthie to have been wished, that the Author himselfe had liv'd, to have set forth, and overseene his own writings; but since it hath bin ordain'd otherwise, and he by death departed from that right, we pray you do not envie his Friends the office of their care, and paine, to have collected and published them; ... absolute in their numbers, as he conceived them, who as he was a happie imitator of Nature, was a most gentle expreser of it, his Mind and Hand went together; and what he thought he uttered with that easinesse, that we have scarse received from him a blot in his papers.

There is beauty and felicity in the words and cadences of these two actors of Shakespeare's company—of his company also of friends. The living Shakespeare is there, the man whose "mind and hand went together; and what he thought, he uttered with ... easinesse," and his friends Heminge and Condell, his perpetuators, are there.

"We cannot go beyond our owne power," they wrote; and so, in the prosecution of their enormous untaught task ("the faults," they said, "ours, if any be committed"), they made enough slips and errata to keep scholars in happy commotion three hundred years later. Yet without the labour of these two men of Aldermanbury, the whole body of Shakespeare's works would not have existed "absolute in their numbers, as he conceived them," either for the schoolmen or for the Great Variety of Readers who now pay their big or little money for lasting joy or an evening's magic, according to their Variety.

I like the advice that occurs in the latter part of their Introduction to the First Folio:

... It is not our province, who only gather his works, and give them you, to praise him. It is yours that reade him. And there we hope, to your divers capacities, you will find enough, both to draw, and hold you: for his wit can no more lie hid, than it could be lost. Reade him, therefore; and againe, and againe: And if you doe not like him, surely you are in some manifest danger, not to understand him.

after READING

UNDERSTANDING THE TEXT

1. a) In your notebook write a clear statement of the central **theme** of Ethel Wilson's **essay**.
   b) Using point-form notes, list details that the writer reveals about herself, her emotions, and her values in this **personal essay**. Compare your statement and list with those of a partner.

2. In a small group, discuss the significance of the introductory information about the taxi ride, the search, and the description of the church and of areas of London.

3. Read carefully the quotations from the writings of Heminge and Condell in the First Folio. Through discussion with your classmates, come to a conclusion about their motives for collecting and publishing Shakespeare's plays.

4. In your notebook, assess the effectiveness of the way in which the essay ends.

EXPLORING IDEAS AND IMPLICATIONS

5. Examine the spelling of various words in the quotations written in 1623, and suggest reasons for the inconsistencies and the differences from current standard spelling. Refer to pages 394–402 on the History and Development of the English Language in The Reference Shelf to check the validity of your reasons.

6. Use print or electronic resources to learn about the theories proposed by some scholars that Shakespeare's plays might have been written by someone else. Discuss your findings in a small group. Reread the essay to discover exactly how Ethel Wilson responds to such theories.

MAKING CONNECTIONS

7. Read "Sonnet 30" by William Shakespeare (page 311). Based on the information about Heminge and Condell from Ethel Wilson's essay, write a letter to Shakespeare from one of the two actors about the ideas on friendship expressed in the **poem**. Compare your letter with letters written by other students. ■

Costa Rica

MICHAEL ZACK

BEFORE READING

1. On a map, identify the location of Costa Rica. With a partner, discuss what you can infer about the geographical features and climate of Costa Rica.

2. Make a list of six or seven common **themes** or subjects for **poetry**. Compare your list with that of a classmate.

The sheaves of poems blew off the deck,
toward the Costa Rican hills.
The one about driving crashed the mangrove and
the good-bye poem disappeared in the banana tree groves.

Some first lines landed on a Pacific beach,   5
some last lines to a Caribbean.
When the sonnet flew by, a cow and a sow
looked up from their grazing. The snowy egret
swooped near the one about Escher's[1] fish.

Everything in life exchanges into something else,   10
especially words. I needed those mangos,
sunsets, howling monkeys in the canopy
could rhyme me to the man who left in the last port.
I needed new adjectives and verbs,
maybe *density* like the river hyacinth,   15
maybe *glide* like the grey osprey.

---

1. Dutch artist Maurits Cornelis Escher (1898–1972)

And when the winds reverse
perhaps those poems will all fly back
rearranged, fonted with this new place,
all the better for their night out in the jungle,   20

so that the one about my childhood
will reminisce about a village,
and the one about you
can begin with the dulcet fragrance of hibiscus.

after READING

UNDERSTANDING THE TEXT

1. In your notebook, list five specific poems identified by form or topic in this **poem**.

2. In a short paragraph, retell the events described in the first two **stanzas**, adding details and explanations where you feel they might help others to understand the poem. Reread both the poem and your retelling to assess whether there are any hints that the events may have occurred in fantasy rather than in reality.

3. Explain in a few sentences your understanding of "Everything in life exchanges into something else, especially words" (lines 10–11). Compare your explanation with that of a classmate.

4. Explain to a partner how the examples "density" and "glide" in lines 15 and 16 are used to illustrate the meaning of line 14: "I needed new adjectives and verbs."

5. a) "Costa Rica" is a poem about writing. In a small group, discuss Michael Zack's observations on writing poetry, paying special attention to the statements in stanzas 3 and 4. In your notebook, record ideas from the discussion.

   b) Use the notes you have recorded to write a paragraph about writing poetry. Ask a member of your discussion group to help you revise your work to include important details and to omit irrelevant information.

EXPLORING IDEAS AND IMPLICATIONS

6. a) Using "Costa Rica" as a model, write a poem about your experiences with school writing (for example, science report, geography and history essay, computer program). Revise and edit your poem for publishing.

   b) As a class, collect all the poems and create an **anthology** entitled "Verses on School Writing."

MAKING CONNECTIONS

7. Read the poem "Postcard" by Margaret Atwood (pages 178–179). Use a **graphic organizer** to identify similarities and differences in the form and content of "Costa Rica" and "Postcard." ■

The Grand Academy of Lagado: An Excerpt From
Gulliver's Travels

JONATHAN SWIFT

"… by his contrivance, the most ignorant person
at a reasonable charge, and with little bodily labour,
may write books in philosophy, poetry, politicks,
law, mathematicks and theology, without the least
assistance from genius or study."

BEFORE READING

With a partner, think of a book, story, film, or television show in which a stranger from another country (or civilization) observes or comments on the behaviours or customs in our society that we seem to take for granted. Discuss the effects of the stranger's observations or comments.

Gulliver's Travels *was written in 1726 at a time of great interest throughout Europe in exploration and discovery in other parts of the world. This passage is taken from Gulliver's third voyage, during which he visits the Island of Balnibarbi. Here the people have been exposed to science and mathematics, and have "fallen into schemes of putting all arts, sciences, languages, and mechanicks upon a new foot." They have established an academy at Lagado where professors are working on numerous projects intended to improve life. The following excerpts are taken from Gulliver's description of his visit to this grand academy.*

The first man I saw, was of a meagre aspect, with sooty hands and face; his hair and beard long, ragged and singed in several places. His cloaths, shirt, and skin, were all of the same colour: he had been eight years upon a project for extracting sun-beams out of cucumbers; which were to be put into vials, hermetically sealed, and let out to warm the air, in raw inclement summers. He told me, he did not doubt, in eight years more, that he should be able to supply the governor's gardens with sun-shine at a reasonable rate; but he complained that his stock was low, and intreated me to give him something as an encouragement to ingenuity, especially since this had been a very dear season for cucumbers: I made him a small present, for my lord had furnished me with money on purpose; because he knew their practice of begging from all who go to see them.

...

We crossed a walk to the other part of the academy, where ... the projectors in speculative learning resided.

The first professor I saw was in a very large room, with forty pupils about him. After salutation, observing me to look earnestly upon a frame, which took up the greatest part of both the length and breadth of the room; he said, perhaps I might wonder to see him employed in a project for improving speculative knowledge by practical and mechanical operations. But the world would soon be sensible of its usefulness; and he flattered himself, that a more noble exalted thought never sprang in any other man's head. Every one knew how laborious the usual method is of attaining to arts and sciences; whereas by his contrivance, the most ignorant person at a reasonable charge, and with little bodily labour, may write books in philosophy, poetry, politicks, law, mathematicks and theology, without the least assistance from genius or study. He then led me to the frame, about the sides whereof all his pupils stood in ranks. It was twenty foot square, placed in the middle of the room. The superficies was composed of several bits of wood, about the bigness of a dye, but some larger than others. They were all linked together by slender wires. These bits of wood were covered on every square with paper pasted on them; and, on these papers were written all the words of their language in their several moods, tenses, and declensions, but without any order. The professor then desired me to observe, for he was going to set his engine at work. The pupils at his command took each of them hold of an iron handle, whereof there were forty fixed round the edges of the frame; and giving them a sudden turn, the whole disposition of the words was entirely changed. He then commanded six and thirty of the lads to read the several lines softly as they appeared upon the frame; and where they found three or four words together that might make part of a sentence, they dictated to the four remaining boys who were scribes. This work was repeated three of four times, and at every turn the engine was so contrived, that the words shifted into new places, as the square bits of wood moved upside down.

Six hours a-day the young students were employed in this labour; and the professor shewed me several volumes in large folio already collected, of broken sentences, which he intended to piece together; and out of those rich materials to give the world a compleat body of all arts and sciences; which, however might still be improved, and much expedited, if the publick would raise a fund for making and employing five hundred such frames in Ladago, and oblige the managers to contribute in common their several collections.

He assured me that this invention had employed all his thoughts from his youth; and that he had emptied the whole vocabulary into his frame, and made the strictest computation of the general proportion there is in books between the numbers of particles, nouns, and verbs, and other parts of speech.

...

We next went to the school of languages, where three professors sat in consultation upon improving that of their own country.

The first project was to shorten discourse by cutting polysyllables into one, and leaving out verbs and participles; because in reality all things are but nouns.

The other, was a scheme for entirely abolishing all words whatsoever: and this was urged as a great advantage in point of health as well as brevity. For, it is plain, that every word we speak is in some degree a diminution of our lungs by corrosion; and consequently contributes to the shortning of our lives. An expedient was therefore offered, that since words are only names for *things*, it would be more convenient for all men to carry about them, such *things* as were necessary to express the particular business they are to discourse on. And this invention would certainly have taken place, to the great ease as well as health of the subject, if the women in conjunction with the vulgar and illiterate had not threatened to raise a rebellion, unless they might be allowed the liberty to speak with their tongues, after the manner of their forefathers: such constant irreconcileable enemies to science are the common people. However, many of the most learned and wise adhere to the new scheme of expressing themselves by *things*; which hath only this inconvenience attending it; that if a man's business be very great, and of various kinds, he must be obliged in proportion to carry a greater bundle of *things* upon his back, unless he can afford one or two strong servants to attend him. I have often beheld two of those sages almost sinking under the weight of their packs, like pedlars among us; who, when they met in the streets would lay down their loads, open their sacks, and hold conversation for an hour together; then put up their implements, help each other to resume their burthens, and take their leave.

But for short conversations, a man may carry implements in his pockets and under his arms, enough to supply him, and in his house he cannot be at a loss; therefore the room where company meet who practise this art, is full of all things ready at hand, requisite to furnish matter for this kind of artificial converse.

Another great advantage proposed by this invention, was, that it would serve as an universal language to be understood in all civilized nations, whose goods and utensils are generally of the same kind, or nearly resembling, so that their uses might easily be comprehended. And thus, embassadors would be qualified to treat with foreign princes or ministers of State, to whose tongues they would be utter strangers.

...

In the school of political projectors, I was but ill entertained; the professors appearing in my judgment wholly out of their senses; which is a scene that never fails to make me melancholy. These unhappy people were proposing schemes for persuading monarchs to chuse favourites upon the score of their wisdom, capacity, and virtue; of teaching ministers to consult the publick good; of rewarding merit, great abilities, and eminent services; of instructing princes to know their true interest, by placing it on the same foundation with that of their people: of choosing for employments persons qualified to exercise them; with many other wild impossible chim-ras, that never entered before into the heart of man to conceive; and confirmed in me the old observation, that there is nothing so extravagant and irrational which some philosophers have not maintained for truth.

after READING

UNDERSTANDING THE TEXT

1. In a group of four, divide the excerpt into four equal parts. Have each member of the group choose a part and read it aloud to the group. After each reading, discuss what you think the part is about. At the end of the reading, **summarize** this excerpt in your notebook.

2. Consult a dictionary to help you **define** the words "superficies," "declensions," "particles," "converse," "projectors," and "chim-ras" as they are used in the **context** of this excerpt. Where required, explain in a sentence for each how Swift's use of the word differs from our modern meaning.

3. In a small group, discuss the **tone** of this excerpt. Locate specific phrases or sentences in the text which reveal the tone to the reader. (You may need to refer to the terms "**irony**" and "**satire**" in the Glossary.)

4. In your notebook, explain how the final paragraph differs in content and technique from the rest of this passage. Compare your ideas with those of your classmates.

5. a) List twelve words in the excerpt that were spelled differently in the 1700s. Next to each, write the current standard spelling of these words. (See The Reference Shelf, pages 400–401.)

   b) In your notebook, rewrite the first paragraph of this excerpt using current spelling, punctuation, sentence structure, and expression. Compare your version with that of another student to see whether your rewritten paragraphs maintain a **voice** and tone similar to the original.

MAKING CONNECTIONS

6. a) Recall one of the films or television shows you discussed in "Before Reading" in which a stranger (or alien) visits our society. Working with a partner, create a **storyboard** for a short scene in which the stranger visits your school, classroom, or local community and observes some behaviour that can be interpreted as strange or unusual.

   b) Write the film or television script for this short scene, including the humour or satire that develops through the observations of the visitor.

   c) Use the comments of another partnership to revise your script. Prepare your script for publication (or videotaping).

7. *Gulliver's Travels* has often been thought of as a children's story, especially Part 1, "A Voyage to Lilliput." Read this section of the book in a complete edition that has not been rewritten for children. With a partner, prepare an oral **report** that includes the following: elements of the **story** that make it appealing to children; descriptions and commentary that would show that it was obviously not written for children; satiric descriptions of rulers of countries, petty human behaviour, religious beliefs or intolerance, and war. ■

CHIP

As a class, discuss humorous misunderstandings you had as a child.

Thach Bùi

"Do you have any CD-ROMs on how to read a book?"

after READING

UNDERSTANDING THE TEXT

1. Use one sentence to explain what is funny about this cartoon.

2. Explain why the cartoonist uses quotation marks around the **caption** to the cartoon. Are all captions on cartoons in quotation marks?

EXPLORING IDEAS AND IMPLICATIONS

 3. Draw your own cartoon based on one of the childhood stories you discussed with the class in the "Before Reading" activity. In a group of four, explain the challenges you encountered in presenting your original idea in a simple drawing and short caption.

MAKING CONNECTIONS

4. As an independent study, write a research **report** on your favourite cartoon series or cartoonist. (See The Reference Shelf, pages 428–433.) Explain at least three characteristics that make the series or cartoonist interesting. Be prepared to present your report to the class, using visual aids if appropriate.

5. Find another cartoon that comments on technology. Be prepared to present it to the class.

And Baby Makes Six Billion

DAVID SUZUKI

"Today there is no ecosystem,
no species on Earth that has not
been affected by human activity."

BEFORE READING

As a class, discuss the effects of rapid population growth. Consider how the effects might be different in various parts of the world.

Last week, somewhere on Earth, human being number six billion was born. There are now three times as many of us on this planet as there were when I was born in 1936. That's an incredible increase, and even though growth rates have slowed somewhat, population will continue to be one of the key factors dictating human and environmental health throughout the next century.

One hundred years ago, we were just one of many species on this planet. Today there is no ecosystem, no species on Earth that has not been affected by human activity. We are everywhere, both literally and through our impact on world systems like the oceans and the atmosphere.

It could have been much worse. Thirty years ago, in his landmark book, *The Population Bomb*, Paul Ehrlich wrote that the world could not sustain the then exploding human population. He created a storm of controversy with predictions of starvation, disease and death due to overpopulation if the high birth rate continued unabated.

Thankfully, Ehrlich wrote his book at what appears to have been the peak of relative world population growth. Since then, extensive birth control campaigns and improved education have had dramatic results, and birth rates have dropped in many countries. Forty years ago, women around the world had an average of five children in their lifetimes. Today that number has dropped to 2.7.

However, lower birth rates only account for two-thirds of the reduction in population growth. The other one-third reduction has a much more ominous source—an increasing death rate. Those of us lucky enough to live in Canada have seen our life expectancy increase steadily over the years. But in some countries, the trend towards longer life spans has made a sharp retreat.

In much of Africa, AIDS is now an epidemic. In Zimbabwe, Botswana and South Africa, close to one-quarter of the adult population is infected with HIV, the virus thought to cause AIDS. These countries are expected to lose 20 per cent of their adult populations to the disease in the next decade. In Zimbabwe, life expectancy has dropped from 61 years less than a decade ago to just 39 years today.

And while population growth rates have slowed in many nations, some still continue to expand rapidly. Pakistan and Nigeria, for example, both expect to see their populations double in the next 50 years. Ethiopia, with the world's highest birth rate, is predicted to almost triple its population. Meanwhile, India is closing in on the one billion mark, fast catching up to China as the world's most populous nation. As the populations of these nations increase, so does the strain on their natural resources. Water tables in India, for example, are falling fast and arable cropland is disappearing in countries like Pakistan and Ethiopia.

Even though many birth rates are declining, we are still in the momentum of population growth, as more than one billion youths are just entering their reproductive years. Adding to the pressure on the resources of our Earth will be the continuing push for an ever-expanding global economy. According to the recent United Nations report, Global Environment Outlook 2000, the continued poverty of the majority of the world's population and the excessive consumption by the minority are the two main causes of environmental degradation, which continues to accelerate.

The world's population is expected to reach about nine billion by 2050. If current trends towards smaller families continue, we will not see another doubling of the population in the coming century. That's a relief, but the six billion people on the planet now are already consuming more than the Earth can replenish. Adding another three billion people will be disastrous unless we start reducing our impact now.

—*Originally published October 20, 1999*

after READING

UNDERSTANDING THE TEXT

1. a) In your notebook, record Suzuki's statement of the **thesis** of this **essay**.
   b) Locate and record a statement from the final paragraph that suggests an action Suzuki wants his readers to take.

2. In your notebook, **summarize** the arguments made in this essay. In point-form notes, record the factual information and the references to authorities used by Suzuki to persuade the reader to accept his argument.

EXPLORING IDEAS AND IMPLICATIONS

3. a) This essay was originally published as one of a series of weekly newspaper columns. With a partner, go to the library and examine a newspaper. Make notes on the differences you observe in the lengths of the paragraphs in various forms of newspaper writing. Consider news **articles**, editorials, and the writing by daily or weekly columnists, and suggest reasons for the different paragraph lengths and styles of writing. Compare paragraph lengths in newspapers with those in **literary essays** by senior secondary-school students.
   b) With a partner, experiment with how the paragraphs of Suzuki's essay could be combined if it had been written as an academic essay instead of a newspaper column.

4. Write a **persuasive essay** on a topic of global significance using factual information and references to authorities to convince the reader. With a partner, revise your essay paying special attention to consistency of **voice**, clarity of expression, and the use of language to convince the reader. Rewrite your paper, and make all the necessary corrections in grammar, spelling, and sentence structure. Format your essay using margins, spacing, and layout appropriate for publication.

MAKING CONNECTIONS

5. a) Read two other selections in the "The Virtual and the Real" unit. Create a print advertisement that either extols science and technology or urges people to return to a simpler life without the influence of science and technology. Consider using a line from one of the selections as a headline or slogan for your ad. Use visuals, fonts, and colours that will attract viewers' attention.
   b) Be prepared to display and explain the message of your ad. As a class, create a form to assess the effectiveness of the ads produced in the class. ■

Food Fight

MARCIA KAYE

"Why are we even growing these crops?"

BEFORE READING

1. Discuss with a partner the ideas or images that are called to mind by the title of this article. Does the title grab your attention?

2. Write in your own words a brief definition of the term "biotechnology." Compare definitions with a partner.

You have never eaten a tomato that has been genetically modified with a fish gene. Or corn with a scorpion gene. Or any vegetable or fruit with any animal gene.

It's very likely, however, that you have eaten a product made from canola, soy, corn or potato that has been genetically modified with, say, a gene from a bacterium to make the plant more resistant to pests. In fact, you may be eating products of genetic engineering every day, whether it's your cornflakes at breakfast, the margarine on your morning toast, the tofu in your stir-fry, your baked potato, or the soy lecithin in your chocolate bar. And you may be wondering if they could affect you.

Is there any proof that these products are dangerous to your health or to the environment?

No.

Then is there proof that these products are 100 per cent safe, for now and for the long term?

No.

What we do know is that this first generation of modified foods, which has been widely available in grocery stores, largely unlabelled, for the past two years, offers no obvious benefits to consumers. The food doesn't taste better, won't last longer, isn't nutritionally superior and isn't cheaper than conventional food. But the next wave of this technology could give us peaches with a longer shelf life, canola oil with a healthier proportion of fats, potatoes that need less oil for frying, decaffeinated coffee beans and vitamin A-enriched rice to prevent blindness in developing countries. The government tells us that the biotech food on the market is as safe as any conventional food, but critics are questioning the entire regulatory process. And while some say this technology could harm the environment, others say it could save it.

The issue of genetically modified foods has become a worldwide food fight. The proponents, including the giant multinational companies (formerly called chemical and pharmaceutical companies but now calling themselves "life sciences" companies), talk about the wonders of "enhanced foods" and "superfoods." Meanwhile, critics wave banners protesting against "Frankenfoods" and "Farmageddon." Somewhere between are those scientists and farmers who say that the technology of transgenics—which means splicing bits of DNA from one organism into another, or even from one species into another—comes with more questions than answers. And stuck in the middle is the hapless consumer.

It's especially hard to know which information to trust—the booklet from the government department that's promoting the products? The speech from the protester in the tomato costume? The words from the university professor whose research is funded by the biotech industry? After several international food disasters, including mad cow disease in England, toxic chocolate in Belgium and deadly E. coli-contaminated water right here in Canada, consumers are naturally wary of any change to their food supply. The worries have brought people together into anti-genetic-engineering groups: Knives

& Forks includes top Ontario chefs Jamie Kennedy, Michael Sullivan and Michael Stradtländer; GE alert includes scientists across the country. The very conservative British Medical Association, which represents more than 110 000 physicians, has called for a moratorium on the commercial planting of genetically modified crops until there's a scientific consensus on their impact.

For most consumers, the No. 1 concern is health. There is no evidence that biotech foods harm people's health, but because they're still relatively new, there are no long-term studies. We simply don't know how these foods may affect us, if at all, 20 years down the road.

The chief short-term health concern is food allergies, particularly among people who have life-threatening reactions to products such as peanuts or fish. So far, there are no foods on the market that have been genetically modified with any nut or fish products. Experiments, however, are ongoing. One U.S. study looked at soybeans that had been engineered with a gene from a Brazil nut to enhance the protein. The study found that blood samples from people with nut allergies tested positive to the engineered soybean, meaning that allergic people could have had serious reactions if they'd actually eaten the soybean. The biotech company immediately dropped any plans to get the product approved for market.

Most of those scientists with concerns about transgenic food are worried not about human health but about the long-term health of the environment. The biggest environmental worry is outcrossing, especially in canola. Outcrossing, which also happens with non-biotech crops, means that through cross-pollination by wind or insects, the traits of one plant spread to another. The concern with canola is that the genetically modified traits of the canola can—and do—transfer to regular canola and to canola's weedy cousins, such as wild mustard, creating "superweeds" that are resistant to the very herbicide that was designed to kill them.

"It was recognized when this technology was in the development stage that outcrossing would be a possibility," says Malcolm Devine of Saskatoon, head of biotechnology research for Aventis CropScience Canada, makers of genetically modified canola. "There's quite a variety of herbicides a farmer can use."

It's not that simple, says Elisabeth Abergel, a Toronto molecular biologist who for her PhD thesis is assessing whether there are environmental risks in growing genetically modified crops. "One of the worst scenarios is, as we've see in Alberta recently, we get strains of canola that are resistant to three different common herbicides. Farmers can't get rid of the stuff." And the ramifications of outcrossing can be international. There was a furor in Europe earlier this year when farmers in Britain, France, Germany and Sweden discovered that the seed they had bought from Canada—seed that was supposed to be GM-free—in fact contained GM material. The unwitting error was apparently a result of cross-pollination in Canada over the last year or two between conventional canola and neighbouring fields of GM canola. Organic farmers whose crops become

victims of outcrossing could lose their organic certification, and their livelihood.

Another potential problem is the loss of diversity that can occur through genetic engineering. Diversity of crops is like an agricultural insurance policy: if an insect infestation or disease wipes out one variety of species, there are plenty more varieties that will survive. "The genetic base we use to grow most of our food crops is already very narrow, and the genetics industry does not prize diversity," Abergel says. A world full of similarly engineered crops could be a great thing if they're all resistant to a certain destructive insect, or it could be a catastrophe if they're all susceptible to it. Just as with the stock market, diversification helps to cover food growers in any eventuality.

Why are we even growing these crops? Supporters say that biotechnology is the only alternative to our current imperfect methods of food production.

"You could argue that the technology has some very nice benefits for the environment," said Don Smith, a crop ecophysiologist and professor in the department of plant sciences at Montreal's McGill University. Smith hastens to state that "I owe nothing to the biotech industry. Genetically modified food is clearly a benefit to the large multinationals and no benefit at all to consumers."

But as Smith explains, even before genetic modification, except for plants like wild blueberries and fiddlehead ferns, our food bore little resemblance to the way Mother Nature intended it. It has been cross-pollinated, hybridized, fertilized and sprayed with toxic pesticides. Smith says that farmland in North America and Europe has reached the saturation point for fertilizers, which are highly polluting, and we're rapidly losing irrigated land. With a world population expected to increase by half in 50 years, we need more crop production. New crops that can be genetically engineered to need less water or less fertilizer could help alleviate those problems. "Biotechnology is about the only thing on the horizon," Smith says.

David Suzuki, the country's best-known geneticist, is one of the most vocal opponents of racing ahead with transgenics. As a scientist who in the 1970s had one of the largest genetics labs in Canada, he admits that he takes a vicarious delight in the new technology. But he says that we know too little about the long-term effects, and he scoffs at the thought that transgenics could ever solve world hunger. He says that global starvation is not a problem of food shortages but of poor distribution of both food and income due to politics, wars, deforestation, lack of family planning and lack of education. "Three billion people in the world live on less than three dollars a day," Suzuki says. "They couldn't afford to buy the food anyway, and don't tell me that we're going to give it away to the poor."

"He's absolutely right," Smith replies. "The World Food Programme cannot deliver food to all those on the brink of starvation. But if you pour more food into the system, the people at the bottom will get more of it."

It's difficult for some to believe that multinational companies could have such altruistic motives, or that the science could be good when the public relations have been so bad. For instance, Monsanto Co., the U.S.-based multinational, hired a public relations firm last year that offered free lunches to people, many of them poor, to carry pro-biotech signs during a demonstration. The employee cafeteria in a Monsanto-owned pharmaceutical company in England serves *no* genetically modified food. And in Canada, Percy Schmeiser of Bruno, Sask., a canola farmer and a former MLA, is being sued by Monsanto for patent infringement by allegedly growing genetically modified canola without a licence; Schmeiser claims that the transgenic seed blew in from a neighbour's field, and he's countersuing Monsanto for allegedly contaminating his non-transgenic canola crop. Schmeiser worries that biotech companies may end up with more control over farming than the farmers have. "If you control the seed supply, you control the food supply," he says. "And if you control the food supply, you control the country."

The biotech companies are so weary of such allegations that some of their executives, such as Ray Mowling, president of Monsanto Canada Inc. of Mississauga, Ont., have all but stopped talking to the media. But in a rare interview Mowling acknowledges, "We've built a reputation a titch on the negative side," and he smiles at the understatement. But he adds, "Despite all that's going on, we're committed to the promise of these technologies. Here's a company that's the world leader in herbicides and we're talking ourselves away from that. If we don't, we're not going to be able to feed ourselves."

Are Canadian consumers ready to eat unknown quantities of transgenic food today for potential benefits tomorrow? Some companies don't think so. McCain Foods of Florenceville, N.B., will accept only non-genetically modified potatoes for its frozen french fries. (Interestingly, the oil in those same french fries may well be from genetically modified canola or soy.) Soyaworld Inc. of Surrey, B.C., the country's leading soy beverage company, uses only non-transgenic soybeans in its top-selling soy drink, necessitating a labour-intensive tracking system that has raised some prices slightly at the grocery store. Both companies are betting that Canadians share the anti-Genetically Modified Organism sentiment existing in the European Union. Indeed, two recent surveys conducted by the polling firm Environics found that three-quarters of Canadians are concerned about the use of biotechnology in food production.

So what's a farmer to do? Many farmers waited till the last minute before spring planting, to see which way the consumer wind was blowing. Dean Moxham, a farmer near Portage la Prairie, Man., started growing genetically modified canola in 1996. The canola had been engineered to be herbicide-resistant, so that when Moxham sprayed his weedy fields, the weeds died but the canola did not. That first year his yield was only average. But the next year was better, and the next even better. Last year he repeated 50 bushes an acre, six or seven bushels more than his conventional yield. Much of his extra profits, however, went to pay for the $15-per-acre "technology charge"

and the fresh seed each year. (The chemical company can tear out the crops if it catches farmers using transgenic seed from the last season.)

While Moxham wasn't thrilled about relinquishing some control over his farming to a chemical company, he did find that the transgenic canola gave him better results than his previous efforts, which included using a variety of herbicides and rotating his crops. But this year, while he planted some genetically modified canola, he grew some regular canola, too, as did many of his fellow farmers. "We've got to grow what we can sell," Moxham explains. "If a guy in the city doesn't want to buy canola oil because it's from a genetically altered crop, where's my market?"

The Canadian Federation of Agriculture, an umbrella organization representing more than 200 000 farm families, supports biotechnology. But the National Farmers Union, which is the country's only voluntary, direct-membership, national farm organization, won't support it until there's more scientific information about its effects on health and environment.

What could those effects possibly be? The government regulatory agencies that have so far approved 43 genetically modified foods in Canada say that rigorous, comprehensive reviews have shown that the products are safe. "What we are saying is that the new products are as safe and nutritious as any products that are currently on the market," says Bart Bilmer, director of the Office of Biotechnology with the Canadian Food Inspection Agency (CFIA). "There's no such thing as 100 per cent safety for any food on the market."

If a company such as Monsanto or Aventis CropScience develops a new food through biotechnology, it must approach the CFIA for permission to do field testing. The CFIA reviews data provided by the company, and if the CFIA is satisfied that it meets government guidelines, small confined field trials begin, using bags to prevent pollen from escaping into the environment. If the company doesn't meet the exact conditions of the field trial, CFIA inspectors can order it to be plowed under.

If the biotech company deems the trial successful, it can apply to commercialize the seed. Before approval, the CFIA looks at both the company's own data and peer-reviewed scientific literature on potential environmental impacts. If the product is intended for animal feed, it goes for review by the CFIA's feed group; if it's intended for human food, it goes for assessment through Health Canada. Neither the CFIA nor Health Canada does original research on these products. They review data, mostly from the biotech company that wants its product approved. Of all the biotech foods that complete the requirements for review, how many has the CFIA refused to approve? None. How many has Health Canada rejected? None.

Criticisms against the regulatory system have come from several fronts. First, since the CFIA reports to Parliament through the Ministry of Agriculture and Agri-Food Canada, it's been accused of a conflict of interest in both promoting and regulating food. "It's like the fox minding the henhouse," says critic Jane Thornthwaite, a North Vancouver dietitian.

Another criticism involves the principle of substantial equivalence, which is the fundamental standard used in crop assessment. Regulators look to see if new products are "substantially equivalent" to their conventional counterparts. Developed jointly in the 1990s by the Food and Agriculture Organization of the United Nations, the World Health Organization and the Organization for Economic Cooperation and Development, the principle of substantial equivalence was condemned as "a pseudo-scientific concept" by three scientists in the Oct. 7, 1999 issue of the prestigious journal *Nature*.

The CFIA defends its regulatory system as thorough and rigorous, but Ann Clark, associate professor in plant agriculture at the University of Guelph in Ontario, says it needs to be more rigorous still. Her recent study claims that according to Health Canada's own information, as well as original industry submissions, 70 per cent of the approved foods have never been analyzed for toxicity and none have been analyzed for allergenicity. Nine senior scientists across the country publicly support those findings, and Clark says that dozens of others support them privately but are afraid to go public for fear of losing jobs at universities. Clark says, "We as a group are not saying the food is not safe. We're saying we don't know."

Right now, most Canadians can't choose whether to buy or to avoid genetically modified foods since, for the most part, the foods aren't labelled. The Council of Canadians, an independent citizens' interest group, and Greenpeace are calling for mandatory labelling. The Food Biotechnology Communications Network, with representatives from industry, government, the Canadian Council of Grocery Distributors and the Consumers' Association of Canada, is pursing voluntary labelling. Some argue that labelling of either kind is costly, since it entails segregating crops from source to market. But it will have to be done anyway for the export market.

While arguments continue to boomerang on both sides of the issue, all parties agree that it is a powerful technology that could have far-reaching implications. McGill's Don Smith says, "I see biotechnology as a potentially useful tool, but it has to be wielded very, very carefully."

Are we being careful enough? That question now goes to consumers, who will answer with their voices and their wallets.

—Originally published October 2000

after READING

UNDERSTANDING THE TEXT

1. In your notebook, write a brief explanation of the significance of the title in relation to the content of the article. Work with a partner to suggest an alternate title. Which title is more successful at attracting the reader's attention? Which title is more appropriate for the content of the article? **Summarize** your discussion in your notebook.

2. a) In your notebook, make two columns headed "pro" and "con." In the first column, list in point-form notes all the arguments from the article that seem to be in favour of genetically modified foods. In the second column, list in point-form notes all the arguments from the article that seem to be opposed to genetically modified foods.

   b) Compare your list with that of another student. Assess whether the writer has successfully covered both sides of the controversy. Summarize your discussion in a few sentences.

   c) Discuss whether you can detect a **bias** on the part of the writer toward one side of the controversy or the other. Consider the writer's **voice** and **tone**, the order of the arguments, and the connotations of specific words. Summarize your ideas and be prepared to provide evidence from the text to support your arguments during a class discussion.

3. In a group of three or four students, discuss the meaning of the terms "Frankenfood" and "Farmageddon" and explain the **allusions** contained in the terms. In your notebook write an evaluation of the effectiveness or impact of these terms.

4. Make a list of technical language that is used in the article. Explain to a partner the reading skills you would use to develop an understanding of these particular words or phrases in the article. Ask your partner to explain to you how a knowledge of root words, prefixes, and suffixes can help you to understand the meaning of some of these terms. (See The Reference Shelf, page 411.)

EXPLORING IDEAS AND IMPLICATIONS

5. a) Locate in the article as many examples as you can find of the writer's use of parentheses, dashes, and hyphens. Review the conventions for the use of these specialized pieces of punctuation (see The Reference Shelf, pages 412–413). Explain to a partner the reasons for the writer's use of the punctuation in the examples you located.

   b) Ask your partner to explain to you the grammatical construction of this sentence from the article: "There's quite a variety of herbicides a farmer can use."

MAKING CONNECTIONS

6. Visit the Web sites of any of the organizations or corporations mentioned in this article (or search for print information from or about them). In addition, visit the Web site of the Council for Biotechnology Information (http://www.whybiotech.com) and other sites located by using a search engine to find "biotechnology." By reading the headings and some of the information at each, identify the **bias** of the writers of the Web site (or print material) and record in your notebook whether it is "for," "against," or "neutral." Using point-form notes, tell how you recognized the particular bias of each Web site.

7. Read "And Baby Makes Six Billion" (pages 98–99). Use a Venn Diagram or other form of **graphic organizer** to show where any of the ideas from Suzuki's essay agree with, overlap, or disagree with the content of "Food Fight." You may wish to compare the two under the following headings: Details to support arguments; Questions/Concerns raised; Solutions/Actions stated; Solutions/Actions implied. ■

In Praise of the Printed Word

KIRI NESBITT

"... or why electronic books will
 never work, at least in the pleasure market."

BEFORE READING

With a partner, identify three **contexts** in which electronic publishing is replacing print-on-paper publishing. In each case, discuss whether print-on-paper publishing will eventually disappear altogether. Be prepared to present your ideas to the class.

It seems that every new way of presenting the written word is touted as the most revolutionary concept since Gutenberg's invention of movable type in the 15th century. Printed material has been pronounced dead so often I'm beginning to suspect some technology writers have undergone a form of aversion therapy that involved being beaten with hardcover books.

The latest development to use the Gutenberg cliché is electronic publishing.

Simply put, electronic publishing is the downloading of typeset material from the Internet. This material can be either printed off, or transferred to a portable device called an e-book reader, for viewing. E-book readers are similar in size, shape and weight to a hardcover novel. The term "electronic book" or "e-book" can refer to either the device itself, or the material that is read on it.

There are some who see a huge future in e-books. [In early January 2000], Microsoft Corp., the largest software maker, announced it had formed an alliance with Barnes & Noble Inc.—the No. 1 U.S. bookseller—and barnesandnoble.com Inc. to sell electronic books that are read using Microsoft software. The companies will set up a Web site to sell the books on the barnesandnoble.com site by the middle of [2000]. And Microsoft is already predicting that sales of electronic books will surpass those of printed books in a decade.

Certainly, the idea for electronic books has been around a long time. In the July, 1945 issue of *The Atlantic Monthly*,

Vannevar Bush mentioned a theoretical device called a memex "in which an individual stores all his books, records, and communications, and which is mechanized so that it may be consulted with exceeding speed and flexibility."

Bush described his memex as follows: "It consists of a desk, and while it can presumably be operated from a distance, it is primarily the piece of furniture at which he works. On the top are slanting translucent screens, on which material can be projected for convenient reading. There is a keyboard, and sets of buttons and levers. Otherwise, it looks like an ordinary desk."

There have been many prototypes since then, none of which proved popular because they were unwieldy and the type was more difficult to read than that of printed books.

In [1999], several companies ... unveiled e-books with improved ergonomic designs....

Nuvomedia's RocketBook weighs a little over half a kilogram and has a 4½- by 3-inch screen. It costs $349 U.S. and can only be used with a PC, although Nuvomedia is working on a Macintosh version. Text is downloaded from Barnes and Noble or Powell's Bookstore Web sites for an average price of about $20 U.S. per book.

SoftBook produced an even fancier e-book reader in August [1999]. It comes with an Ethernet card and a modem so it can be directly connected to servers for downloading text. It has a larger—8- by 6-inch—screen than RocketBook and weighs about 1.3 kilograms. At $699.95 U.S. it is also pricier, but you can get it for less if you agree to buy a certain number of e-books per month....

Are these changes likely to have an impact on the publishing industry? Dick Brass, vice-president of Technology Development at Microsoft, certainly thinks so. He predicts that electronic publishing is set to become a vast and lucrative new industry in the next century.

"In less than 15 years, more than half of all titles sold will be electronic," he predicted at a press conference [in] August [1999].

Not everyone is as enthusiastic. In his Oct. 23 [1999] *Toronto Star* column, book critic Philip Marchand reported that Brass' prediction about printed books becoming history by the year 2006 was greeted with skepticism at the Frankfurt Book Fair. Small presses such as Porcupine's Quill, a Canadian publisher of literary books, respond coldly to the idea of electronic publishing.

Even computer book publisher Tim O'Reilly is cautious. "Online information delivery is a better mousetrap for the user, but we need to figure out how to make it work for authors and publishers as well," he says.

"Right now, there are a lot of people who are suggesting business models that are, quite frankly, short-sighted and destructive to the industry."

The prices for RocketBook and SoftBook readers put them out of reach for many people who currently enjoy paperbacks. Added to the expense of e-book readers is the cost of buying the books themselves. Inexplicably, the e-books I looked at on the Barnes and Noble Web site cost several dollars more than the hardcover editions. These costs will need to be significantly reduced in order to compete with printed matter.

However, we have already seen the prices of PCs drop dramatically over the last two decades, and it is possible that e-book readers will do the same if hardware manufacturers become convinced that this is a growth market.

Not everyone uses special hardware for reading e-books. Peanut Press gives away free software for reading its books on Palmtop computers. Users get the portability of an e-book reader without having to fork out several hundred dollars for a separate hardware device.

Cost is important not only to consumers, but also to the publishers and authors who create books. It is often said that electronic publishing reduces the cost of manufacturing a book and this should make it attractive to publishers concerned about the bottom line.

This is not true. Many of the costs involved in producing a paper book (author royalties, editing, typesetting, marketing, etc.) exist for e-books, too.

Nor do e-books eliminate the need for storage space, as some proponents claim. Instead of being kept in a warehouse, the e-book is stored on a server's hard drive, and megabytes cost money.

Even if e-books could be produced quicker and at less financial risk than printed books, it still would not be enough to lure some publishers into the realm of electronic publishing.

Tim Inkster, co-owner of Porcupine's Quill, would rather have quality than quantity.

"I think our in-house production facility is a good check and restraint on the enthusiasm of our editorial staff. I don't want to produce more books at lower cost. That is a slippery slope that leads to sloth and financial ruin."

There are other problems e-books need to overcome. The latest e-book readers are as portable as paper books; you can curl up in bed with them. But they are still not as easy to read as a printed page. In spite of recent advances such as sharper text and type that can be increased in size to suit your needs, there is no getting around the fact that you are reading from a screen.

When it comes to the advantages of e-books, two features are always mentioned: shipping and updating content. E-books are definitely easier to get a hold of than the paper versions. Once ordered, an e-book can be delivered as quickly as an e-mail. They can also be easily updated, which is very useful for reference material.

I spent a fortune on textbooks for university, only to find that their resale value at the end of five years was negligible because most of them were obsolete. This is one of the reasons why the Texas Board of Education started a pilot program in 1999 to replace printed books with e-books.

The ability to update text is only an advantage if the authors, editors and publishers involved are available and willing to do the work. This might not always be the case. O'Reilly points out that failure to keep books up-to-date is more often due to authors' time constraints rather than the lag imposed by print production.

Another concern with e-books is the lack of common standards in the industry. You can buy periodicals issued by any publisher from any bookstore and be able to read them. This is not the case with e-books. A book purchased from SoftBook cannot be read on the RocketBook reader and vice versa.

Those in the electronic publishing industry are aware of this problem and have taken steps to deal with it. Several companies including Microsoft, Adobe, IBM, Nuvomedia and SoftBook have been working together to write specifications for e-books.

In September, 1999, they released version 1.0 of the Open eBook (OEB) Publication Structure. This document provides guidelines for formatting and displaying electronic books. It suggests using XML and HTML to format content, which would make e-book pages look similar to Web pages.

OEB reading devices need to support certain MIME media types and Unicode characters. MIME is a standard for transferring non-textual data such as graphics electronically. Unicode was developed by the International Standards Organization (ISO) to combine character sets for different languages into one large, multilingual character set.

The problem with standards is that they are only good if everyone uses them. The protocol for standard HTML was supposed to ensure constancy among Web pages and browsers.

Unfortunately, few people have complied with this and the browsers with the biggest market shares, *Netscape Navigator* and *Internet Explorer*, do not support standard HTML. The result is that many Web sites do not look their best unless you are using a particular browser.

In spite of the problems involved, some large publishing houses have taken a chance on electronic publishing. In September [1999], Macmillan USA released its first e-book: *The Inmates Are Running the Asylum*, by Alan Cooper. Macmillan's editors must have an ironic sense of humour, as the book is about the frustrations people have with modern technology.

Random House also has e-books for sale, but its stock is limited to reference material, which is probably the safest bet for those who want to publish electronically.

When it comes to reading for pleasure, I can't see e-books having much impact. Paper books have a lot of sentimental value. They are passed on from generation to generation, from one friend to another. They are desirable because others have read them and will continue to read them in the future.

William Gass summed this up in an article that appeared in the November [1999] issue of *Harper's*. "We shall not understand what a book is, and why a book has the value many persons have, if we forget how important is its body."

A printed book gives us the history of everyone who has read it. All that an e-book can give us is information.

—*Originally published January 13, 2000*

after READING

UNDERSTANDING THE TEXT

1. Make a list of the three most positive features of e-books. In each case, give a reason for your choice.

2. Make a list of three problems with e-books that need to be solved before they can become popular with a large number of people.

3. In a paragraph, explain why you think the overall **tone** of this **article** has a positive, negative, or balanced view of electronic publishing. Cite evidence to support your position. In a small group, compare the paragraphs written by the members of the group.

4. With a partner, discuss whether electronic publishing, as it is described in this article, better serves the interests of the reader or the publisher. Be prepared to present your ideas to the class.

EXPLORING IDEAS AND IMPLICATIONS

5. In a small group, research the invention of printing from movable type by Gutenberg. (See The Reference Shelf, page 398.) Prepare an oral **report** on the various ways his invention has been credited with changing the course of history. Be sure to
   - clearly outline each group member's task
   - have the group convene at certain stages to report on progress
   - use both electronic and print sources to gather information
   - keep bibliographical information of all the sources you use
   - use visuals and technology as part of your presentation

6. Have members of the class research the International Standardization Organization (ISO) to find out other areas in which it sets standards. On chart paper, record the findings about its major work and contribution to society. Post the findings around the classroom.

MAKING CONNECTIONS

7. Stephen King has experimented with publishing stories and novels electronically on the Internet. Research his experience with this new form of publishing fiction and prepare a written report on your findings. ■

Long Distance Calling

LENORA STEELE

BEFORE READING

Interview your parents, guardians, or grandparents who remember when a long-distance telephone call was a difficult, expensive, and out-of-the-ordinary event. Ask them to recall the actions of family members when making or receiving a long-distance telephone call. Be prepared to present your findings to the class.

The cost of calling
is affordable these days, I
talked with Judy last night
for one hour and
twenty minutes; the distance   5
between the Maritimes and Upper
Canada has been shortened.
When someone in the house
calls, "It's long distance," I no
longer travel with break-   10
neck speed to get to
the receiver, but I
remember how, when
my brother would sometimes

call from Toronto, we would flee   15
from the four corners of
the house, leave water
running, kettles boiling, friends
turning ropes by
themselves to crowd around   20
the little stand at the end
of the stairs, waiting our
turns. Mum, her hands
waving, saying, "Quick,
quick." Putting words in our   25
mouths, "Tell him what you
made in school today" "Tell
him you had the measles" "Tell
him Uncle Ross bought a new
Ford" "Ask him if he has been   30
to see the Maple Leafs" It
used to be something, my
brother so far away, his
voice transported across
unfathomable wires, it used   35
to be magic once or twice
a year ... my brother calling
all the way from Toronto.

after READING

1. "... it used/to be magic once or twice/a year ..." (lines 35–37). In your notebook, list details from the **poem** that illustrate that receiving a long-distance telephone call used to be a special event. Compare these details with your findings in the "Before Reading" activity.

2. a) Explain to a partner the meaning of the statement "the distance/between the Maritimes and Upper/Canada has been shortened." (lines 5–7)

   b) Ask your partner to explain to you the meaning of lines 20–22, "... to crowd around/the little stand at the end/of the stairs ...."

EXPLORING IDEAS AND IMPLICATIONS

3. a) Review what you already know about the characteristics of free verse. (See The Reference Shelf, page 423.)

   b) In a small group, discuss the poet's use of line length, suggesting reasons for beginning or ending lines where she does.

   c) In your notebook, experiment with rewriting the first 23 lines of the poem, breaking the lines where you can identify a unit of thought. Also, experiment with rewriting lines 23–38 in **prose** using conventional punctuation.

   d) Compare your "rewritten" versions with the original poem, discussing the appeal and impact of each.

4. a) In a small group, use print and/or electronic sources to research the developments in communication over long distances in the past 25 years. Be sure to include satellite communication, computers and the Internet, fax, e-mail, and cellular or digital telephones.

   b) In a panel discussion present your findings on recent changes in communication, including a prediction about long-distance communication in the next 25 years.

MAKING CONNECTIONS

5. Compare "Long Distance Calling" with another free verse poem such as "When I Heard the Learn'd Astronomer" (page 116) or "Polaris" (page 118). Use a Venn diagram (or another type of **graphic organizer**) to outline the similarities and differences between the form and the content of the two poems. Display your graphic on chart paper. ■

When I Heard the Learn'd Astronomer

WALT WHITMAN

BEFORE READING

Using print and/or electronic sources, look up **biographical** information about Walt Whitman. Be prepared to present interesting details about his life and works to the class.

When I heard the learn'd astronomer,
When the proofs, the figures, were ranged in columns before me,
When I was shown the charts and diagrams, to add, divide, and
    measure them,
When I sitting heard the astronomer where he lectured with much   5
    applause in the lecture-room,
How soon unaccountable I became tired and sick,
Till rising and gliding out I wander'd off by myself,
In the mystical moist night-air, and from time to time,
Look'd up in perfect silence at the stars.   10

after READING

●

UNDERSTANDING THE TEXT

1. In your notebook, describe how the **narrator** feels about the astronomer and the science of astronomy.

2. Make a list of the words and phrases associated with the astronomer and those associated with the narrator once he or she has left the lecture. Show how these words differ in meaning and in sound and how the differences have an impact on the reader's understanding of the **poem**. Compare your observations with those of other class members.

3. This poem starts with a series of subordinate clauses within a periodic sentence. (See The Reference Shelf, page 409.) In a well-developed paragraph, prove these are effective constructions to use in this poem.

EXPLORING IDEAS AND IMPLICATIONS

4. This poem was published in 1865. Research the scientific advancements that were being made at that time and explain why Whitman would be concerned with science taking precedence over nature. Make notes for a possible oral **report** to the class.

5. a) With a partner, make a list of products this poem could be used to sell. Choose the best idea and create a television commercial using the poem. Target a specific **audience**. Using a shooting script, which includes camera shots, narration, and sound, capture your commercial.

   b) Present your commercial to the class and be prepared to defend your choice of products and your production design.

MAKING CONNECTIONS

6. a) In a small group, choose a scientific development you have heard about that you think may not be beneficial to humankind or to the environment. Have each member of the group research the topic, finding arguments and examples that demonstrate both sides of the issue. Sort, distribute, and share the research to members of the group. Each group member should prepare a **speech** focusing on his or her specific area of the investigation.

   b) Present a panel discussion to the class in which each group member takes the part of an expert on one aspect of the **topic**.

   c) Have the class create an evaluation form and assess each panel discussion. ■

Polaris

ZOE LANDALE

BEFORE READING

With a partner, list the names of as many planets, stars, and other "heavenly bodies" as you can without looking up the information. As a class, make a master list. How impressed were you with your class's knowledge of astronomy?

My daughter found Polaris the other night,
out her window in the sky beyond
the Douglas firs. *My first constellation*
she kept saying, as if her recognition were a lustrous
thing, remarkable in its sudden condensation   5
of meaning.

Now she wants a telescope
and the starry January sky is a mystical whirl of shapes
with lighted innards that pass by her own room
every evening after dinner.   10
A celestial join-the-dots to find the figure.
The North Star is a marker for escaped slaves:
a dreamy luminosity for my daughter to hang
reveries on. The book she is reading about
a black woman who escaped to Canada—   15
the child sees herself as The True North Strong and Free—
and cheers Polaris on. Good Work.

Obedient star. Lawful star, to light the way
across borders and through glass, to tweak
an eleven-year-old heart who has never been lost   20
in a dark country outside all protection.
Though she tries hard to imagine the alienness
of hemlock and alder swamps lit by the Big Dipper,
the moon
Night noises. Only last week she saw a yellow   25
stalking cat sign on a store door:
Cougar alert
Four minutes from home.

Though my daughter tries to stay with Polaris,
her imagination betrays her.   30
The dark Earth draws her back
to the escaped slave, the cougar
who may or may not be coming this way,
who wisps above the crisp ground
silent as mist   35
with paws that drive the hexagonal frost crystals
an inch down into the path.

No wonder she wants a telescope:
she wants to fall through her eyes
into that strange parade of luminosities   40
in the sky
with no more distractions.
Let the Archer, the Scorpion
tell her their stories of light.

after READING

1. As a class, brainstorm a list of **themes** in this **poem**. Select one of the themes and in your notebook explain how it is developed in the poem.

2. Select three **images** in the poem. For each, explain how the image conveys a "sudden condensation of meaning."

3. Create a **graphic organizer** that illustrates the connections and relationships among the various people, places, and things talked about in this poem.

4. In a short **essay**, describe three characteristics of the **narrator** of this poem. Provide evidence from the poem for each characteristic. Compare your essay with that of a partner.

EXPLORING IDEAS AND IMPLICATIONS

5. Write a diary entry by the 11-year-old daughter in this poem that reveals both her aspirations and fears after an evening of stargazing.

6. a) Research the life of Harriet Tubman. Write a poem about Polaris from her **point of view**.
   b) Revise and edit your poem. As a class, collect all the poems and create a class **anthology**. Use photographs, drawings, or electronically generated artwork to illustrate the anthology, if appropriate.

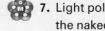

7. Light pollution in urban areas is making it increasingly difficult for people to see stars with the naked eye. With a partner, research the idea of "night sky preserves." Create a question-answer **brochure** describing the concept and explaining why it is or is not a good idea. Display your pamphlet on a bulletin board in the classroom.

MAKING CONNECTIONS

8. Read the poem "When I Heard the Learn'd Astronomer" (page 116). In a paragraph, explain whether the narrator of "Polaris" would or would not agree with the narrator of Whitman's poem. In a second paragraph, explain how you think the narrator of "When First I Heard the Learn'd Astronomer" would react to the ideas expressed in "Polaris." ■

Small Change Can Add Up to a Big Loss

ELLEN ROSEMAN

"With a little planning, you can avoid costly transactions."

BEFORE READING

As a class, brainstorm the pros and cons of a student in Grade 11 having access to a credit card or a bank debit card.

You're short of money, so you stop at an automated teller machine, or ATM, to make a withdrawal. That quick cash can often cost you $1, $2, even $3 a pop, depending on whose ATM you use and what kind of account you have. Do it every weekend and you may pay $150 a year in fees.

That's no small change.

Even virtual institutions that advertise "no-fee accounts" still charge for each withdrawal you make at another institution's ATM.

And if you use one of the new generic or "white label" machines, you'll pay an additional $1 to $2, on top of the $1.25 fee for Interac, the national electronic payments network shared by the country's financial institutions.

If you want to save money, check into whose slot you're sliding your card. With a little planning, you can avoid costly transactions.

As a frequent ATM user, you should have a bank account that provides a number of services for a flat monthly fee, or keep the minimum balance your bank requires in order to waive certain fees. Without one or the other, you may pay 30 cents to $1 for each ATM transaction.

Deal with an institution whose ATMs are convenient to your home, office or shopping areas. Count up the Interac charges on your monthly statements. Consider switching if the cost is too high.

Industry Canada, which publishes an annual report on bank service charges, has developed five typical consumer profiles.

One customer has two monthly ATM withdrawals at institutions other than his or her own bank. So does the connected consumer, who never goes into a branch.

White-label machines are multiplying fast. Thousands are in stores, shopping malls and restaurants, operated by private firms.

You can find out whether you're dealing with a generic ATM. A message on the screen asks if you're aware of the extra charge and allows you to abort the transaction.

Use your bank debit card to pay for purchases wherever possible. When you swipe a card through a point-of-sale terminal and key in a personal identification number or PIN, money is automatically transferred from your account to the store's account.

You should have a service package that includes debit-card transactions.

When using a bank card at an ATM or at a store, shield your PIN as you enter it. Someone who looks over your shoulder to get your PIN and later steals your card can take everything from your account.

With a stolen debit card, you may be on the hook for the full amount lost. You're more likely to be held liable if you haven't taken care of your PIN. It's your electronic signature.

Many people don't realize they have unlimited liability. They think stolen debit cards are treated the same way as credit cards, where you're on the hook for $50 at most if you report the theft right away.

But the convenience consumer, whose time is at a premium and who disregards where transactions are made, makes eight withdrawals a month from another institution's ATM.

If you fit that profile, find a bank with ATMs on your normal route. Recognize you won't go out of your way if the weather is chilly or you're in a hurry.

after READING

UNDERSTANDING THE TEXT

1. Create a **glossary** of terms used in this **article** for someone unfamiliar with banking in general and electronic banking in particular.

2. In your notebook, identify one piece of advice presented in this article and explain why you agree or disagree with it.

3. Using a single sentence, write an alternative headline for this article. Justify your title.

4. In your notebook, copy sentences from this article that illustrate the following: a simple sentence, a complex sentence, a compound sentence, and a compound-complex sentence. In each case, explain why the sentence you chose is an example of the kind of sentence structure. (See The Reference Shelf, page 410.)

EXPLORING IDEAS AND IMPLICATIONS

5. With a partner, make a list of 10 acronyms that you know. Working with another pair, see how many of their acronyms you can accurately provide the words for.

6. Write an **opinion essay** explaining why you think Canada will or will not become a "cash-less society." Be prepared to present your opinion to the class.

7. With a partner, conduct a survey of students in your school to find out how many of them have access to a credit card or bank debit card. Prepare a **report** that correlates access with characteristics such as age and gender. (Remember, in order to make a correlation, you need to collect information about the characteristic you are planning to correlate with.) Be prepared to present your findings to the class.

8. **Debate** the following resolution: Be It Resolved that Young People Today Know the Value of a Dollar. (See The Reference Shelf, pages 455–458.) You may need to do research to prepare your arguments.

MAKING CONNECTIONS

9. Find another newspaper or magazine article that presents financial advice that you think is relevant for teenagers. Present a synopsis of the article to the class and explain why the information is important. ■

Will We Plug Computers into Our Brains?

WILLIAM GIBSON

"Our hardware ... is likely to turn into something like us a lot faster than we are likely to turn into something like our hardware."

BEFORE READING

With a partner, identify one piece of today's technology that would be most amazing to a person born in the year 1900. Prepare a list of reasons to convince the rest of the class that your choice would be the most amazing to that imaginary person from the past.

Will we plug computers into our brains? Maybe.

But only once or twice, and probably not for very long.

With their sharp black suits and their surgically implanted silicon chips, the cyberpunk hard guys of '80s science fiction (including the characters in my early novels and short stories) already have a certain nostalgic romance about them. These information highwaymen were so heroically attuned to the new technology that they laid themselves open to its very cutting edge. They became it; they took it within themselves.

Meanwhile, in case you somehow haven't noticed, we are all becoming it; we seem to have no choice but to take it within ourselves.

In hindsight, the most memorable images of science fiction often have more to do with our anxieties in the past (that is to say, the writer's present) than with those singular and ongoing scenarios that make up our life as a species—our real future, our ongoing present.

Many of us, even today, or most particularly today, must feel as though we already have silicon chips embedded in our brains. Some of us, certainly, are not entirely happy with that feeling. Some of us must wish that ubiquitous computation would simply go away and leave us alone. But that seems increasingly unlikely.

That does not, however, mean that we will one day, as a species, submit to the indignity of the chip—if only because the chip is likely to shortly be as quaint an object as the vacuum tube or the slide rule.

From the viewpoint of bioengineering, a silicon chip is a large and rather complex shard of glass. Inserting a silicon chip into the human brain involves a certain irreducible inelegance of scale. It's scarcely more elegant, relatively, than inserting a steam engine into the same tissue. It may be technically possible, but why should we even want to attempt such a thing?

I suspect that mainstream medicine and the military will both find reasons for attempting such a thing, at least in the short run, and that medicine's reasons may at least serve to counter some disability, acquired or inherited. If I were to lose my eyes, I would quite eagerly submit to some sort of surgery that promised a video link to the optic nerves. (And once there, why not insist on full-channel cable and a Web browser?) The military's reasons for chip insertion would probably have something to do with what I suspect is the increasingly archaic job description of "fighter pilot," or with some other aspect of telepresent combat, in which weapons in the field are remotely controlled by distant operators. At least there's still a certain macho frisson to be had in the idea of embedding a tactical shard of glass in your head, and crazier things, really, have been done in the name of king and country.

But if we do it at all, I doubt we'll be doing it for very long, as various models of biological and nanomolecular computing are looming rapidly in view. Rather than plug a piece of hardware into our gray matter, how much more elegant to extract some brain cells, plop them into a Petri dish and graft on various sorts of gelatinous computing goo. Slug it all back into the skull and watch it run on blood sugar, the way a human brain's supposed to. Get all the functions and features you want, without that clunky-junky 20th century hardware thing. You really don't need complicated glass to crunch numbers, and computing goo probably won't be all that difficult to build. (The trickier aspect here may be turning data into something brain cells can understand. If you knew how to get brain cells to manage pull-down menus, you'd probably know everything you needed to know about brain cells.)

Our hardware, I think, is likely to turn into something like us a lot faster than we are likely to turn into something like our hardware. Our hardware is evolving at the speed of light, while we are still the product, for the most part, of unskilled labor.

But there is another argument against the need to implant computing devices, be they glass or goo. It's a very simple one, so simple that some have difficulty grasping it. It has to do with a certain archaic distinction we still tend to make, a distinction between computing and "the world." Between, if you like, the virtual and the real.

I very much doubt that our grandchildren will understand the distinction between that which is a computer and that which isn't.

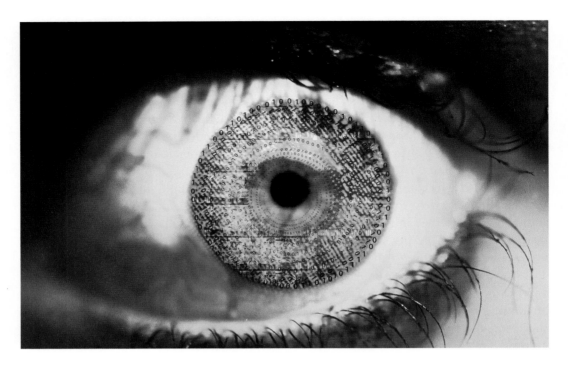

Or to put it another way, they will not know "computers" as a distinct category of object or function. This, I think, is the logical outcome of genuinely ubiquitous computing, of the fully wired world. The wired world will consist, in effect, of a single unbroken interface. The idea of a device that "only" computes will perhaps be the ultimate archaism in a world in which the fridge or the toothbrush is potentially as smart as any other object, including you, a world in which intelligent objects communicate, routinely and constantly, with one another and with us.

In this world, there may be no need for the physical augmentation of the human brain, as the most significant, and quite unthinkably powerful, augmentation will have taken place beyond geographic boundaries, via distributed processing. You won't need smart goo in your brain, because your fridge and your toothbrush will be very smart indeed, enormously smart, and they will be there for you, constantly and always.

So it won't, I don't think, be a matter of computers crawling buglike into the most intimate chasms of our being, but of humanity crawling buglike out into the mingling light and shadow of the presence of that which we will have created, which we are creating now, and which seems to be in the process of re-creating us.

—Originally published June 19, 2000

after READING

UNDERSTANDING THE TEXT

1. In a single sentence, identify and explain the main point of this **essay**.

2. Select one idea in this essay that you do not agree with and explain why you disagree with it.

3. Although most of this essay is written in full and complete sentences, paragraphs 1 and 2 are not written as sentences. In your notebook, write a paragraph explaining why you think these two paragraphs are or are not effective.

4. As a class, create a **glossary** of words in this essay that might be challenging for a Grade 11 student.

EXPLORING IDEAS AND IMPLICATIONS

5. William Gibson created the terms "cyberspace" and "cyberpunk" in the 1980s. Based on this essay and on your own research, write an explanation of these terms in your notebook.

6. In a small group, discuss why medicine and the military are areas of human endeavour that would be most likely to insert a silicon chip into the human brain. Be prepared to present your ideas to the class.

7. In your notebook, write a short essay explaining one way in which "our hardware is turning into something like us" (paragraph 11 on page 125).

8. **Debate** one of the following resolutions: Be It Resolved That Technology Is Making Human Life Better or Be It Resolved That Technology Has Improved Life for Women More Than for Men. (See The Reference Shelf, pages 455–458.) You may need to do research to prepare your arguments.

MAKING CONNECTIONS

9. Read a science fiction **novel** or watch a science fiction movie. Write a **review** of it for the school newspaper. Revise your review, focusing on **diction**, **voice**, and effectiveness of argument. Then edit it for grammar, spelling, and punctuation.

10. Read the excerpt from "The Grand Academy of Lagado" (pages 91–94). Using it as a model, write a **satire** of our computerized world. Revise and edit after the first draft. Be prepared to submit your work to your teacher. ■

The Broken Globe

HENRY KREISEL

"A toy ... you bring me a toy here, not bigger
than my hand, and it is supposed to be the world,
this little toy here, with the printed words on
coloured paper, this little cardboard ball."

BEFORE READING

Using print and/or electronic sources, investigate what is studied in geophysics.

Since it was Nick Solchuk who first told me about the opening in my field at the University of Alberta, I went up to see him as soon as I received word that I had been appointed. He lived in one of those old mansions in Pimlico that had once served as town houses for wealthy merchants and aristocrats, but now housed a less moneyed group of people—stenographers, students, and intellectuals of various kinds. He had studied at Cambridge and got his doctorate there and was now doing research at the Imperial College and rapidly establishing a reputation among the younger men for his work on problems which had to do with the curvature of the earth.

His room was on the third floor, and it was very cramped, but he refused to move because he could look out from his window and see the Thames and the steady flow of boats, and that gave him a sense of distance and of space also. Space, he said, was what he missed most in the crowded city. He referred to himself, nostalgically, as a prairie boy, and when he wanted to demonstrate what he meant by space he used to say that when a man stood and looked out across the open prairie, it was possible for him to believe that the earth was flat.

"So," he said, after I had told him my news, "you are going to teach French to prairie boys and girls. I congratulate you." Then he cocked his head to one side, and looked me over and said: "How are your ears?"

"My ears?" I said. "They're all right. Why?"

"Prepare yourself," he said. "Prairie voices trying to speak French—that will be a great experience for you. I speak from experience. I learned my French pronunciation in a little one-room school in a prairie village. From an extraordinary girl, mind you, but her mind ran to science. Joan McKenzie—that was her name. A wiry little thing, sharp-nosed, and she always wore brown dresses. She was particularly fascinated by earthquakes. 'In 1755 the city of Lisbon, Portugal, was devastated. 60,000 persons died; the shock was felt in Southern France and North Africa; and inland waters of Great Britain and Scandinavia were agitated.' You see, I still remember that, and I can hear her voice too. Listen: 'In common with the entire solar system, the earth is moving through space at the rate of approximately 45,000 miles per hour, toward the constellation of Hercules. Think of that, boys and girls.' Well, I thought about it. It was a lot to think about. Maybe that's why I became a geophysicist. Her enthusiasm was infectious. I knew her at her peak. After a while she got tired and married a solid farmer and had eight children."

"But her French, I take it, was not so good," I said.

"No," he said. "Language gave no scope to her imagination. Mind you, I took French seriously enough. I was a very serious student. For a while I even practised French pronunciation at home. But I stopped it because it bothered my family. My mother begged me to stop. For the sake of peace."

"Your father's ears were offended," I said.

"Oh, no," Nick said, "not his ears. His soul. He was sure that I was learning French so I could run off and marry a French girl.... Don't laugh. It's true. When once my father believed something, it was very hard to shake him."

"But why should he have objected to your marrying a French girl anyway?"

"Because," said Nick, and pointed a stern finger at me, "because when he came to Canada he sailed from some French port, and he was robbed of all his money while he slept. He held all Frenchmen responsible. He never forgot and he never forgave. And, by God, he wasn't going to have that cursed language spoken in his house. He wasn't going to have any non-sense about science talked in his house either." Nick was silent for a moment, and then he said, speaking very quietly, "Curious man, my father. He had strange ideas, but a strange kind of imagination, too. I couldn't understand him when I was going to school or to the university. But then a year or two ago, I suddenly realized that the shape of the world he lived in had been forever fixed for him by some medieval priest in the small Ukrainian village where he was born and where he received an education of sorts when he was a boy. And I suddenly realized that he wasn't mad, but that he lived in the universe of the medieval church. The earth for him was the centre of the universe, and the centre was still. It didn't move. The sun rose in the East and it set in the West, and it moved perpetually around a still earth. God had made this earth specially for man, and man's function was to perpetuate himself and to worship God.

My father never said all that in so many words, mind you, but that is what he believed. Everything else was heresy."

He fell silent.

"How extraordinary," I said.

He did not answer at once, and after a while he said, in a tone of voice which seemed to indicate that he did not want to pursue the matter further, "Well, when you are in the middle of the Canadian West, I'll be in Rome. I've been asked to give a paper to the International Congress of Geophysicists which meets there in October."

"So I heard," I said. "Wilcocks told me the other day. He said it was going to be a paper of some importance. In fact, he said it would create a stir."

"Did Wilcocks really say that?" he asked eagerly, his face reddening, and he seemed very pleased. We talked for a while longer, and then I rose to go.

He saw me to the door and was about to open it for me, but stopped suddenly, as if he were turning something over in his mind, and then said quickly, "Tell me—would you do something for me?"

"Of course," I said. "If I can."

He motioned me back to my chair and I sat down again. "When you are in Alberta," he said, "and if it is convenient for you, would you—would you go to see my father?"

"Why, yes," I stammered, "why, of course. I—I didn't realize he was still ..."

"Oh, yes," he said, "he's still alive, still working. He lives on his farm, in a place called Three Bear Hills, about sixty or seventy miles out of Edmonton. He lives alone. My mother is dead. I have a sister who is married and lives in Calgary. There were only the two of us. My mother could have no more children. It was a source of great agony for them. My sister goes to see him sometimes, and then she sometimes writes to me. He never writes to me. We—we had—what shall I call it—differences. If you went to see him and told him that I had not gone to the devil, perhaps ..." He broke off abruptly, clearly agitated, and walked over to his window and stood staring out, then said, "Perhaps you'd better not. I—I don't want to impose on you."

I protested that he was not imposing at all, and promised that I would write to him as soon as I had paid my visit.

I met him several times after that, but he never mentioned the matter again.

I sailed from England about the middle of August and arrived in Montreal a week later. The long journey West was one of the most memorable experiences I had ever had. There were moments of weariness and dullness. But the very monotony was impressive. There was a grandeur about it. It was monotony of a really monumental kind. There were moments when, exhausted by the sheer impact of the landscape, I thought back with longing to the tidy, highly cultivated countryside of England and of France, to the sight of men and women working in the fields, to the steady succession of villages and towns, and everywhere the consciousness of nature humanized. But I also began to understand why Nick Solchuk was always longing for more space and more air, especially when we moved into the prairies, and the land became flatter until there seemed nothing, neither hill nor tree nor bush, to disturb the vast unbroken flow of land until in the far distance a thin, blue line marked the point where the prairie merged into the sky. Yet over all there was a strange tranquillity, all motion seemed suspended, and only the sun moved steadily, imperturbably West, dropping finally over the rim of the horizon, a blazing red ball, but leaving a superb evening light lying over the land still.

I was reminded of the promise I had made, but when I arrived in Edmonton, the task of settling down absorbed my time and energy so completely that I did nothing about it. Then, about the middle of October, I saw a brief report in the newspaper about the geophysical congress which had opened in Rome on the previous day, and I was mindful of my promise again. Before I could safely bury it in the back of my mind again, I sat down and wrote a brief letter to Nick's father, asking him when I could come out to visit him. Two weeks passed without an answer, and I decided to go and see him on the next Saturday without further formalities.

The day broke clear and fine. A few white clouds were in the metallic autumn sky and the sun shone coldly down upon the earth, as if from a great distance. I drove south as far as Wetaskiwin and then turned east. The paved highway gave way to gravel and got steadily worse. I was beginning to wonder whether I was going right, when I rounded a bend and a grain elevator hove like a signpost into view. It was now about three o'clock and I had arrived in Three Bear Hills, but, as Nick had told me, there were neither bears nor hills there, but only prairie, and suddenly the beginning of an embryonic street with a few buildings on either side like a small island in a vast sea, and then all was prairie again.

I stopped in front of the small general store and went in to ask for directions. Three farmers were talking to the storekeeper, a bald, bespectacled little man who wore a long, dirty apron and stood leaning against his counter. They stopped talking and turned to look at me. I asked where the Solchuk farm was.

Slowly scrutinizing me, the storekeeper asked, "You just new here?"

"Yes," I said.

"From the old country, eh?"

"Yes."

"You selling something?"

"No, no," I said. "I—I teach at the University."

"That so?" He turned to the other men and said, "Only boy ever went to University from around here was Solchuk's boy. Nick. Real brainy young kid, Nick. Two of 'em never got on together. Too different. You know."

They nodded slowly.

"But that boy of his—he's a real bigshot scientist now. You know them addem bombs and them hydrergen bombs. He helps make 'em."

"No, no," I broke in quickly. "That's not what he does. He's a geophysicist."

"What's that?" asked one of the men.

But before I could answer, the little storekeeper asked excitedly, "You know Nick?"

"Yes," I said, "we're friends. I've come to see his father."

"And where's he now? Nick, I mean."

"Right now he is in Rome," I said. "But he lives in London, and does research there."

"Big-shot, eh," said one of the men laconically, but with a trace of admiration in his voice, too.

"He's a big scientist, though, like I said. Isn't that so?" the storekeeper broke in.

"He's going to be a very important scientist indeed," I said, a trifle solemnly.

"Like I said," he called out triumphantly. "That's showing 'em. A kid from Three Bear Hills, Alberta. More power to him!" His pride was unmistakable. "Tell me, mister," he went on, his voice dropping, "does he remember this place sometimes? Or don't he want to know us no more?"

"Oh, no," I said quickly. "He often talks of this place, and of Alberta, and of Canada. Some day he plans to return."

"That's right," he said with satisfaction. He drew himself up to full height, banged his fist on the table and said, "I'm proud of that boy. Maybe old Solchuk don't think so much of him, but you tell him old Mister Marshall is proud of him." He came from behind the counter and almost ceremoniously escorted me out to my car and showed me the way to Solchuk's farm.

I had about another five miles to drive, and the road, hardly more now than two black furrows cut into the prairie, was uneven and bumpy. The land was fenced on both sides of the road, and at last I came to a rough wooden gate hanging loosely on one hinge, and beyond it there was a cluster of small wooden buildings. The largest of these, the house itself, seemed at one time to have been ochre-coloured, but the paint had worn off and it now looked curiously mottled. A few chickens were wandering about, pecking at the ground, and from the back I could hear the grunting and squealing of pigs.

I walked up to the house and, just as I was about to knock, the door was suddenly opened, and a tall, massively built old man stood before me.

"My name is ..." I began.

But he interrupted me. "You the man wrote to me?" His voice, though unpolished, had the same deep timbre as Nick's.

"That's right," I said.

"You a friend of Nick?"

"Yes."

He beckoned me in with a nod of his head. The door was low and I had to stoop a bit to get into the room. It was a large, low-ceilinged room. A smallish window let in a patch of light which lit up the middle of the room but did not spread into the corners, so that it seemed as if it were perpetually dusk. A table occupied the centre, and on the far side there was a large wood stove on which stood a softly hissing black kettle. In the corner facing the entrance there was an iron bedstead, and the bed was roughly made, with a patchwork quilt thrown carelessly on top.

The old man gestured me to one of the chairs which stood around the table.

"Sit."

I did as he told me, and he sat down opposite me and placed his large calloused hands before him on the table. He seemed to study me intently for a while, and I scrutinized him. His face was covered by a three-days' stubble, but in spite of that, and in spite of the fact that it was a face beaten by sun and wind, it was clear that he was Nick's father. For Nick had the same determined mouth, and the same high cheek bones and the same dark, penetrating eyes.

At last he spoke. "You friend of Nick."

I nodded my head.

"What he do now?' he asked sharply. "He still tampering with the earth?"

His voice rose as if he were delivering a challenge, and I drew back involuntarily. "Why—he's doing scientific research, yes," I told him. "He's ..."

"What God has made," he said sternly, "no man should touch."

Before I could regain my composure, he went on, "He sent you. What for? What he want?"

"Nothing," I said, "Nothing at all. He sent me to bring you greetings and to tell you he is well."

"And you come all the way from Edmonton to tell me?"

"Yes, of course."

A faint smile played about his mouth, and the features of his face softened. Then suddenly he rose from his chair and stood towering over me. "You are welcome in this house," he said.

The formality with which he spoke was quite extraordinary and seemed to call for an appropriate reply, but I could do little more than stammer a thank you, and he, assuming again a normal tone of voice, asked me if I cared to have coffee. When I assented he walked to the far end of the room and busied himself about the stove.

It was then that I noticed, just under the window, a rough little wooden table and on top of it a faded old globe made of cardboard, such as little children use in school. I was intrigued to see it there and went over to look at it more closely. The cheap metal mount was brown with rust, and when I lifted it and tried to turn the globe on its axis, I found that it would not rotate because part of it had been squashed and broken. I ran my hand over the deep dent, and suddenly the old man startled me.

"What you doing there?" Curiosity seemed mingled with suspicion in his voice and made me feel like a small child surprised by its mother in an unauthorized raid on the pantry. I set down the globe and turned. He was standing by the table with two big mugs of coffee in his hands.

"Coffee is hot," he said.

I went back to my chair and sat down, slightly embarrassed.

"Drink," he said, pushing one of the mugs over to me.

We both began to sip the coffee, and for some time neither of us said anything.

"That thing over there," he said at last, putting down his mug, "that thing you was looking at—he brought it home one day—he was a boy then—maybe thirteen-year-old Nick. The other day I found it up in the attic. I was going to throw it in the garbage. But I forgot. There it belongs. In the garbage. It is a false thing." His voice had now become venomous.

"False?" I said. "How is it false?"

He disregarded my question. "I remember," he went on, "he came home from school one day and we was all here in this room—all sitting around this table eating supper, his mother, his sister and me and Alex, too—the hired man like. And then sudden like Nick pipes up, and he says, we learned in school today, he says, how the earth is round like a ball, he says, and how it moves around and around the sun and never stops, he says. They learning you rubbish in school, I say. But he says, no, Miss McKenzie never told him no lies. Then I say she does, I say, and a son of mine shouldn't believe it. Stop your ears! Let not Satan come in!" He raised an outspread hand and his voice thundered as if he were a prophet armed. "But he was always a stubborn boy—Nick. Like a mule. He never listened to reason. I believe it, he says. To me he says that— his father, just like that, I believe it, he says, because science has proved it and it is the truth. It is false, I cry, and you will not believe it. I believe it, he says. So then I hit him because he will not listen and will not obey. But he keeps shouting and shouting and shouting. "She moves," he shouts, "she moves, she moves!"

He stopped. His hands had balled themselves into fists, and the remembered fury sent the blood streaming into his face. He seemed now to have forgotten my presence and he went on speaking in a low murmuring voice, almost as if he were telling the story to himself.

"So the next day, or the day after, I go down to that school, and there is this little Miss McKenzie, so small and so thin that I could have crush her with my bare hands. What you teaching my boy Nick? I ask her. What false lies you stuffing in his head? What you telling him that the earth

is round and that she moves for? Did Joshua[1] tell the earth to stand still, or did he command the sun? So she says to me, I don't care what Joshua done, she says, I will tell him what science has discovered. With that woman I could get nowhere. So then I try to keep him away from school, and I lock him up in the house, but it was no good. He got out, and he run to the school like, and Miss McKenzie she sends me a letter to say she will send up the inspectors if I try to keep him away from the school. And I could do nothing."

His sense of impotence was palpable. He sat sunk into himself as if he were still contemplating ways of halting the scientific education of his son.

"Two, three weeks after," he went on, "he comes walking in this door with a large paper parcel in his hand. Now, he calls out to me, now I will prove it to you, I will prove that she moves. And he tears off the paper from the box and takes out this—this thing, and he puts it on the table here. Here, he cries, here is the earth, and look, she moves. And he gives that thing a little push and it twirls around like. I have to laugh. A toy, I say to him, you bring me a toy here, not bigger than my hand, and it is supposed to be the world, this little toy here, with the printed words on coloured paper, this little cardboard ball. This Miss McKenzie, I say to him, she's turning you crazy in that school. But look, he says, she moves. Now I have to stop my laughing. I'll soon show you she moves, I say, for he is beginning to get me mad again. And I go up to the table

1. Biblical character who, during a battle, made the sun, moon, and stars stand still upon calling out God's name.

and I take the toy thing in my hands and I smash it down like this."

He raised his fists and let them crash down on the table as if he meant to splinter it.

"That'll learn you, I cry. I don't think he could believe I had done it, because he picks up the thing and he tries to turn it, but it don't turn no more. He stands there and the tears roll down his cheeks and then, sudden like, he takes the thing in both his hands and he throws it at me. And it would have hit me right in the face, for sure, if I did not put up my hand. Against your father, I cry, you will raise up your hand against your father. Asmodeus![2] I grab him by the arm, and I shake him and I beat him like he was the devil. And he makes me madder and madder because he don't cry or shout or anything. And I would have kill him there, for sure, if his mother didn't come in then and pull me away. His nose was bleeding, but he didn't notice. Only he looks at me and says, you can beat me and break my globe, but you can't stop her moving. That night my wife she make me swear by all that's holy that I wouldn't touch him no more. And from then on I never hit him again nor talk to him about this thing. He goes his way and I go mine."

He fell silent. Then after a moment he snapped suddenly, "You hold with that?"

"Hold with what?" I asked, taken aback.

"With that thing?" He pointed behind him at the little table and at the broken globe. His gnarled hands now tightly interlocked, he leaned forward in his chair and his dark, brooding eyes sought an answer from mine in the twilight of the room.

Alone with him there, I was almost afraid to answer firmly. Was it because I feared that I would hurt him too deeply if I did, or was I perhaps afraid that he would use violence on me as he had on Nick?

I cleared my throat. "Yes," I said then. "Yes, I believe that the earth is round and that she moves. That fact has been accepted now for a long time."

I expected him to round on me but he seemed suddenly to have grown very tired, and in a low resigned voice he said, "Satan has taken over all the world." Then suddenly he roused himself and hit the table hard with his fist, and cried passionately, "But not me! Not me!"

It was unbearable. I felt that I must break the tension, and I said the first thing that came into my mind. "You can be proud of your son in spite of all that happened between you. He is a fine man, and the world honours him for his work."

He gave me a long look. "He should have stayed here," he said quietly. "When I die, there will be nobody to look after the land. Instead he has gone off to tamper with God's earth."

His fury was now all spent. We sat for a while in silence, and then I rose. Together we walked out of the house. When I was about to get into my car, he touched me lightly on the arm. I turned. His eyes surveyed the vast expanse of sky and land, stretching far into the distance, reddish clouds in the sky and blue shadows on the

2. Appears in the Book of Tobias (iii, 8) as the king of demons; also an evil spirit.

land. With a gesture of great dignity and power he lifted his arm and stood pointing into the distance, at the flat land and the low-hanging sky.

"Look," he said, very slowly and very quietly, "she is flat, and she stands still."

It was impossible not to feel a kind of admiration for the old man. There was something heroic about him. I held out my hand and he took it. He looked at me steadily, then averted his eyes and said, "Send greetings to my son."

I drove off quickly, but had to stop again in order to open the wooden gate. I looked back at the house, and saw him still standing there, still looking at his beloved land, a lonely, towering figure framed against the darkening evening sky.

after READING

UNDERSTANDING THE TEXT

1. From the first two pages, locate at least three statements that **foreshadow** the **conflict** of the **story**. Record these in your notebook.

2. Explain in a few sentences the importance to the story of the detailed descriptions of the Canadian prairie.

3. The storekeeper said, "Only boy ever went to University from around here was Solchuk's boy. Real brainy young kid, Nick. Two of 'em never got on together. Too different. You know." Explain to a partner the importance of these statements to the central conflict in the story. Locate and discuss two other significant statements about the **character** of Nick or his father.

4. As the title suggests, the broken globe is a central **symbol** in the story. In a small group, come to a **consensus** about the globe and its significance to the **plot**, characterization, and **theme** of the story. Suggest reasons why the father had not thrown the "thing" away. In your notebook, **summarize** the ideas from your discussion.

5. Find two examples of deliberate use of incorrect grammar in the speech of the characters in the story. Discuss with a partner what is added to the story by the use of ungrammatical expression. In your notebook, write a corrected version of the expressions.

6. Use **interviews**, or print and/or electronic sources, to research groups in North America that still believe that the world is flat. Make notes for a possible oral **report** to the class on their beliefs and on the arguments they use as proof.

7. Choose one of the following scenes from the story:
   • Nick and the narrator in London (page 128)
   • the narrator, the farmers, and the storekeeper (page 131)
   • the narrator and Nick's father at the farm (page 132)

   In a small group, develop a shooting script for a film or videotaped version of the scene. Indicate clearly where you would use long shots, medium shots, close-ups, and high-angle and low-angle shots. (See The Reference Shelf, pages 462–463.) Discuss the effects on the viewer of each of the shots used in your shooting script, and revise your script as necessary. Select one member of the group to present your final version to the class.

MAKING CONNECTIONS

8. Read "When I Heard the Learn'd Astronomer" (page 116). Write a few paragraphs comparing the conflict in this **poem** with that in "The Broken Globe." Be prepared to share your observations with the class. ■

To Set Our House in Order

MARGARET LAURENCE

"she's had troubles in her life ... that's why she gets migraine sometimes ..."

BEFORE READING

Think of a time when, as a child, you discovered a family secret. Without disclosing confidential information, write a short paragraph in your notebook describing how you felt when you made the discovery.

When the baby was almost ready to be born, something went wrong and my mother had to go into hospital two weeks before the expected time. I was wakened by her crying in the night, and then I heard my father's footsteps as he went downstairs to phone. I stood in the doorway of my room, shivering and listening, wanting to go to my mother but afraid to go lest there be some sight there more terrifying than I could bear.

"Hello—Paul?" my father said, and I knew he was talking to Dr. Cates. "It's Beth. The waters have broken, and the fetal position doesn't seem quite—well, I'm only thinking of what happened the last time, and another like that would be—I wish she were a little huskier, damn it—she's so—no, don't worry, I'm quite all right. Yes, I think that would be the best thing. Okay, make it as soon as you can, will you?"

He came back upstairs, looking bony and dishevelled in his pyjamas, and running his fingers through his sand-colored hair. At the top of the stairs, he came face to face with Grandmother MacLeod, who was standing there in her quilted black satin dressing gown, her slight figure held straight and poised, as though she were unaware that her hair was bound grotesquely like white-feathered wings in the snare of her coarse night-time hairnet.

"What is it, Ewen?"

"It's all right, Mother. Beth's having—a little trouble, I'm going to take her into the hospital. You go back to bed."

"I told you," Grandmother MacLeod said in her clear voice, never loud, but distinct and ringing like the tap of a sterling teaspoon on a crystal goblet, "I did tell you, Ewen, did I not, that you should have got a girl in to help her with the housework? She would have rested more."

"I couldn't afford to get anyone in," my father said. "If you thought she should've rested more, why didn't you ever—oh God, I'm out of my mind tonight—just go back to bed, Mother, please. I must get back to Beth."

When my father went down to the front door to let Dr. Cates in, my need overcame my fear and I slipped into my parents' room. My mother's black hair, so neatly pinned up during the day, was startlingly spread across the white pillowcase. I stared at her, not speaking, and then she smiled and I rushed from the doorway and buried my head upon her.

"It's all right, honey," she said. "Listen, Vanessa, the baby's just going to come a little early, that's all. You'll be all right. Grandmother MacLeod will be here."

"How can she get the meals?" I wailed, fixing on the first thing that came to mind. "She never cooks. She doesn't know how."

"Yes, she does," my mother said. "She can cook as well as anyone when she has to. She's just never had to very much, that's all. Don't worry—she'll keep everything in order, and then some."

My father and Dr. Cates came in, and I had to go, without ever saying anything I had wanted to say. I went back to my own room and lay with the shadows all around me. I listened to the night murmurings that always went on in that house, sounds which never had a source, rafters and beams contracting in the dry air, perhaps, or mice in the walls, or a sparrow that had

flown into the attic through the broken skylight there. After a while, although I would not have believed it possible, I slept.

The next morning I questioned my father. I believed him to be not only the best doctor in Manawaka, but also the best doctor in the whole of Manitoba, if not in the entire world, and the fact that he was not the one who was looking after my mother seemed to have something sinister about it.

"But it's always done that way, Vanessa," he explained. "Doctors never attend members of their own family. It's because they care so much about them, you see, and—"

"And what?" I insisted, alarmed at the way he had broken off. But my father did not reply. He stood there, and then he put on that difficult smile with which adults seek to conceal pain from children. I felt terrified, and ran to him, and he held me tightly.

"She's going to be fine," he said. "Honestly she is. Nessa, don't cry—"

Grandmother MacLeod appeared beside us, steel-spined despite her apparent fragility. She was wearing a purple silk dress and her ivory pendant. She looked as though she were all ready to go out for afternoon tea.

"Ewen, you're only encouraging the child to give way," she said. "Vanessa, big girls of ten don't make such a fuss about things. Come and get your breakfast. Now, Ewen, you're not to worry. I'll see to everything."

Summer holidays were not quite over, but I did not feel like going out to play with any of the kids. I was very superstitious, and I had the feeling that if I left the house, even for a few hours, some disaster would overtake my mother. I did not, of course, mention this feeling to Grandmother MacLeod, for she did not believe in the existence of fear, or if she did, she never let on. I spent the morning morbidly, in seeking hidden places in the house. There were many of these—odd-shaped nooks under the stairs, small and loosely nailed-up doors at the back of clothes closets, leading to dusty tunnels and forgotten recesses in the heart of the house where the only things actually to be seen were drab oil paintings stacked upon the rafters, and trunks full of outmoded clothing and old photograph albums. But the unseen presences in these secret places I knew to be those of every person, young or old, who had ever belonged to the house and had died, including Uncle Roderick who got killed on the Somme, and the baby who would have been my sister if only she had managed to come to life. Grandfather MacLeod, who had died a year after I was born, was present in the house in more tangible form. At the top of the main stairs hung the mammoth picture of a darkly uniformed man riding upon a horse whose prancing stance and dilated nostrils suggested that the battle was not yet over, that it might indeed continue until Judgment Day. The stern man was actually the Duke of Wellington, but at the time I believed him to be my Grandfather MacLeod, still keeping an eye on things.

We had moved in with Grandmother MacLeod when the Depression got bad and she could no longer afford a house-keeper, but the MacLeod house never seemed like home to me. Its dark red brick was grown over at the front with Virginia creeper that turned crimson in the fall, until you could hardly tell brick from leaves. It boasted a small tower in which Grandmother MacLeod kept a weedy collection of anemic ferns. The veranda was embellished with a profusion of wrought-iron scrolls, and the circular rose-window upstairs contained glass of many colors which permitted an outlooking eye to see the world as a place of absolute sapphire or emerald, or if one wished to look with a jaundiced eye, a hateful yellow. In Grandmother MacLeod's opinion, these features gave the house style.

Inside, a multitude of doors led to rooms where my presence, if not actually forbidden, was not encouraged. One was Grandmother MacLeod's bedroom, with its stale and old-smelling air, the dim reek of medicines and lavender sachets. Here resided her monogrammed dresser silver, brush and mirror, nail-buffer and button hook and scissors, none of which must even be fingered by me now, for she meant to leave them to me in her will and intended to hand them over in the same flawless and unused condition in which they had always been kept. Here, too, were the silver-framed photographs of Uncle Roderick—as a child, as a boy, as a man in his Army uniform. The massive walnut spool bed had obviously been designed for queens or giants, and my tiny grand-mother used to lie within it all day when she had migraine, contriving somehow to look like a giant queen.

The living room was another alien territory where I had to tread warily, for many valuable objects sat just-so on tables and mantel-piece, and dirt must not be tracked in upon the blue Chinese carpet with its birds in eternal motionless flight and its water-lily buds caught forever just before the point of opening. My mother was always nervous when I was in this room.

"Vanessa, honey," she would say, half apologetically, "why don't you go and play in the den, or upstairs?"

"Can't you leave her, Beth?" my father would say. "She's not doing any harm."

"I'm only thinking of the rug," my mother would say, glancing at Grand-mother MacLeod, "and yesterday she nearly knocked the Dresden shepherdess off the mantel. I mean, she can't help it, Ewen, she has to run around—"

"Goddamn it, I know she can't help it," my father would growl, glaring at the smirking face of the Dresden shepherdess.

"I see no need to blaspheme, Ewen," Grandmother MacLeod would say quietly, and then my father would say he was sorry, and I would leave.

The day my mother went to the hospital, Grandmother MacLeod called me at lunch-time, and when I appeared, smudged with dust from the attic, she looked at me distastefully as though I had been a cockroach that had just crawled impertinently out of the woodwork.

"For mercy's sake, Vanessa, what have you been doing with yourself? Run and get washed this minute. Here, not that way—you use the back stairs, young lady. Get along now. Oh—your father phoned."

I swung around. "What did he say? How is she? Is the baby born?"

"Curiosity killed a cat," Grandmother MacLeod said, frowning. "I cannot under-stand Beth and Ewen telling you all these things, at your age. What sort of vulgar person you'll grow up to be, I dare not think. No, it's not born yet. Your mother's just the same. No change."

I looked at my grandmother, not want-ing to appeal to her, but unable to stop myself. "Will she—will she be all right?"

Grandmother MacLeod straightened her already-straight back. "If I said definitely yes, Vanessa, that would be a lie, and the MacLeods do not tell lies, as I have tried to impress upon you before. What happens is God's will. The Lord giveth, and the Lord taketh away."

Appalled, I turned away so she would not see my face and my eyes. Surprisingly, I heard her sigh and felt her papery white and perfectly manicured hand upon my shoulder.

"When your Uncle Roderick got killed," she said, "I thought I would die. But I didn't die, Vanessa."

At lunch, she chatted animatedly, and I realized she was trying to cheer me in the only way she knew.

"When I married your Grandfather MacLeod," she related, "he said to me, 'Eleanor, don't think because we're going to the prairies that I expect you to live roughly. You're used to a proper house, and you shall have one.' He was as good as his word. Before we'd been in Manawaka three years, he'd had this place built. He earned a good deal of money in his time, your grandfather. He soon had more patients than either of the other doctors. We ordered our dinner service and all our silver from Birks in Toronto. We had resident help in those days, of course, and never had less than twelve guests for dinner parties. When I had a tea, it would always be twenty or thirty. Never any less than half a dozen different kinds of cake were ever served in this house. Well, no one seems to bother much these days. Too lazy, I suppose."

"Too broke," I suggested: "That's what Dad says."

"I can't bear slang," Grandmother MacLeod said. "If you mean hard up, why don't you say so? It's mainly a question of management, anyway. My accounts were always in good order, and so was my house. No unexpected expenses that couldn't be met, no fruit cellar running out of preserves before the winter was over. Do you know what my father used to say to me when I was a girl?"

"No," I said. "What?"

"God loves Order," Grandmother MacLeod replied with emphasis. "You remember that, Vanessa. God loves Order—he wants each one of us to set our house in order. I've never forgotten those words of my father's. I was a MacInnes before I got married. The MacInnes is a very ancient clan, the lairds of Morven and the constables of the Castle of Kinlochaline. Did you finish that book I gave you?"

"Yes," I said. Then, feeling some additional comment to be called for, "It was a swell book, Grandmother."

This was somewhat short of the truth. I had been hoping for her cairngorm brooch on my tenth birthday, and had received instead the plaid-bound volume entitled *The Clans and Tartans of Scotland.* Most of it was too boring to read, but I had looked up the motto of my own family and those of some of my friends' families. *Be then a wall of brass. Learn to suffer. Consider the end. Go carefully.* I had not found any of these slogans reassuring. What with Mavis Duncan learning to suffer, and Laura Kennedy considering the end, and Patsy Drummond going carefully, and I spending my time in being a wall of brass, it did not seem to me that any of us were going to lead very interesting lives. I did not say this to Grandmother MacLeod.

"The MacInnes motto is *Pleasure Arises from Work,*" I said.

"Yes," she agreed proudly. "And an excellent motto it is, too. One to bear in mind."

She rose from the table, rearranging on her bosom the looped ivory beads that held the pendant on which a full-blown ivory rose was stiffly carved.

"I hope Ewen will be pleased," she said.

"What at?"

"Didn't I tell you?" Grandmother MacLeod said. "I hired a girl this morning, for the housework. She's to start tomorrow."

When my father got home that evening, Grandmother MacLeod told him her good news. He ran one hand distractedly across his forehead.

"I'm sorry, Mother, but you'll just have to unhire her. I can't possibly pay anyone."

"It seems distinctly odd," Grandmother MacLeod snapped, "that you can afford to eat chicken four times a week."

"Those chickens," my father said in an exasperated voice, "are how people are paying their bills. The same with the eggs and the milk. The scrawny turkey that arrived yesterday was for Logan MacCardney's appendix, if you must know. We probably eat better than any family in Manawaka, except Niall Cameron's. People can't entirely dispense with doctors or undertakers. That doesn't mean to say I've got any cash. Look, Mother, I don't know what's happening with Beth. Paul thinks he may have to do a Caesarean. Can't we leave all this? Just leave the house alone. Don't touch it. What does it matter?"

"I have never lived in a messy house, Ewen," Grandmother MacLeod said, "and I don't intend to begin now."

"Oh Lord," my father said. "Well, I'll phone Edna, I guess, and see if she can give us a hand, although God knows she's got enough, with the Connor house and her parents to look after."

"I don't fancy having Edna Connor in to help," Grandmother MacLeod objected.

"Why not?" my father shouted. "She's Beth's sister, isn't she?"

"She speaks in such a slangy way," Grandmother MacLeod said. "I have never believed she was a good influence on Vanessa. And there is no need for you to raise your voice to me, Ewen, if you please."

I could barely control my rage. I thought my father would surely rise to Aunt Edna's defence. But he did not.

"It'll be all right," he soothed her. "She'd only be here for part of the day, Mother. You could stay in your room."

Aunt Edna strode in the next morning. The sight of her bobbed black hair and her grin made me feel better at once. She hauled out the carpet sweeper and

the weighted polisher and got to work. I dusted while she polished and swept, and we got through the living room and front hall in next to no time.

"Where's her royal highness, kiddo?" she inquired.

"In her room," I said. "She's reading the catalogue from Robinson & Cleaver."

"Good Glory, not again?" Aunt Edna cried. "The last time she ordered three linen tea-cloths and two dozen serviettes. It came to fourteen dollars. Your mother was absolutely frantic. I guess I shouldn't be saying this."

"I knew anyway," I assured her. "She was at the lace handkerchiefs section when I took up her coffee."

"Let's hope she stays there. Heaven forbid she should get onto the banqueting cloths. Well, at least she believes the Irish are good for two things—manual labor and linen-making. She's never forgotten Father used to be a blacksmith, before he got the hardware store. Can you beat it? I wish it didn't bother Beth."

"Does it?" I asked, and immediately realized this was a wrong move, for Aunt Edna was suddenly scrutinizing me.

"We're making you grow up before your time," she said. "Don't pay any attention to me, Nessa. I must've got up on the wrong side of the bed this morning."

But I was unwilling to leave the subject.

"All the same," I said thoughtfully, "Grandmother MacLeod's family were the lairds of Morven and the constables of the Castle of Kinlochaline. I bet you didn't know that."

Aunt Edna snorted. "Castle, my foot. She was born in Ontario, just like your

Grandfather Connor, and her father was a horse doctor. Come on, kiddo, we'd better shut up and get down to business here."

We worked in silence for a while.

"Aunt Edna—" I said at last, "what about Mother? Why won't they let me go and see her?"

"Kids aren't allowed to visit maternity patients. It's tough for you, I know that. Look, Nessa, don't worry. If it doesn't start tonight, they're going to do the operation. She's getting the best of care."

I stood there, holding the feather duster like a dead bird in my hands. I was not aware that I was going to speak until the words came out.

"I'm scared," I said.

Aunt Edna put her arms around me, and her face looked all at once stricken and empty of defences.

"Oh, honey, I'm scared, too," she said.

It was this way that Grandmother MacLeod found us when she came stepping lightly down into the front hall with the order in her hand for two dozen lace-bordered handkerchiefs of pure Irish linen.

I could not sleep that night, and when I went downstairs, I found my father in the den. I sat down on the hassock beside his chair, and he told me about the operation my mother was to have the next morning. He kept on saying it was not serious nowadays.

"But you're worried," I put in, as though seeking to explain why I was.

"I should at least have been able to keep from burdening you with it," he said in a distant voice, as though to himself.

"If only the baby hadn't got itself twisted around—"

"Will it be born dead, like the little girl?"

"I don't know," my father said. "I hope not."

"She'd be disappointed, wouldn't she, if it was?" I said bleakly, wondering why I was not enough for her.

"Yes, she would," my father replied. "She won't be able to have any more, after this. It's partly on your account that she wants this one, Nessa. She doesn't want you to grow up without a brother or sister."

"As far as I'm concerned, she didn't need to bother," I retorted angrily.

My father laughed. "Well, let's talk about something else, and then maybe you'll be able to sleep. How did you and Grandmother make out today?"

"Oh, fine, I guess. What was Grandfather MacLeod like, Dad?"

"What did she tell you about him?"

"She said he made a lot of money in his time."

"Well, he wasn't any millionaire," my father said, "but I suppose he did quite well. That's not what I associate with him, though."

He reached across to the bookshelf, took out a small leatherbound volume and opened it. On the pages were mysterious marks, like doodling, only much neater and more patterned.

"What is it?" I asked.

"Greek," my father explained. "This is a play called *Antigone*. See, here's the title in English. There's a whole stack of them on the shelves there. *Oedipus Rex*. *Electra*. *Medea*. They belonged to your

Grandfather MacLeod. He used to read them often."

"Why?" I inquired, unable to understand why anyone would pore over those undecipherable signs.

"He was interested in them," my father said. "He must have been a lonely man, although it never struck me that way at the time. Sometimes a thing only hits you a long time afterwards."

"Why would he be lonely?" I wanted to know.

"He was the only person in Manawaka who could read these plays in the original Greek," my father said. "I don't suppose many people, if anyone, had even read them in English translations. Maybe he would have liked to be a classical scholar— I don't know. But his father was a doctor, so that's what he was. Maybe he would have liked to talk to somebody about these plays. They must have meant a lot to him."

It seemed to me that my father was talking oddly. There was a sadness in his voice that I had never heard before, and I longed to say something that would make him feel better, but I could not, because I did not know what was the matter.

"Can you read this kind of writing?" I asked hesitantly.

My father shook his head. "Nope. I was never very intellectual, I guess. Rod was always brighter than I, in school, but even he wasn't interested in learning Greek. Perhaps he would've been later, if he'd lived. As a kid, all I ever wanted to do was go into the merchant marine."

"Why didn't you, then?"

"Oh well," my father said offhandedly, "a kid who'd never seen the sea wouldn't have made much of a sailor. I might have turned out to be the seasick type."

I had lost interest now that he was speaking once more like himself.

"Grandmother MacLeod was pretty cross today about the girl," I remarked.

"I know," my father nodded. "Well, we must be as nice as we can to her, Nessa, and after a while she'll be all right."

Suddenly I did not care what I said.

"Why can't she be nice to us for a change?" I burst out. "We're always the ones who have to be nice to her."

My father put his hand down and slowly tilted my head until I was forced to look at him.

"Vanessa," he said, "she's had troubles in her life which you really don't know much about. That's why she gets migraine sometimes and has to go to bed. It's not easy for her these days, either—the house is still the same, so she thinks other things should be, too. It hurts her when she finds they aren't."

"I don't see—" I began.

"Listen," my father said, "you know we were talking about what people are interested in, like Grandfather MacLeod being interested in Greek plays? Well, your grandmother was interested in being a lady, Nessa, and for a long time it seemed to her that she was one."

I thought of the Castle of Kinlochaline, and of horse doctors in Ontario.

"I didn't know—" I stammered.

"That's usually the trouble with most of us," my father said. "You go on up to bed now. I'll phone tomorrow from the hospital as soon as the operation's over."

I did sleep at last, and in my dreams I could hear the caught sparrow fluttering in the attic and the sound of my mother crying, and the voices of the dead children.

My father did not phone until afternoon. Grandmother MacLeod said I was being silly, for you could hear the phone ringing all over the house, but nevertheless I refused to move out of the den. I had never before examined my father's books, but now, at a loss for something to do, I took them out one by one and read snatches here and there. After I had been doing this for several hours, it dawned on me that most of the books were of the same kind. I looked again at the titles.

Seven-League Boots. Arabia Deserta. The Seven Pillars of Wisdom. Travels in Tibet. Count Lucknor the Sea Devil. And a hundred more. On a shelf by themselves were copies of the *National Geographic* magazine, which I looked at often enough, but never before with the puzzling compulsion which I felt now, as though I were on the verge of some discovery, something which I had to find out and yet did not want to know. I riffled through the picture-filled pages. Hibiscus and wild orchids grew in a soft-petalled confusion. The Himalayas stood lofty as gods, with the morning sun on their peaks of snow. Leopards snarled from the vined depths of a thousand jungles. Schooners buffeted their white sails like the wings of giant angels against the great sea winds.

"What on earth are you doing?" Grandmother MacLeod inquired waspishly, from the doorway. "You've got everything scattered all over the place. Pick it all up this minute, Vanessa, do you hear?"

So I picked up the books and magazines, and put them all neatly away, as I had been told to do.

When the telephone finally rang, I was afraid to answer it. At last I picked it up. My father sounded faraway, and the relief in his voice made it unsteady.

"It's okay, honey. Everything's fine. The boy was born alive and kicking after all. Your mother's pretty weak, but she's going to be all right."

I could hardly believe it. I did not want to talk to anyone. I wanted to be by myself, to assimilate the presence of my brother, towards whom, without ever having seen him yet, I felt such tenderness and such resentment.

That evening, Grandmother MacLeod approached my father, who, still dazed with the unexpected gift of neither life now being threatened, at first did not take her seriously when she asked what they planned to call the child.

"Oh, I don't know. Hank, maybe, or Joe. Fauntleroy, perhaps."

She ignored his levity.

"Ewen," she said, "I wish you would call him Roderick."

My father's face changed. "I'd rather not."

"I think you should," Grandmother MacLeod insisted, very quietly, but in a voice as pointed and precise as her silver nail-scissors.

"Don't you think Beth ought to decide?" my father asked.

"Beth will agree if you do."

My father did not bother to deny something that even I knew to be true. He did not say anything. Then Grandmother

MacLeod's voice, astonishing, faltered a little.

"It would mean a great deal to me," she said.

I remembered what she had told me—*When your Uncle Roderick got killed, I thought I would die. But I didn't die.* All at once, her feeling for that unknown dead man became a reality for me. And yet I held it against her, as well, for I could see that it had enabled her to win now.

"All right," my father said tiredly. "We'll call him Roderick."

Then alarmingly, he threw back his head and laughed.

"Roderick Dhu!" he cried. "That's what you'll call him, isn't it? Black Roderick. Like before. Don't you remember? As though he were a character out of Sir Walter Scott, instead of an ordinary kid who—"

He broke off, and looked at her with a kind of desolation in his face.

"God, I'm sorry, Mother," he said. "I had no right to say that."

Grandmother MacLeod did not flinch, or tremble, or indicate that she felt anything at all.

"I accept your apology, Ewen," she said.

My mother had to stay in bed for several weeks after she arrived home. The baby's cot was kept in my parents' room, and I could go in and look at the small creature who lay there with his tightly closed fists and his feathery black hair. Aunt Edna came in to help each morning, and when she had finished the housework, she would have coffee with my mother. They kept the door closed, but this did not prevent me from eavesdropping, for there was an air register in the floor of the spare room, which was linked somehow with the register in my parents' room. If you put your ear to the iron grille, it was almost like a radio.

"Did you mind very much, Beth?" Aunt Edna was saying.

"Oh, it's not the name I mind," my mother replied. "It's just the fact that Ewen felt he had to. You knew that Rod had only had the sight of one eye, didn't you?"

"Sure, I knew. So what?"

"There was only a year and a half between Ewen and Rod," my mother said, "so they often went around together when they were youngsters. It was Ewen's air-rifle that did it."

"Oh Lord," Aunt Edna said heavily. "I suppose she always blamed him?"

"No, I don't think it was so much that, really. It was how he felt himself. I think he even used to wonder sometimes if—but people shouldn't let themselves think like that, or they'd go crazy. Accidents do happen, after all. When the war came, Ewen joined up first. Rod should never have been in the Army at all, but he couldn't wait to get in. He must have lied about his eyesight. It wasn't so very noticeable unless you looked at him closely, and I don't suppose the medicals were very thorough in those days. He got in as a gunner, and Ewen applied to have him in the same company. He thought he might be able to watch out for him, I guess, Rod being—at a disadvantage. They were both only kids. Ewen was nineteen and Rod was eighteen when they went to France. And then the Somme. I don't know, Edna, I think Ewen felt that if Rod had had proper sight, or if he hadn't been in the same outfit and had been sent somewhere else—you know how people always think these things afterwards, not that it's ever a bit of use. Ewen wasn't there when Rod got hit. They'd lost each other somehow, and Ewen was looking for him, not bothering about anything else, you know, just frantically looking. Then he stumbled across him quite by chance. Rod was still alive, but—"

"Stop it, Beth," Aunt Edna said. "You're only upsetting yourself."

"Ewen never spoke of it to me," my mother went on, "until once his mother showed me the letter he'd written to her at the time. It was a peculiar letter, almost formal, saying how gallantly Rod had died, and all that. I guess I shouldn't have, but I told him she'd shown it to me. He was very angry that she had. And then, as though for some reason he were terribly ashamed, he said—*I had to write something to her, but men don't really die like that, Beth. It wasn't that way at all.* It was only after the war that he decided to come back and study medicine and go into practice with his father."

"Had Rod meant to?" Aunt Edna asked.

"I don't know," my mother said slowly. "I never felt I should ask Ewen that."

Aunt Edna was gathering up the coffee things, for I could hear the clash of cups and saucers being stacked on the tray.

"You know what I heard her say to Vanessa once, Beth? *The MacLeods never tell lies.* Those were her exact words. Even then, I didn't know whether to laugh or cry."

"Please, Edna—" my mother sounded worn-out now. "Don't."

"Oh Glory," Aunt Edna said remorsefully, "I've got all the delicacy of a two-ton truck. I didn't mean Ewen, for heaven's sake. That wasn't what I meant at all. Here, let me plump up your pillows for you."

Then the baby began to cry, so I could not hear anything more of interest. I took my bike and went out beyond Manawaka, riding aimlessly along the gravel highway. It was late summer, and the wheat had changed color, but instead of being high and bronzed in the fields, it was stunted and desiccated, for there had been no rain again this year. But in the bluff where I stopped and crawled under the barbed wire fence and lay stretched out on the grass, the plentiful poplar leaves were turning to a luminous yellow and shone like church windows in the sun. I put my head down very close to the earth and looked at what was going on there. Grasshoppers with enormous eyes ticked and twitched around me, as though the dry air were perfect for their purposes. A ladybird labored mightily to climb a blade of grass, fell off, and started all over again, seeming to be unaware that she possessed wings and could have flown up.

I thought of the accidents that might easily happen to a person—or, of course, might not happen, might happen to somebody else. I thought of the dead baby, my sister, who might as easily have been I. Would she, then, have been lying here in my place, the sharp grass making its small toothmarks on her brown arms, the sun warming her to the heart? I thought of the leatherbound volumes of Greek, and the six different kinds of iced cakes that used to be offered always in the MacLeod house, and the pictures of leopards and green seas. I thought of my brother, who had been born alive after all, and now had been given his life's name.

I could not really comprehend these things, but I sensed their strangeness, their disarray. I felt that whatever God might love in this world, it was certainly not order.

after READING

UNDERSTANDING THE TEXT

1. In your notebook, make a list of the discoveries that Vanessa, the young **narrator**, makes about the backgrounds of her grandmother, her mother's family, her father, and her uncle Roderick. Discuss your list with another student and make additions and clarifications as required.

2. After reading this **story**, use the **context** in which they appear to help you write a **definition** of the following words: "morbidly," "tangible," "anemic," "jaundiced," "hassock," "undecipherable," and "desiccated." Discuss with a partner what strategies you use to help you understand words or phrases while reading. If necessary, use a dictionary to verify any of the definitions.

3. In a few paragraphs, refer to details from this story to explain the **irony** of the grandmother's words: "If I said definitely yes, Vanessa, that would be a lie, and the MacLeods do not tell lies, as I have tried to impress upon you before."

4. In a small group, discuss the importance of the final two paragraphs in understanding the main point of this story. After the discussion, write a clear statement of **theme** for this story in your notebook.

EXPLORING IDEAS AND IMPLICATIONS

5. a) Write a paragraph describing the narrative **voice** and **style** of the story, including observations on the vocabulary, sentence structure, and expression. In a second paragraph, assess the age of the narrator at the time she is telling her story and at the time the events in the story occur.

b) With a partner, select one of the scenes between Grandmother MacLeod and her son, Ewen. Discuss the effect on the reader of having the scene told in the voice of Vanessa, who is observing the interaction. Decide what different information the reader would learn if the scene had been narrated in the voice of one of the other **characters**.

c) Rewrite the scene from the **point of view** of Vanessa's grandmother; have your partner rewrite the same scene using the point of view of Vanessa's father.

d) Read and discuss what your partner has written, making suggestions for improving the narrative voice. Compare your versions with the original. In your notebook, write a paragraph on the effects of the original narrative voice used in telling a story.

6. Use print and/or electronic resources to research information about the social and economic conditions that existed in western Canada during the 1930s. In your notebook, record details from the story that illustrate what you have learned from research.

MAKING CONNECTIONS

 7. As an independent study, use the Internet or reference books on Canadian literature to find out about the life and literary works of Margaret Laurence. (See The Reference Shelf, pages 429–433.) Are there other stories or novels by Laurence that use Manawaka as a **setting**? Make notes for an oral presentation on your findings to the class. ■

Unnatural Causes

LILLIAN ALLEN

BEFORE READING

Canada has frequently been cited by the United Nations as the best country in the world in which to live. As a class, discuss whether you agree with this assessment.

The wind howled and cussed
it knew no rest
when it ran free
it was a hurricane
to be watched and silenced   5

silence makes you sit and rot
even cactus fades
against persistent drought

they hope the poor will become acclimatized
see how they look at skyrises   10
and call them mountain peaks
see how the sun greets them first
in the city
makes a rolling shadow

Somewhere in this silvered city   15
hunger rails beneath the flesh
... and one by one, they're closing shops in the city
... the Epicure, the Rivoli on the porch ...
No Small Affair
... No Small Affair—the Sequel ... Le Petit Café   20
The Bamboo ...

The city, a curtained metropolitan glare
grins a diamond sparkle sunset
it cuts a dashing pose

"The picture you sent on the postcard was wonderful!   25
It reminded me of a fairy land,
where everything is so clean
a place where everyone is happy
and well taken care of
... and the sky ... the sky ... it seems so round, so huge   30
and so indifferent."

Indifference passes through the wind
the wind, it rains a new breed
breeds a new passion
the passion of inaction   35
the inaction of politicians
the art of avoiding issues
the issues of culture
the culture of exclusion
the exclusion of the "political" and the powerless   40

Somewhere in this our city
in our governing chambers
a watershed of indelight
of neutered niceties, unctuous
click////click////click   45
postcard perfect

Dry rivers in the valley
the thirst at the banks of plenty
the room at the street-car shelter
a bus stop bed   50
a bus stop bed
a bus stop bed

You can make it through winter if you're ice
You can make it through winter if you're ice

gone frozen   55
on many things

bare back. no shelter
iced hearts in the elements
impassioned is the wind

All people are created equal except in winter   60
All people are created equal except in winter

Right here
on the front steps of abundance
Caroline Bungle tugs her load
stakes a place, invites a little company of sleep   65
unclick////
this my dear is very unpostcardlike

Not inclined to poses
posturing only her plight
a dungle of terror   70
of lost hope
abandonment
an explorer in the arctic of our culture
a straggler adrift
cross our terrain of indifference   75
a life unravelled
seeks a connection
a soul outstretched to the cosmos

Can you spare a little social change, please?
a cup of tea   80
    a cup of tea
a place to sleep
a job
    a job
       a job ... ???   85

"The last postcard you sent was kinda weird
... poor people, sleeping at the bus stop!??
Surely you don't have that there ..."

"... anyways, I'm dying to come to Canada
I'm a pioneer!"   90

after READING

UNDERSTANDING THE TEXT

1. Describe the contrast between the two postcards in this **poem**. Write a paragraph explaining which best represents the reality of a large Canadian city today.

2. With a partner, discuss the relationship of the lines in quotation marks and the lines in italics to the rest of the poem. Record your conclusions in your notebook.

3. In a group of four, discuss the significance of the following phrases found near the end of the poem.
   - "the arctic of our culture" (line 73)
   - "Can you spare a little social change, please?" (line 79)
   - "I'm a pioneer." (line 90)

4. Find examples of parallel structures and repetition in the poem. Explain the effectiveness of these devices in developing the ideas presented in the poem.

5. In a small group, prepare an oral reading of the poem to present to the class. Be prepared to explain what methods you used to make your presentation of the poem effective and to emphasize a certain interpretation of the lines.

EXPLORING IDEAS AND IMPLICATIONS

6. As a class, brainstorm issues surrounding homelessness. With a partner, choose one of the issues to do a research **report**. Be prepared to present your report to the class. Use visuals to enhance your presentation.

7. Create a newspaper advertisement for publication in another country inviting immigrants to come and make their home in Canada or an advertisement that warns people considering emigration to Canada to reconsider their decision.

8. Take a photograph in your community that you think could be used on a postcard. Mount the photograph on a sheet of 8½" x 11" paper and below it explain why you think a postcard with the picture you took on it would be popular with tourists visiting your community.

MAKING CONNECTIONS

9. Read "Small Place" (pages 170–176). With a partner, create a **dialogue** between Jamaica Kincaid and Lillian Allen. Consider the message(s) in "Small Place" and "Unnatural Causes." Revise and edit your dialogue before you role-play it to the class. ■

The 1st

LUCILLE CLIFTON

BEFORE READING

In your notebook, record the feelings or emotions you experienced when your family moved to another residence, or when one of your friends moved.

What I remember about that day
is boxes stacked across the walk
and couch springs curling through the air
and drawers and tables balanced on the curb
and us, hollering,   5
leaping up and around
happy to have playground;

nothing about the emptied rooms
nothing about the emptied family

after READING

1. In your notebook, list details in the **poem** that tell you what is happening to the family.

2. Reread the poem and list words used by the **narrator** to describe himself or herself and the other children (lines 5–7). In a paragraph, explain the emotional effect of these descriptive words.

3. **a)** In a few sentences, explain how the last two lines change the emotional feeling of the poem.

   b) Explain why the **mood** of the children is in contrast with that of the ending of the poem.

4. **a)** Explain to a partner how the **connotation** of "emptied rooms" (line 8) is different from the connotation of "emptied family" (line 9).

   b) Ask your partner to explain to you the effects of the repetition in the last two lines. (See The Reference Shelf, page 425.)

   c) In your notebook, record the ideas from your discussion.

 5. Examine the poet's use of punctuation. In your notebook, identify the function of the commas and the semicolon. Also, explain the effect on the reader of the lack of punctuation in the final two lines of the poem.

EXPLORING IDEAS AND IMPLICATIONS

 6. **a)** Imagine that you are making a filmed or videotaped documentary about the family's situation described in the poem. In a small group, develop a shooting script to record the details in lines 1–7. Use a combination of long shots, middle shots, and close-ups to establish the situation and to capture important details and emotions.

   b) Compare your shooting script with one developed by another group and assess which script most accurately conveys the mood and visual details of the poem.

MAKING CONNECTIONS

7. Read "Fern Hill" (pages 288–289). Based on this poem and "The 1st," create a poster depicting the innocence and carefreeness of youth. Include a slogan (you may use lines from one of the poems) and a visual that will grab the attention of viewers. Post your poster on a bulletin-board display in the classroom. ■

Going Up (and Down) in the World

ALEX SHPRINTSEN

"There is a very clean and orderly
system of promotion on elevators ..."

BEFORE READING

In a group of four students, develop a short script and **role-play** the behaviour of people riding an elevator in a high-rise building.

All men—and women—are created equal. Then something happens. And by about the age of three days, we begin our respective life-long journeys into various stages of inequality. In fact, as far as I can tell, there is only one place where equality upon creation is maintained throughout—elevators. You know, those things—elevating devices, lifts, ascenseurs, etc.

As you go through life dealing with all its injustices, various tasks take you into high-rise buildings. That is when you meet the great equalizer, the elevator.

And you are in luck. You do not need to apply, send your resumé or even go through an interview. Nor do you bring references from elevator riders in other buildings in order to get on. And connections are redundant. Knowing the elevator repairman or building superintendent will not get you any farther than a guy off the street—just to the penthouse, or at best, the laundry room.

Once you are on, it is back to square one for all the riders. Whether you are English or French, black or white, a man or a woman, the elevator will understand your instructions the same way. So, if you are the chief executive officer of Otis and need to get to your office on the 72nd floor, the janitor who is going to the second will get there before you.

There is a very clean and orderly system of promotion on elevators—one floor at a time—and no amount of nepotism, patronage or corruption will help you. Even being a Liberal senator will do you no good.

And while you are at it, you do not even need to produce. You will not get kicked out for making a mistake, like pressing the wrong button. Some people go so far as to sabotage the entire ride by pressing all the buttons—and get away with it.

I have ridden elevators all around the world, and have never encountered a constitutional crisis involving these machines, even though these things do break down from time to time. In all those experiences, I have seen no written rules about riding, with the exception of one indelibly written inside your mind—to avoid eye contact with fellow passengers at all costs.

This, I believe, has led to the incredible spirit of co-operation between riders, no matter what religion, political regime or baseball team they support: stares pose threats. And so, you never hear of territorial disputes inside elevators. On the contrary, everyone tries to occupy as little room as possible, as though the United Nations had threatened to impose sanctions on the other side of the door of every floor.

Now you may think that other modes of transportation possess the same properties. Well, there are no class separations on elevators, nor are they ever hijacked. The only regularly occurring hostage-taking incidents have to do with the breakdown of air conditioning, or of other technological gadgets.

Finally, there is a kind of emotional neutrality on elevators that helps maintain that initial state of equality. Somehow, during our journey up or down, we tend to suspend whatever hatred we harbored toward whomever before getting on. The only exception to that is the collective sense of outrage we feel toward the true elevator terrorists—the cowards who press the buttons for all the floors. *They* are nobody's freedom fighters.

At the same time, unspoken civility shows itself in the most unlikely of circumstances. I bet that if Saddam Hussein and George Bush found themselves on the same elevator, and the U.S. President had groceries in one hand and the nuclear-button briefcase in the other, the Iraqi strongman would no doubt ask, without making eye contact: "Which floor, my dear guest?"

I have heard somewhere that we will all be equal again in heaven (or in hell, I suppose). That is why I cannot wait for the Japanese to build that 200-story tower of theirs. Not only will that reward us with a longer "equality" ride than on the CN Tower, but it will also give us the hope of, some day, building the elevator to heaven.

after READING

UNDERSTANDING THE TEXT

1. In the group that you worked with on the "Before Reading" activity, discuss the extent to which the writer's observations in this **essay** matched the behaviours from your role-playing.

2. In your notebook, record the central idea or **thesis** of this essay. Compare your written statement with that of a classmate, and defend it with specific references to the essay. As a result of the discussion, revise or amend your statement if necessary.

3. Write **definitions** of the words "redundant," "nepotism," "patronage," and "sabotage" as they are used in the **context** of this essay. In some cases, you may need to use a dictionary to verify your definitions.

4. In your notebook, make brief notes about the organizational pattern of the essay, identifying definite sections, and the connections of the sections to the essay's **thesis** and to each other. Discuss your observations with a partner, and revise your notes as necessary.

EXPLORING IDEAS AND IMPLICATIONS

5. **a)** Using Shprintsen's observations about the behaviour of people in elevators as a model, in a small group, brainstorm other observed patterns of human behaviour in specific situations in your school or community. Do any of the behaviours lead to generalizations about people or society?

   b) Individually, plan and write the first draft of a reflective essay about one of the ideas your group discussed. Ask a partner to read your draft and to make suggestions for revision to improve the content and organization of the essay. Rewrite the paper and edit it for submission or publication.

   c) Have the class develop a rubric for assessing the ideas, organization, and **style** of expression in these essays.

MAKING CONNECTIONS

6. Read "Those Anthropologists" (page 80). With a partner, discuss what the anthropologists or sociologists might have to say about the behaviours described in this essay. Using "Those Anthropologists" as a model, compose a free-verse poem from the **point of view** of the people riding the elevators, who are commenting on the observations of the anthropologists or sociologists. Be prepared to read your poem aloud to the class. ■

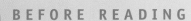

Many Canadians Are Made to Feel Like Strangers in Their Homeland

SHELLENE DRAKES

"It bothers me that people assume I'm not Canadian."

BEFORE READING

1. In your notebook, write down one question that people often ask that you wish they would stop asking.

2. Read the title of this **article**. Make a list of questions people ask that might make a Canadian feel like a stranger in his or her own homeland.

Being an outsider in your own country can hurt.

It's not the sharp kind of hurt that you feel after someone slings a nasty comment your way, but a deep, long-suffering hurt that, with time, becomes a part of you. You expect it, but you never get used to it.

"It bothers me that people assume I'm not Canadian," said Dayo Kefentse, 25. She is quiet for a moment, then begins to explain.

"When I worked at a news agency there was a woman, a senior employee, who asked me—the typical question—where are you from? I told her that I'm from Toronto. I knew what she was getting at, but I didn't want to play into her hands. So she asked where did my family come from and I said Barbados."

What bothered Kefentse was the assumption she had to have come from somewhere else. It is a feeling that many in the black community share, a lack of acceptance. Kefentse was born in Toronto to parents who immigrated to Canada in the late 1960s.

She confronted the woman.

"She was very taken back and realized what she said wasn't politically correct. She said 'I'm just white bread from Brantford and I don't know better,' " said Kefentse. "I'm Canadian of Bajan (Barbadian) parentage. I won't allow anyone to deny me my Canadian (heritage)."

Sehrab Grewal never felt like an outsider.

The 24-year-old, who is of South Asian descent, feels she is accepted as a Canadian. She hears the question "Where are you from?" very differently—it's not a slight to her Canadian heritage, but a part of the expression of a multicultural Canada. Everybody comes from somewhere.

"I think that's the beauty in this country. In America if you say to a person, where do you come from, where are your roots? They say, oh, I'm an American," she said. "In Canada, the fact that I can say I'm Canadian, what ethnicity are you, I'm East Indian, that's a beauty. There are so many different cultures in this country and people wear their cultures on their sleeves here."

Grewal's family originated in India but her parents moved to Canada more than 45 years ago and were one of the first Sikh families in their community.

"When people ask me where I'm from I say Canada. If they ask me what nationality I am, I say I'm Canadian," she explained. "I was born here. I have never been back to India. The rest of my family have and they have strong ties there, but my ties are here in this country. If there's a person who calls me an immigrant, even if they meant it in a derogatory way, hey, to me, it's a big plus."

The 1996 census found that more than three million Canadians are people of colour. Many of them are immigrants, but 29 per cent were born here. Sixty-five per cent of people of Japanese origin are native born, 42 per cent of blacks were born in Canada and 29 per cent of people of South Asian descent were born here.

Ruby Lee, a Canadian of Chinese descent, doesn't feel the need to defend her Canadian heritage. Her great-grandfathers came from China at the turn of the century to build the Canadian Pacific Railway.

"I consider myself more Canadian than anything else," she said. "From looking at me, you can tell that I'm of Asian descent. But I've never had the feeling that people viewed me as an immigrant."

She has never felt the hurt of someone assuming that she had to be from somewhere besides Canada. Lee, 24, who was born in Toronto, grew up in Mississauga and now lives in Scarborough, has had mainly positive experiences.

"I can't speak for (all Canadians), but the people I have surrounded myself with, they've never treated me differently."

While Lee and Grewal feel that they've been accepted in Canadian society, some blacks of Caribbean descent, who were born in Canada, don't feel they belong or that they ever did.

The immigration of people of colour to Canada didn't start yesterday—they've had a long, rich history in this country. African-Americans, and people from China, Japan, India and from other parts of the world, came to Canada generations ago.

But neither Lee nor Kefentse ever learned about the histories of people of colour while they were in school. Visible minorities were talked about in terms of recent immigration or mere footnotes on the pages of their history books.

Lee's family could not reunite with her great-grandfathers in Canada until the 1960s. Racist immigration policy required Chinese-Canadians to pay high head-taxes to bring their families into the country.

"I wasn't aware of the major contributions of Chinese-Canadians until a couple of years ago," said Lee. "But I don't think I was interested (when I was younger). By history, Canada was founded by mainly the English and French—aside from the Native peoples—they just figured this was their land and anyone else who came in after was either a minority or second class."

You can hear it in the term "visible minority," said Kefentse. It divides Canadians into two groups: the minority, which clearly is designated, and the majority, which really isn't defined.

"I hate the term 'minority,' " she said. "First of all, statistically it's not correct. Secondly, it implies that you have to put yourself against others to define yourself. Who's the majority? It makes me feel less than a person. I feel like I'm something to be defined instead of a person."

The tag "visible minority" and hyphenated terms like Jamaican-Canadian or Chinese-Canadian, can play a part in making some people feel they aren't accepted in the community.

"It may have something to do with it. As much as it's not the right thing to do,

people think in terms of colour, ethnicity and culture. It kind of leads to certain presumptions of people," said Lee.

Not so, said Grewal. Her parents faced much ignorance and racism when they first arrived in Canada. There weren't many people of colour and Canadians did not want to accept what they didn't know. Grewal won't say she has been immune to ignorance, but it was never serious. She has always felt accepted by most of the people she came into contact with.

Besides, she said, younger people are more accepting of change and people of various races and nationalities.

"I just don't think it makes a difference in Canada these days, especially to my generation. I think maybe 50 years ago, or even 10 years ago, race and all of this would have been a relevant issue," said Grewal. "Maybe I would have felt a little bit out of place, but nowadays, the world is so global. It's an international community and because of that it's not an issue for my generation."

Toronto's a good place to live, said Kefentse, but when will she feel like she's accepted as a Canadian and not have to endure prodding questions about where she's from?

"I think slowly it's changing," said Kefentse, "but I still wonder when the day will come when someone will look at me and not ask the question, 'Where do you come from?' "

—*Originally published January 29, 2000*

after READING

UNDERSTANDING THE TEXT

1. a) Name the people the writer **interviewed** during her research and record each of their attitudes toward the topic of the article.

b) Based on your reading of the article, decide whether or not the headline is an accurate indication of the content. List three other possible titles for the article.

2. a) With a partner, make an outline of this article.

b) Identify any places within the article where the writer strays from the **topic**, adds unnecessary information, or interrupts the flow of ideas.

c) Write point-form notes explaining whether the order is effective.

 3. a) Choose three medium-sized paragraphs from the article. Analyze Drakes's writing under the following topics: average number of words per paragraph, sentence type, sentence order, number of words with three or more syllables, number of quotations used.

b) With a partner, examine your findings. Explain how Drakes's writing **style** makes the article easy or difficult to read.

4. In your notebook, record the purpose and **audience** of this article. Refer to the writer's style and her vocabulary level to provide reasons for your choice of purpose and audience. In a paragraph, explain whether you think the writer has been successful in reaching the audience you have identified.

EXPLORING IDEAS AND IMPLICATIONS

5. a) In a small group, create a poster that warns against making assumptions. You can use the assumption Kayo Kefentse finds objectionable or you can raise awareness about different types of assumptions people make that create discomfort in others. In your poster, include both **implicit** and **explicit meanings**, clear visual and written messages, and effective **layout** and design.

b) Be sure to follow the creative process including idea gathering, thumbnail sketches, drafts, revisions, and an assessment of the final product.

c) Display your poster along with your rough work and assessment in your classroom.

d) As a class, design an evaluation form and assess the work of each group.

MAKING CONNECTIONS

6. Using electronic and/or print resources, investigate which contributions to Canada's history by minorities are included in the social studies or history curriculum. ■

Stereotypes Are for "Others"

MARIA COLETTA MCLEAN

"Where do the stereotypes come from?
Who fuels them? Why?"

BEFORE READING

As a class, brainstorm a list of stereotypes associated with teenagers in our society.
Discuss the fairness and possible origins of these stereotypes.

My friend Lisa is black; her husband is white. [In spring 1993], they had their first baby. A girl with fair skin, blue eyes and a batch of red hair.

Lisa is enjoying the first few months with her daughter, except for one thing. When she takes her baby out for a walk, people stop to admire her. "What a sweet baby! Look at that red hair!" they say to the baby. To Lisa, they say, "Are you the nanny?"

I told this to my university class. Judith recalled a similar story. She has a friend who teaches literary theory and writes poetry: she's a tenured professor and she's South Asian.

One day, they rode the elevator to the seventh floor; they carried books and essays; they talked about the spring exam schedule. A man interrupted their conversation and said to the South Asian professor,

"Are you the one responsible for cleaning the fifth floor?"

I told these stories to my family at dinner but my son didn't understand why people assume that a South Asian woman is a cleaning woman or why a black woman is a nanny.

I recalled a story from the '70s when people believed that all Italians were associated with the Mafia. At first, we used to joke among ourselves, "I'm going to make you a proposition...." but soon it wasn't funny anymore. Italian friends graduated from law school, but couldn't get jobs with established law firms because of the perceived Mafia association.

WHITE GARBAGEMEN!

My husband reminded me about the competitive swimmers from Florida that we met a few years ago. Three of them spent the weekend at our house while they competed in a swim meet at the Etobicoke Olympium.

Friday morning, one young man looked out the front window and became very excited. He called to his friends, "Come here, quick! You won't believe it!" We looked but all I saw was the garbagemen picking up the garbage, just like every Friday morning. "What's the big deal?" I asked.

"Are you kidding?" the swimmer replied, "Look! Those garbagemen are white! I've never seen a white garbageman in my life!"

I told this story to my university class. It was a communication, education and mass media course. Where do the stereotypes come from? Who fuels them? Why?

We played a game together. Dividing into three groups: black, yellow and white, we performed skits highlighting stereotypes. All Chinese people have cellular phones, know martial arts, can't drive but can recommend a good Chinese restaurant. All blacks are on welfare, can dance and sing and are recent immigrants from Jamaica. White people can't jump.

Why was it difficult to find stereotypes for white people; easy to find them for "others?"

As I drove home from school that day, I followed the same car for a few blocks. It was a gray Chrysler, driven by a man wearing a turban. Something was wrong with the car. It bothered me all the way to Sheppard Ave.

Then, it struck me. A man wearing a turban was driving a car that was not a taxi.

Aren't all South Asians cab drivers?

—*Originally published September 6, 1994*

after READING

UNDERSTANDING THE TEXT

1. The main point of this **article** is developed through a series of examples. Identify the main idea in this article and explain which one example best captures it.

2. In your notebook, identify the **tone** of this article and explain why you think it is or is not a good tone for the subject matter of this article.

3. In a small group, discuss the "game" the writer had her university class participate in. Assess the appropriateness of this activity for understanding racial stereotypes.

EXPLORING IDEAS AND IMPLICATIONS

4. In a small group, discuss whether an article like this in a newspaper is more likely to put a stop to stereotyping or to perpetuate the stereotypes it describes. Be prepared to present the ideas of your group to the class.

MAKING CONNECTIONS

5. Identify any stereotypes that are presented in a novel or **drama** you are studying in class. Write an essay explaining the appropriate and inappropriate uses of stereotypes in fiction.

Picture of Erick off Baranof Island, Alaska

NANCY PAGH

BEFORE READING

Describe a memorable photograph or short clip from a video taken of a friend or family member. Try to capture in your description what the photographer/videographer was thinking when taking the picture.

This one I took when halibut season closed.
Thirty-four hours straight, little brother,
and we saw fluked brown diamonds
every time we closed our eyes
for a week.   5
Pacific halibut, Greenland turbot, yellowfin sole—
flat panting monsters all over the deck.
Well you were too tired to smile,
too tired to sit.
You stood against the rail, smoking all the way in   10
to Sitka,
straight like a totem.

This photo remembers dark ruffled water,
white coastal mountains,
uneasy pink sky.   15
You leaning into it in tall boots, blue jeans,
your torn Norwegian sweater
with nothing underneath.

Show this one to your college friends.
Show them where you go when they ski.   20
Tell them what this gear can do
to an eye or an arm.
Show them how we're cut, little brother.
Straight
as a diamond   25
as the halibut.

after READING

1. In your notebook, write a response to this **poem**. Focus on your emotional reaction and try to explain that reaction, referring to the poem as much as possible.

2. With a partner, answer the following questions about the content of the poem:
   - Who is the **narrator** in relation to the young man she has photographed?
   - When was the photograph taken?
   - What is the feeling you get from the description of the man in the photograph (lines 8–18)?
   - How does the narrator feel about Erick's college friends?
   - What is the significance of the last **stanza** of the poem?

3. Divide the poem into stanzas by grouping lines with the same **topic** and starting a new stanza when the subject, **setting**, or time changes. Give each stanza a subtitle that reflects the function and content of those lines within the poem.

4. The poet uses the expression "This photo remembers ..." (line 13). Suggest some different words she could have used in place of "remembers." Explain why the poet's word or one of your own is the best choice for the poem. Keep in mind **tone**, meaning, **voice**, and content when choosing.

5. In a paragraph, explain a possible reason for the poet's repeated use of imperative sentences in the last stanza of her poem. (See The Reference Shelf, page 425.)

EXPLORING IDEAS AND IMPLICATIONS

6. Using Nancy Pagh's poem as a model, write your own poem about the person in the photograph or video from your "Before Reading" activity. Take your poem through the revision process with a focus on capturing a specific tone and **mood** in the poem. Prepare your poem for publication.

7. With a partner, **role-play** the conversation that might take place between Erick and a college friend who has seen the picture of Erick taken on the boat. Consider how Erick might feel about his friend knowing his heritage and the nature of his life at home and how the friend might see Erick differently after finding out about his other life away from school. Compare your interpretation of the situation with those of the other partnerships in your class.

MAKING CONNECTIONS

8. Read "Snow White" (pages 204–209). The protagonist of this short story and Erick here have some things in common. Make a list of the elements common to both. Write a **thesis** based on your findings and create an outline for a **literary essay** you could write using your thesis. Exchange outlines with a partner and critique each other's outlines, focusing on the strength of the main and supporting ideas. ■

Small Place

JAMAICA KINCAID

"A tourist is an ugly human being."

BEFORE READING

With a partner, discuss the best foreign vacation spot for a Canadian tourist with a small budget.

If you go to Antigua as a tourist, this is what you will see. If you come by airplane, you will land at the V.C. Bird International Airport. Vere Cornwall (V.C.) Bird is the Prime Minister of Antigua. You may be the sort of tourist who would wonder why a Prime Minister would want an airport named after him—why not a school, why not a hospital, why not some great public monument? You are a tourist and you have not yet seen a school in Antigua, you have not yet seen the hospital in Antigua, you have not yet seen a public monument in Antigua. As your plane descends to land, you might say, What a beautiful island Antigua is—more beautiful than any of the other islands you have seen, and they were very beautiful, in their way, but they were much too green, much too lush with vegetation, which indicated to you, the tourist, that they got quite a bit of rainfall, and rain is the very thing that you, just now, do not want, for you are thinking of

the hard and cold and dark and long days you spent working in North America (or, worse, Europe), earning some money so that you could stay in this place (Antigua) where the sun always shines and where the climate is deliciously hot and dry for the four to ten days you are going to be staying there; and since you are on your holiday, since you are a tourist, the thought of what it might be like for someone who had to live day in, day out in a place that suffers constantly from drought, and so has to watch carefully every drop of fresh water used (while at the same time surrounded by a sea and an ocean—the Caribbean Sea on one side, the Atlantic Ocean on the other), must never cross your mind.

You disembark from your plane. You go through customs. Since you are a tourist, a North American or European— to be frank, white—and not an Antiguan black returning to Antigua from Europe or North America with cardboard boxes of much needed cheap clothes and food for relatives, you move through customs swiftly, you move through customs with ease. Your bags are not searched. You emerge from customs into the hot, clean air: immediately you feel cleansed, immediately you feel blessed (which is to say special); you feel free. You see a man, a taxi driver; you ask him to take you to your destination; he quotes you a price. You immediately think that the price is in the local currency, for you are a tourist and you are familiar with these things (rates of exchange) and you feel even more free, for things seem so cheap, but then your driver ends by saying, "In U.S. currency." You may say, "Hmmmm, do you have a formal sheet that lists official prices and destinations?" Your driver obeys the law and shows you the sheet, and he apologizes for the incredible mistake he has made in quoting you a price off the top of his head which is so vastly different (favouring him) from the one listed. You are driven to your hotel by this taxi driver in his taxi, a brand new Japanese-made vehicle. The road on which you are travelling is a very bad road, very much in need of repair. You are feeling wonderful, so you say, "Oh, what a marvellous change these bad roads are from the splendid highways I am used to in North America." (Or, worse, Europe.) Your driver is reckless; he is a dangerous man who drives in the middle of the road when he thinks no other cars are coming in the opposite direction, passes other cars on blind curves that run uphill, drives at sixty miles an hour on narrow, curving roads when the

road sign, a rusting, beat-up thing left over from colonial days, says 40 MPH. This might frighten you (you are on your holiday; you are a tourist); this might excite you (you are on your holiday; you are a tourist), though if you are from New York and take taxis you are used to this style of driving: most of the taxi drivers in New York are from places in the world like this. You are looking out the window (because you want to get your money's worth); you notice that all the cars you see are brand-new, or almost brand-new, and that they are all Japanese-made. There are no American cars in Antigua—no new ones, at any rate; none that were manufactured in the last ten years. You continue to look at the cars and you say to yourself, Why, they look brand-new, but they have an awful sound, like an old car—a very old, dilapidated car. How to account for that? Well, possibly it's because they use leaded gasoline in these brand-new cars whose engines were built to use non-leaded gasoline, but you mustn't ask the person driving the car if this is so, because he or she has never heard of unleaded gasoline. You look closely at the car; you see that it's a model of a Japanese car that you might hesitate to buy; it's a model that's very expensive; it's a model that's quite impractical for a person who has to work as hard as you do and who watches every penny you earn so that you can afford this holiday you are on. How do they afford such a car? And do they live in a luxurious house to match such a car? Well, no. You will be surprised, then, to see that most likely the person driving this brand-new car filled with the wrong gas lives in a house that, in comparison, is far beneath the status of the car; and if you were to ask why you would be told that the banks are encouraged by the government to make loans available for cars, but loans for houses not so easily available; and if you ask again why, you will be told that the two main car dealerships in Antigua are owned in part or outright by ministers in government. Oh, but you are on holiday and the sight of these brand-new cars driven by people who may or may not have really passed their driving test (there was once a scandal about driving licenses for sale) would not really stir up these thoughts in you. You pass a building sitting in a sea of dust and you think, It's some latrines for people just passing by, but when you look again you see the building has written on it PIGGOT'S SCHOOL. You pass the hospital, the Holberton Hospital, and how wrong you are not to think about this, for though you are a tourist on your holiday, what if your heart should miss a few beats? What if a blood vessel in your neck should break? What if one of those people driving those brand-new cars filled with the wrong gas fails to pass safely while going uphill on a curve and you are in the car going in the opposite direction? Will you be comforted to know that the hospital is staffed with doctors that no actual Antiguan trusts; that Antiguans always say about the doctors, "I don't want them near me"; that Antiguans refer to them not as doctors but as "the three men" (there are three of them); that when the Minister of Health himself doesn't feel well he takes the first plane to New York to see a real doctor; that if any one of the

ministers in government needs medical care he flies to New York to get it?

It's a good thing that you brought your own books with you, for you couldn't just go to the library and borrow some. Antigua used to have a splendid library, but in The Earthquake (everyone talks about it that way—The Earthquake; we Antiguans, for I am one, have a great sense of things, and the more meaningful one thing, the more meaningless we make it) the library building was damaged. This was in 1974, and soon after that a sign was placed on the front of the building saying, THIS BUILDING WAS DAMAGED IN THE EARTHQUAKE OF 1974. REPAIRS ARE PENDING. The sign hangs there, and hangs there more than a decade later, with its unfulfilled promise of repair, and you might see this as a sort of quaintness on the part of these islanders, these people descended from slaves—what a strange, unusual perception of time they have. REPAIRS ARE PENDING, and here it is, many years later, but perhaps in a world that is twelve miles long and nine miles wide (the size of Antigua) twelve minutes and twelve days are all the same. The library is one of those splendid old buildings from colonial times, and the sign telling of the repairs is a splendid old sign from colonial times. Not long after The Earthquake Antigua got its independence from Britain, making Antigua a state in its own right, and Antiguans are so proud of this that each year, to mark the day, they go to Church and thank God, a British God, for this. But you should not think of the confusion that must lie in all that and you must not think of the damaged library. You have brought your own books with you, and among them is one of those new books about economic history, one of those books explaining how the West (meaning Europe and North America after its conquest and settlement by Europeans) got rich: the West got rich not from free (free—in this case, meaning got-for-nothing) and then undervalued labour, for generations, of the people like me you see walking around you in Antigua but from the ingenuity of small shopkeepers in Sheffield and Yorkshire and Lancashire, or wherever; and what a part the invention of the wristwatch played in it, for there was nothing noble-minded men could not do when they discovered they could slap time on their wrists just like that (isn't that the last straw; for not only did we have to suffer the unspeakableness of slavery, but the satisfaction to be had from "We made you bastards rich" is taken away, too), and so you needn't let that slightly funny feel-ing you have from time to time about exploitation, oppression, domination develop into full-fledged unease, discom-fort; you could ruin your holiday. They are not responsible for what you have; you owe them nothing; in fact, you did them a big favour, and you can provide one hundred examples. For here you are now, passing by Government House. And here you are now, passing by the Prime Minister's Office and the Parliament Building, and overlooking these, with a splendid view of St. John's Harbour, the American Embassy. If it were not for you, they would not have the Government House, and Prime Minister's Office, and

Parliament Building and embassy of a powerful country. Now you are passing a mansion, an extraordinary house painted the colour of cow dung, with more aerials and antennas attached to it than you will see even at the American Embassy. The people who live in this house are a mer-chant family who came to Antigua from the Middle East less than twenty years ago. When this family first came to Antigua they sold dry goods door to door from suitcases they carried on their backs. Now they own a lot of Antigua; they regularly lend money to the government, they build enormous (for Antigua), ugly (for Antigua), concrete buildings in Antigua's capital, St. John's, which the government then rents for huge sums of money; a member of their family is the Antiguan Ambassador to Syria; Antiguans hate them. Not far from this mansion is another mansion, the home of a drug smuggler. Everybody knows he's a drug smuggler, and if just as you were driving by he stepped out of his door your driver might point him out to you as the notorious person that he is, for this drug smuggler is so rich people say he buys cars in tens—ten of this one, ten of that one—and that he bought a house (another mansion) near Five Islands, con-tents included, with cash he carried in a suitcase: three hundred and fifty thousand American dollars, and, to the surprise of the seller of the house, lots of American dollars were left over. Overlooking the drug smuggler's mansion is yet another mansion, and leading up to it is the best paved road in all of Antigua—even better than the road that was paved for the

Queen's visit in 1985 (when the Queen came, all roads that she would travel on were paved anew, so that the Queen might have been left with the impression that riding in a car in Antigua was a pleasant experience). In this mansion lives a woman sophisticated people in Antigua call Evita. She is a notorious woman. She's young and beautiful and the girlfriend of somebody high up in the government. Evita is notorious because her relationship with this high government official has made her the owner of boutiques and property and given her a say in cabinet meetings, and all sorts of other privileges such a relationship would bring a beautiful young woman.

Oh, but by now you are tired of all this looking, and you want to reach your destination—your hotel, your room. You long to refresh yourself; you long to eat some nice lobster, some nice local food. You take a bath, you brush your teeth. You get dressed again; as you get dressed, you look out the window. That water— have you ever seen anything like it? Far out, to the horizon, the colour of the water is navy-blue; nearer, the water is the colour of the North American sky. From there to the shore, the water is pale, silvery, clear, so clear, that you can see its pinkish-white sand bottom. Oh, what beauty! Oh, what beauty! You have never seen anything like this. You are so excited. You breathe shallow. You breathe deep. You see a beautiful boy skimming the water, godlike, on a Windsurfer. You see an incredibly unattractive, fat, pastrylike-fleshed woman enjoying a walk on the beautiful sand, with a man, an incredibly

unattractive, fat, pastrylike-fleshed man; you see the pleasure that they're taking in their surroundings. Still standing, looking out the window, you see yourself lying on the beach, enjoying the amazing sun (a sun so powerful and yet so beautiful, the way it is always overhead as if on permanent guard, ready to stamp out any cloud that dares to darken and so empty rain on you and ruin your holiday; a sun that is your personal friend). You see yourself meeting new people (only they are new in a limited way, for they are people just like you). You see yourself eating some delicious, locally grown food. You see yourself, you see yourself.... You must not wonder what exactly happened to the contents of your lavatory when you flushed it. You must not wonder where your bathwater went when you pulled out the stopper. You must not wonder what happened when you brushed your teeth. Oh, it might all end up in the water you are thinking of taking a swim in; the contents of your lavatory might, just might, graze gently against your ankle as you wade carefree in the water, for you see, in Antigua, there is no proper sewage-disposal system. But the Caribbean Sea is very big and the Atlantic Ocean is even bigger; it would amaze even you to know the number of black slaves this ocean has swallowed up. When you sit down to eat your delicious meal, it's better that you don't know that most of what you are eating came off a plane from Miami. And before it got on a plane in Miami, who knows where it came from? A good guess is that it came from a place like Antigua first, where it was grown dirt-cheap, went to Miami, and came back. There is a world of something in this, but I can't go into it right now.

The thing you have always suspected about yourself the minute you become a tourist is true: A tourist is an ugly human being. You are not an ugly person all the time; you are not an ugly person ordinarily; you are not an ugly person day to day. From day to day, you are a nice person. From day to day, all the people who are supposed to love you on the whole do. From day to day, as you walk down a busy street in the large and modern and prosperous city in which you work and love, dismayed, puzzled (a cliché, but only a cliché can explain you) at how alone you feel in this crowd, how awful it is to go unnoticed, how awful it is to go unloved, even as you are surrounded by more people than you could possibly get to know in a lifetime that lasted for millennia, and then out of the corner of your eye you see someone looking at you and absolute pleasure is written all over that person's face, and then you realize that you are not as revolting a presence as you think you are (for that look just told you so). And so, ordinarily, you are a nice person, an attractive person, a person capable of drawing to yourself the affection of other people (people just like you), a person at home in your own skin (sort of; I mean, in a way; I mean, your dismay and puzzlement are natural to you, because people like you just seem to be like that, and so many of the things people like you find admirable about yourselves— the things you think about, the things you think really define you—seem rooted in

these feelings): a person at home in your own house (and all its nice house things), with its nice back yard (and its nice back-yard things), at home on your street, your church, in community activities, your job, at home with your family, your relatives, your friends—you are a whole person. But one day, when you are sitting somewhere, alone in that crowd, and that awful feeling of displacedness comes over you, and really, as an ordinary person you are not well equipped to look too far inward and set yourself aright, because being ordinary is already so taxing, and being ordinary takes all you have out of you, and though the words "I must get away" do not actually pass across your lips, you make a leap from being that nice blob just sitting like a boob in your amniotic sac of the modern experience to being a person visiting heaps of death and ruin and feeling alive and inspired at the sight of it; to being a person lying on some faraway beach, your stilled body stinking and glistening in the sand, looking like something first forgotten, then remembered, then not important enough to go back for; to being a person marvelling at the harmony (ordinarily, what you would say is the backwardness) and the union these other people (and they are other people) have with nature. And you look at the things they can do with a piece of ordinary cloth, the things they fashion out of cheap, vulgarly coloured (to you) twine, the way they squat down over a hole they have made in the ground, the hole itself is something to marvel at, and since you are being an ugly person this ugly but joyful thought will swell inside you: their ancestors were not clever in the way yours were and not ruthless in the way yours were, for then would it not be you who would be in harmony with nature and backwards in that charming way? An ugly thing, that is what you are when you become a tourist, an ugly, empty thing, a stupid thing, a piece of rubbish pausing here and there to gaze at this and taste that, and it will never occur to you that the people who inhabit the place in which you have just paused cannot stand you, that behind their closed doors they laugh at your strangeness (you do not look the way they look); the physical sight of you does not please them; you have bad manners (it is their custom to eat their food with their hands; you try eating their way, you look silly; you try eating the way you always eat, you look silly); they do not like the way you speak (you have an accent); they collapse helpless from laughter, mimicking the way they imagine you must look as you carry out some everyday bodily function. They do not like you. *They do not like me?* That thought never actually occurs to you. Still, you feel a little uneasy. Still, you feel a little foolish. Still, you feel a little out of place. But the banality of your own life is very real to you; it drove you to this extreme, spending your days and your nights in the company of people who despise you, people you do not like really, people you would not want to have as your actual neighbour. And so you must devote yourself to puzzling out how much of what you are told is really true. (Is ground-up bottle glass in peanut sauce really a delicacy around here, or will it do just what you think ground-up bottle glass will do? Is this rare, multicoloured, snout-mouthed fish really an aphrodisiac, or will it cause you to fall asleep permanently?) Oh, the hard work all of this is, and is it any wonder, then, that on your return home you feel the need of a long rest, so that you can recover from your life as a tourist?

That the native does not like the tourist is not hard to explain. For every native of every place is a potential tourist, and every tourist is a native of somewhere. Every native everywhere lives a life of overwhelming and crushing banality and boredom and desperation and depression, and every deed, good and bad, is an attempt to forget this. Every native would like to find a way out, every native would like a rest, every native would like a tour. But some natives—most natives in the world—cannot go anywhere. They are too poor. They are too poor to go anywhere. They are too poor to escape the reality of their lives; and they are too poor to live properly in the place where they live, which is the very place you, the tourist, want to go—so when the natives see you, the tourist, they envy you, they envy your ability to leave your own banality and boredom, they envy your ability to turn their own banality and boredom into a source of pleasure for yourself.

after READING

UNDERSTANDING THE TEXT

1. In your own words, explain what Jamaica Kincaid means when she writes "A tourist is an ugly human being."

2. Individually, find examples of **irony** and **sarcasm** in this **essay**. Compare your examples with a partner. Be prepared to explain your choices to your partner.

3. a) There are a number of long sentences in this essay. With a partner, analyze the sentence starting with the words "As your plane descends to land ..." in the first paragraph. Consider the following questions:
   - Is the sentence grammatically correct?
   - Why might the writer have decided to construct such a long sentence at this point in the essay?
   - How could the sentence be broken into shorter sentences?

   b) Find another long sentence in the essay and make a similar analysis of it.

   c) Write a paragraph evaluating the use of sentence variety in this essay.

EXPLORING IDEAS AND IMPLICATIONS

4. Write a letter to Jamaica Kincaid explaining why, after reading her essay, you would or would not consider vacationing in Antigua. Be prepared to read your letter to the class.

5. With a partner, using print and/or electronic sources, obtain tourist information about Antigua. Prepare a presentation for the class comparing and contrasting the way Antigua is presented in the tourist information with the way it is presented in this essay.

6. Have a class discussion debating the pros and cons of poor countries developing resort areas for rich tourists. In your notebook, summarize the class **debate**.

MAKING CONNECTIONS

7. Create a bibliography of print and electronic materials for a research essay on Jamaica Kincaid. Divide the bibliography into two sections: primary sources and secondary sources. (See The Reference Shelf, pages 431–433.) ■

Postcard

MARGARET ATWOOD

BEFORE READING

In a group of three or four students, brainstorm reasons why people send postcards.
Set your list of reasons aside for future reference.

I'm thinking of you. What else can I say?
The palm trees on the reverse
are a delusion; so is the pink sand.
What we have are the usual
fractured coke bottles and the smell   5
of backed-up drains, too sweet,
like a mango on the verge
of rot, which we have also.
The air clear sweat, mosquitos
& their tracks; birds, blue & elusive.   10

Time comes in waves here, a sickness, one
day after the other is rolling on;
I move up, it's called
awake, then down into the uneasy
nights but never   15
forward. The roosters crow
for hours before dawn, and a prodded
child howls & howls
on the pocked road to school.
In the hold with the baggage   20
there are two prisoners,
their heads shaved by bayonets, & ten crates
of queasy chicks. Each spring
there's a race of cripples, from the store

to the church. This is the sort of junk   25
I carry with me; and a clipping
about democracy from the local paper.
Outside the window
they're building the damn hotel,
nail by nail, someone's   30
crumbling dream. A universe that includes you
can't be all bad, but
does it? At this distance
you're a mirage, a glossy image
fixed in the posture   35
of the last time I saw you.
Turn you over, there's the place
for the address. Wish you were
here. Love comes
in waves like the ocean, a sickness which goes on 40
& on, a hollow cave
in the head, filling and pounding, a kicked ear.

after READING

UNDERSTANDING THE TEXT

1. In your notebook, explain the contrast described in the first **stanza**.

2. Make a list of unpleasant details used by the poet in the second stanza to describe her location. Write a short paragraph describing the effect of these details on the reader.

3. In a small group, discuss whether this **poem** reflects any of the reasons for sending post-cards that you identified in the "Before Reading" activity. What is the importance of the postcard in the poem? In your notebook, record the group's ideas.

4. In your own words, describe the ideas about the loved one and about love expressed in the final 10 lines of the poem.

EXPLORING IDEAS AND IMPLICATIONS

5. In a small group, discuss Atwood's use of free verse and ampersands. Does the writing **style** seem appropriate for the content of the poem? Would the use of a regular metrical pattern and rhymed lines add to the poem's impact or detract from it? (See The Reference Shelf, pages 423–427.) Make notes on the group's ideas and be prepared to share them with the rest of the class.

MAKING CONNECTIONS

6. Read "Sonnet 30" (page 307). In a small group, use a chart to compare "Postcard" and "Sonnet 30" under the headings "Poet's Mood," "Changes in Mood," and "Poetic Form and Techniques." Choose one group member to present the ideas to the class.

 7. As an independent study, use the Internet or reference books on Canadian literature to find out about the life and writings of Margaret Atwood. (See The Reference Shelf, pages 429–433.) Research her importance as a poet, novelist, storywriter, and literary critic. Write an **essay** and prepare an oral presentation for the class. ■

The Average

W.H. AUDEN

BEFORE READING

As a class, discuss the idea of an "average person." Do you consider the term a compliment? How many people can be above average?

His peasant parents killed themselves with toil
To let their darling leave a stingy soil
For any of those smart professions which
Encourage shallow breathing and grow rich.

The pressure of their fond ambition made   5
Their shy and country-loving child afraid
No sensible career was good enough,
Only a hero could deserve such love.

So here he was without maps or supplies,
A hundred miles from any decent town;   10
The desert glared into his blood-shot eyes;

The silence roared displeasure: looking down,
He saw the shadow of an Average Man
Attempting the exceptional, and ran.

after READING

1. In a sentence, express the main idea or **theme** of this **poem**.

2. Look up the word "fond" in the dictionary. Explain why you think the word, as it is used in line 5 of the poem, is or is not well chosen.

3. With a partner, discuss the predicament of the main **character** at the end of the poem. Consider where he is, what he is doing there, and where he will run to. Be prepared to present your ideas to the class.

4. a) Identify the **rhyme scheme** of this poem.
   b) Identify the stressed and unstressed syllables in the first quatrain of the poem. Identify the meter of the poem. (See The Reference Shelf, page 426.)

5. Explain how line 12 belongs in one way with the three lines that precede it and in another way with the last two lines of the poem. If you were making the decision, explain why you would set up the poem on the page to end with two tercets or with a third quatrain and a couplet.

EXPLORING IDEAS AND IMPLICATIONS

6. Look up the characteristics of a sonnet in The Reference Shelf (page 423). Identify the characteristics of a sonnet this poem has and those it lacks. Identify the kind of sonnet this is and explain the reasons for your choice.

7. Write an **opinion essay** explaining whether parents today put too much pressure on their children to be successful. Have a partner make revision and editing suggestions before your final draft.

MAKING CONNECTIONS

8. Find the poems "Richard Cory" and "Miniver Cheevy," both by Edwin Arlington Robinson, and write a comparison/contrast **essay** explaining why the two title **characters** are similar to or different from "The Average" described by W.H. Auden. Have a partner read your essay for clarity of expression, use of transitions, and organization. Revise and edit your essay for submission. ∎

Zits

JERRY SCOTT AND JIM BORGMAN

BEFORE READING

Discuss the following statement in a small group: "For teenagers, peer pressure makes it difficult to maintain individuality."

after READING

UNDERSTANDING THE TEXT

1. **a)** In your notebook, **summarize** the efforts of the comic strip's central **character** to conform to a set of perceived standards.

   b) Explain the meaning of his "new motto." Assess whether it applies to situations from your own experience. Discuss your explanation and assessment with a classmate.

 2. Examine the combinations of adjectives and nouns used by the central character. Explain whether or not they are effective. (See "oxymoron" in The Reference Shelf, page 419.)

EXPLORING IDEAS AND IMPLICATIONS

3. **a)** Based on the "Before Reading" discussion, write a **personal essay** on what is more important to you: to be accepted (which may mean conforming) or to maintain your individuality (which may mean going against the standards of your friends and peers).

   b) Illustrate your essay with a comic strip that captures a key point you have made.

MAKING CONNECTIONS

 4. Compare this comic strip with the Bizarro cartoon (page 42). In a small group, discuss each cartoonist's depiction of teenagers. Do you agree or disagree with each of the views?

5. Compare this comic strip with another cartoon or comic strip that appears regularly in newspapers or magazines. With a partner, discuss the extent to which the meaning or impact of the particular cartoon installment is able to stand on its own or is dependent on the reader's familiarity with the characters or the situation. ■

The Life and Work of Al Purdy

"The only thing that equals
    writing what you think is a good poem,
  is to write another just as good."

BEFORE READING

Using an encyclopedia or electronic sources for your research, find information about the Dorset people who lived in northern Canada. Share your findings with the class.

National Icon Was Larger Than Life

VAL ROSS

Irascible, loud-mouthed, hard-living, talented Alfred Wellington Purdy, who died of cancer at age 82 in April 2000, was one of the last of the generation of angry, left-leaning, restless poets which included Purdy's friends Milton Acorn and Earle Birney.

A robust nationalist who identified strongly with the small-town central Ontario landscape of his birth, Purdy won two Governor-General's awards for poetry (in 1965 and again in 1986 for his *Collected Poems*) and was appointed to the Order of Canada. Over the last half century, he published more than 40 books; his final volume of poetry, *Beyond Remembering*, will be published in September by Harbour Publishing of B.C.

Like Acorn (whose poetry Purdy selected and edited in a volume titled *I've Tasted My Blood*) Purdy was one of the rowdymen of Canadian literature. He was once famously spritzed by the young Margaret Atwood with a beer during

a heated literary discussion over—what else?—poetry. "I shook my own beer hard and swizzled her with it," he wrote in his memoir *Reaching for the Beaufort Sea* in 1993. "The battle was joined."

In later years he tried to soften his reputation, and in 1993 told the *Globe and Mail*, "I'm not a brawler, I'm a sober, god-fearing Presbyterian, well, not exactly god-fearing. But what would you do if someone called you an [unprintable]? I'll hit him no matter how old I am. There are times when there doesn't seem to be anything else to do ... but you know, I've been timid for much of my life." Still, that didn't stop him from scrapping with other poets, such as Louis Dudek, and even lowly journalists (after I interviewed him in 1993, he fired off a corrective letter, protesting "I do not brag and boast." My apologetic reply prompted a second note— Purdy gallantly forgiving me and looking forward to more jousts in the future.)

Born in 1918 of what he described as "degenerate Loyalist stock," on a farm just north of Trenton in central Ontario, Purdy once boasted (in the introduction to his *Collected Poems*) "If I were in a rowboat, afloat on all the beer I've drunk, I couldn't see the shore." His father died in 1921 and his adoring mother moved with him to town, where his earliest childhood memories were dominated by his cussing, whisky-drinking, poker-playing grandfather.

As Purdy described him in his auto-biography *Reaching for the Beaufort Sea*, the old man "had cold watery eyes and a look of calm ferocity ... that ferocity, that smoldering and burning self, concealed or half-concealed in rotting flesh! … I couldn't imagine him ever defeated or humbled." In Purdy's later years, he could have applied this description to himself.

He dropped out of school in Belleville in 1936 at age 17. He already stood 6 feet 3 inches tall and fearlessly decided to hop a freight train west, brawling and scribbling poetry on scraps of paper as he rode. He rode the rails in 1937 and 1938 (in the 1965 poem *Transients*, he wrote with typical Purdy exuberance: "Riding the boxcars out of Winnipeg / morning after rain so close to / the violent sway of the fields it's / like running and running / naked with summer in your mouth").

The young vagabond finally settled in Vancouver, where he found work in a mattress factory, and then, when war was declared, joined the air force. In the summer of 1941, Corporal Purdy began courting Eurithe Mary Jane Parkhurst; they married and returned to Vancouver. Their son Jimmy was born in 1945.

The marriage lasted through wild times (travelling around Mexico) and lean times back in Ontario where the Purdys eventually collected scrap wood and built a small A-frame house on the shores of Roblin Lake. Still, Eurithe Purdy remains a shadow in Purdy's writings. Throughout his life, Purdy always sought other men with whom he could test his mettle, from his father-in-law with whom he once shared a taxi-driving company, to colleagues such as George Bowering, George Woodcock, Layton and Acorn. When speaking of them, he'd sometimes use the word "love."

But words themselves were Purdy's true love. In an essay in *The Oxford Companion to Canadian Literature*, George Woodcock wrote that Purdy's work was "a type of poetry that is really a philosophical continuum where the here-and-now, immediately perceived, becomes the Blakean grain wherein, if not the world, at least universal values are reflected."

Purdy brought out his first volume of poetry, *The Enchanted Echo*, in 1944. He wrote magazine articles, radio and television plays, and wrote and edited volumes of polemic essays (*The New Romans*, a critique of the United States). In *The Last Canadian Poet: An Essay on Al Purdy*, [published in early 2000], Sam Solecki places Purdy high among the major figures of this country's literature.

"The only thing that equals writing what you think is a good poem, is to write another just as good," the poet wrote on the last page of his autobiography. "It is like coming home after a long absence, and knowing the trees and water and land are yours, your land; or waking up with the woman you have known all your life and knowing she is your life; to feel the boundaries of yourself widen and expand in the sober drunkenness of your brain …"

—*Originally published April 24, 2000*

Lament for the Dorsets

(Eskimos extinct in the 14th century A.D.)

AL PURDY

Animal bones and some mossy tent rings
scrapers and spearheads   carved ivory swans
all that remains of the Dorset giants
who drove the Vikings back to their long ships
talked to spirits of earth and water   5
—a picture of terrifying old men
so large they broke the backs of bears
so small they lurk behind bone rafters
in the brain of modern hunters
among good thoughts and warm things   10
and come out at night
to spit on the stars
The big men with clever fingers
who had no dogs and hauled their sleds
over the frozen northern oceans   15
awkward giants
                    killers of seal
they couldn't compete with little men
who came from the west with dogs
Or else in a warm climatic cycle   20
the seals went back to cold waters
and the puzzled Dorsets scratched their heads
with hairy thumbs around 1350 A.D.
—couldn't figure it out
went around saying to each other   25
plaintively
          "What's wrong? What happened?
          Where are the seals gone?"
And died

Twentieth century people   30
apartment dwellers
executives of neon death
warmakers with things that explode
—they have never imagined us in their future

how could we imagine them in the past   35
squatting among the moving glaciers
six hundred years ago
with glowing lamps?
As remote or nearly
as the trilobites and swamps   40
when coal became
or the last great reptile hissed
at a mammal the size of a mouse
that squeaked and fled

Did they ever realize at all   45
what was happening to them?
Some old hunter with one lame leg
a bear had chewed
sitting in a caribou skin tent
—the last Dorset?   50
Let's say his name was Kudluk
carving 2-inch ivory swans
for a dead grand-daughter
taking them out of his mind
the places in his mind   55
where pictures are
He selects a sharp stone tool
to gouge a parallel pattern of lines
on both sides of the swan
holding it with his left hand   65
bearing down and transmitting
his body's weight
from brain to arm and right hand
and one of his thoughts
turns to ivory   70
The carving is laid aside
in beginning darkness
at the end of hunger
after a while wind
blows down the tent and snow   75
begins to cover him
After 600 years
the ivory thought
is still warm

after READING

UNDERSTANDING THE TEXT

1. a) In your notebook, explain the two possible reasons suggested by the poet for the disappearance of the Dorsets (lines 13–29).
   b) Record details from the **poem** that describe the Dorset people or their lifestyle.

2. Explain the emotional impact of identifying the last Dorset as "Kudluk" (lines 45–74).

3. With a partner, discuss the importance of the "carved ivory swans" as a symbol in the poem. Be prepared to share your discussion with the class.

4. a) In your notebook, list a chronological **summary** of events in Al Purdy's life.
   b) List details from the **obituary** that create the impression of Al Purdy as a rowdy or argumentative poet, as a responsible citizen and family man, and as a prolific and respected Canadian writer.
   c) Select two examples of oxymoron from this obituary—one by the author, Val Ross, and one from Purdy's own writing—and explain their effectiveness in describing the complexity of Purdy's **character**.

EXPLORING IDEAS AND IMPLICATIONS

5. Use a dictionary to clarify your understanding of the term "lament." Make a chart of details from the poem that *do* and *do not* qualify this poem as a "lament."

6. The **tone** and language of an obituary should reflect the life and character of the person. Select and record examples of a particular tone in the language from this obituary. Discuss the tone we might expect an obituary to be written for a famous person who was not a writer (for example, a popular television actor; an esteemed member of the royal family).

7. The author of this obituary comments that "if not the world, at least universal values are reflected in Purdy's poetry." Write a short **essay** assessing whether this statement is valid for "Lament for the Dorsets." Write a draft of your essay and work with a partner to improve the arguments, organization, and expression. Prepare a final draft for publication.

MAKING CONNECTIONS

8. Read "Those Anthropologists" (page 80). In a small group, prepare an oral **report** that the narrator of the poem might make on Purdy's portrayal of the Dorset people. Select one member of your group to present the report to the class. ■

Ain't I a Woman?

SOJOURNER TRUTH

"I could work as much and eat as much
as a man ... and bear the lash as well!"

BEFORE READING

In your notebook, recall a **speech** that made you think. In your writing, explain how the occasion, the ideas presented, and the speaker's delivery style made an impact on you.

Well, children, where there is so much racket there must be something out of kilter. I think that 'twixt the negroes of the South and the women at the North, all talking about rights, the white men will be in a fix pretty soon. But what's all this here talking about?

That man over there says that women need to be helped into carriages, and lifted over ditches, and to have the best place everywhere. Nobody ever helps me into carriages, or over mud-puddles, or gives me any best place! And ain't I a woman? Look at me! Look at my arm! I have ploughed and planted, and gathered into barns, and no man could head me! And ain't I a woman? I could work as much and eat as much as a man—when I could get it—and bear the lash as well! And ain't I a woman? I have borne thirteen children, and seen them most all sold off to slavery and when I cried out with my mother's grief, none but Jesus heard me! And ain't I a woman?

Then they talk about this thing in the head; what's this they call it? [Intellect, someone whispers.] That's it, honey. What's that got to do with women's rights or negro's rights? If my cup won't hold but a pint, and yours holds a quart, wouldn't you be mean not to let me have my little half-measure full?

Then that little man in black there, he says women can't have as much rights as men, 'cause Christ wasn't a woman! Where did your Christ come from? Where did your Christ come from? From God and a woman! Man had nothing to do with Him.

If the first woman God ever made was strong enough to turn the world upside down all alone, these women together ought to be able to turn it back, and get it right side up again! And now they is asking to do it, the men better let them.

Obliged to you for hearing me, and now old Sojourner ain't got nothing more to say.

after READING

UNDERSTANDING THE TEXT

1. a) In a paragraph, explain whether this speech appeals more to reason or emotion in making its points to the **audience**. Give reasons for your answer.

b) Select the most effective argument presented in this speech and write it in your own words.

2. Some parts of this speech are not in standard Canadian English. With a partner, discuss whether this makes the speech more or less effective. Be prepared to present your ideas to the class.

EXPLORING IDEAS AND IMPLICATIONS

3. Prepare an oral reading of this speech to present to the class. Before delivering the speech, consider its **tone** and how you think Sojourner Truth might have presented it. Practise it aloud on your own before presenting it to the class.

4. In the role of one of the following individuals, write a diary entry made after hearing this speech by Sojouner Truth in 1851:
- a black woman
- a white woman
- a black man
- a white man

5. Write a speech on a social issue that you feel strongly about. After the first draft, read your speech to a classmate to help you revise and edit it. Rehearse your final speech and present it to the class.

 6. a) Research the life and times of Sojourner Truth and create a Web site on your findings.

b) Write an **opinion essay** indicating whether today's sophisticated media technology has or has not improved the opportunity for average people to present their ideas to their fellow citizens.

MAKING CONNECTIONS

7. Find a copy of Martin Luther King's famous "I Have a Dream" speech. Make a list of rhetorical devices that both he and Sojourner Truth have used in their respective speeches. Discuss whether any of these devices can be used only to express ideas about human rights issues or if they could be adapted and used in speeches on any topic. Be prepared to present your conclusions to the class. ■

Archetypes

SUNITI NAMJOSHI

BEFORE READING

As a class, define **"archetype."** Make a list of archetypes you have studied and/or heard about.

Sisyphus rolled his boulder to the top
    then he kicked it down, since he was
    at heart a simple artist, who greatly
    delighted in the sound of thunder.
But Penelope was a housewife. What   5
    governed her? Mere habit perhaps?
    Or shortage of wool? Or the desire to attain
    an impossible perfection? Sometimes
    I have thought it was ordinary rage.
    Virtuous women punish themselves.   10

after READING

UNDERSTANDING THE TEXT

1. **a)** Look up the **stories** of Sisyphus and Penelope. (You will find Sisyphus in Greek mythology and Penelope in Homer's *The Odyssey*.) Make brief point-form notes on each one.
   b) Identify the details the poet has changed about each of these stories.

2. **a)** With a partner, develop a statement of the **theme** for this **poem**.
   b) The poet uses a declarative sentence when describing Sisyphus, but a series of questions when describing Penelope. Explain how these sentence types help emphasize the theme of the poem.

EXPLORING IDEAS AND IMPLICATIONS

3. Having read Penelope's story, work with a partner to **role-play** a radio **interview** with her **character**. You can use Namjoshi's questions and observations as a starting point, but you should branch out to include more of your own. Cover some of the issues you believe a modern **audience** would like to hear about.

MAKING CONNECTIONS

4. **a)** Using electronic and/or print resources, research one of the following archetypes: the hero, the martyr, the quest or the journey, and the fall.
   b) After your research, make conclusions about the usefulness of knowing archetypes when studying literature. ∎

Turning Points

SUSAN KLAUBER

BEFORE READING

By looking only at the title of this **essay**, predict what it will be about. Share your predictions with a classmate, and discuss how you arrived at them. In your notebook, make notes on the ideas that came from your discussion.

The picks on a figure skate had always been my friend. Not in the same way Kurt Browning or Elvis Stojko used their power to leap and spin through the air, suspending every imaginable moment of grace and beauty, and then punctuating that freedom with a sharp and precise landing, an incision in the ice, held firm by the strength of that faithful friend, the pick.

No, mine was not like those feats of the giants, for my figure skates had always been used in a different way. Oh, maybe for a year as a six-year-old, I'd stuttered around the ice in a frilly cotton costume and made the gestures of a grown-up figure skater, but my real passion was hockey. My skates were for that.

Dad was a fanatic fan. He and Mom had season tickets to the local main attraction every Friday evening, the hockey game—the biggest and only traffic jam all week.

To watch those heroes play became the highlight of my life—their speed, their grace, their artistry of passing. It was quick moves, agile minds, the joy of competition at lightning speeds, and above all, fun!

Dad made us a rink in our backyard that became the gathering point for the neighborhood. Every winter day, as soon as school was over, we'd rush to get out there and play. Darkness came early in Northern Ontario, but a lone light strung up on Mom's clothesline, high above the rink, let the games carry on well into suppertime. Mom used to get annoyed when we'd eat with our skates on, tucked away under the table, secure in their guards. We'd run out after supper and play some more. Only bedtime pried us away from our passion.

We learned it all from Dad, just by listening to him screaming out instructions at the Friday night games. But my sister was my closest hero, my mentor. It was she who told me to file the bottom pick off my skates so we could stride out forcefully like all the hockey players.

I always listened to her. She was such a good player.

We did leave some picks, though, just enough to rely on for sharp turns and stops in the corners when the play got tight—or to make that fake left and then the quick push off to the right to dash around someone. The picks were always there when you needed them.

Deep down, I knew that real hockey players had real hockey skates, but then, girls didn't look very girl-like with big, black hockey skates. They were for boys!

So, right on through the University of Toronto, as a varsity girls' hockey star, I kept my picks; even had them autographed by Frank Mahovlich and Eddie Shack. We put nail polish over the signatures to preserve them.

They stayed shiny and clear through the ensuing hiatus—my "grown up" years of travel, work, marriage—eighteen years with no skates.

But they were just asleep I guess, for they did reawaken—in my late thirties—married and all—on a frozen Iowa pond. I dusted off the picks and stick teaching my husband the love of the game, which has become our great winter sport for ten years now.

Sadly, after only a few upstart years, I had to retire my old figure skates. The thought did come up briefly again— "hockey skates?" But it was a definitive "no." To my delight, they had developed new ladies' free style skates—a hard boot that was a bonus when a bullet-like puck bounced off them without even a twinge of pain—bold white boots with picks! I was in heaven.

I briefly tried out hockey skates, when they were the only choice available, on one of my spiritual pilgrimages, when you seem to open up to new challenges. But this was just for skating. I had my picks at home for hockey.

My rebirth expanded from pond games to league competition three hours away in the big indoor rinks—full equipment, real hockey games—with men! I felt guided to the big reunion game with the university women's alumnae playing against varsity.

I'd heard the girls had progressed in twenty-four years and even played like guys! It'd be great to see. I wondered how I'd fare playing 800 miles away in my old rink.

My sister was just as anxious to see me play. She took me to The Hockey Shoppe to sharpen my skates in preparation for the game. The man behind the counter was world famous for his hockey knowledge. Everyone in the store bantered back and forth their love of hockey.

"I don't mind if the sharpener has to smooth down the bottom pick, but leave some of the others," I explained to the clerk, and returned to the kibitzing.

I wasn't prepared for the view when the skates came back. They sat on the counter—glistening—not a pick left!

In some recess of my mind, I registered, "no picks!" and just as swiftly, was consumed by an empty thud. It became awfully quiet deep in my soul. The banter and talk kept on as loud as ever, but inside felt like an eternity away—stilled, stunned!

My outward self dutifully went through the motions of polite conversation, paid the man, and picked up my skates, but all

I was thinking was, "How am I going to play the biggest game of my female hockey career with no picks?"

As I left, my sister said I had been so cavalier in instructing him to file the picks! I almost disliked her at that moment, but, somehow she always pulled out my courage.

The girls were awesome—in another league. Four times I fell flat on the ice—shocked—surprised—but, I kept getting up.

My sister summed up my performance to her daughter. "Your old auntie Susie hasn't got the moves any more, but she still has the instincts and anticipates like a pro." The next day, in quieter moments, she blurted, "Cut that damned stick, and get some good hockey skates. You have to learn lateral mobility!"

She had a way of thrusting me into the truth before I even realized it.

It took me only a few days before I went to Canadian Tire, tried them on and bought them—boys size six, Bauer Supreme Classics.

My feet took a while to forget my old friends.

My heart took longer.

I'm still learning new tricks and new ways to move, but the challenge has become fun and the game more rewarding.

I smile at my skates now, the ones that miss the old turning points. But you know, I never even noticed they were black.

after READING

UNDERSTANDING THE TEXT

1. In your notebook, assess the extent to which your "Before Reading" predictions were accurate. How did the essay differ from your predictions?

2. **Summarize** the ways in which the writer was influenced by her father and her sister.

3. In a few sentences, explain at least two possible interpretations of the title "Turning Points" in relation to the ideas in the essay.

EXPLORING IDEAS AND IMPLICATIONS

4. Using print and/or electronic sources, research the names of skaters and hockey players mentioned in the essay. Write a short paragraph explaining what these names add to the reader's response to the essay.

5. a) With a partner, examine the author's use of paragraphs in the essay. Suggest reasons for her use of so many short paragraphs.

b) This essay was originally published in a book subtitled *Poems and Prose by Susan Klauber*. Discuss with a partner the extent to which some of the paragraphs in the essay seem to be poetic. Which paragraphs could have been part of a free verse poem? (See The Reference Shelf, page 423.) Share your ideas with the class.

6. a) Write a **personal essay** about a change in your life. The essay could be modelled on "Turning Points." Consider topics such as "Farewell Training Wheels," "Driving Solo," and "Starting My New Job."

b) With a partner, revise your first draft to include more interesting details and emotions, as well as clear expression. Rewrite and edit your essay for publication, for submission to the teacher, or to be read aloud to your classmates.

MAKING CONNECTIONS

7. Read "99" (page 199). Using your research from activity 4, write your own **poem** about one of the athletes mentioned in this essay. Revise and edit your poem. As a class, collect all the poems and create a class poetry **anthology** of "Great Canadians on Ice." ■

99

MARK COCHRANE

BEFORE READING

As a class, brainstorm a list of films, novels, **short stories**, and **poems** about sports or sports heroes. Discuss to what extent you feel these art forms are able to capture the essence of sports.

Speed, force of weapon, musculature:
there sleep armies of men who possess these
in bruter proportion—knight, bishop

& rook. On the grid of his mind glitters
an optic calculus. A triangulation   5
of the probable. He views each square

yet circles beyond rank, & without opposite.
Even the master who would be his mirror,
his nemesis to the sixes, read only

bad oracles. Despair. No logic & no art   10
honed on the ice by flat-earthers
can foil a wizard who is arranging the stars.

after READING

UNDERSTANDING THE TEXT

1. In a brief paragraph, explain the relationship between the title of this poem and the poem itself.

2. This poem uses **imagery** borrowed from the game of chess. In a paragraph for each, identify the point being made by any two of these images. In a final paragraph, explain whether the chess images are effective in developing the poet's ideas about the main subject of the poem.

3. In the last **stanza** the word "Despair" forms a single-word sentence. Explain how that word relates to the words and sentence on either side of it.

EXPLORING IDEAS AND IMPLICATIONS

4. One of the characteristics of **poetry** is concise wording—saying a lot in very few words. Select one phrase or word in this poem and make a list of the ideas and information it conveys. Explain your ideas to a partner. With your partner, discuss to what extent this economy of language confuses or engages readers in making meaning out of the poem.

5. Imagine you are the sports hero described in this poem. Write a letter to the poet who wrote this poem expressing your reaction on finding it in an **anthology** of literature being studied in an English classroom.

6. Read **biographical** information about the sports hero described in this poem. Assess the imagery and accuracy of the ideas and descriptions in the poem in light of the information you read. Share your findings with the class.

MAKING CONNECTIONS

7. Find another poem related to sports. Write a **review** of the poem explaining what you do or do not like about it. Prepare a display of the poem and your comments to post as part of a bulletin board display about sports-related poetry. ■

Ex-Basketball Player

JOHN UPDIKE

BEFORE READING

As a class, discuss whether you know of a student who has become a highly paid professional athlete. Has the student continued her or his education to prepare for a career after sports?

Pearl Avenue runs past the high-school lot,
Bends with the trolley tracks, and stops, cut off
Before it has a chance to go two blocks,
At Colonel McComsky Plaza. Berth's Garage
Is on the corner facing west, and there,   5
Most days, you'll find Flick Webb, who helps Berth out.

Flick stands tall among the idiot pumps—
Five on a side, the old bubble-head style,
Their rubber elbows hanging loose and low.
One's nostrils are two S's, and his eyes   10
An E and O. And one is squat, without
A head at all—more of a football type.

Once Flick played for the high-school team, the Wizards.
He was good: in fact, the best. In '46
He bucketed three hundred ninety points,   15
A county record still. The ball loved Flick.
I saw him rack up thirty-eight or forty
In one home game. His hands were like wild birds.

He never learned a trade, he just sells gas,
Checks oil, and changes flats. Once in a while,   20
As a gag, he dribbles an inner tube,
But most of us remember anyway.
His hands are fine and nervous on the lug wrench.
It makes no difference to the lug wrench, though.

Off work, he hangs around Mae's Luncheonette.   25
Grease-grey and kind of coiled, he plays pinball,
Sips lemon cokes, and smokes those thin cigars;
Flick seldom speaks to Mae, just sits and nods
Beyond her face toward bright applauding tiers
Of Necco Wafers, Nibs, and Juju Beads.   30

after READING

POEM | Ex-Basketball Player 203

UNDERSTANDING THE TEXT

1. **a)** Summarize in three or four sentences the ideas expressed in the **poem**. Then write a single sentence that states the **theme** of the poem. Compare your sentence with that of a partner, and revise it if necessary.

   b) Review the ideas developed in your "Before Reading" discussion. Assess whether any of them can be applied to this poem.

2. In your notebook, record three or four details in the poem that help to establish the approximate historical period in which the events take place. With a partner, compare your findings.

3. In a small group, discuss whether the poem presents a sympathetic description of Flick Webb. Refer to specific details from the poem to defend your ideas. Work toward reaching a **consensus**, and present your group's observations to the class.

EXPLORING IDEAS AND IMPLICATIONS

4. **a)** Symbols are important to poetic expression. (See The Reference Shelf, page 419.) In a small group, identify three symbols used by the poet to describe Flick Webb's situation. Discuss the effect of these **symbols**, making notes during the discussion.

   b) Individually, develop the outline and the first draft of an **essay** on the poet's use of symbols in "Ex-Basketball Player." Have a partner read your draft, and discuss possible revisions to improve the content and expression of your essay. Rewrite and edit your essay for submission or publication.

5. Write a motivational **speech** that Flick might give to Grade 11 students. With a partner, rehearse and revise your speech. Video- or audiotape your speech to present to the class.

MAKING CONNECTIONS

6. Read the poem "99" (page 199). Using a chart or **graphic organizer**, compare the two poems, paying special attention to each narrator's attitude to the central **character** and to the poetic devices used in each poem. Be prepared to share your observations with the class. ■

Snow White

GRACE HU

"... kids have learned to be mean in that silent, adult way."

BEFORE READING

The writer of this **story** says at one point that as we get older, we learn to be mean in a "silent, adult way" (page 205). As a class, discuss ways teenagers are mean to other teens whom they perceive as "different" from themselves.

I finished dabbing a generous coat of Noxzema on my face and yanked on the chain that extinguishes the harsh bathroom lights. My pink robe dropped to the floor as I slowly stepped into the tub, stirring the water with my big toe first, to test the temperature. The moon snuck in through the slats of the window shutters and I could see my ghost-white reflection glowing in the mirror. I wetted a washcloth and scrubbed, scrubbed, scrubbed my face. When I was done, I snuck a glance in the mirror to make sure I was still there; still there, still ghost-white, perfectly still. White as snow and pure as Ivory soap. Then I relaxed and sunk into the tub. I enjoy this part of my day the most. I get some of my best thinking done here. My mother thinks it's some sort of weird "ritualistic behavior" but she indulges me a lot since she has become a crusader to "protect my right to self-expression." She

uses a lot of euphemisms in her everyday speech. My mother also takes on her role of protectress with quite a religious zeal, though this was not always so.

Once, when I was six, I heard her behind a semi-closed bedroom door, sobbing, "My poor, poor baby, it's all my fault." She was holding the package of school portraits I had just brought home. Scientifically, the way I see it, it's both of their faults. They are both heterozygous carriers with a one-in-four chance of producing a homozygous albino individual. My two older brothers turned out tan and freckled, respectively, then bingo, they hit the genetic jackpot with me. My father opts to avoid the entire subject, like a nervous man who wears gloves to prevent his old vice of nail biting. Which is okay by me. When I was little, kids would tease me by singing, "Mary, Mary, quite contrary, how'd ya get so white and scary?"

The whole thing kind of bored me. My brother Joe once gave me some apple-flavored candy that turned my tongue green. He told me to stick out my tongue when the kids started, and if any of them still stuck around after that he'd come and beat them up. We had a good laugh. Now my brothers are away at school and kids have learned to be mean in that silent, adult way. Actually most of them aren't mean, they're more semi-apathetic. That is, they don't really care, except they sure are glad they aren't me. You can read relief off their faces as soon as they pass in the hallways, shouting overly cheerful hellos to avoid staring. I guess it hasn't helped that my mother has always been overprotective in an apologetic way, practically passing out flyers on the subject matter to mothers of curious children at the playground. When I told this to my brother Ben, he laughed. "Oh, God. Don't give her any ideas." My brothers always make me feel special too, but in a good way. I miss them when they're away.

So what I'm basically trying to say is that I've never had a lot of real "social interaction with other kids my age." This is what the school counselor suggested is the root of all my problems. Considering it was the third time I had been called into her office in two weeks, she said she was a little disappointed "in my effort to modify my antisocial behavior." She must have taken a course in polite speech with my mother, since that roughly translates into: This is the third time in two weeks I have been caught eating lunch in the library. I told the librarian that I am very careful about eating and reading without staining the books (which is pretty easy as I detest all condiments). Ms. Kleghorn, aforementioned counselor, whined, "But we have such a nice courtyard. Everyone else enjoys eating on the green." The Weeping Willow High green has seen better seasons.

Basically I have only one friend. Sometimes you'll find that one good friend is really all you need. Anyway, Karen is the real reason I've been eating lunch in the library. She started dating a rather popular individual a few weeks ago and has started eating lunch with him and his friends. The whole first week of her relationship she would come looking for me at lunch and I'd hide behind some lockers and duck into the library when she wasn't looking. Finally I just told her that I'd started a macrobiotic diet in preparation for the Weeping Willow Marathon I'm training for and have to run home for lunch every day. I'm not sure this plan of mine is a good idea, but I don't want to ruin her chances of making some more friends, and I'd rather we not have some sort of awkward conversation about the whole matter.

I take a big gulp of air and sink all the way into the tub. Even under water I can hear my mother's shrill voice calling, "MMmmmaary! Phone call! MMmmmaary!" How I could have floated inside her for nine months listening to that voice at such close range, I'll never know.

"Hello?" I said, clutching my make-shift towel sarong with one hand and the phone with the other. My hair kept dripping pitter-pat dots on the lime-green pile carpet.

"Mary? It's Karen. Sorry to interrupt your bath." I wasn't too surprised it was her, since she's the only one besides my brothers who ever calls me.

"That's okay. What's going on? Did Clara want to talk to me?" I teased. Clara is Karen's 11-month-old sister, the product of the joyous union of Karen's mother and Herbert, Karen's stepfather. We have an ongoing contest to see who can teach her to say their name first.

"Yeah, right," she laughed. "Listen, what are you doing next Friday?"

"Halloween? Dressing up and scaring people. Like always," I said, half serious.

"Well, listen to this. I'm having a party and you're coming," Karen said. I could hear the excitement in her voice but I didn't know what to say.

"Hmmm. I don't know, Karen. I had other plans," I lied. My only plan was to dress up for the trick-or-treaters who would come to our house.

"C'mon. It'll be fun; you can come early and help me decorate. Besides, I'm serving crudités." I thought about the costume I had been designing. Maybe it would be fun to actually wear it out and see the reaction.

"Okay. You got me. I'll go, if only for the crudités. Your stepfather makes a mean onion dip. But I can't come early; my costume takes a long time to put together," I answered.

"What is it?" Karen wondered.

"You'll see. Listen, I've got to go. I'm getting the carpet all wet."

"Hey, Mary?"

"Yes?"

"Are you still on that macrobiotic diet?"

"Sure am. Tastes like gourmet gerbil fare, but it's really improving my endurance," I said.

"Well, I'll see you later then. Maybe you can run on over here after school tomorrow and help me brainwash Clara. I think she tried to say 'Mama' today."

"Okay," I laughed and hung up. As I finished drying myself and putting on my pajamas, I wondered what I had gotten myself into. Past Halloweens I had dressed up in the expected costumes: Lady Macbeth, Albino Killer Rabbit, Teenage Mutant Zombie. This year, though, I had decided on a different kind of costume. I had decided to dress up as a life-size, anatomically correct Weeping Willow High cheerleader, brain cells not included. I fell asleep thinking about my costume and dreamed I was tossed onto a giant trampoline hovering over a large crowd, with no way down except to jump through a series of flaming hoops.

I turned to Dr. Capra with one contact in each eye. I had narrowed down my choice to two colors: "Acquiescing Aqua" and "Vociferous Violet."

"Which one do you think is the real me?" I asked jokingly.

"Oh, little one," he answered. "Neither. But if I must choose one, I prefer the aqua."

"Me too," I agreed, examining myself closely with a hand-held mirror. "It brings out the color in my veins, don't you think?" Dr. Capra smiled and shook his head. About a year ago, I started coming into his shop every two weeks or so to try on all the different colors. When he realized that I was not really interested in actually purchasing a pair of Chameleon Vision lenses, Dr. Capra offered me a job. Mainly I answer phones and help customers with sample frames while Dr. Capra is in the examining room with patients. It was here that I first thought of my costume.

In Dr. Capra's well-lit, mirrored office I have spent many an afternoon placing and plucking colored lenses in and out of my eyes. In moments of unrelenting, undisturbed narcissism I would see myself through different eyes and wonder if I could have been the head cheerleader, the Winter Snow Ball Queen, the desired one. And each time these thoughts would creep up on me and send me into a whirling world that belonged to fairies and make-believe. And each time I would be shocked awake when I realized that these were my mother's thoughts sneaking into my head; her secret daydreams, her dress-up-world way of thinking that made me sick.

Indirectly, my mother had been helping me out with my costume. Up in the attic, in her cedar chest, neatly sandwiched between layers of moth-resistant tissue paper, was her white and blue Weeping Willow Class of '69 cheerleading uniform. I remembered an old photo we had, where it looked marvelous on her, accentuating her golden tan, blue-green eyes and straw-berry blond ponytail with only a flash of white being emitted from her high wattage smile. Karen had been asking me about my costume all week. She refused to tell me what she was dressing up as, to punish me for my own secrecy. She also told me she knew I wasn't on a macrobiotic diet. "You hate brown rice," was all she said.

We went out to lunch on Friday, thor-oughly enjoying our bacon cheeseburgers and mocha mint milkshakes.

Late Friday afternoon I helped Dr. Capra close the shop early and left his office with a quickened step, my heart beating fast. In my jacket pocket, the two little glass vials clinked against each other in celebration. He had lent me a pair of the aqua lenses for my costume. When I got home I went straight to the bath-room and locked the door. Following the directions on the back of the bottle of haircoloring, I saturated my lifeless locks with dye solution and shoved it into an old shower cap before settling down into a steaming bath. Even the hot water did nothing to calm my nerves; I was running on a kind of nervous, excited energy that I had never experienced before. After 15 minutes of soaking, I shampooed and dried my hair, gently wrapping it up into a turban. The bath left my skin sweet-smelling and sunburnt-looking. I opened the paper bag full of supplies that I had bought at the drugstore. I began sponging on a creamy "Alabaster Beige" base on my face and neck. Next I opened the sterile vials and popped two beautiful irises onto my own. I blinked at the mirror. Though I told myself I was doing this as a big joke, another part of me was really enjoying the whole ritual. I carefully applied eye makeup, replete with two coats of brown mascara, copying the way I had seen my mother do it all the times I had watched her when I was little. When I was all powdered and done, I pulled off the towel and a mass of clingy, wet, strawberry blond curls tumbled out. I put on the uniform and a pair of "Naughty Nude" pantyhose underneath. In a glance, I saw my mother in the mirror; the way she looked in the group portrait in the attic, enthusiasm spilling over, electric jolts of energy flying out of each ringlet. I hoped no one would wonder why I'd be wearing white gloves in October.

"Mary! You look beautiful!" my mother gasped as I came downstairs. A hot flush of annoyance moved through me but subsided quickly, to my surprise. I even let her take a few snapshots before I headed outside.

"Have a good time, sweetheart!" she called out behind me, waving furiously. She looked as though she might cry. Outside the air felt cool and I felt good. But as I neared Karen's house, my steps became hesitant. I told myself not to sweat because it would cause my makeup to run down my neck in orangey rivulets. I took a deep breath and entered the open door. The typical ghouls and boys from school were milling about the darkened living room, their feet tapping to the beat of the music. Several people smiled and said hello; clearly they did not recognize me. At first I mocked my mother's fake cheerleader smile, but after a while I relaxed and actually had conversations with various classmates before I spotted Karen, dressed as Julius Caesar, arranging a fresh plate of vegetables and dip on the coffee table. She had always been adamantly proud of her rather aquiline nose.

"Psst, Karen," I whispered.

"Yes?" she said. Then, "Mary? Is that you? I cannot believe it!" she laughed. "Wow, you look great." She walked in a circle around me before she fingered my hair to see if it was real.

"Is it permanent?" Karen asked, her eyes glazed like doughnuts.

"Nope. The hair color comes out in a few washes and the contacts are due in the office tomorrow." I smiled. Karen shook her head at me.

"You really are something, you know that?" Karen took my arm in hers and introduced me to some people, including Marcus, her boyfriend. Everyone was surprisingly nice. I was having a better time than I had ever imagined and I hadn't even had any of Herbert's onion dip yet. But all good things come to an end.

At midnight, there was a sudden uproar of laughter and commotion at the door. In came a boy I faintly recognized, with a face painted white, an equally white shoulder-length wig on his head. In his hand he held an empty can.

"Hey! Toss me another Miller Lite," he said to his friend behind him.

"You mean, Miller White?" his friend answered, laughing heartily, stumbling over his words. Not until then did I realize who he was dressed up as. Then I noticed he was wearing a "Mr. Bubble" T-shirt, just like the one I wore to school every other Monday. Hot tears rushed fiercely to my eyes as I pushed my way through the crowd and out the door. Behind me I could hear Karen calling my name, but even then I didn't stop. The whole way home the cold wind helped hold the tears back; I didn't want to stain my mother's uniform. I could have run forever but after three blocks my house pulled up in front of me. As soon as I reached the bathroom I locked the door and peeled off the costume part by part. I scrubbed my face as hard as I could, crying under the running faucet. What did it matter that I was Technicolor for a night? Like Cinderella, my night of revelry would fade by morning and I hadn't even been clever enough to leave behind a sneaker for my prince. Those boys probably didn't even know my name, much less think that I was going to be at the party. My face burned in anger and shame. Much worse than their teasing, I had let myself believe I had found the magic solution, a panacea in a two-dollar bottle of hair dye. I wonder if this is how Cinderella felt as she walked home, bare-foot and ragged. I jumped into the shower and washed my hair three times, but it only faded to a sickly pink. I grabbed the scissors from the cabinet and began to cut, feeling lighter as each lock dropped to the floor. When only an inch was left on my head, I pulled out the shears and shaved the rest. I gazed into the mirror and had to laugh. I looked completely ridiculous. For an instant I almost felt sorry for my mother; I could see her staring in horror and disbelief. I shook my head; it felt so light and free. I put on my favorite T-shirt and climbed into bed. I don't think I dreamt at all.

Saturday morning Karen came by the house. She knocked on my bedroom door.

"Mary? Open up. It's me. Are you okay?" Before I could clear the sticky quietness that settles in your mouth from hours of sleep, she answered herself. "Of course you are. Will you just open the door?" I opened the door and stood square in front of her.

"You shaved your head," she nodded, barely concealing a smirk.

"Yeah. I did," I agreed.

"So ... you want to go downtown and buy a hat?" she asked.

"Nope. I already got one." I pointed to the bedpost with my gleaming globe of a head.

"Want to go downtown anyway and scare all the salesladies?" she asked.

"Sure," I answered and smiled as I grabbed my old baseball cap. Like I said, one friend is really all you need.

after READING

1. In your notebook, record your reaction to this **story**.

2. In a group of four, discuss how each of the following relates to the **narrator**. Rank them from most to least supportive. Be prepared to present your ranking and your reasons for it to the class.
   - the narrator's mother
   - Karen
   - her father
   - Ms. Kleghorn
   - her brothers

3. Write an analysis of the effectiveness of the first paragraph of this story.

4. Compare and contrast the two long paragraphs dealing with the narrator's preparations for the Halloween party and her departure from the party in terms of vocabulary, sentence structure, and **mood**.

5. With a partner, create a **dramatization** of the scene between the narrator and Ms. Kleghorn in the guidance office. Rehearse and present the scene to the class.

6. This story won first prize in an "Earn Your Place in Literary History" contest. Writing as one of the contest judges, explain three aspects of this story that qualify it for the prize. Use specific references to the story to illustrate your points. Compare your observations with those of your classmates.

EXPLORING IDEAS AND IMPLICATIONS

7. Write an **opinion essay** explaining why you agree or disagree with the narrator's statement "one friend is really all you need." Find a classmate who has taken the opposing stance to yours and compare your views.

8. In a group of four, discuss why people tease and make fun of others. To what extent should society fight this behaviour? Be prepared to present the ideas raised in your discussion to the class.

MAKING CONNECTIONS

9. Write a **report** on a film or television program that you have seen that deals with the **theme** of an outsider. Explain whether you felt it was as effective in presenting ideas on the topic as "Snow White." Revise and edit your report in preparation for submission. ■

Tattooed

WILLIAM PLOMER

BEFORE READING

In a small group, write down as many reasons as you can think of for getting a tattoo. If possible, use prior knowledge about the history of tattoos and the stereotypes associated with tattoos.

On his arms he wears
Diagrams he chose,
A snake inside a skull,
A dagger in a rose,

And the muscle playing   5
Under the skin
Makes the rose writhe
And the skull grin.

He is one who acts his dreams
And these emblems are a clue   10
To the wishes in his blood
And what they make him do,

These signs are truer
Than the wearer knows:
The blade vibrates   15
In the vulnerable rose,

Anthers bend, and carmine curly
Petals kiss the plunging steel,
Dusty with essential gold
Close in upon the thing they feel.   25

Moistly once in bony sockets
Eyeballs hinted at a soul,
In the death's head now a live head
Fills a different role;

Venomous resilience sliding   30
In the empty cave of thought,
Call it instinct ousting reason,
Or a reptile's indoor sport.

The flower's pangs, the snake
    exploring,
The skull, the violating knife,   35
Are the active and the passive
Aspects of his life,

Who is at home with death
More than he guesses;
The rose will die, and a skull   40
Gives back no caresses.

after READING

1. Based on this **poem**, sketch the tattoos drawn on this man's arms. Compare your concept of them with the rest of the class and come to a **consensus** about how they look.

2. In a small group, choose one of the tattoos and explain the symbolism of the elements of that tattoo as described by the **narrator**.

3. a) In a paragraph, describe how the narrator feels about the tattoo wearer. Explain how the poet gives that impression.
   b) Do you agree or disagree with the narrator? Explain your **point of view**.

4. Write a statement of **theme** for this poem in your notebook. Back up your statement with proof from the poem.

5. a) The poet has used a specific **rhyme scheme** throughout the poem. Identify the rhyme scheme and state whether or not this enhances or detracts from the poem.
   b) Show how the poet's use of enjambment changes the way the reader reads the rhyme. (See The Reference Shelf, page 425.)

EXPLORING IDEAS AND IMPLICATIONS

6. Design a tattoo for yourself that symbolizes the different aspects of your personality. Write an explanation of the tattoo.

MAKING CONNECTIONS

7. Research and write a **report** on body adornment in one other culture. With a partner, revise and edit your work. Be prepared to present the report to the class. ■

Barn Door Detail

ROB FILGATE

BEFORE READING

Write about someone you admire, explaining why you admire him or her.

It has been years since my grandfather stood
before this barn door, since his calloused hands

worked free the chain latched on a bent nail.
I wonder what he thought, early on a winter

morning while he forked hay to the animals   5
and drew milk from the eight cows. Or during

the day when he cut down frozen trees by hand,
removed the limbs with an axe, and hooked

the logs to a team of Clydesdales to skid them out
on the snow, back to the farm where drifts   10

hid them until spring. And each night, returning
to the barn by lantern, alone among the animals,

where he talked in a foreign tongue, words
frozen in moonlight, stories of how his sons

had drifted away to Edmonton one by one,   15
how the farm had taken the third finger

on his right hand, the cold ache in the hollow
of his bones, his words slipping from stall

to stall, his life hanging in the frigid air
like the breath of horses.   20

after READING

UNDERSTANDING THE TEXT

1. In your notebook, make a list from the **poem** of at least five details we discover about the **narrator**'s grandfather.

2. With a partner, describe the **mood** in the poem. Explain words and/or phrases that create that mood. Record the ideas from your discussion in your notebook.

3. In a small group explore how each of the following decisions made by the poet affects the way the poem is read and understood:
   - the two-line **stanzas**
   - the use of two sentence fragments
   - the length of the final sentence of the poem

4. Explain the **image** in the final phrase of the poem.

EXPLORING IDEAS AND IMPLICATIONS

5. Explain how this poem fits into this unit called "The Average."

 6. Imagine this poem is going to be included as a **monologue** in the opening scene of a movie. Create a shooting script starting with a series of at least three camera shots to set the scene and the mood, and then move to the monologue itself. In the sound column, suggest music to underscore the scene.

MAKING CONNECTIONS

7. a) Read "The Broken Globe" (pages 128–135). From this story and "Barn Door Detail," make some conclusions about the way farmers have been portrayed in some literature.
   b) Create a **thesis** on the one common feature shared by each of these rural **characters** and, in a **literary essay**, show how the writers have developed that feature in their characters.
   c) Have a partner offer suggestions for revisions focusing on the depth and clarity of the controlling idea, the use of supporting details, the connections between ideas, and the integration of quotations from the literature into the essay.
   d) Revise and edit your essay for submission. ■

Excerpt From
Murder on Location

HOWARD ENGEL

"Then I saw it. A black shape moving out away from the ice-jammed boarding area. It was climbing up on the ice bridge."

BEFORE READING

1. With a partner, make a list of several famous fictional detectives. For each, describe a familiar trait (or traits) associated with the **character**. Be prepared to describe one of the characters on your list to the class.

2. As a class, discuss why the mystery/crime/detective genre is a traditional favourite with **audiences**.

Set in Niagara Falls, Ontario, Murder on Location *follows private investigator Benny Cooperman as he searches for a woman—the wife of a prominent businessman—who has disappeared from a nearby town. Cooperman's search leads him to the set of a Hollywood movie being shot near the Falls. In this excerpt, Cooperman catches up with film-maker Jim Sayre. Sayre himself is on the trail of another man who is blackmailing him. Both of these men's lives are connected, in some way, to the missing woman.*

Outside it was dark once you got out from under the bright marquee of the hotel entrance. Melt-waters were running from crevasses in the frozen snow near the fire hydrant; the gutter was moving water and silt to the sewer grating. It spoke of glaciers and drumlins and eskers, and I kicked a dam of slush across the flow, a peevish gesture because I was in a hurry without knowing where I was going. I crossed Falls Avenue to the entrance of the Rainbow Bridge. It was business as usual, with the guards asking the same familiar questions. I turned right and walked along the damp sidewalk toward the falls. The park, twinkling with a filigree of coloured lights caught in the trees, smacked of left-over Christmas pudding. By now I could hear far-off police sirens moving away from

the curb near a shuttered souvenir kiosk. Before it was properly halted, a figure came out of the shadows by the *Maid of the Mist* ticket booth. It ran up the slight rise to the cab and was opening the back door when I caught up to Ed Noonan and piled in after him.

"Cooperman! Get the hell out of here! I got no time." He was flushed with running and he shouted in short bursts.

"Not before you tell me where you've been," I said, cocking my head toward the river, as though I already knew some of it.

"I want no part of this, Cooperman. I'm getting as far away from here as possible. They can kill each other as far as I'm concerned. It's none of my business. Now, clear out. I'm not joking."

"You mean Furlong and Sayre? Where are they? The whole town is looking for them. You'd better fess up, or it'll bite you where it hurts. Furlong's wanted by the police for murder and you don't want to aid and abet a fugitive, do you?" Noonan's mouth dropped and I got a look at some surprised tonsils along with a whiff of stale rye.

"Oh, so that's what it is. Furlong asked me to get the gate unlocked, and no sooner had I done that when Mr. Sayre came after him. He had a gun in his hand. Furlong took off down the hill toward the *Maid of the Mist* landing."

"How long ago was this?"

"Five minutes, maybe ten. Did I tell you? Sayre had a gun."

"Who called the taxi?"

"I did. I called from the hotel twenty minutes ago. I didn't know how bad I was going to need it. Close the door or get

the hotel in different directions. The only quiet place seemed to be right where I was standing. That's the way I liked it. I looked over the parapet and down into the gorge below. The ice was grey except where the illumination from the falls painted it. I noticed that the spray from the falls was reaching further downstream than it had all week. And it wasn't freezing. There was a thaw in the air. It had been there all day.

Traffic was thin along the Niagara Parkway. What there was of it came out of or disappeared into the sticky mist. I watched a taxi slow down and stop at the hell out, Cooperman. I don't want any part of this."

The driver had been watching us in his rear-view mirror. He wasn't in a hurry and the meter flag had been engaged. To him this was just another rear-view melodrama. I climbed out of the car and Noonan nearly slammed the door on my coat-tail.

The *Maid of the Mist* ticket booth was stone like the kiosk, built to harmonize with the rest of the un-commercial look that had been decreed for the view leading up to the falls. Stone baffles and steel pipes were arranged to handle the heavy summer crowds past the ticket window and forward to the incline railway that slanted steeply down to the boarding dock. The red and yellow cars looked hung up to dry. The crowd-control devices made the place all the more desolate tonight. Not quite parallel to the funicular, and upstream slightly, a narrow road pointed down toward the power plant at the foot of the Canadian falls. It clung closely to the wall of the gorge and sometimes was overhung by it. I started down that unilluminated black line.

The high wire gate was standing open. A padlock hanging unfastened on a plastic-covered chain didn't stop me. A few yards more and there was a sign that warned pedestrians like me to proceed no further. The ice underfoot was still frozen in irregular lumps. I skidded a few times and came down with a crash that took the skin from the heel of my hand. As I worked my way down, I could feel the temperature moving down beside me. I realized that on the Parkway it had been almost balmy. Very strange weather for

January. Once under the lee of the cliff it was easier to see the way ahead. The lights from the town above and behind me lit up the edge of the gorge, but didn't help much down here, except for reflections from the surface of the ice below.

There was no snow on the roadway, only frozen slush that had hardened in the shape of bootprints and tire treads. It was slippery going and I was beginning to feel a little silly, when I thought I heard something almost directly below me. I tried to see where the sound was coming from, but I saw shapes all over the place. Under me I could make out the form of four *Maids of the Mist*, mounted on frames. I kept moving down as fast as I could, leaving the shapes behind me. By now I was feeling pain in the front of each shin. Downhill does that to me. A few hundred feet beyond the ships, the road divided: one fork continued straight ahead under the cliff toward the power plant, the other made a sharp descending hairpin aimed back toward the dark shapes of the ferries. I cleared the *Maid of the Mist* office and came out toward the ice between that and the dry-docked ships.

Then I saw it. A black shape moving out away from the ice-jammed boarding area. It was climbing up on the ice bridge.

"Sayre!" I shouted. I heard the echo play around with the sound, and thought I heard the ice begin to growl where it touched the shoreline. I thought that the silence was going to settle back in place when I heard another voice out on the ice. It was far away and sounded like the parting shot from a dead battery. About a hundred yards ahead I could see another figure making its way across the ice. It looked like all the other shadows on the ice, except that it was moving diagonally across from me toward the far abutment of the Rainbow Bridge. If there was any place where a man might be able to climb out of the river gorge, it was here. I watched the shape move, Sayre moving quickly after it. I called to Sayre again.

"Cooperman! Go back. Don't come any closer! I've got a gun!"

"To hell with your gun. Are you crazy? This thing isn't safe. You can't go out there!"

"Get back, Ben. This is between me and him. He's out there and I'm going to get him. I've been studyin' this ice for a week now."

"I can see him from here. Let him go. Come on back." I hadn't stopped moving. By now I was able to see Sayre more clearly, moving steadily out across the river on the packed ice. At the shoreline the snow and ice were firm like in the Christmas carol: deep and crisp and even. But from there the bridge slowly mounted, like a vault over a gigantic sports palace, running from the up-river side of the American falls to beyond the Rainbow Bridge. It had the shopworn reflection of a grey and threatening sky, with darker shadows like coal sacks marking gaps and crevasses. Attached at the up-river and down-river ends, cleaner ice was visible. These sections looked newer than the band that ran from shore to shore in front of me and were formed of ice more recently swept over the falls. Downstream, this less dense flotilla had been forced under the ice bridge by water power difficult to imagine.

I could see a gap where Sayre had jumped from the boarding dock to the bridge. He was moving forward ahead of me, steadily and without looking back. I called again, but he didn't turn. I thought a moment then jumped after him. By now Furlong was about half-way across. He'd reached the high point of the bridge and from then on I could only see him as he rounded some high eminence. His path took him to the edge of the older ice, dangerously close to the smaller, less compact floes that stretched down toward the international bridge. My eyes were becoming cleverer in the dark, and my feet, though both freezing and soaked, helped me move safely over the unreliable surface. Twice a solid-enough path gave way under my weight, which taught me to look closer before investing all one hundred and sixty pounds of me in one place. Ahead, and to the right, I could see the pale ghost of one of the wonders of the world looming straight as a wall and going up two hundred feet in the air. I knew the American falls were less than that, but you try being precise from where I was. From time to time I could see movement in the newer ice to my left. One floe jumped eight feet in the air and came crashing down in a shower of fragments on the floes that had already moved to fill its place. I felt like I was walking on an eggshell with hobnail boots. Over my shoulder I could see how far I'd come from the ice reaching up to touch the sterns of the four *Maids of the Mist*.

By now I was nearing the top round of the ice bridge vault. Below me, Sayre had been shortening the distance between himself and Furlong. I tried calling again.

"Sayre, don't be a fool! He's not worth it!" Fifty yards ahead of me Jim Sayre looked back over his shoulder.

"I'm going to get that son of a bitch!"

"If you're doing this for Peggy, you're crazy."

"You just don't know what it's all about. Stay back!" Sayre was looking ahead, trying to find the dark shadow in front of him. The falls were getting to sound like the biggest broken air-conditioner on earth. I couldn't make myself look up at them.

"I talked to Claudia in La Jolla," I shouted. "I figured it out from there." He was leaning on a piece of timber, part of a broken log-boom that annually attempts to control the ice from Lake Erie. It looked like it had been through a shredder; one end was rounded like the top of a bullrush. He levelled the gun at Furlong, then changed his mind, starting on again down the sloping roof of ice toward the American side. I climbed, slipped and crouched my way after them. We were all walking on the down-river edge of the old ice. Suddenly I heard what sounded like a shot over my shoulder. More like a cannon than a revolver.

"What the hell was that?" Sayre called. I looked ahead to see whether it had been Furlong. Sayre saw me and shook his head. "It's not him. This is his gun." Both of us were puzzled and paused. Then I saw it.

"It's the ice, Sayre. It's breaking up!" To my right a long fault ran parallel to the edge of the ice. If the whole ice bridge wasn't falling apart, at least it was shedding the piece the three of us were crawling over. The gap was widening. Between the two parts, I could see a strip of black water many feet below. The huge piece of ice we were on was very slowly moving away from the main mass. I yelled again: "You crazy old galoot, you'll never stop him. He can't get across. The ice is breaking up. The river will get the two of you!"

I felt like I was standing on a huge slice of meatloaf that was being slowly tilted over out of the pan and onto a plate. I could see the crack getting bigger. I turned and ran back to the break. By now it was too wide to jump. Back in the direction of the ferry landing, the crack was less pronounced. The ice was still locked together. I took a run and leaped across the gap. Below me it felt like the ice was actually pulling apart beneath me, like a seam was being ripped out and I was trying to jump at the point where the material was just letting go. One leg landed safe and dry. The other pulled me down toward the water reaching up for my galoshes. I had to roll up to the other side.

I lay there, not even feeling the cold, my face resting roughly on the scratchy surface of the ice below my cheek. When I'd caught my breath, I stood up. Sayre had almost caught Furlong, who had come to the end of the disengaging ice cake. They both stood about ten feet above the level of the flotilla of brighter ice floes that told where the water level was. Furlong had got about three-quarters of the way to the American shore. Between him and shore ran a curve of looser ice running close to the main mass. He was standing at the edge when Sayre got to him. The older man reached out and pulled Furlong around to face him. Neil punched out awkwardly at Sayre who doubled up.

Going down, he grabbed Furlong's knees. Now they were rolling over one another. I couldn't make out who was on top. I couldn't hear anything above the roar of the falls. It was like watching television with the sound turned down; even wrestling looks like ballet. A dependable feeling in the back of my knees told me to get back to the Canadian shore. The ice bridge was deceptive. It looked like it would last a thousand years. It already looked at least a hundred. But it was slipping away whenever you were distracted for a minute.

Furlong was standing over Sayre. I could see that the yellow Anorak was spread out on the ice. That had to be my last look, because I thought I could hear the ice growling a warning. I turned around and ran, skipping and skidding, back to the *Maid of the Mist* dock. The ice was now further from the shoreline. It meant a jump of about two yards. It wouldn't stand thinking about so I did it at a fast clip. I felt myself falling, then landing flat against the shore-side of the broken-away bridge. I seemed to be sticking on the slanted surface by invisible suction cups. For a moment I was suspended there, holding fast with my face and fingernails. When the slide began, it was like all my contact points were being rejected at once. Down I went into the water of the river. Luckily, there was more ice just under the surface, and the second after I felt that, a hand reached down over the shore and caught my flailing arm.

"Easy does it," a voice said, and up I came suddenly eye to eye with a rough, weather-worn face with a mariner's wool cap over grey hair. I squeegeed water from my shoes and trouser cuffs and looked back across the river. It was good to feel solid, if frozen, ground underfoot again. I couldn't make out anything on the ice bridge. Both Furlong and Sayre were on the side sloping away from us. I could see more ice coming over the falls. The rest of the ice was holding fast. Above Goat Island a new noise joined the parade: a helicopter was throbbing and blinking its riding lights out in the dark. For a moment we listened to the noise, then I let myself be led up the steps and into the *Maid of the Mist* office by the man who had grabbed me. It was warm inside, and I saw the makings of coffee before I began to shiver.

after READING

UNDERSTANDING THE TEXT

1. Select one part of the excerpt that you found suspenseful. In your notebook, briefly explain how the writer created the **suspense**.

2. Select a descriptive paragraph from this excerpt and assess its effectiveness in terms of **diction**, **imagery**, appeal to the senses, and **tone**.

EXPLORING IDEAS AND IMPLICATIONS

3. Make a list of the characteristics associated with mystery or crime novels. Give examples of any of these characteristics that are present in this excerpt. Compare your list with a partner's.

4. Detectives in crime fiction come from all walks of life and are increasingly diverse to appeal to all kinds of audiences. Write a character study of Benny Cooperman based on information in this excerpt and explain what **audience** he would appeal to. Discuss your character study with a small group of classmates.

5. The background setting for the novel *Murder on Location* is the filming of a Hollywood movie on location in Niagara Falls, Ontario. With a partner, write a film script of the events in this excerpt. Submit your script to another partnership to assess as a film project they would be willing to invest in. Revise and edit your script, if necessary, based on your peers' comments.

6. Read the rest of the novel from which this excerpt is taken. Prepare an oral **report** to the class on the most interesting events of the novel.

7. Write a short suspenseful **story** of a **conflict** that takes place in a Canadian **setting** that many readers would recognize. In a small group, have a "read-around" of your first draft. Then revise and edit your story based on your group members' comments. Be prepared to submit the final version of your story to the teacher.

MAKING CONNECTIONS

8. As an independent study, read at least three mystery novels written by different writers and prepare a written report on the variations they present on some key characteristics of the genre. (See The Reference Shelf, pages 429–433.) ■

The Road Not Taken

ROBERT FROST

BEFORE READING

In your notebook, describe a decision you have made that has had an important impact on your life.

Two roads diverged in a yellow wood,
And sorry I could not travel both
And be one traveller, long I stood
And looked down one as far as I could
To where it bent in the undergrowth;   5

Then took the other, as just as fair,
And having perhaps the better claim,
Because it was grassy and wanted wear;
Though as for that the passing there
Had worn them really about the same,   10

And both that morning equally lay
In leaves no step had trodden black.
Oh, I kept the first for another day!
Yet knowing how way leads on to way,
I doubted if I should ever come back.   15

I shall be telling this with a sigh
Somewhere ages and ages hence:
Two roads diverged in a wood, and I—
I took the one less travelled by,
And that has made all the difference.   20

after READING

1. a) **Summarize** the sequence of events in the **poem**.
   b) Describe the **tone** of each **stanza**, supporting your description with specific references to words and phrases in the poem.
   c) In a single sentence, state the **theme** of "The Road Not Taken."

2. With a partner, explore three patterns (such as rhythm, **rhyme**, repetition) in the poem and analyze their effectiveness in relation to the topic and theme of the poem.

3. a) The first two and a half stanzas are all one sentence. In your notebook, explain the relationship of this single sentence to the main idea of the poem.
   b) Compare your observations with those of others in the class. Discuss how the poet's choices made an impact on your reactions to and feelings about the poem.

EXPLORING IDEAS AND IMPLICATIONS

4. a) Look back at the writing you did in "Before Reading." Create a **graphic organizer** that charts the decision you made and the outcomes of that decision. Chart, as well, decisions you could have made and the possible outcomes of those decisions.
   b) In a paragraph, reflect on the intelligence of your choice and what you have learned from that particular decision-making process.

5. a) In the poem, the **narrator** says he "doubted if [he] should ever come back." In a small group, research differences in the workforce and educational opportunities before the 1960s and since the 1960s. Create a group **report** directed to your peers in which you compare and contrast conditions in the two periods. In the final section of your report, explain why your generation is more likely to keep "the first [road] for another day."
   b) Have another group read your report and give you feedback on the quality of sources used, integration of researched information, depth of analysis, organization, and **voice**.
   c) Revise and edit your own work in preparation for submission.

MAKING CONNECTIONS

6. Read the "Is this a dagger …" soliloquy from Shakespeare's *Macbeth* (II, i). With a partner, create a **dialogue** between Macbeth and Frost's narrator in which they discuss the decision-making process. Be sure to maintain the feelings both have in their own "soliloquies" along with a new understanding they come to through their discussion. ■

Which Is Better: College or University?

ANN EBY

"... you are fortunate to have so many options before you."

BEFORE READING

Conduct a survey among your classmates to discover their opinions on the following topics:

- Which is better: college or university?
- Who has an easier time finding jobs: college graduates or university graduates?
- Which reasons determine the choice of college or university programs: employment statistics, parental influence, personal interests, peer influences, personal skills, or abilities?

From the e-mail and letters I get it appears our youth have recurring questions that reflect a lot of angst about their future prospects in the job market. Periodically, I will devote a column to answering their letters.

The following letter illustrates an issue facing many young people and their parents today.

My dad comes from a school of thought that believes a university degree is everything while a college diploma is meaningless. I beg to differ, for in the case of computer graphics/multimedia/graphic design, a lot of college grads are getting placements. Am I correct?

My problem is that I have to provide my dad with factual information regarding these placements and the opportunities available, so that I can convince him a college diploma is worth investing in.

So Ann, I would really appreciate it if you can suggest resources I can consult. I need to convince my dad it will be worth it for me to get a college education.

—Erika

Let me start by saying you have three things going for you already. You know what you are interested in and you have options; you have a caring parent who wants the best for you; and economic forecasts are favourable for the next few years, which will benefit both college and university graduates.

However, whether it's better to go to college or university is a loaded question. Only you have the answer to this. Both avenues will lead you to the job market provided you can convince an employer you can do something to help their business. And whether you can "do something" has as much to do with you as it does your education.

To answer your question about computer graphics design, yes it is a real "hot" area right now due to the increasing use of computer technology. Graduates in this field are getting jobs, and information on their hiring success is available.

For instance, community colleges all have Web sites that will give you information on the placement experience of their recent graduates. But looking at numbers alone can be a waste of time without talking to someone who has an understanding about what the numbers mean. Don't base your decision to enroll in a course solely on the placement results.

What I would recommend is that you also call the colleges and ask to speak to someone who can tell you about job prospects in the computer design graphics field. It could be an instructor, a senior student or someone in a career centre on campus.

If you live close to one of the colleges go and visit and sit in on a senior class in the design field. Speak to those currently attending. The students should have some ideas on job prospects at graduation. I think instructors should also know where jobs are to be found. Ask them.

Another source of graduate placement information for both university and college is a World Wide Web site that is maintained by the Federal government, *http://www.hrdc-drhc.gc.ca/jobfutures/english/index.htm.*

It features a program called Job Futures Volume 2, which offers the outlook and experience of graduates surveyed in 1992, two years after graduation. Keep in mind, the economy was different when these graduates were surveyed and the economic outlook needs to be up-dated.

In spite of this, the information is still useful. The description of the courses, the opinions of the graduates and where they found work can give you an idea of what you can expect.

Next you might consider looking at courses offered at university that require an artistic or design element. You may like them better. The same advice applies here as with community colleges. Check

Web sites, connect with people and ask questions.

Here's another option to think about. Many students today are choosing to go to university first, and then to college later. Combining an undergraduate degree in arts, business or science with technical design training from college later would give you another dimension to offer an employer. Having a combination of design and technical skills with broad-based learning would position you well in any field you choose. Looking at the pros and cons of a variety of scenarios will help you to make a better career choice. One that may suit both you and your dad.

Good luck and remember you are fortunate to have so many options before you.

If you are a student and have questions or information you think would help others, please write to me at *The Star* or via e-mail. Let me know your age and how to reach you if I need clarification. And it doesn't matter how young you are, I want to hear from you. Your input may very well help others, just like you.

—Originally published January 29, 2000

after READING

UNDERSTANDING THE TEXT

1. Using specific information from this **article**, discuss with a partner whether the writer answers the question in the title.

2. In a newspaper column that answers questions from individual readers, a writer must combine information that responds directly to the specific question with information that is designed to interest a wide range of readers. In your notebook, list details in Ann Eby's response, under the headings "Specific Information for the Questioner" and "More General Information for All Readers."

3. Explain to a partner the grammatical reasons for the use of the word "better" in the title. Ask a partner to explain to you the reasons for the use of semicolons and commas in the first paragraph of the response to Erika's question. (See The Reference Shelf, page 412.)

EXPLORING IDEAS AND IMPLICATIONS

4. **Interview** university and college students to discover the writing and oral presentation skills required for success in postsecondary programs. Make a point-form analysis of areas in which you need to improve your own skills in writing and oral presentation.

5. Visit a series of Web sites of colleges and universities, and the Web site mentioned in this article. Choose one of the institutions that most appealed to you, and create an informational **brochure** targeted for high-school students who are going into postsecondary education. Use a computer program, if one is available, to help you design the brochure. Consider the use of interesting typefaces and visuals to enhance your message. Display your brochure on a bulletin board for the class to see.

6. **Debate** the following resolution: Be It Resolved That the Purpose of Postsecondary Education Is to Prepare for Employment. (See The Reference Shelf, pages 455–458.) You may use your findings from activities 4 and 5 to prepare your arguments.

MAKING CONNECTIONS

7. Read other advice columns or question-and-answer columns in newspapers and magazines. Write a paragraph containing your observations on the balance between specific information and information that would appeal to a wide range of readers in these columns. Be prepared to present your observations to the class. ∎

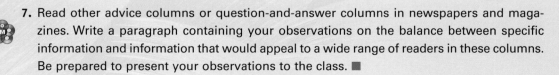

Leaving

M.G. VASSANJI

"... you will lose your son."

BEFORE READING

As a class, brainstorm the challenges an individual and his or her family encounter when qualifying for, selecting, and financing a postsecondary education. Consider whether the challenges are surmountable for most families and worth the sacrifices involved.

Kichwele Street was now Uhuru Street. My two sisters had completed school and got married and Mother missed them sometimes. Mehroon, after a succession of wooers, had settled for a former opening batsman of our school team and was in town. Razia was a wealthy housewife in Tanga, the coastal town north of Dar.[1] Firoz dropped out in his last year at school, and everyone said that it was a wonder he had reached that far. He was assistant bookkeeper at Oriental Emporium, and brought home stationery sometimes.

Mother had placed her hopes on the youngest two of us, Aloo and me, and she didn't want us distracted by the chores that always needed doing around the store. One evening she secured for the last time the half a dozen assorted padlocks on the sturdy panelled doors and sold the store. This was exactly one week after the wedding party had driven off with a tearful Razia, leaving behind a distraught mother in the stirred-up dust of Uhuru Street.

We moved to the residential area of Upanga. After the bustle of Uhuru Street, our new neighbourhood seemed quiet. Instead of the racket of buses, bicycles and cars on the road, we now heard the croaking of frogs and the chirping of insects. Nights were haunting, lonely and desolate and took some getting used to. Upanga Road emptied after seven in the evening and the sidestreets became pitch dark, with no illumination. Much of the area was as yet uninhabited and behind the housing developments there were overgrown bushes, large, scary baobab trees, and mango and coconut groves.

---

1. Dar es Salaam is the capital of the African nation of Tanzania.

Sometimes in the evenings, when Mother felt sad, Aloo and I would play two-three-five with her, a variation of whist for three people. I had entered the University by then and came back at weekends. Aloo was in his last year at school. He had turned out to be exceptionally bright in his studies—more so than we realised.

That year Mr Datoo, a former teacher from our school who was also a former student, returned from America for a visit. Mr Datoo had been a favourite with the boys. When he came he received a tumultuous welcome. For the next few days he toured the town like the Pied Piper followed by a horde of adulating students, one of whom was Aloo.

The exciting event inspired in Aloo the hope that not only might he be admitted to an American university, but he could also win a scholarship to go there. Throughout the rest of the year, therefore, he wrote to numerous universities, culling their names from books at the USIS, often simply at random or even only by the sounds of their names.

Mother's response to all these efforts was to humour him. She would smile. "Your uncles in America will pay thousands of shillings just to send you to college," she would say. Evidently she felt he was wasting his time, but he would never be able to say that he did not have all the support she could give him.

Responses to his enquiries started coming within weeks and a handful of them were guardedly encouraging. Gradually Aloo found out which were the better places, and which among them the truly famous. Soon a few catalogues arrived, all looking impressive. It seemed that the more involved he became with the application process, the more tantalising was the prospect of going to an American university. Even the famous places did not discourage him. He learnt of subjects he had never heard of before: genetics, cosmology, artificial intelligence: a whole universe was out there waiting for him if only he could reach it. He was not sure if he could, if he was good enough. He suffered periods of intense hope and hopeless despair.

Of course, Aloo was entitled to a place at the local university. At the end of the year, when the selections were announced in the papers, his name was on the list. But some bureaucratic hand, probably also corrupt, dealt out a future prospect for him that came as a shock. He had applied to study medicine, he was given a place in agriculture. An agricultural officer in a rural district somewhere was not what he wanted to become however patriotic he felt. He had never left the city except to go to the national parks once on a school trip.

When Aloo received a letter from the California Institute of Technology offering him a place with a scholarship, he was stupefied at first. He read and reread the letter, not believing what it seemed to be saying, afraid that he might be reading something into it. He asked me to read it for him. When he was convinced there was no possibility of a mistake he became elated.

"The hell I'll do agriculture!" he grinned.

But first he had to contend with Mother.

Mother was incredulous. "Go, go," she said, "don't you eat my head, don't tease me!"

"But it's true!" he protested. "They're giving me a scholarship!"

We were at the table—the three of us—and had just poured tea from the thermos. Mother sitting across from me stared at her saucer for a while then she looked up.

"Is it true?" she asked me.

"Yes, it's true," I said. "All he needs is to take 400 dollars pocket money with him."

"How many shillings would that make?" she asked.

"About three thousand."

"And how are we going to raise this three thousand shillings? Have you bought a lottery? And what about the ticket? Are they going to send you a ticket too?"

As she said this Aloo's prospects seemed to get dimmer. She was right, it was not a little money that he needed.

"Can't we raise a loan?" he asked. "I'll work there. Yes, I'll work as a waiter. A waiter! —I know you can do it, I'll send the money back!"

"You may have uncles in America who would help you," Mother told him, "but no one here will."

Aloo's shoulders sagged and he sat there toying with his cup, close to tears. Mother sat drinking from her saucer and frowning. The evening light came in from the window behind me and gave a glint to her spectacles. Finally she set her saucer down. She was angry.

"And why do you want to go away, so far from us? Is this what I raised you for—so you could leave me to go away to a foreign place? Won't you miss us, where

you want to go? Do we mean so little to you? If something happens ..."

Aloo was crying. A tear fell into his cup, his nose was running. "So many kids go and return, and nothing happens to them ... Why did you mislead me, then? Why did you let me apply if you didn't want me to go ... why did you raise my hopes if only to dash them?" He raised his voice to her, the first time I saw him do it, and he was shaking.

He did not bring up the question again and he prepared himself for the agricultural college, waiting for the term to begin. At home he would slump on the sofa putting away a novel a day.

If the unknown bureaucrat at the Ministry of Education had been less arbitrary, Aloo would not have been so broken and Mother would not have felt compelled to try and do something for him.

A few days later, on a Sunday morning, she looked up from her sewing machine and said to the two of us: "Let's go and show this letter to Mr Velji. He is experienced in these matters. Let's take his advice."

Mr Velji was a former administrator of our school. He had a large egg-shaped head and a small compact body. With his large forehead and big black spectacles he looked the caricature of the archetypal wise man. He also had the bearing of one. The three of us were settled in his sitting-room chairs staring about us and waiting expectantly when he walked in stiffly, like a toy soldier, to welcome us.

"How are you, sister?" he said. "What can I do for you?"

Aloo and I stood up respectfully as he sat down.

"We have come to you for advice ..." Mother began.

"Speak, then," he said jovially and sat back, joining his hands behind his head.

She began by giving him her history. She told him which family she was born in, which she had married into, how she had raised her kids when our father died. Common relations were discovered between our families. "Now this one here," she pointed at me, "goes to university here, and *that* one wants to go to America. Show him the documents," she commanded Aloo.

As if with an effort, Aloo pushed himself out of the sofa and slowly made his way to place the documents in Mr Velji's hands. Before he looked at them Mr Velji asked Aloo his result in the final exam.

At Aloo's answer, his eyes widened. "Henh?" he said, "All A's?"

"Yes," replied Aloo, a little too meekly.

Mr Velji flipped the papers one by one, cursorily at first. Then he went over them more carefully. He looked at the long visa form with the carbon copies neatly bound behind the original; he read over the friendly letter from the Foreign Student Adviser; he was charmed by the letters of invitation from the fraternities. Finally he looked up, a little humbled.

"The boy is right," he said. "The university is good, and they are giving him a bursary. I congratulate you."

"But what should I do?" asked Mother anxiously. "What is your advice? Tell us what we should do."

"Well," said Mr Velji, "it would be good for his education." He raised his hand to clear his throat. Then he said, a little slowly: "But if you send him, you will lose your son.

"It's a far place, America," he concluded, wiping his hands briskly at the finished business. "Now what will you have—tea? orange squash?"

His wife appeared magically to take orders.

"All the rich kids go every year and they are not lost," muttered Aloo bitterly as we walked back home. Mother was silent.

That night she was at the sewing machine and Aloo was on the couch, reading. The radio was turned low and through the open front door a gentle breeze blew in to cool the sitting room. I was standing at the door. The banana tree and its offspring rustled outside, a car zoomed on the road, throwing shadows on neighbouring houses. A couple out for a stroll, murmuring, came into sight over the uneven hedge; groups of boys or girls chattered before dispersing for the night. The intermittent buzz of an electric motor escaped from Mother's sewing machine. It was a little darker where she sat at the other end of the room from us.

Presently she looked up and said a little nonchalantly, "At least show me what this university looks like—bring that book, will you?"

Mother had never seen the catalogue. She had always dismissed it, had never shown the least bit of curiosity about the place Aloo wanted so badly to visit. Now the three of us crowded around the glossy pages, pausing at pictures of the neoclassic façades and domes, columns towering over humans, students rushing about in a dither of activity, classes held on lush lawns in ample shade. It all looked so awesome and yet inviting.

"It's something, isn't it?" whispered Aloo, hardly able to hold back his excitement. "They teach hundreds of courses there," he said. "They send rockets into space ... to other worlds ... to the moon—"

"If you go away to the moon, my son, what will become of me?" she said humorously, her eyes gleaming as she looked up at us.

Aloo went back to his book and Mother to her sewing.

A little later I looked up and saw Mother deep in thought, brooding, and as she often did at such times she was picking her chin absent-mindedly. It was, I think, the first time I saw her as a person and not only as our mother. I thought of what she must be going through in her mind, what she had gone through in bringing us up. She had been thirty-three when Father died, and she had refused several offers of marriage because they would all have entailed one thing: sending us all to the "boarding"—the orphanage. Pictures of her before his death showed her smiling and in full bloom: plump but not excessively fat, hair puffed fashionably, wearing high heels and make-up. There was one picture, posed at a studio, which Father had had touched up and enhanced, which now hung beside his. In it she stood against a black background, holding a book stylishly, the nylon pachedi painted a light green, the folds falling gracefully down, the borders decorated with sequins. I had never seen her like that. All I had seen of her was the stern face getting sterner with time as the lines set permanently and the hair thinned, the body turned squat, the voice thickened.

I recalled how Aloo and I would take turns sleeping with her at night on her big bed; how she would squeeze me in her chubby arms, drawing me up closer to her breast until I could hardly breathe—and I would control myself and hope she would soon release me and let me breathe.

She looked at me looking at her and said, not to me, "Promise me ... promise me that if I let you go, you will not marry a white woman."

"Oh Mother, you know I won't!" said Aloo.

"And promise me that you will not smoke or drink."

"You know I promise!" He was close to tears.

Aloo's first letter came a week after he left, from London where he'd stopped over to see a former classmate. It flowed over with excitement. "How can I describe it," he wrote, "the sight from the plane ... mile upon mile of carefully tilled fields, the earth divided into neat green squares ... even the mountains are clean and civilised. And London ... Oh London! It seemed that it would never end ... blocks and blocks of houses, squares, parks, monuments ... could any city be larger? How many of our Dar es Salaams would fit here, in this one gorgeous city ...?"

A bird flapping its wings: Mr Velji nodding wisely in his chair, Mother staring into the distance.

after READING

UNDERSTANDING THE TEXT

1. Both Aloo and his mother are described as having conflicting emotions in this **story**. In your notebook, describe the **conflict** each feels within himself or herself and explain the degree of resolution each is able to achieve.

2. In your notebook, write a paragraph explaining the significance of each of the three parts of the final sentence of this story.

3. The **narrator** of this story is a member of the family the story is about. Write a paragraph explaining whether this first-person **point of view** presents an objective or subjective account of the **characters** and events.

4. "He had applied to study medicine, he was given a place in agriculture" (paragraph 9 on page 229). With a partner, discuss the following:
   - What is the punctuation error in this sentence called?
   - How could it be corrected?
   - Is there an artistic reason that would allow the writer to claim "artistic licence" for writing the sentence the way it is?
   - Is this particular rule of punctuation being changed because writers are no longer adhering to it?

   Be prepared to present your answers to these questions to the class.

EXPLORING IDEAS AND IMPLICATIONS

5. This story takes place in the city of Dar es Salaam in the country now known as Tanzania in Africa. Identify details in the story that indicate the society being described is in the midst of a shift from colonial to postcolonial status.

6. In a group of three, discuss which aspects of this story are universal enough to be true for you and your family when you graduate from high school and go to university or college.

7. Look up the tale of the Pied Piper of Hamelin. In a paragraph, explain why this allusion is or is not appropriate as used in this story.

8. a) With a partner, research the concept of the "brain drain" as it applies to Canadians going to the United States and immigrants coming to Canada. Based on your research, write a newspaper **report**. Remember to use a headline that would grab your reader's attention and include graphs to show statistical information.

b) With another partnership, read your newspaper reports and discuss whether they reflect any kind of **bias**. Be prepared to discuss your conclusions as a class.

MAKING CONNECTIONS

9. Look at the catalogue and other promotional literature for a university or college you think you might like to attend. Write an **essay** indicating the impression the institution is trying to present of itself. Provide examples to support your opinion. ■

Gravity

ALISHYA SCHRAUWEN

BEFORE READING

With a partner, look at the layout of this poem and its title. Discuss what you think this poem is about.

In real life
 reactions are

 irreversible.
 You can't return the infant
 to the womb   5
 or mend a splintered mirror

 Or a shattered trust.

 A bloom holds not
 the promise of a bud.
 Regret cannot make careless words   10
 unsaid.

 No river
 Will ever

 flow

 up   15
 the

 mountain

 And after I walk out this door alone,

 Though often you may pull me close again,
 You'll never hold   20
 your child.

after READING

UNDERSTANDING THE TEXT

1. In a small group, discuss the issues that are raised in this **poem** that other young people may have experienced. Survey the class to find out whether both males and females go through these same experiences.

2. Explain how the images of the "womb" and "bud" emphasize the **theme** of the poem.

3. With a partner, examine the **layout** of the poem. For each line explain why the poet might have chosen that line length and division and whether or not you think it is effective. Be prepared to present your partnership's findings to the rest of the class.

EXPLORING IDEAS AND IMPLICATIONS

4. **a)** Using "Gravity" as a model, write your own poem to a person about leaving childhood or leaving home.
   b) Have a partner read your poem and comment on **tone**, language, line length and division, and literary devices. Revise and edit your poem. Be prepared to publish your poem in an appropriate way.

MAKING CONNECTIONS

5. Read "Leaving" (pages 228–233). How does the **theme** of this **short story** compare with "Gravity?" Create a Venn diagram that shows the similarities and differences in the themes of the two works. ■

She, Plural

BIBIANA TOMASIC

BEFORE READING

As a class, discuss which of the following are, in general, more generous to the needy in society: youth or adults; men or women.

I am alone when I spot her.
She and her two sons, the leafless tree
they stand under make an unreal family, oddly lit

by the store's abounding light. Dark tresses,
the boy's dark eyes honest when she asks   5
for spare change. *I don't have my wallet.*

I explain apologetically and with an emphatic
OK she shoulders my guilt, places it in her
back pocket with the ease of her smile.

I climb in the van, my children surprisingly   10
quiet in the back seat, wait for my husband to pay
at the cashier. He walks past and looks

the other way. I lose my head in the jumble
of my purse, shake all the bus dollars into my palm.
She opens hers without disgrace. Her face   15

saves mine by remaining calm
and questionless at this turn of fortune.
Do you have a place to stay I say

without considering her reply. *Yes, but*
we're out of food. I look at hers, turn to my   20
children staring out the car. Nothing bars

my sons' eager agreement and with one arm
I swoop the bag, the Styrofoam still warm
from what is rightly left over. Her older son's eyes

shower sparks beneath the naked tree. Grateful   25
she stuffs the food into her bag, offers me sincerity
with such light that I and my fumbling are humbled

into shadow. Driving away, out the back window
I see her, them, the night's row of women, children in tow.
I look at my children's eyes grown round and shining.   30

We look away.

after READING

UNDERSTANDING THE TEXT

1. In a group of three, discuss the significance of the following lines in the **poem**. Be prepared to present your ideas to the class.
   - "She and her two sons, the leafless tree/they stand under make an unreal family" (lines 2 and 3)
   - "she shoulders my guilt" (line 8)
   - "the Styrofoam still warm from what is rightly left over" (line 23)
   - "I and my fumbling are humbled" (line 27)

2. In your notebook, describe the impression the poem creates of the family without food. Explain which words the poet uses to create that impression.

3. In your notebook, identify one characteristic you would associate with the mother, the father, and the children in the van. Explain which words the poet uses to establish characteristics for each member of the family for the reader.

4. Explain the significance of the words in italics in the poem. What other punctuation could have been used for those words?

EXPLORING IDEAS AND IMPLICATIONS

5. In your notebook, explain whether you think this poem deals in stereotypes. Provide reasons for the position you take.

6. With a partner, create a **storyboard** for a film or video presentation of the events in this poem. Present your storyboard to the class and explain what techniques you have used to convey the emotions and ideas behind the events.

7. Using print and/or electronic sources, research the plight of the poor and/or homeless in our society. Based on your findings, create an informational **brochure** that educates people about the subject. If a computer is available, design your brochure using appropriate software. Use headings and statistical data to organize your information. Display your brochure on a class bulletin board.

MAKING CONNECTIONS

8. Read "A Visit of Charity" (pages 252–257) and "Excerpt From *Fugitive Pieces*" (pages 326–331). Each of these works deals with an act of charity. Explain which act you consider the most and the least noble. Give reasons from the works to support your choices. ■

The Bucket Rider

FRANZ KAFKA

"... there's nothing here; I see nothing, I hear nothing ..."

BEFORE READING

In a group of four, discuss how you and other members of society respond to people who beg for money on the street. To what extent do members of your group feel a sense of responsibility to the less fortunate members of society? Be prepared to present your ideas to the class.

Coal all spent; the bucket empty; the shovel useless; the stove breathing out cold; the room freezing; the leaves outside the window rigid, covered with rime; the sky a silver shield against any one who looks for help from it. I must have coal; I cannot freeze to death; behind me is the pitiless stove, before me the pitiless sky, so I must ride out between them and on my journey seek aid from the coal-dealer. But he has already grown deaf to ordinary appeals; I must prove irrefutably to him that I have not a single grain of coal left, and that he means to me the very sun in the firmament. I must approach like a beggar, who, with the death-rattle already in his throat, insists on dying on the doorstep, and to whom the grand people's cook accordingly decides to give the dregs of the coffee-pot; just so must the coal-dealer, filled with rage, but acknowledging the command, "Thou shalt not kill," fling a shovelful of coal into my bucket.

My mode of arrival must decide the matter; so I ride off on the bucket. Seated on the bucket, my hands on the handle, the simplest kind of bridle, I propel myself with difficulty down the stairs; but once down below my bucket ascends, superbly, superbly; camels humbly squatting on the ground do not rise with more dignity, shaking themselves under the sticks of their drivers. Through the hard frozen streets we go at a regular canter; often I am upraised as high as the first story of a house; never do I sink as low as the house doors. And at last I float at an extraordinary height above the vaulted cellar of the dealer, whom I see far below crouching over his table, where he is writing; he has opened the door to let out the excessive heat.

"Coal-dealer!" I cry in a voice burned hollow by the frost and muffled in the cloud made by my breath, "please, coal-dealer, give me a little coal. My bucket is so light that I can ride on it. Be kind. When I can I'll pay you."

The dealer puts his hand to his ear. "Do I hear rightly?" he throws the question over his shoulder to his wife. "Do I hear rightly? A customer."

"I hear nothing," says his wife, breathing in and out peacefully while she knits on, her back pleasantly warmed by the heat.

"Oh, yes, you must hear," I cry. "It's me; an old customer; faithful and true; only without means at the moment."

"Wife," says the dealer, "it's someone; it must be; my ears can't have deceived me so much as that; it must be an old, a very old customer, that can move me so deeply."

"What ails you, man?" says his wife, ceasing from her work for a moment and pressing her knitting to her bosom. "It's nobody, the street is empty, all our customers are provided for; we could close down the shop for several days and take a rest."

"But I'm sitting up here on the bucket," I cry, and unfeeling frozen tears dim my eyes. "Please look up here, just once; you'll see me directly; I beg you, just a shovelful; and if you give me more it'll make me so happy that I won't know what to do. All the other customers are provided for. Oh, if I could only hear the coal clattering into the bucket!"

"I'm coming," says the coal-dealer, and on his short legs he makes to climb the steps of the cellar, but his wife is already beside him, holds him back by the arm, and says: "You stay here; seeing you persist in your fancies I'll go myself. Think of the bad fit of coughing you had during the night. But for a piece of business, even if it's one you've only fancied in your head, you're prepared to forget your wife and child and sacrifice your lungs. I'll go."

"Then be sure to tell him all the kinds of coal we have in stock; I'll shout out the prices after you."

"Right," says his wife, climbing up to the street. Naturally she sees me at once. "Frau Coal-dealer," I cry, "my humblest greetings; just one shovelful of coal; here in my bucket; I'll carry it home myself. One shovelful of the worst you have. I'll pay you in full for it, of course, but not just now, not just now." What a knell-like sound the words "not just now" have, and how bewilderingly they mingle with the evening chimes that fall from the church steeple near by!

"Well, what does he want?" shouts the dealer. "Nothing," his wife shouts back, "there's nothing here; I see nothing, I hear nothing; only six striking, and now we must shut up the shop. The cold is terrible; tomorrow we'll likely have lots to do again."

She sees nothing and hears nothing; but all the same she loosens her apron-strings and waves her apron to waft me away. She succeeds, unluckily. My bucket has all the virtues of a good steed except powers of resistance, which it has not; it is too light; a woman's apron can make it fly through the air.

"You bad woman!" I shout back, while she, turning into the shop, half-contemptuous, half-reassured, flourishes her fist in the air. "You bad woman! I begged you for a shovelful of the worst coal and you would not give it me." And with that I ascend into the regions of the ice mountains and am lost forever.

after READING

UNDERSTANDING THE TEXT

1. Compare and contrast the response of the coal-dealer and his wife to the plight of the **narrator**.

2. The second paragraph of this **story** introduces an air of fantasy. In a group of four, discuss the following questions: Did the narrator actually go to the coal-dealer's home? Why could the coal-dealer hear the narrator, but his wife could not? What happens to the narrator at the end of the story?

3. Individually, write an **opinion essay** explaining whether the surreal elements of "The Bucket Rider" do or do not enhance the story for you as a reader. With a partner, revise your essay focusing on clarity of expression, strength of arguments, and use of evidence. Prepare your final draft for submission.

4. The translator of this story uses a large number of semicolons. With a partner, review the rules for the use of the semicolon and assess their use in this story. (See also The Reference Shelf, page 412.)

EXPLORING IDEAS AND IMPLICATIONS

5. This story was originally written in Prague in 1917 and published in 1921. In a paragraph, describe the effect you think Kafka might have hoped it would have on his fellow citizens. Be prepared to present your ideas to the class.

6. Research the life and work of Franz Kafka. Write a short **essay** explaining how knowledge about Kafka helps the reader understand "The Bucket Rider." Revise and edit your essay before submitting it.

MAKING CONNECTIONS

7. Read the poem "She, Plural" (pages 237–238). With a partner, reflect back on your "Before Reading" activity. Then create a short radio commercial, to be aired during Thanksgiving or another festive season, asking people to give to the less fortunate. Write the script, rehearse, and present your commercial either live or taped. Use sound effects to enhance your message.

8. Research the characteristics of literature that is classified as surrealism, fantasy, or magic realism. Read at least two works in one category for an independent study project on the genre. (See The Reference Shelf, pages 429–433.) Create a written and oral **report** to share your findings with the class. ■

A Family Supper

KAZUO ISHIGURO

"It felt quite soft, quite fleshy against my tongue."

BEFORE READING

As a class, discuss the reasons why many parents want their children to stay close to home and family.

Fugu is a fish caught off the Pacific shores of Japan. The fish has held a special significance for me ever since my mother died through eating one. The poison resides in the sexual glands of the fish, inside two fragile bags. When preparing the fish, these bags must be removed with caution, for any clumsiness will result in the poison leaking into the veins. Regrettably, it is not easy to tell whether or not this operation has been carried out successfully. The proof is, as it were, in the eating.

Fugu poisoning is hideously painful and almost always fatal. If the fish has been eaten during the evening, the victim is usually overtaken by pain during his sleep. He rolls about in agony for a few hours and is dead by morning. The fish became extremely popular in Japan after the war. Until stricter regulations were imposed, it was all the rage to perform the hazardous gutting operation in one's own kitchen, then to invite neighbours and friends round for the feast.

At the time of my mother's death, I was living in California. My relationship with my parents had become somewhat strained around that period, and consequently I did not learn of the circumstances surrounding her death until I returned to Tokyo two years later. Apparently, my mother had always refused to eat fugu, but on this particular occasion she had made an exception, having been invited by an old schoolfriend whom she was anxious not to offend. It was my father who supplied me with the details as we drove from the airport to his house in the Kamakura district. When we finally arrived, it was nearing the end of a sunny autumn day.

"Did you eat on the plane?" my father asked. We were sitting on the tatami floor of his tea-room.

"They gave me a light snack."

"You must be hungry. We'll eat as soon as Kikuko arrives."

My father was a formidable-looking man with a large stony jaw and furious black eyebrows. I think now in retrospect that he much resembled Chou En-lai, although he would not have cherished such a comparison, being particularly proud of the pure samurai blood that ran in the family. His general presence was not one which encouraged relaxed conversation; neither were things helped much by his odd way of stating each remark as if it were the concluding one. In fact, as I sat opposite him that afternoon, a boyhood memory came back to me of the time he had struck me several times around the head for "chattering like an old woman." Inevitably, our conversation since my arrival at the airport had been punctuated by long pauses.

"I'm sorry to hear about the firm," I said when neither of us had spoken for some time. He nodded gravely.

"In fact the story didn't end there," he said. "After the firm's collapse, Watanabe killed himself. He didn't wish to live with the disgrace."

"I see."

"We were partners for seventeen years. A man of principle and honour. I respected him very much."

"Will you go into business again?' I asked.

"I am—in retirement. I'm too old to involve myself in new ventures now. Business these days has become so different. Dealing with foreigners. Doing things their way. I don't understand how we've come to this. Neither did Watanabe." He sighed. "A fine man. A man of principle."

The tea-room looked out over the garden. From where I sat I could make out the ancient well which as a child I had believed haunted. It was just visible now through the thick foliage. The sun had sunk low and much of the garden had fallen into shadow.

"I'm glad in any case that you've decided to come back," my father said. "More than a short visit, I hope."

"I'm not sure what my plans will be."

"I for one am prepared to forget the past. Your mother too was always ready to welcome you back—upset as she was by your behaviour."

"I appreciate your sympathy. As I say, I'm not sure what my plans are."

"I've come to believe now that there were no evil intentions in your mind," my father continued. "You were swayed by certain—influences. Like so many others."

"Perhaps we should forget it, as you suggest."

"As you will. More tea?"

Just then a girl's voice came echoing through the house.

"At last." My father rose to his feet. "Kikuko has arrived."

Despite our difference in years, my sister and I had always been close. Seeing me again seemed to make her excessively excited and for a while she did nothing but giggle nervously. But she calmed down somewhat when my father started to question her about Osaka and her university. She answered him with short formal replies. She in turn asked me a few questions, but she seemed inhibited by the fear that her questions might lead to awkward topics. After a while, the conversation had become even sparser than prior to Kikuko's arrival. Then my father stood up, saying: "I must attend to the supper. Please excuse me for being burdened down by such matters. Kikuko will look after you."

My sister relaxed quite visibly after he had left the room. Within a few minutes, she was chatting freely about her friends in Osaka and about her classes at university. Then quite suddenly she decided we should walk in the garden and went striding out onto the veranda. We put on some straw sandals that had been left along the veranda rail and stepped out into the garden. The daylight had almost gone.

"I've been dying for a smoke for the last half-hour," she said, lighting a cigarette.

"Then why didn't you smoke?"

She made a furtive gesture towards the house then grinned mischievously.

"Oh I see," I said.

"Guess what? I've got a boyfriend now."

"Oh yes?"

"Except I'm wondering what to do. I haven't made up my mind yet."

"Quite understandable."

"You see, he's making plans to go to America. He wants me to go with him as soon as I finish studying."

"I see. And you want to go to America?"

"If we go, we're going to hitchhike." Kikuko waved a thumb in front of my face. "People say it's dangerous, but I've done it in Osaka and it's fine."

"I see. So what is it you're unsure about?"

We were following a narrow path that wound through the shrubs and finished by the old well. As we walked, Kikuko persisted in taking unnecessarily theatrical puffs on her cigarette.

"Well. I've got lots of friends now in Osaka. I like it there. I'm not sure I want to leave them all behind just yet. And Suichi—I like him, but I'm not sure I want to spend so much time with him. Do you understand?"

"Oh perfectly."

She grinned again, then skipped on ahead of me until she had reached the well. "Do you remember," she said, as I came walking up to her, "how you used to say this well was haunted?"

"Yes, I remember."

We both peered over the side.

"Mother always told me it was the old woman from the vegetable store you'd seen that night," she said. "But I never believed her and never came out here alone."

"Mother used to tell me that too. She even told me once the old woman had confessed to being the ghost. Apparently she'd been taking a short cut through our garden. I imagine she had some trouble clambering over these walls."

Kikuko gave a giggle. She then turned her back to the well, casting her gaze about the garden.

"Mother never really blamed you, you know," she said, in a new voice. I remained silent. "She always used to say to me how it was their fault, hers and Father's, for not bringing you up correctly. She used to tell me how much more careful they'd been with me, and that's why I was so good." She looked up and the mischievous grin had returned to her face. "Poor Mother," she said.

"Yes. Poor Mother."

"Are you going back to California?"

"I don't know. I'll have to see."

"What happened to—to her? To Vicki?"

"That's all finished with," I said. "There's nothing much left for me now in California."

"Do you think I ought to go there?"

"Why not? I don't know. You'll probably like it." I glanced towards the house. "Perhaps we'd better go in soon. Father might need a hand with supper."

But my sister was once more peering down into the well. "I can't see any ghosts," she said. Her voice echoed a little.

"Is Father very upset about his firm collapsing?"

"Don't know. You can never tell with Father." Then suddenly she straightened up and turned to me. "Did he tell you about Watanabe? What he did?"

"I heard he committed suicide."

"Well, that wasn't all. He took his whole family with him. His wife and his two little girls."

"Oh yes?"

"Those two beautiful little girls. He turned on the gas while they were all asleep. Then he cut his stomach with a meat knife."

"Yes, Father, was just telling me how Watanabe was a man of principle."

"Sick." My sister turned back to the well.

"Careful. You'll fall right in."

"I can't see any ghost," she said. "You were lying to me all that time."

"But I never said it lived down the well."

"Where is it then?"

We both looked around at the trees and shrubs. The light in the garden had grown very dim. Eventually I pointed to a small clearing some ten yards away.

"Just there I saw it. Just there."

We stared at the spot.

"What did it look like?"

"I couldn't see very well. It was dark."

"But you must have seen something."

"It was an old woman. She was just standing there, watching me."

We kept staring at the spot as if mesmerized.

"She was wearing a white kimono," I said. "Some of her hair had come undone. It was blowing around a little."

Kikuko pushed her elbow against my arm. "Oh be quiet. You're trying to frighten me all over again." She trod on the remains of her cigarette, then for a brief moment stood regarding it with a perplexed expression. She kicked some pine needles over it, then once more displayed her grin. "Let's see if supper's ready," she said.

We found my father in the kitchen. He gave us a quick glance, then carried on with what he was doing.

"Father's become quite a chef since he's had to manage on his own," Kikuko said with a laugh. He turned and looked at my sister coldly.

"Hardly a skill I'm proud of," he said. "Kikuko, come here and help."

For some moments my sister did not move. Then she stepped forward and took an apron hanging from a drawer.

"Just these vegetables need cooking now," he said to her. "The rest just needs watching." Then he looked up and regarded me strangely for some seconds. "I expect you want to look around the house," he said eventually. He put down the chopsticks he had been holding. "It's a long time since you've seen it."

As we left the kitchen I glanced back towards Kikuko, but her back was turned.

"She's a good girl," my father said quietly.

I followed my father from room to room. I had forgotten how large the house was. A panel would slide open and another room would appear. But the rooms were all startlingly empty. In one of the rooms the lights did not come on, and we stared at the stark walls and tatami in the pale light that came from the windows.

"This house is too large for a man to live in alone," my father said. "I don't have much use for most of these rooms now."

But eventually my father opened the door to a room packed full of books and papers. There were flowers in vases and pictures on the walls. Then I noticed something on a low table in the corner of the room. I came nearer and saw it was a plastic model of a battleship, the kind constructed by children. It had been placed on some newspaper; scattered around it were assorted pieces of grey plastic.

My father gave a laugh. He came up to the table and picked up the model.

"Since the firm folded," he said, "I have a little more time on my hands." He laughed again, rather strangely. For a moment his face looked almost gentle. "A little more time."

"That seems odd," I said. "You were always so busy."

"Too busy perhaps." He looked at me with a small smile. "Perhaps I should have been a more attentive father."

I laughed. He went on contemplating his battleship. Then he looked up. "I hadn't meant to tell you this, but perhaps it's best that I do. It's my belief that your mother's death was no accident. She had many worries. And some disappointments."

We both gazed at the battleship.

"Surely," I said eventually, "my mother didn't expect me to live here for ever."

"Obviously you don't see. You don't see how it is for some parents. Not only must they lose their children, they must lose them to things they don't understand." He spun the battleship in his fingers. "These little gunboats here could have been better glued, don't you think?"

"Perhaps. It looks fine."

"During the war I spent some time on a ship rather like this. But my ambition was always the air force. I figured it like this. If your ship was struck by the enemy, all you could do was struggle in the water hoping for a lifeline. But in the airplane—well—there was always the final weapon." He put the model back on the table. "I don't suppose you believe in war."

"Not particularly."

He cast an eye around the room. "Supper should be ready by now," he said. "You must be hungry."

Supper was waiting in a dimly lit room next to the kitchen. The only source of light was a big lantern that hung over the table, casting the rest of the room into shadow. We bowed to each other before starting the meal.

There was little conversation. When I made a polite comment about the food, Kikuko giggled a little. Her earlier nervousness seemed to have returned to her. My father did not speak for several minutes. Finally he said:

"It must feel strange for you, being back in Japan."

"Yes, it is a little strange."

"Already, perhaps, you regret leaving America."

"A little. Not so much. I didn't leave behind much. Just some empty rooms."

"I see."

I glanced across the table. My father's face looked stony and forbidding in the half-light. We ate on in silence.

Then my eye caught something at the back of the room. At first I continued eating, then my hands became still. The others noticed and looked at me. I went on gazing into the darkness past my father's shoulder.

"Who is that? In that photograph there?"

"Which photograph?" My father turned slightly, trying to follow my gaze.

"The lowest one. The old woman in the white kimono."

My father put down his chopsticks. He looked at the photograph, then at me.

"Your mother." His voice had become very hard. "Can't you recognize your own mother?"

"My mother. You see, it's dark. I can't see it very well."

No one spoke for a few seconds, then Kikuko rose to her feet. She took the photograph off the wall, then came back to the table and gave it to me.

"She looks a lot older," I said.

"It was taken shortly before her death," said my father.

"It was the dark. I couldn't see it very well."

I looked up and noticed my father holding out a hand. I gave him the photograph. He looked at it intently, then held it towards Kikuko. Obediently, my sister rose to her feet once more and returned the picture to the wall.

There was a large pot left unopened at the centre of the table. When Kikuko had seated herself again, my father reached forward and lifted the lid. A cloud of steam rose up and curled towards the lantern. He pushed the pot a little towards me.

"You must be hungry," he said. One side of his face had fallen into shadow.

"Thank you." I reached forward with my chopsticks. The steam was almost scalding. "What is it?"

"Fish."

"It smells very good."

In amidst the soup were strips of fish that had curled almost into balls. I picked one out and brought it to my bowl.

"Help yourself. There's plenty."

"Thank you." I took a little more, then pushed the pot towards my father. I watched him take several pieces to his bowl then we both watched as Kikuko served herself.

My father bowed slightly. "You must be hungry," he said again. He took some fish to his mouth and started to eat. Then I chose a piece and put it in my mouth. It felt quite soft, quite fleshy against my tongue.

"Very good," I said, "What is it?"

"Just fish."

"It's very good."

The three of us ate on in silence. Several minutes went by.

"Some more?"

"Is there enough?"

"There's plenty for all of us." My father lifted the lid and once more steam rose up. We all reached forward and helped ourselves.

"Here," I said to my father, "you have this last piece."

"Thank you."

When we finished the meal, my father stretched out his arms and yawned with an air of satisfaction. "Kikuko," he said. "Prepare a pot of tea, please."

My sister looked at him, then left the room without comment. My father stood up.

"Let's retire to the other room. It's rather warm in here."

I got to my feet and followed him into the tea-room. The large sliding windows had been left open, bringing in a breeze from the garden. For a while we sat in silence.

"Father," I said, finally.

"Yes?"

"Kikuko tells me Watanabe-San took his whole family with him."

My father lowered his eyes and nodded. For some moments he seemed in deep thought. "Watanabe was very devoted to his work," he said at last. "The collapse of the firm was a great blow to him. I fear it must have weakened his judgement."

"You think what he did—it was a mistake?"

"Why, of course. Do you see it otherwise?"

"No, no. Of course not."

"There are other things besides work."

"Yes."

We fell silent again. The sounds of the locusts came in from the garden. I looked out into the darkness. The well was no longer visible.

"What do you think you will do now?" my father asked. "Will you stay in Japan for a while?"

"To be honest, I hadn't thought that far ahead."

"If you wish to stay here, I mean this house, you would be very welcome. That is, if you don't mind living with an old man."

"Thank you. I'll have to think about it."

I gazed out once more into the darkness.

"But of course," said my father, "this house is so dreary now. You'll no doubt be returning to America before long."

"Perhaps. I don't know yet."

"No doubt you will."

For some time my father seemed to be studying the back of his hands. Then he looked up and sighed.

"Kikuko is due to complete her studies next spring," he said. "Perhaps she will want to come home then. She's a good girl."

"Perhaps she will."

"Things will improve then."

"Yes, I'm sure they will."

We fell silent once more, waiting for Kikuko to bring the tea.

after READING

UNDERSTANDING THE TEXT

1 Write a personal response to the issues raised in this **story**. Compare your responses with those of a partner.

2. Referring specifically to the story, describe the different techniques the author uses to build **suspense**.

3. Decide whether or not the fish served by the father is fugu. In your notebook, explain your decision, referring specifically to the story. Compare your decision with those of your classmates.

4. Describe the **character** of the father by examining and making notes on the way the writer describes him, the things the father says about himself and others, and the reactions of both the son and daughter to him. Bring your notes to a small group and discuss the effectiveness of the writer's character development.

EXPLORING IDEAS AND IMPLICATIONS

5. In your notebook, explain the significance of the description of the ghost and the description of the mother in the photograph. Be sure to research the significance of the colour white in Japanese culture.

6. Write a critique of "A Family Supper." (See The Reference Shelf, pages 443–444.) Have a partner revise your work, focusing on content, **voice**, and language. Have a different partner edit your work for spelling, grammar, and punctuation.

7. Imagine that the father in "A Family Supper" does serve the poisonous fish for supper. In a group of three, prepare a **report** of the tragedy for television news. Rely on the story for details. Include all three group members when writing and performing the script. Have another group see your broadcast and critique its production values and content. Rehearse and polish in preparation for presentation.

MAKING CONNECTIONS

8. Read the excerpt from *The Pearl* (pages 275–283). In a small group, discuss the similarities between the excerpt and "A Family Supper." Make notes using chart paper or Presentation software and be prepared to present your work to the class. ■

A Visit of Charity

EUDORA WELTY

"I'm a Campfire Girl. ... I have to pay a visit to some old lady."

BEFORE READING

As a class, discuss a community service you have performed (or plan to perform) as a requirement for school, or for a club or an organization to which you belong. How do you feel about performing community service?

It was mid-morning—a very cold, bright day. Holding a potted plant before her, a girl of fourteen jumped off the bus in front of the Old Ladies' Home, on the outskirts of town. She wore a red coat, and her straight yellow hair was hanging down loose from the pointed white cap all the little girls were wearing that year. She stopped for a moment beside one of the prickly dark shrubs with which the city had beautified the Home, and then proceeded slowly toward the building, which was of whitewashed brick and reflected the winter sunlight like a block of ice. As she walked vaguely up the steps she shifted the small pot from hand to hand; then she had to set it down and remove her mittens before she could open the heavy door.

"I'm a Campfire Girl.[1] ... I have to pay a visit to some old lady," she told the nurse at the desk. This was a woman in a white uniform who looked as if she were cold; she had close-cut hair which stood up on the very top of her head exactly like a sea wave. Marian, the little girl, did not tell her that this visit would give her a minimum of only three points in her score.

"Acquainted with any of our residents?" asked the nurse. She lifted one eyebrow and spoke like a man.

"With any old ladies? No—but—that is, any of them will do," Marian stammered. With her free hand she pushed her hair behind her ears, as she did when it was time to study science.

The nurse shrugged and rose. "You have a nice *multiflora cineraria* there," she remarked as she walked ahead down the hall of closed doors to pick out an old lady.

---

1. An American organization founded in 1912 for girls aged five to 18.

There was loose, bulging linoleum on the floor. Marian felt as if she were walking on the waves, but the nurse paid no attention to it. There was a smell in the hall like the interior of a clock. Everything was silent until, behind one of the doors, an old lady of some kind cleared her throat like a sheep bleating. This decided the nurse. Stopping in her tracks, she first extended her arm, bent her elbow, and leaned forward from the hips—all to examine the watch strapped to her wrist; then she gave a loud double-rap on the door.

"There are two in each room," the nurse remarked over her shoulder.

"Two what?" asked Marian without thinking. The sound like a sheep's bleating almost made her turn around and run back.

One old woman was pulling the door open in short gradual jerks, and when she saw the nurse a strange smile forced her old face dangerously awry. Marian, suddenly propelled by the strong, impatient arm of the nurse, saw next the side-face of another old woman, even older, who was lying flat in bed with a cap on and a counterpane drawn up to her chin.

"Visitor," said the nurse, and after one more shove she was off up the hall.

Marian stood tongue-tied; both hands held the potted plant. The old woman, still with that terrible, square smile (which was a smile of welcome) stamped on her bony face, was waiting.... Perhaps she said something. The old woman in bed said nothing at all, and she did not look around.

Suddenly Marian saw a hand, quick as a bird claw, reach up in the air and pluck the white cap off her head. At the same time, another claw to match drew her all the way into the room, and the next moment the door closed behind her.

"My, my, my," said the old lady at her side.

Marian stood enclosed by a bed, a washstand, and a chair; the tiny room had altogether too much furniture. Everything smelled wet—even the bare floor. She held onto the back of the chair, which was wicker and felt soft and damp. Her heart beat more and more slowly; her hands got colder and colder, and she could not hear whether the old women were saying anything or not. She could not see them very clearly. How dark it was! The window shade was down, and the only door was shut. Marian looked at the ceiling.... It was like being caught in a robbers' cave, just before one was murdered.

"Did you come to be our little girl for a while?" the first robber asked.

Then something was snatched from Marian's hand—the little potted plant.

"Flowers!" screamed the old woman. She stood holding the pot in an undecided way. "Pretty flowers," she added.

Then the old woman in bed cleared her throat and spoke. "They are not pretty," she said, still without looking around, but very distinctly.

Marian suddenly pitched against the chair and sat down in it.

"Pretty flowers," the first old woman insisted. "Pretty—pretty ..."

Marian wished she had the little pot back for just a moment—she had forgotten to look at the plant before giving it away. What did it look like?

"Stinkweeds," said the other old woman sharply. She had a bunchy white forehead and red eyes like a sheep. Now she turned them toward Marian. The fogginess seemed to rise in her throat again, and she bleated, "Who—are—you?"

To her surprise, Marian could not remember her name. "I'm a Campfire Girl," she said finally.

"Watch out for the germs," said the old woman like a sheep, not addressing anyone.

"One came out last month to see us," said the first old woman.

A sheep or a germ? wondered Marian dreamily, holding onto the chair.

"Did not!" cried the other old woman.

"Did so! Read to us out of the Bible, and we enjoyed it!" screamed the first.

"Who enjoyed it!" said the woman in bed. Her mouth was unexpectedly small and sorrowful, like a pet's.

"We enjoyed it," insisted the other. "You enjoyed it—I enjoyed it."

"We all enjoyed it," said Marian, without realizing that she had said a word.

The first old woman had just finished putting the potted plant high, high on the top of the wardrobe, where it could hardly be seen from below. Marian wondered how she had ever succeeded in placing it there, how she could ever have reached so high.

"You mustn't pay any attention to old Addie," she now said to the little girl. "She's ailing today."

"Will you shut your mouth?" said the woman in bed. "I am not."

"You're a story."

"I can't stay but a minute—really I can't," said Marian suddenly. She looked down at the wet floor and thought that if she were sick in here they would have to let her go.

With much to-do the first old woman sat down in a rocking chair—still another piece of furniture!—and began to rock. With the fingers of one hand she touched a very dirty cameo pin on her chest. "What do you do at school?" she asked.

"I don't know ..." said Marian. She tried to think but she could not.

"Oh, but the flowers are beautiful," the old woman whispered. She seemed to rock faster and faster; Marian did not see how anyone could rock so fast.

"Ugly," said the woman in bed.

"If we bring flowers—" Marian began, and then fell silent. She had almost said that if Campfire Girls brought flowers to the Old Ladies' Home, the visit would count one extra point, and if they took a Bible with them on the bus and read it to the old ladies, it counted double. But the old woman had not listened, anyway; she was rocking and watching the other one, who watched back from the bed.

"Poor Addie is ailing. She has to take medicine—see?" she said, pointing a horny finger at a row of bottles on the table, and rocking so high that her black comfort shoes lifted off the floor like a little child's.

"I am no more sick than you are," said the woman in bed.

"Oh yes you are!"

"I just got more sense than you have, that's all," said the other old woman, nodding her head.

"That's only the contrary way she talks when *you all* come," said the first old lady with sudden intimacy. She stopped the rocker with a neat pat of her feet and leaned toward Marian. Her hand reached over—it felt like a petunia leaf, clinging and just a little sticky.

"Will you hush? Will you hush!" cried the other one.

Marian leaned back rigidly in her chair.

"When I was a little girl like you, I went to school and all," said the old woman in the same intimate, menacing voice. "Not here—another town ..."

"Hush!" said the sick woman. "You never went to school. You never came and you never went. You never were any-where—only here. You never were born! You don't know anything. Your head is empty, your heart and hands and your old black purse are all empty, even that little old box that you brought with you you brought empty—you showed it to me. And yet you talk, talk, talk, talk, talk all the time until I think I'm losing my mind! Who are you? You're a stranger— a perfect stranger! Don't you know you're a stranger? Is it possible that they have actually done a thing like this to anyone— sent them in a stranger to talk, and rock, and tell away her whole long rigmarole? Do they seriously suppose that I'll be able to keep it up, day in, day out, night in, night out, living in the same room with a terrible old woman—forever?"

Marian saw the old woman's eyes grow bright and turn toward her. This old woman was looking at her with despair and calculation in her face. Her small lips suddenly dropped apart, and exposed a half circle of false teeth with tan gums.

"Come here, I want to tell you some-thing," she whispered. "Come here!"

Marian was trembling and her heart nearly stopped beating altogether for a moment.

"Now, now, Addie," said the first old woman. "That's not polite. Do you know what's really the matter with old Addie today?" She, too, looked at Marian; one of her eyelids drooped low.

"The matter?" the child repeated stupidly. "What's the matter with her?"

"Why, she's mad because it's her birth-day!" said the first old woman, beginning to rock again and giving a little crow as though she had answered her own riddle.

"It is not, it is not!" screamed the old woman in bed. "It is not my birthday, no one knows when that is but myself, and will you please be quiet and say nothing more, or I'll go straight out of my mind!" She turned her eyes toward Marian again, and presently she said in the soft, foggy voice, "When the worst comes to the worst, I ring this bell, and the nurse comes." One of her hands was drawn out from under the patched counterpane—a thin little hand with enormous black freckles. With a finger which would not hold still she pointed to a little bell on the table among the bottles.

"How old are you?" Marian breathed. Now she could see the old woman in bed very closely and plainly, and very abruptly, from all sides, as in dreams. She wondered about her—she wondered for a moment as though there was nothing else in the world to wonder about. It was the first time such a thing had happened to Marian.

"I won't tell!"

The old face on the pillow, where Marian was bending over it, slowly gathered and collapsed. Soft whimpers came out of the small open mouth. It was a sheep that she sounded like—a little lamb. Marian's face drew very close, the yellow hair hung forward.

"She's crying!" She turned a bright, burning face up to the first old woman.

"That's Addie for you," the old woman said spitefully.

Marian jumped up and moved toward the door. For the second time, the claw almost touched her hair, but it was not quick enough. The little girl put her cap on.

"Well, it was a real visit," said the old woman, following Marian through the doorway and all the way out into the hall. Then from behind she suddenly clutched the child with her sharp little fingers. In an affected, high-pitched whine she cried, "Oh, little girl, have you a penny to spare for a poor old woman that's not got anything of her own? We don't have a thing in the world—not a penny for candy—not a thing! Little girl, just a nickel—a penny—"

Marian pulled violently against the old hands for a moment before she was free. Then she ran down the hall, without looking behind her and without looking at the nurse, who was reading *Field and Stream* at her desk. The nurse, after another triple motion to consult her wristwatch, asked automatically the question put to visitors in all institutions: "Won't you stay and have dinner with *us*?"

Marian never replied. She pushed the heavy door open into the cold air and ran down the steps.

Under the prickly shrub she stooped and quickly, without being seen, retrieved a red apple she had hidden there.

Her yellow hair under the white cap, her scarlet coat, her bare knees all flashed in the sunlight as she ran to meet the big bus rocketing through the street.

"Wait for me!" she shouted. As though at an imperial command, the bus ground to a stop.

She jumped on and took a big bite out of the apple.

after READING

UNDERSTANDING THE TEXT

1. With a partner, discuss whether the experiences or emotions of Marian in the **story** matched any of the experiences or feelings the class talked about in the "Before Reading" activity. In your notebook, record three details from the beginning of the story that reveal Marian's attitude toward her visit.

2. In a group of four, read the **dialogue** from the story aloud, each taking the part of one of the four **characters**. After the reading, discuss whether this story would be successful as a **drama**. What would be missing from the dramatic version? What would be added for the **audience** that is not in the story? In your notebook, record the results of your discussion.

3. Use a chart or a Venn diagram to record details that show the similarities and differences in character and behaviour of the two old women.

EXPLORING IDEAS AND IMPLICATIONS

4. a) Carefully reread the **narrative** sections (not the dialogue) in the story. Make a list of observations about the author's narrative **style** and language. Include observations about any literary techniques or devices used effectively by the author.
   b) Compare your observations and explanations with those of a peer.
   c) Select four **similes** from the story, and explain in a few sentences for each what the comparison adds to the story.

5. a) In a group of three, have each member of the group select one of the characters: Marian, the first old woman, and Addie. Then do the following tasks:
   - In the role of Marian, one group member writes a diary entry describing the visit.
   - In the roles of the first old woman and Addie, the other two group members write letters to a relative describing their impressions of Marian's visit.
   b) After writing, read aloud the diary entry and letters within the group to see what differences there are, if any, in the viewpoints of the three characters. Discuss the following questions: How would you account for the differences? Are they true to the characters in the story?
   c) Then revise your work to ensure that the writing has captured the unique character of the individual based on details from the story.
   d) After the letters and diary have been revised, read them aloud to the rest of the class.

6. a) In a small group, develop a shooting script for a film or videotaped version of the scene between Marian and the two old ladies in their room. Ensure your script indicates clearly where you would use long shots, medium shots, close-ups, and high-angle and low-angle shots. Discuss the effects on the viewer of each of the shots used in your shooting script, and revise your script as necessary.

b) Role-play the scene and videotape it, as planned on the shooting script. Present your video to the class for assessment.

MAKING CONNECTIONS

7. Interview a caregiver such as a nurse, social worker, chaplain, or food service worker. Research information about the benefits (or disadvantages) to the people who receive visits from volunteers. Be prepared to make a brief oral **report** of your findings to the class.

8. Read three other stories by Eudora Welty. Then imagine that the three stories, along with "A Visit of Charity," are going to appear in a book collection of Welty's stories. Write a book jacket copy, which briefly describes each story in an interesting way. (You may wish to examine other book jackets for ideas.) Read your book jacket to a small group to see how members react to the copy. Would they buy the book based on your description of the stories? Why or why not? Revise and edit your book jacket for submission. ■

You Are What You Play

VINCENT BOZZI

"... people ... may choose [sports] whose symbolism
is appropriate to their desired social identity."

BEFORE READING

As a class, brainstorm a list of characteristics associated with the athletes who play certain sports in your school. Based on the characteristics associated with each sport, rank the sports in order of their prestige within the school.

Just as we don't buy cars simply for transportation or houses solely for shelter, we don't always play a particular sport just because we like it or are good at it. The game also helps us project a certain image or identify with a certain crowd. Do we want to be known as active and daring? Skiing can help. Calm and honest? Try golf.

Arizona State University psychologists Darwyn Linder, Edward Sadalla and Bradley Jenkins gave 250 college students the description of a man or woman strongly interested in one of five common sports: golf, bowling, tennis, snow skiing and motocross (a type of motorcycle racing). The skier, for example, was depicted this way:

"John belongs to a local snow skiing club and skis frequently. He participates in club competitions and spends a lot of time working on his technique. He subscribes to a couple of ski magazines and generally socializes with other skiers."

With this as a guide, the students thought about what kind of person the athlete was likely to be and rated him or her on a 5-point scale (1 being highest and 5 lowest) for 70 characteristics—such as intelligence, courage, patience, confidence and aggression—that the researchers grouped into five overall categories: active-daring, cultured-sophisticated, calmness, honesty and sensual-attractive.

The chart [on page 260] summarizes what the researchers reported in the *Journal of Sport & Exercise Psychology*—a series of widely shared stereotypes:

Bowlers are considered the least daring and sensual, and the second-least cultured. But they are rated as very honest and among the most calm and relaxed.

Tennis players are seen as sensual and attractive, highly cultured, moderately

You Are What You Play

This chart shows an average rating in each category for each sport.

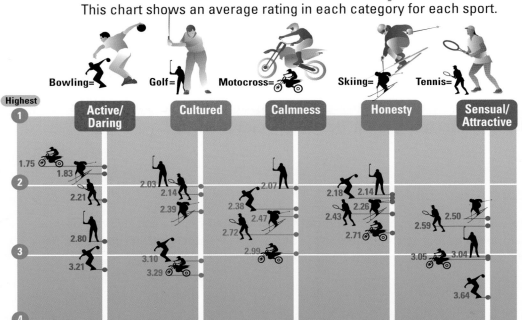

Bowling=   Golf=   Motocross=   Skiing=   Tennis=

Highest					
1	Active/ Daring	Cultured	Calmness	Honesty	Sensual/ Attractive

Active/Daring: 1.75, 1.83, 2.21, 2.80, 3.21
Cultured: 2.03, 2.14, 2.39, 3.10, 3.29
Calmness: 2.07, 2.38, 2.47, 2.72, 2.99
Honesty: 2.18, 2.14, 2.26, 2.43, 2.71
Sensual/Attractive: 2.50, 2.59, 3.05, 3.04, 3.64

4

5 — Lowest

active and daring, but among the least calm or honest.

Golfers are quite similar to tennis players, the researchers found, but have the distinction of being ranked the most cultured, calm and honest of all the players.

The most sensual and attractive group is skiers, also considered the second-most active and daring. They are right in the middle on culture, calmness and honesty.

"Motocross racing is the most variable sport," Linder reported. Considered the most active and daring, "motocross racers were rated lowest on the cultured, calmness and honesty scales."

If people sense that particular sports suggest particular character traits, Linder points out, they may choose ones "whose symbolism is appropriate to their desired social identity." So an executive who wants to be known as a simple, down-to-earth guy may take up bowling. The man who likes to think of himself as a rugged risk-taker dons a leather jacket and gets into motocross racing.

Perhaps we should paraphrase the Bible verse this way: "By their sports ye shall know them" ... or at least know what they want ye to know about them.

after READING

UNDERSTANDING THE TEXT

1. With a partner, review the chart in this **article** to determine possible reasons why each sport was ranked the way it was in the survey. Discuss whether the rankings are based on stereotypes or offer insights into the sports and the people who play them. Individually, write a critique (See The Reference Shelf, pages 443–444) of the study based on the ideas discussed with your partner.

2. In a group of three, review the description of the research study in this article and discuss whether the results of the study are valid, and whether you think any changes should have been made to the study. Be prepared to present ideas raised in your discussion to the class.

3. On the basis of the description of the research study in this article, create the first page of the study's questionnaire dealing with bowling. Compare your page with that of one of your classmates.

EXPLORING IDEAS AND IMPLICATIONS

4. In your notebook, identify which of the sports profiled best matches the characteristics you associate or would like others to associate with yourself. Explain whether the sport that seems to best suit your characteristics is one that you enjoy playing or would consider taking up in a serious way.

5. In a paragraph, explain whether the statements in the first paragraph of this article are as true for professional athletes as they are for amateurs.

6. a) Write an **opinion essay** explaining the benefits of playing a sport or engaging in another form of extracurricular activity. Indicate on what basis you would recommend that someone select the most appropriate activity for his or her participation.
   b) Work with a partner to revise and edit your essay for submission.

7. Find and bring to class an advertisement that is trying to get people to sign up for a club or activity. Explain how the advertisement appeals to a certain image its readers might want to convey or a certain group they might want to be associated with.

MAKING CONNECTIONS

8. With a partner, read "99" (page 199) and "Ex-Basketball Player" (page 201). Discuss where you think hockey and basketball would have placed on the chart had they been used as part of this study. Provide reasons for your ideas to the class. ■

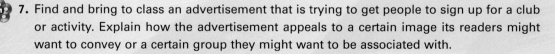

Forbidden Clothes

JAMILA GAVIN

"They are taking her away ... taking her away ..."

BEFORE READING

With a partner, discuss whether you or your partner have ever had a **conflict** with your parents over the style of clothing you want to wear to "fit in" with your peers. Assess the extent to which this conflict is based on cultural or religious values that your parents hold. How have you managed to deal with this conflict?

"They are taking her away from us."

Mrs Khan articulated her words in a flat, monotone voice but, as she spoke, she leaned forward and stared intensely into the eyes of her volunteer English teacher, Margot Henderson.

Margot stared back, momentarily shocked out of her boredom. This was the first English sentence Mrs Khan had put together herself after nearly six weeks of lessons.

"What do you mean?" asked Margot.

Still leaning forward, Mrs Khan spoke again. She repeated the same sentence, hammering it out with staccato precision.

"They are taking her away from us."

"Who is taking who away from you?" asked Margot, looking round.

Then she met the large, dark eyes of the fifteen-year-old girl in the school photograph. It sat alone on the mantelpiece, testifying to the reverence and devotion accorded to an only child.

She wasn't beautiful. Her face had been left to fend for itself, framed only by a severe headscarf which swept her hair away out of sight. Her nose was too long and narrow, her cheekbones too angular, her mouth too broad. Yet there was something compelling about the way she looked almost defiantly into the camera, as if she was trying to say, "Yes, this is me. There's more to me than meets the eye."

"Nasreen." Mrs Khan whispered her daughter's name.

"Ah, yes! Nasreen!" Repeated Margot, brightly. "How is she getting on at school?" Margot asked her question loudly and slowly as if the woman were deaf.

Mrs Khan opened her mouth and drew in her breath sharply as she struggled to find the words.

"She ... she ... not ... fine. Fine ..." She shrugged helplessly and slumped back in her seat, drawing her veil across her face.

Margot felt the irritation rising up in her. Mrs Khan was not her favourite pupil. She was a slow learner, and she resented the sense of dumb depression which seemed to envelop the woman, slowing down her movements and imprinting an expression of wooden despair on her face.

"Don't just say 'fine,' Mrs Khan. Put it in a sentence," urged Margot with exaggerated patience. "Nasreen is fine."

"No!" exclaimed Mrs Khan sharply. "Nasreen is ... no ... fine ..." she struggled desperately.

"You mean, Nasreen is *not* fine," corrected Margot.

"Nasreen is *not* fine," repeated Mrs Khan obediently.

"Is something wrong at school?" asked Margot. She glanced at her watch and noted with relief that their time was up.

Mrs Khan saw the movement. She stood up, twisting the ends of her veil in her fingers.

"Yes, it is time for me to go," said Margot, thankfully. She was really not in the mood for trying to extricate sufficient English out of Mrs Khan to find out what was bothering her.

"If you have a problem with Nasreen, the best thing to do is talk to the school," said Margot. "Perhaps your husband can. He speaks good English, doesn't he?" Then, giving her a kindly pat on the arm, she gathered up her text book.

"Try and work through the exercises we have covered today, OK? and I'll see you next week." Then she made her own way to the front door and opened it.

"Goodbye, Mrs Khan."

Mrs Khan didn't reply, but stood in the semi-darkness at the rear of the hall. She looked as if she were being swallowed up within her satin tunic and pyjamas, as she clutched the veil around herself.

"By-ee!" repeated Margot, giving a cheery wave, and shut the front door behind her.

"Nasreen! Nasreen! Come on, we'll miss the bus!" Louise Dibben danced impatiently at her friend's elbow, as she stood in front of the long mirror, fluffing out her hair and squirting clouds of hair lacquer into it.

"How do I look?" asked Nasreen, twisting her head to examine her profile.

"You look great, really great! Now come on. If we miss the bus it will all be for nothing."

"OK, I'm coming." She gave a last critical glance at herself. The transformation was pretty good. From her demure, sexless school uniform with headscarf and slacks for modesty, she had squeezed herself into a tight elasticated pair of jeans for which she had secretly saved up for weeks to buy. They flattered her figure, she thought, emphasising her long legs and narrow waist.

"Does my bum look too big?" she asked, turning sideways.

"You look great, I tell you," insisted Louise, "and I like your top an' all," she added. "You got better boobs than me, lucky thing. But hurry up."

"We're all right for time," said Nasreen, glancing at her watch. "Stop panicking!

We've got five minutes yet. I've got to do me eyes."

Louise sighed and sat on her bed. "God! If your mum and dad could see you now they'd have a blooming fit."

"My dad would kill me," murmured Nasreen, as she brushed the mascara on to her eyelashes.

Nasreen had taken to coming back to Louise's house most days after school. Gradually she had built up a secret wardrobe of leggies and low-cut tops, of miniskirts and T-shirts, sometimes plain and sometimes with slogans brazened across her chest.

"My forbidden clothes," she would laugh. She felt like Cinderella transforming herself to go out and have a ball, then rushing back to change into her uniform, headscarf and dull slacks, so that when she went back home she would once more be the demure, innocent little girl her parents thought she was.

Nasreen still shuddered when she remembered the pain of those early days at Merton Close. She had never been made to feel different before. But now all people seemed to see were her differences: her different coloured skin, her different clothes, her different voice and, most of all, her different religion. She was nothing but a Paki, until Louise decided to be her friend.

Louise was brash, Louise was loud, Louise was a leader. People listened to her. She seemed so grown-up. She was the first to perm her hair and wear tight, short skirts; she was the first to have a boyfriend and sit smoking in the bus shelter with

him. She had opinions, and talked back to teachers, so Nasreen was astonished when, one day, Louise marched up to her with a maths book and said, "Hey, Nasreen! You're good at maths. Help me with this."

They began going to each other's houses, but Nasreen knew her mother didn't like Louise and thought she was a bad influence so, instead, she only went round to Louise's house.

Nasreen loved the Dibben household. It was so different from her own clean, silent, scrupulously tidy home. Here it looked as if a tornado had struck it most of the time: always buried under a rubble of toys and washing, of babies' bottles and half-chewed rusks. Yet it was a good-natured chaos, and no one minded if she and Louise slumped across the sofa watching television and munching sandwiches.

"Wanna go with me to the disco?" Louise asked her one day.

"Oh, no! I couldn't!" Nasreen looked shocked at the prospect, then disappointed because she wished she could go. "I'd never be allowed," she said, sadly.

"Don't tell 'em then," snapped Louise, bold as brass.

"Anyway, I've got no clothes," added Nasreen. "I couldn't go like this!"

"Borrow mine," retorted Louise. Then she shrieked excitedly. "Hey! Let me dress you up! Please, Nasreen! Just for fun!"

So that's how it all started.

"There! OK?" She turned round to show her friend her face with her painted eyelids, stiff, blackened lashes, the hint of blusher on her cheeks and just the right shade of lipstick to tone in.

"Beautiful!" exclaimed Louise, generously. "Now let's go!"

The two girls clattered downstairs.

An admiring whistle rang out from the kitchen. Louise's younger brother, Craig, gave a cheeky wave. "Like your jeans, Nasreen! Sexeee!"

"Oh shut up!" squealed Nasreen, but she was pleased.

Sitting at the back of the bus, Nasreen and Louise admired each other and laughed at the world they had set out to conquer. In ten minutes they had alighted in the centre of town and made their way along to the precinct where they knew all their friends would be congregating.

"Carl's there," Louise hissed at her friend.

"So?" exclaimed Nasreen, flushing.

"You know you want to get off with him, and he's just split up with Denise."

"Has he?" cried Nasreen. "Why didn't you tell me before? Oh God, how do I look?"

"I've told you. You look fabulous. If he doesn't fall for you, he's a blind dope. Oh good, there's Mark," Louise squealed, and ran over to join her boyfriend.

The telephone rang. "It's me ..."

"Where are you?" wailed Mrs Khan. "Why weren't you on the bus?"

"Mum, I went back to Louise's house. We're doing our homework together. She's miles better at geography than me, and she's helping me," explained Nasreen, convincingly.

"But what about tea?" asked Mrs Khan. "I've got yours all ready here."

"Sorry, Mum," said Nasreen. "Louise's mum gave me some, so I'm fine. Must go. We've got tons to get done."

"When will you be home?" asked Mrs Khan quickly, trying to hang on to her daughter's voice.

"Well ..." Nasreen answered vaguely. "I think we've got another hour or two's work, because after geography, I said I'd help Louise with her maths. I'm better at that than her. OK?"

Mrs Khan hesitated, trying desperately to assert her authority.

"Get back before your dad does, won't you?"

"Of course I will, Mum. Must go. Bye!" And the phone went dead.

"OK?" asked Carl as she came out of the phone booth.

"Yeh!" Nasreen smiled sweetly at him, and slipped her arm in his.

"Have we time to go to the Flamingo? Have a quick drink?" asked Carl. "Louise and Mark have gone on ahead."

"Of course!" cried Nasreen, happily. "But I've got to be changed and on that eight o'clock bus home. Me dad gets in at nine, and I've got to make it before he does, or else there'll be hell to pay."

Mrs Khan stood in the bay window. Although darkness had fallen, she hadn't put on the light, but had drawn aside the net curtains to gaze, invisibly, up and down the empty street outside.

A hard lump of anxiety pressed into her chest so that it hurt to breathe. She was afraid, but then she realised she had always been afraid. Ever since Nasreen had moved up into secondary school, things had changed.

They used to walk together, side by side, friends; but then Nasreen took to going on ahead or dawdling behind her mother. Even the way she walked changed. Instead of the leisurely, shy walk, she now strode, long-legged, looking more and more like a western girl despite her head-scarf and the slacks under her school uniform. On approaching the school gates she would suddenly see her friends and, tossing out the word "goodbye" as if to no one in particular, she would disappear into the school, arms linked and immersed in the sound of gossip and laughter. She never looked back these days.

That was when the lump of misery took residence in Mrs Khan's heart.

"They are taking her away ... taking her away ..." She hissed the words out in English, as if someone would hear and understand her fears.

She felt a sudden surge of anger as she remembered her English teacher.

"They? Who's they?" Mrs Khan could hear the indifferent voice as Margot Henderson asked the question.

"They? Why the Dibbens of course!" Mrs Khan answered it now to the empty room, spotlessly clean, neat and devoid of any signs of human activity—just as Mr Khan liked to have it when he came home.

The Dibbens. Mrs Khan clasped her arms tightly around her body, straitjacketing herself, as if afraid if she did not she might scream at the world: "I'm lonely! I'm lonely! And they're taking my child away from me."

"Nasreen?" The sound of the front door sent her scurrying to the hall. Nasreen tossed her schoolbag inside, and kicked the front door closed.

"Hi, Mum!" she said indifferently, and did not look her in the eye. "Sorry I'm late, we had tons of homework. I'm going to my room. I'm tired and I just want to flop!"

"Nasreen!" Mrs Khan reached out and touched her daughter's cheek. She wanted to clasp her, reclaim her. "Did you have supper?" she asked. "I made your favourite pakoras. Come to the kitchen and have some."

"No, Mum!" Nasreen refused impatiently. "I'm not hungry. I had plenty to eat at Louise's. Just let me go to my room," and she shook herself free from her mother's grasp and rushed upstairs.

Once in her room, she hastily removed the rest of her forbidden clothes. She carefully folded them into a carrier bag and tucked it right at the back of her wardrobe.

Then she sat in front of her mirror. Had her mother noticed remnants of make-up? She leaned forward to scrutinise herself and looked into her own eyes. They were still shining with excitement.

Carl had seen her home. Carefully, of course, because it wouldn't do for any of the neighbours to see her—especially anyone from her own community. They had hidden in a bus shelter while she took off her jeans and put back her school slacks under her uniform.

"What about the headscarf?" he asked, after she had shaken out her hair and re-plaited it. But she dropped her head with embarrassment. "Oh that doesn't matter," she said.

Of course, it did, and when he said "goodbye" to her at the corner—he kissed her till she felt she would faint—and hurriedly walked away, she tied on her headscarf when he was out of sight and went home slowly, giving time for her flushed cheeks to calm down.

Now, as she stared at her reflection, she felt guilty. She didn't like feeling guilty; it made her angry. She didn't want to think about the shock and disappointment her father would feel if he knew what she was doing; she didn't want to think of how she was hurting her mother. At the moment, it was her mother, above all, who made her angry. She was so pliable, so pathetically vulnerable; her whole life was devoted to serving. Serving her husband; serving her daughter. Nothing she did was for her own benefit. She allowed herself to be a victim.

"I won't be like that! I won't, I won't!" Nasreen swore to herself.

Suddenly, Nasreen heard the front door. She heard her mother's puzzled footsteps hurry into the hall.

"Nasreen! Nasreen!" It was her father's voice, rough with anger.

"Nasreen's up in her room," she heard her mother say nervously. "You're back early. Is everything all right?"

He ignored her and called again. "Nasreen! Get down here! I wish to speak to you." Fiercely he switched on all the lights.

Nasreen slowly descended the stairs, pausing halfway down, her pale face looming over the bannister.

"Hi, Dad!" She tried to sound unconcerned.

"Get down here." He prodded his finger into the air space before him.

She continued her descent, meeting her mother's puzzled eyes at the bottom. Then she faced her father.

"Here!" He prodded the air in front of him.

"Nasreen!" Mrs Khan touched her daughter's arm. She had never seen Mr Khan look so angry. Mrs Khan wanted to protect her. She clung to her arm, pulling her back.

"What is it, Rashid? What has she done? Please don't harm her!"

"Let go of her!" His voice was cold and determined. "Nasreen has shamed me and her family and her community, and she must be made to realise what she has done."

"How?" cried Mrs Khan. "What has she done? Nasreen?" She turned pitifully to her daughter. "What have you done?"

"She has been seen in the town without her veil and slacks, dressed like one of those loose English girls, wearing a tight miniskirt, high heels and made up like a prostitute. How dare you! How dare you do this to us." He began to remove his leather belt.

"No, Rashid, no!" begged Mrs Khan. "I'm sure Nasreen won't do this again, will you, Nasreen?"

"And it's not the first time." Mr Khan's voice choked with emotion. "I now hear that this has been going on for months. Everyone in the community knows about it. Everyone has been talking about it behind our backs. You have ridiculed me!"

"Nasreen!" She looked at her daughter for some sign of repentance. But to her amazement Nasreen stood before her father, upright and unflinching as he raised his arm, moved round her, and brought the belt down across her back.

"Why are you doing this, Nasreen?" the head of her school pleaded with her.

"Why do you go on behaving in a way which upsets your mother and father and your whole community. All you get is a beating. Is it really worth it?"

Usually, Nasreen took her beatings and remonstrations sullenly, and without a word, but this time she looked up at her head teacher and said quietly, "Sir, I'll be sixteen in two months' time. That's all the time I have left to be free. When I'm sixteen, they'll marry me off; I expect it'll be to some bloke from Pakistan who I've never met. I'm clever enough to go to university, aren't I? But I won't be allowed. I'll have to stay at home and have babies and be nothing but a good little house-wife, sewing and ironing and having a meal ready in the evening. That's how it'll be when I'm sixteen. That's how it'll be for the rest of my life. Well, sir, I've got two months left, and I don't care how often I get beaten, I'm going to go into town, and dress as I like, and smoke in shop doorways, and my dad'll have to kill me before he stops me having what free-dom is left."

"Did you ever find out what that Mrs Khan meant when she said, 'They are taking her away from me?'" asked the colleague.

She and Margot Henderson had met again in the precinct coffee shop.

"Funny you should ask," said Margot, putting down her coffee cup. "After I last saw you, I got a message to say that Mrs Khan wanted to give up the lessons. Can't say I was disappointed. The last I heard was that the daughter, Nasreen, had run away and gone to live with her best friend."

"What are you doing?" Louise woke and stared into the darkness. "It's the middle of the night. Are you ill?"

She could just make out Nasreen, standing in the centre of the bedroom.

"Nasreen!" She sat up in bed and switched on her table lamp. "What are you doing? Where are you going?"

Nasreen was fully dressed, but in her tunic, pyjamas and veil. By her side was a suitcase. She picked it up and moved towards the bedroom door.

"That's it for me now, Louise," she said quietly. "It's my birthday tomorrow."

"Yeh! I know. Me and the gang, we've all got a smashing party organised for you," cried Louise.

"Well, you'll have to have it without me," said Nasreen. "I'm going home. Don't try and stop me. Please—" She put out a resisting hand, as Louise flung her legs out of bed and made to hold her back.

"Just let me go. I know what I'm doing. I've had my fun, but it had to end. I made a pact with myself that when I'm sixteen I return to my community. It's where I really belong. Don't make it hard for me, Louise. Please. Thank you for everything you've done for me. Thank

your parents, too. I'll make it up to you one day. Promise. Meantime, just let me go without any fuss."

Then she slipped out of the door and was gone.

It wasn't quite dawn, yet Mrs Khan woke to see a rosy glow through the bedroom window. She had barely slept all night long, as she had barely slept since Nasreen left home. Now, with a dull curiosity, she slid out of bed without disturbing her sleeping husband, and went to the window.

"Rashid!" she called out uncontrollably.

He awoke instantly, alerted by the urgency in her voice. He went to her side and looked out of the window.

Nasreen had lit a bonfire. The flames shot upwards into the night sky. They could see her figure silhouetted against the firelight as from time to time she bent down and, taking a garment from the open suitcase, tossed it on to the fire. Sparks flew upwards, scattering like fireflies.

When she had emptied the suitcase, she stood transfixed for a while, staring into the embers, then, pulling her veil over her head and drawing it tightly round her shoulders, she turned towards the house.

"Nasreen! Nasreen!" whispered her mother. "At last! You have come back to us!"

after READING

UNDERSTANDING THE TEXT

1. With a partner, discuss the conflicts in this **story** between Nasreen and her parents, between Nasreen and her cultural background, and between Nasreen and herself. Do any of these conflicts compare directly with those you discussed in the "Before Reading" activity? In your notebook, **summarize** the conflicts in the story and how they are resolved.

2. Using a dictionary where necessary, write a **definition** of the words "staccato," "demure," "scrupulously," "rusks," and "precinct" as they are used in the **context** of this story. Add to this list definitions for any other words from the story that you had difficulty understanding.

3. Find examples of prejudice and racism in this story. Write brief statements in your notebook about the **characters** who exhibit this behaviour and how it makes the other characters feel. Identify characters in the story who seem to be completely free of any prejudicial or racist behaviour. Explain in a few sentences how they exhibit understanding and acceptance.

4. In a small group, discuss the feelings that readers have for Nasreen, her mother, her father, Margot Henderson, and Louise Dibben. How do our feelings toward the characters change as the events of the story unfold? In your notebook, summarize the main points of the group's discussion.

EXPLORING IDEAS AND IMPLICATIONS

5. a) This story takes place in England, and therefore it contains many British expressions and spellings. Make a two-column chart, writing words or expressions from the story that are examples of British English in the first column; in the second column write the equivalent word or expression from standard Canadian English. Begin your chart with "bloke," "maths," and "hair lacquer."

   b) Using the same type of chart, record in the first column words that are spelled differently in British English; in the second column rewrite the word using standard Canadian spelling. Begin your spelling chart with "Mrs" and "realised." You may wish to consult a Canadian dictionary.

6. Write a friendly letter from Nasreen to Louise that might have been sent about two weeks after Nasreen returned home. Explain in Nasreen's own **voice** why she chose to return to her parents' home and culture and why she burned her "forbidden clothes." With a partner, revise your letter, paying special attention to using relevant references to the events of the story and maintaining a consistent voice throughout. Rewrite your letter and be prepared to submit it for evaluation.

MAKING CONNECTIONS

7. Read the poem "Gravity" (page 235). With a partner, write a short **dialogue** between Nasreen and Louise in which they discuss the ideas in this **poem**. Include a statement from each about why she likes or dislikes the poem based on your understanding of her character from the story. Work with another partnership to revise and improve your dialogue. Rewrite the dialogue and be prepared to **role-play** it to the class. ■

Slaughtering Chickens

CHARLES FINN

"The life of the rooster was going
and there was no way to catch it."

BEFORE READING

As a class, brainstorm a list of arguments made by both vegetarians and meat eaters for their dietary decisions.

Two weeks ago, I stopped my neighbour Rick on the dirt road that winds through the community where we live in southeastern British Columbia. We leaned elbows out our respective pickup-truck windows and breathed in the clear pine-scented air. Rick is a quiet, likable man. One of the true gentle souls. He lives on a small homestead where he raises chickens, ducks, geese, goats and sheep. When I asked if he was going to be slaughtering chickens any time soon, there was a narrowing of his hazel-grey eyes.

For seven years I'd been a vegetarian. This past year I'd fallen off the wagon. I was eating meat and, if it was to continue, I thought I should at least do my own killing. Hypocrisy, I told Rick, had always been one of my strong suits—and I was hoping to change that.

On the morning Rick told me to come by, he was spreading a plastic red-and-white tablecloth over the circular dining-room table. A large wood stove pumped dense, friendly heat. He told me the table is where we would pluck the chickens' feathers after dipping the carcasses in hot water. We would gut and then hang the birds up to dry before wrapping. Because a day of slaughtering on the farm is no different from weeding carrots (they are all part of the cycle) we took time to chat and gossip. Rick offered me coffee. Because a day of slaughtering *is* different than weeding carrots, we indulged in a few extra jokes, trying to hold down the rising tide of anxiety.

The night before, Rick had caught the 10 chickens he wanted to slaughter. He'd put them in large paper feed sacks and tied the tops closed with orange baling twine. In the hen house, the bag Rick gave me was bright white with "Pro-Form Feeds" written in block letters across it. It was light as a feather.

Nearly everyone I know has at one point been vegetarian. I get the impression from some it's like experimenting with drugs. Philosophically, many are opposed to the battery-cage life commercially raised chickens go through, or the fear and growth hormones that live on in the animals' cells. I was here because an hour's drive away at the nearest IGA, a package of chicken comes shrink-wrapped in plastic on a Styrofoam tray, with an absorbent pad to soak up the blood.

I wasn't after blood. I was after owning up to the truth. Behind the woodshed, Rick swung an axe lazily and said, "This is your truth."

At my feet was the chopping block. It was a half-round of firewood with two nails tapped in it. The nail heads were sticking up, an inch apart, and I was to put the chicken's neck between them and pull back on the feet. The bird I had was a rooster. Its feathers were an orangey-gold, red like a woman's hair. In that moment, sun coming through the trees, it was one of the most beautiful things I had ever seen.

Was I really going to do this? Since being a boy, I'd never willfully killed another living thing. I'd never hunted or fished. Raising the axe over my head, I drew in a deep breath and whispered, "I'm sorry." I felt I was doing something intrinsically wrong.

North America has a strange relationship with death. It avoids it at all costs. Death used to be a part of everyday life. It used to be respected. Now it's ketchup on TV. It's shut away in nursing homes and hidden from view. As the axe came down, I closed my eyes. I did not hear the chop.

When I opened my eyes, I was surprised to see the hind end of the rooster had come away in my hand. I felt a wave of relief and then renewed panic. The feet exploded in a frenzy of kicking and shot straight up in the air. The neck was red and thick as a thumb; blood spurted from it. The only thing I could think to do was look at the head.

The rooster's head rested on the log exactly as it had before. The beak was draped over the far side and the eyes remained open. The feathers had fallen back to cover where the neck had been severed and, except for the blood sprayed on the ground, nothing appeared different. Then the light started to go.

A grey film crept into its eyes. It was like a spotlight turned off but still faintly glowing. I leaned closer and could see the rooster's life spiralling away. It was like watching water spin down a drain. The life of the rooster was going and there was no way to catch it. I stood not making a sound and watched what is indisputably a miracle. The light behind the eye faded and a grey eyelid rose up and covered the pupil. The rooster was dead.

That day I came away with a better understanding not of death, but of life. I can't say exactly what it is, but I feel it deep in my nature.

The chicken Rick gave me sits in my freezer. It will get eaten, but I'm waiting to have some friends over. What has changed is not my renewed vegetarianism, but the length of the grace I say before meals.

Now when a carnivore friend I know regales me with stories of great steaks he has known, I simply nod. He says not a single tofu has died to keep his skinny butt alive. I agree, and then when he's done, I tell him of the rooster.

Of the light leaving its eye.

after READING

UNDERSTANDING THE TEXT

1. a) Make a two-column chart in your notebook. In the first column, record the details from the **essay** that come directly from the writer's personal experience. In the second column, record statements of opinion made by the writer in the essay.
    b) Use your chart to discuss with a partner whether you consider "Slaughtering Chickens" to be a personal essay or an opinion piece. Compare your decision with the rest of the class.

2. In your notebook, write short **definitions** of "hypocrisy" and "intrinsically" as they are used in the **context** of this essay. Use a dictionary to verify or correct your definition.

EXPLORING IDEAS AND IMPLICATIONS

3. In your notebook, explain the **connotation** of the word "slaughtering" as it is used in the title and the essay. Make a list of other connotative language used by the author, and of details that are used to appeal to the emotions of the reader. Compare your list with that of a classmate.

4. In your notebook, explain the author's **explicit** and **implicit meanings** in the sentences, "That day I came away with a better understanding not of death, but of life" and "What has changed is not my renewed vegetarianism, but the length of the grace I say before meals."

5. Create an advertisement in which you advocate either vegetarianism or meat eating. Use a slogan, fonts, and visuals that will capture the attention of viewers. Present and explain your ad to your classmates. As a class, create a form to assess the effectiveness of each ad.

MAKING CONNECTIONS

6. Read "Forbidden Clothes" (pages 262–269). In a short essay, compare the **theme** of this **short story** with that of "Slaughtering Chickens." Revise and edit your essay in preparation for submission. ■

Excerpt From
The Pearl

JOHN STEINBECK

> "... he could feel the dark creeping things waiting for him
> to go out into the night. It was shadowy and dreadful, and yet
> it called to him and threatened him and challenged him."

BEFORE READING

In your notebook, write about what you would do if you won a million dollars.

The Pearl *follows the life of Kino, a poor pearl diver who discovers a large, absolutely perfect pearl on the bottom of the sea. He hopes that it will provide him with the means of supporting his family, but he soon learns that wealth can bring out the darkest evils in human nature.*

It is wonderful the way a little town keeps track of itself and all its units. If every single man and woman, child and baby, acts and conducts itself in a known pattern and breaks no walls and differs with no one and experiments in no way and is not sick and does not endanger the ease and peace of mind or steady unbroken flow of the town, then that unit can disappear and never be heard of. But let one man step out of the regular thought or the known and trusted pattern, and the nerves of the townspeople ring with nervousness and communication travels over the nerve lines of the town. Then every unit communicates to the whole.

Thus, in La Paz, it was known in the early morning through the whole town that Kino was going to sell his pearl that day. It was known among the neighbors in the brush huts, among the pearl fishermen; it was known among the Chinese grocery-store owners; it was known in the church, for the altar boys whispered about it. Word of it crept in among the nuns; the beggars in front of the church spoke of it, for they would be there to take the tithe of the first fruits of the luck. The little boys knew about it with excitement, but most of all the pearl buyers knew about it, and when the day had come, in the offices of the pearl buyers, each man sat alone with his little black velvet tray, and each man rolled the pearls about with his fingertips and considered his part in the picture.

It was supposed that the pearl buyers were individuals acting alone, bidding against one another for the pearls the fishermen brought in. And once it had been so. But this was a wasteful method, for often, in the excitement of bidding for a fine pearl, too great a price had been paid to the fishermen. This was extravagant and not to be countenanced. Now there was only one pearl buyer with many hands, and the men who sat in their offices and waited for Kino knew what price they would offer, how high they would bid, and what method each one would use. And although these men would not profit beyond their salaries, there was excitement among the pearl buyers, for there was excitement in the hunt, and if it be a man's function to break down a price, then he must take joy and satisfaction in breaking it as far down as possible. For every man in the world functions to the best of his ability, and no one does less than his best, no matter what he may think about it. Quite apart from any reward they might get, from any word of praise, from any promotion, a pearl buyer was a pearl buyer, and the best and happiest pearl buyer was he who bought for the lowest prices.

The sun was hot yellow that morning, and it drew the moisture from the estuary and from the Gulf and hung it in shimmering scarves in the air so that the air vibrated and vision was insubstantial. A vision hung in the air to the north of the city—the vision of a mountain that was over two hundred miles away, and the high slopes of this mountain were swaddled with pines and a great stone peak arose above the timber line.

And the morning of this day the canoes lay lined up on the beach; the fishermen did not go out to dive for pearls, for there would be too much happening, too many things to see when Kino went to sell the great pearl.

In the brush houses by the shore Kino's neighbors sat long over their breakfasts, and they spoke of what they would do if they had found the pearl. And one man said that he would give it as a present to the Holy Father in Rome. Another said that he would buy Masses for the souls of his family for a thousand years. Another thought he might take the money and distribute it among the poor of La Paz; and a fourth thought of all the good things one could do with the money from the pearl, of all the charities, benefits, of all the rescues one could perform if one had money. All of the neighbors hoped that sudden wealth would not turn Kino's head, would not make a rich man of him, would not graft onto him the evil limbs of greed and hatred and coldness. For Kino was a well-liked man; it would be a shame if the pearl destroyed him. "That good wife Juana," they said, "and the beautiful baby Coyotito, and the others to come. What a pity it would be if the pearl should destroy them all."

For Kino and Juana this was the morning of mornings of their lives, comparable only to the day when the baby had been born. This was to be the day from which all other days would take their arrangement. Thus they would say, "It was two years before we sold the pearl," or, "It was six weeks after we sold the pearl." Juana, considering the matter, threw caution to the winds, and she dressed Coyotito in the clothes she had prepared for his baptism, when there would be money for his baptism. And Juana combed and braided her hair and tied the ends with two little bows of red ribbon, and she put on her marriage skirt and waist. The sun was quarter high when they were ready. Kino's ragged white clothes were clean at least, and this was the last day of his raggedness. For tomorrow, or even this afternoon, he would have new clothes.

The neighbors, watching Kino's door through the crevices in their brush houses, were dressed and ready too. There was no self-consciousness about their joining Kino and Juana to go pearl selling. It was expected, it was an historic moment, they would be crazy if they didn't go. It would be almost a sign of unfriendship.

Juana put on her head shawl carefully, and she draped one long end under her right elbow and gathered it with her right hand so that a hammock hung under her arm, and in this little hammock she placed Coyotito, propped up against the head shawl so that he could see everything and perhaps remember. Kino put on his large straw hat and felt it with his hand to see that it was properly placed, not on the back or side of his head, like a rash, unmarried, irresponsible man, and not flat as an elder would wear it, but tilted a little forward to show aggressiveness and seriousness and vigor. There is a great deal to be seen in the tilt of a hat on a man. Kino slipped his feet into his sandals and pulled the thongs up over his heels. The great pearl was wrapped in an old soft piece of deerskin and placed in a little leather bag, and the leather bag was in a pocket in Kino's shirt. He folded his blanket carefully and draped it in a narrow strip over his left shoulder, and now they were ready.

Kino stepped with dignity out of the house, and Juana followed him, carrying Coyotito. And as they marched up the freshet-washed alley toward the town, the neighbors joined them. The houses belched people; the doorways spewed out children. But because of the seriousness of the occasion, only one man walked with Kino, and that was his brother, Juan Tomás.

Juan Tomás cautioned his brother. "You must be careful to see they do not cheat you," he said.

And, "Very careful," Kino agreed.

"We do not know what prices are paid in other places," said Juan Tomás. "How can we know what is a fair price, if we do not know what the pearl buyer gets for the pearl in another place."

"That is true," said Kino, "but how can we know? We are here, we are not there."

As they walked up toward the city the crowd grew behind them, and Juan Tomás, in pure nervousness, went on speaking.

"Before you were born, Kino," he said, "the old ones thought of a way to get more money for their pearls. They thought it would be better if they had an agent who took all the pearls to the capital and sold them there and kept only his share of the profit."

Kino nodded his head. "I know," he said. "It was a good thought."

"And so they got such a man," said Juan Tomás, "and they pooled the pearls, and they started him off. And he was never heard of again and the pearls were lost. Then they got another man, and they started him off, and he was never heard of again. And so they gave the whole thing up and went back to the old way."

"I know," said Kino. "I have heard our father tell of it. It was a good idea, but it was against religion, and the Father made that very clear. The loss of the pearl was punishment visited on those who tried to leave their station. And the Father made it clear that each man and woman is like a soldier sent by God to guard some part of the castle of the Universe. And some are in the ramparts and some far deep in the darkness of the walls. But each one must remain faithful to his post and must not go running about, else the castle is in danger from the assaults of Hell."

"I have heard him make that sermon," said Juan Tomás. "He makes it every year."

The brothers, as they walked along, squinted their eyes a little, as they and their grandfathers and their great-grandfathers had done for four hundred years, since first the strangers came with argument and authority and gunpowder to back up both. And in the four hundred years Kino's people had learned only one defense—a slight slitting of the eyes and a slight tightening of the lips and a retirement. Nothing could break down this wall, and they could remain whole within the wall.

The gathering procession was solemn, for they sensed the importance of this day,

and any children who showed a tendency to scuffle, to scream, to cry out, to steal hats and rumple hair, were hissed to silence by their elders. So important was this day that an old man came to see, riding on the stalwart shoulders of his nephew. The procession left the brush huts and entered the stone and plaster city where the streets were a little wider and there were narrow pavements beside the buildings. And as before, the beggars joined them as they passed the church; the grocers looked out at them as they went by; the little saloons lost their customers and the owners closed up shop and went along. And the sun beat down on the streets of the city and even tiny stones threw shadows on the ground.

The news of the approach of the procession ran ahead of it, and in their little dark offices the pearl buyers stiffened and grew alert. They got out papers so that they could be at work when Kino appeared, and they put their pearls in the desks, for it is not good to let an inferior pearl be seen beside a beauty. And word of the loveliness of Kino's pearl had come to them. The pearl buyers' offices were clustered together in one narrow street, and they were barred at the windows, and wooden slats cut out the light so that only a soft gloom entered the offices.

A stout slow man sat in an office waiting. His face was fatherly and benign, and his eyes twinkled with friendship. He was a caller of good mornings, a ceremonious shaker of hands, a jolly man who knew all jokes and yet who hovered close to sadness, for in the midst of a laugh he could remember the death of your aunt, and his eyes could become wet with sorrow for your loss. This morning he had placed a flower in a vase on his desk, a single scarlet hibiscus, and the vase sat beside the black velvet-lined pearl tray in front of him. He was shaved close to the blue roots of his beard, and his hands were clean and his nails polished. His door stood open to the morning, and he hummed under his breath while his right hand practiced legerdemain. He rolled a coin back and forth over his knuckles and made it appear and disappear, made it spin and sparkle. The coin winked into sight and as quickly slipped out of sight, and the man did not even watch his own performance. The fingers did it all mechanically, precisely, while the man hummed to himself and peered out the door. Then he heard the tramp of feet of the approaching crowd, and the fingers of his right hand worked faster and faster until, as the figure of Kino filled the doorway, the coin flashed and disappeared.

"Good morning, my friend," the stout man said. "What can I do for you?"

Kino stared into the dimness of the little office, for his eyes were squeezed from the outside glare. But the buyer's eyes had become as steady and cruel and unwinking as a hawk's eyes, while the rest of his face smiled in greeting. And secretly, behind his desk, his right hand practiced with the coin.

"I have a pearl," said Kino. And Juan Tomás stood beside him and snorted a little at the understatement. The neighbors peered around the doorway, and a line of little boys clambered on the window bars and looked through. Several little boys, on their hands and knees, watched the scene around Kino's legs.

"You have a pearl," the dealer said. "Sometimes a man brings in a dozen. Well, let us see your pearl. We will value it and give you the best price." And his fingers worked furiously with the coin.

Now Kino instinctively knew his own dramatic effects. Slowly he brought out the leather bag, slowly took from it the soft and dirty piece of deerskin, and then he let the great pearl roll into the black velvet tray, and instantly his eyes went to the buyer's face. But there was no sign, no movement, the face did not change, but the secret hand behind the desk missed in its precision. The coin stumbled over a knuckle and slipped silently into the dealer's lap. And the fingers behind the desk curled into a fist. When the right hand came out of hiding, the forefinger touched the great pearl, rolled it on the black velvet; thumb and forefinger picked it up and brought it near to the dealer's eyes and twirled it in the air.

Kino held his breath, and the neighbors held their breath, and the whispering went back through the crowd. "He is inspecting it—No price has been mentioned yet— They have not come to a price."

Now the dealer's hand had become a personality. The hand tossed the great pearl back in the tray, the forefinger poked and insulted it, and on the dealer's face there came a sad and contemptuous smile.

"I am sorry, my friend," he said, and his shoulders rose a little to indicate that the misfortune was no fault of his.

"It is a pearl of great value," Kino said.

The dealer's fingers spurned the pearl so that it bounced and rebounded softly from the side of the velvet tray.

"You have heard of fool's gold," the dealer said. "This pearl is like fool's gold. It is too large. Who would buy it? There is no market for such things. It is a curiosity only. I am sorry. You thought it was a thing of value, and it is only a curiosity."

Now Kino's face was perplexed and worried. "It is the Pearl of the World," he cried. "No one has ever seen such a pearl."

"On the contrary," said the dealer, "it is large and clumsy. As a curiosity it has interest; some museum might perhaps take it to place in a collection of seashells. I can give you, say, a thousand pesos."

Kino's face grew dark and dangerous. "It is worth fifty thousand," he said. "You know it. You want to cheat me."

And the dealer heard a little grumble go through the crowd as they heard his price. And the dealer felt a little tremor of fear.

"Do not blame me," he said quickly. "I am only an appraiser. Ask the others. Go to their offices and show your pearl—or better let them come here, so that you can see there is no collusion. Boy," he called. And when his servant looked through the rear door, "Boy, go to such a one, and such another one and such a third one. Ask them to step in here and do not tell them why. Just say that I will be pleased to see them." And his right hand went behind the desk and pulled another coin from his pocket, and the coin rolled back and forth over the knuckles.

Kino's neighbors whispered together. They had been afraid of something like this. The pearl was large, but it had a strange color. They had been suspicious of it from the first. And after all, a thousand pesos was not to be thrown away. It was comparative wealth to a man who was not wealthy. And suppose Kino took a thousand pesos. Only yesterday he had nothing.

But Kino had grown tight and hard. He felt the creeping of fate, the circling of wolves, the hover of vultures. He felt the evil coagulating about him, and he was helpless to protect himself. He heard in his ears the evil music. And on the black velvet the great pearl glistened, so that the dealer could not keep his eyes from it.

The crowd in the doorway wavered and broke and let the three pearl dealers through. The crowd was silent now, fearing to miss a word, to fail to see a gesture or an expression. Kino was silent and watchful. He felt a little tugging at his back, and he turned and looked in Juana's eyes, and when he looked away he had renewed strength.

The dealers did not glance at one another nor at the pearl. The man behind the desk said, "I have put a value on this pearl. The owner here does not think it fair. I will ask you to examine this—this thing and make an offer. Notice," he said to Kino, "I have not mentioned what I have offered."

The first dealer, dry and stringy, seemed now to see the pearl for the first time. He took it up, rolled it quickly between thumb and forefinger, and then cast it contemptuously back into the tray.

"Do not include me in the discussion," he said dryly. "I will make no offer at all. I do not want it. This is not a pearl—it is a monstrosity." His thin lips curled.

Now the second dealer, a little man with a shy soft voice, took up the pearl, and he examined it carefully. He took a glass from his pocket and inspected it under magnification. Then he laughed softly.

"Better pearls are made of paste," he said. "I know these things. This is soft and chalky, it will lose its color and die in a few months. Look—." He offered the glass to Kino, showed him how to use it, and Kino, who had never seen a pearl's surface magnified, was shocked at the strange-looking surface.

The third dealer took the pearl from Kino's hands. "One of my clients likes such things," he said. "I will offer five hundred pesos, and perhaps I can sell it to my client for six hundred."

Kino reached quickly and snatched the pearl from his hand. He wrapped it in the deerskin and thrust it inside his shirt.

The man behind the desk said, "I'm a fool, I know, but my first offer stands. I still offer one thousand. What are you doing?" he asked, as Kino thrust the pearl out of sight.

"I am cheated," Kino cried fiercely. "My pearl is not for sale here. I will go, perhaps even to the capital."

Now the dealers glanced quickly at one another. They knew they had played too hard; they knew they would be disciplined for their failure, and the man at the desk said quickly, "I might go to fifteen hundred."

But Kino was pushing his way through the crowd. The hum of talk came to him dimly, his rage blood pounded in his ears, and he burst through and strode away. Juana followed, trotting after him.

When the evening came, the neighbors in the brush houses sat eating their corn-cakes and beans, and they discussed the great theme of the morning. They did not know, it seemed a fine pearl to them, but they had never seen such a pearl before, and surely the dealers knew more about the value of pearls than they. "And mark this," they said. "Those dealers did not discuss these things. Each of the three knew the pearl was valueless."

"But suppose they had arranged it before?"

"If that is so, then all of us have been cheated all of our lives."

Perhaps, some argued, perhaps it would have been better if Kino took the one thousand five hundred pesos. That is a great deal of money, more than he has ever seen. Maybe Kino is being a pig-headed fool. Suppose he should really go to the capital and find no buyer for his pearl. He would never live that down.

And now, said other fearful ones, now that he had defied them, those buyers will not want to deal with him at all. Maybe Kino has cut off his own head and destroyed himself.

And others said, Kino is a brave man and a fierce man; he is right. From his courage we may all profit. These were proud of Kino.

In his house Kino squatted on his sleeping mat, brooding. He had buried his pearl under a stone of the fire hole in his house, and he stared at the woven tules of his sleeping mat until the crossed design danced in his head. He had lost one world and had not gained another. And Kino was afraid. Never in his life had he been far from home. He was afraid of strangers and of strange places. He was terrified of that monster of strangeness they called the capital. It lay over the water and through the mountains, over a thousand miles, and every strange terrible mile was frightening. But Kino had lost his old world and he must clamber on to a new one. For his dream of the future was real and never to be destroyed, and he had said "I will go," and that made a real thing too. To determine to go and to say it was to be halfway there.

Juana watched him while he buried his pearl, and she watched him while she cleaned Coyotito and nursed him, and Juana made the corncakes for supper.

Juan Tomás came in and squatted down beside Kino and remained silent for a long time, until at last Kino demanded, "What else could I do? They are cheats."

Juan Tomás nodded gravely. He was the elder, and Kino looked to him for wisdom. "It is hard to know," he said. "We do know that we are cheated from birth to the overcharge on our coffins. But we survive. You have defied not the pearl buyers, but the whole structure, the whole way of life, and I am afraid for you."

"What have I to fear but starvation?" Kino asked.

But Juan Tomás shook his head slowly. "That we must all fear. But suppose you are correct—suppose your pearl is of great value—do you think then the game is over?"

"What do you mean?"

"I don't know," said Juan Tomás, "but I am afraid for you. It is new ground you are walking on, you do not know the way."

"I will go. I will go soon," said Kino.

"Yes," Juan Tomás agreed. "That you must do. But I wonder if you will find it any different in the capital. Here, you have friends and me, your brother. There, you will have no one."

"What can I do?" Kino cried. "Some deep outrage is here. My son must have a chance. That is what they are striking at. My friends will protect me."

"Only so long as they are not in danger or discomfort from it," said Juan Tomás. He arose, saying, "Go with God."

And Kino said, "Go with God," and did not even look up, for the words had a strange chill in them.

Long after Juan Tomás had gone Kino sat brooding on his sleeping mat. A lethargy had settled on him, and a little gray hopelessness. Every road seemed blocked against him. In his head he heard only the dark music of the enemy. His senses were burningly alive, but his mind went back to the deep participation with all things, the gift he had from his people. He heard every little sound of the gathering night, the sleepy complaint of settling birds, the love agony of cats, the strike and withdrawal of little waves on the beach, and the simple hiss of distance. And he could smell the sharp odor of exposed kelp from the receding tide. The little flare of the twig fire made the design on his sleeping mat jump before his entranced eyes.

Juana watched him with worry, but she knew him and she knew she could help him best by being silent and by being near. And as though she too could hear the Song of Evil, she fought it, singing softly the melody of the family, of the safety and warmth and wholeness of the family. She held Coyotito in her arms and sang the song to him, to keep the evil out, and her voice was brave against the threat of the dark music.

Kino did not move nor ask for his supper. She knew he would ask when he wanted it. His eyes were entranced, and he could sense the wary, watchful evil outside the brush house; he could feel the dark creeping things waiting for him to go out into the night. It was shadowy and dreadful, and yet it called to him and threatened him and challenged him. His right hand went into his shirt and felt his knife; his eyes were wide; he stood up and walked to the doorway.

Juana willed to stop him; she raised her hand to stop him, and her mouth opened with terror. For a long moment Kino looked out into the darkness and then he stepped outside. Juana heard the little rush, the grunting struggle, the blow. She froze with terror for a moment, and then her lips drew back from her teeth like a cat's lips. She set Coyotito down on the ground. She seized a stone from the fireplace and rushed outside, but it was over by then. Kino lay on the ground, struggling to rise, and there was no one near him. Only the shadows and the strike and rush of waves and the hiss of distance. But the evil was all about, hidden behind the brush fence, crouched beside the house in the shadow, hovering in the air.

Juana dropped her stone, and she put her arms around Kino and helped him to his feet and supported him into the house. Blood oozed down from his scalp and there was a long deep cut in his cheek from ear to chin, a deep, bleeding slash. And Kino was only half conscious. He shook his head from side to side. His shirt was torn open and his clothes half pulled off. Juana sat him down on his sleeping mat and she wiped the thickening blood from his face with her skirt. She brought him pulque to drink in a little pitcher, and still he shook his head to clear out the darkness.

"Who?" Juana asked.

"I don't know," Kino said. "I didn't see."

Now Juana brought her clay pot of water and she washed the cut on his face while he stared dazed ahead of him.

"Kino, my husband," she cried, and his eyes stared past her. "Kino, can you hear me?"

"I hear you," he said dully.

"Kino, this pearl is evil. Let us destroy it before it destroys us. Let us crush it between two stones. Let us—let us throw it back in the sea where it belongs. Kino, it is evil, it is evil!"

And as she spoke the light came back in Kino's eyes so that they glowed fiercely and his muscles hardened and his will hardened.

"No," he said. "I will fight this thing. I will win over it. We will have our chance." His fist pounded the sleeping mat. "No one shall take our good fortune from us," he said. His eyes softened then and he raised a gentle hand to Juana's shoulder. "Believe me," he said. "I am a man." And his face grew crafty.

"In the morning we will take our canoe and we will go over the sea and over the mountains to the capital, you and I. We will not be cheated. I am a man."

"Kino," she said huskily, "I am afraid. A man can be killed. Let us throw the pearl back into the sea."

"Hush," he said fiercely. "I am a man. Hush." And she was silent, for his voice was command. "Let us sleep a little," he said. "In the first light we will start. You are not afraid to go with me?"

"No, my husband."

His eyes were soft and warm on her then, his hand touched her cheek. "Let us sleep a little," he said.

after READING

UNDERSTANDING THE TEXT

1. Create a chart like the one below in which you record how this excerpt makes you feel about Kino, Juana, and the pearl buyers.

Character	Your Feelings	Reason for Your Feelings
Kino		
Juana		
Pearl Buyers		

2. a) With a partner, examine the description of the pearl dealer on page 278. Make a list of words that reveal the **character** of this person. Label as either positive or negative the **connotation** of each of the words. Compare your list with those of the rest of the class.

   b) Name at least three other ways we learn about the characters in this excerpt. Give an example of each method used.

3. Explain the purpose of Juan Tomás telling Kino the story of the old ones hiring the agent (pages 277–278). Consider the effects of this story on both Kino and on the reader.

4. Reread the first two sentences of paragraph 2. Defend Steinbeck's use of the passive **voice** to emphasize the meaning of his sentences.

EXPLORING IDEAS AND IMPLICATIONS

5. a) In a small group, list at least three options that Kino has once he leaves the pearl buyers in La Paz. For each of the options show the possible outcomes.

b) Imagine you are the author of this novel. Choose one option from your list and develop a detailed **plot** line for the rest of the book. Share your plot line with the rest of the class.

6. Each chapter in a novel serves several purposes. Outline the purposes of this chapter in the novel.

7. "The people of the village are ruled by both religion and superstition. Both conspire to keep the villagers in their rightful place." Write an **argumentative essay** agreeing or disagreeing with the second statement. Use cause and effect as an organizer in at least one of your paragraphs. (See The Reference Shelf, page 438.)

8. a) With a partner, prepare a news broadcast for radio in which you report the events of the day covered in the chapter. Decide the interpretation you want to take and write your report using words that will encourage your **audience** to see the events in the same way you do.

b) Exchange your **report** with another partnership. Make revision suggestions about the content, voice, and organization. Revise, rehearse, and present your news report to the class.

c) As a class, create an evaluation form for oral performances. Assess each performance based on your evaluation form.

MAKING CONNECTIONS

9. a) Compare the description of the pearl buyers' practices (page 276) with the way some modern businesses and multinational corporations function.

b) Prepare a **speech** to the villagers in which you explain the practices of the pearl buyers and suggest ways for them to deal with the current situation. (Remember: The villagers have been dealing with these same buyers for many years. They are not going to be happy hearing they have been cheated all these years.) ■

Kate's Poem

JEAN LITTLE

BEFORE READING

As a class, discuss the following question: Which is better: sticking to what you know, or taking a risk on an unknown course of action that could result in something better or worse than what you have?

When I opened my eyes this morning,
The day belonged to me.
The sky was mine and the sun,
And my feet got up dancing.
The marmalade was mine and the squares of sidewalk　　5
And all the birds in the trees.
So I stood and I considered
Stopping the world right there,
Making today go on and on forever.
But I decided not to.　　　　　　　　　　　10
I let the world spin on and I went to school.
I almost did it, but then, I said to myself,
"Who knows what you might be missing tomorrow?"

after READING

UNDERSTANDING THE TEXT

1. Describe the attitude of the **narrator** in the **poem**. Support your opinion with references to the text.

2. **a)** Define "omnipotence." Explain how the narrator captures the feeling that she's omnipotent.

   b) Consult an **etymological** dictionary to discover the origins of the word "omnipotence." In your notebook, write three other words that begin with the prefix "omni." Also, write five English words that are constructed from the same root word as "omnipotence." (See The Reference Shelf, pages 394–402.)

3. With a partner, examine the **voice**, vocabulary, and **diction** of the poem. From your examination, determine the age of the narrator and the **audience** she is addressing. Be sure to support your opinion with direct references to the poem.

4. In line 12, the pronoun "it" could refer to two things. In your notebook, explain why the use of the pronoun in this way is or is not confusing to the reader.

EXPLORING IDEAS AND IMPLICATIONS

5. Rewrite this poem in the third-person **point of view**. Reread it in its new form and describe in what ways the poem is more or less effective written this way.

MAKING CONNECTIONS

6. **a)** Using the "Zits" cartoon on page 183 as a model, create a comic strip of this poem using Jeremy as the main **character**.

   b) Write an explanation of how you have created both **implicit** and **explicit meanings** through the visuals and the printed word. Display your finished cartoon and your explanation.

   c) As a class, create an assessment form for each comic strip. ■

Fern Hill

DYLAN THOMAS

BEFORE READING

With a partner, choose one **stanza** from the **poem** and practise reading it aloud to each other. Pay particular attention to the punctuation for clues to the rhythm of the lines and appropriate pauses. Read your stanza aloud to the class in the same order as the poem. As a class, discuss the variations in the readings.

Now as I was young and easy under the apple boughs
About the lilting house and happy as the grass was green,
  The night above the dingle starry,
   Time let me hail and climb
  Golden in the heydays of his eyes,   5
And honoured among wagons I was prince of the apple towns
And once below a time I lordly had the trees and leaves
   Trail with daisies and barley
  Down the rivers of the windfall light.

And as I was green and carefree, famous among the barns 10
About the happy yard and singing as the farm was home,
  In the sun that is young once only,
   Time let me play and be
  Golden in the mercy of his means,
And green and golden I was huntsman and herdsman, the calves 15
Sang to my horn, the foxes on the hills barked clear and cold,
   And the sabbath rang slowly
  In the pebbles of the holy streams.

All the sun long it was running, it was lovely, the hay
Fields high as the house, the tunes from the chimneys, it was air   20
   And playing, lovely and watery
      And fire green as grass.
   And nightly under the simple stars
As I rode to sleep the owls were bearing the farm away,
All the moon long I heard, blessed among stables, the nightjars   25
   Flying with the ricks, and the horses
      Flashing into the dark.

And then to awake, and the farm, like a wanderer white
With the dew, come back, the cock on his shoulder: it was all
   Shining, it was Adam and maiden,   30
      The sky gathered again
   And the sun grew round that very day.
So it must have been after the birth of the simple light
In the first, spinning place, the spellbound horses walking warm
   Out of the whinnying green stable   35
      On to the fields of praise.

And honoured among foxes and pheasants by the gay house
Under the new made clouds and happy as the heart was long,
   In the sun born over and over,
      I ran my heedless ways,   40
   My wishes raced through the house high hay
And nothing I cared, at my sky blue trades, that time allows
In all his tuneful turning so few and such morning songs
   Before the children green and golden
      Follow him out of grace,   45

Nothing I cared, in the lamb white days, that time would take me
Up to the swallow thronged loft by the shadow of my hand,
   In the moon that is always rising,
      Nor that riding to sleep
   I should hear him fly with the high fields   50
And wake to the farm forever fled from the childless land.
Oh as I was young and easy in the mercy of his means,
      Time held me green and dying
   Though I sang in my chains like the sea.

after READING

1. Summarize the poem in a sentence starting, "This poem is about ..." In a small group, discuss your **summaries** and arrive at a common understanding of the poem.

2. In your notebook, write a statement of the **theme** of "Fern Hill."

3. Make a list of words that were unfamiliar to you when you first read the poem. Include a short **definition** beside each word.

4. a) Form an "expert" group consisting of all the people who read the same stanza as you did in "Before Reading." With your group members, explore that stanza for the following things:
   - references to colours or to objects that have colours closely associated with them
   - the significance of the colours in light of the subject of the poem
   - the **mood** in the stanza and the words and phrases that create that mood
   - religious references and their meanings

   b) Form new groups with one person from each "expert" group. Share the observations you made with your new group members. Take notes as each presenter speaks.

   c) At the end of the presentations, combine your observations about individual stanzas to make general observations about the whole poem. Record these observations on chart paper or on the board for the class to discuss.

EXPLORING IDEAS AND IMPLICATIONS

5. a) Identify the age of the child in the poem and the age of the **narrator** as he or she is telling about the experience. Explain the significance of the distance in age difference between the experience and the telling of the experience to the meaning of the poem.

   b) Explain why it is essential for us not to know we are "green and dying" when we are young.

   c) Write a letter to a much younger person, gently telling that person the things you think are essential for him or her to know in life. With a partner, revise and edit your letter.

MAKING CONNECTIONS

6. Find another poem that addresses the same theme as "Fern Hill." Bring your poem to class and have a "read-around" listening to each person's poem. Word-process your poem and, using electronic or print resources, find an illustration that complements the poem's main idea. Create a class **anthology** and post it in the classroom. ■

Wild Horse Shakes Her Mane

SANDY SHREVE

from "T'ai Chi Variations"

"The same techniques that were capable of developing internal power for combat also proved to be effective as life prolonging, healing and rejuvenating exercises."

—Master Liang Shou-Yu and Wu Wen-Ching

BEFORE READING

With a partner, discuss the difference between wild and domestic animals. Consider whether all wild animals can be domesticated. Discuss whether human beings can be divided into the same two categories: wild and domestic.

Everyone thought you were broken
in, tamed like that russet mare
standing in the pasture, her calm eye
on a man fixing the fence.

Everyone thought you were living   5
content within normal borders, but you
leave unnoticed,
wander unharnessed into the first
yellow strands of dawn, hear

distant violins linger over an oboe,   10
proclaim spring in the Appalachians.

You shed winter from your limbs,
reach into air as if to hold
sound in your open hands,
then give it to the wind again   15
and follow.

after READING

UNDERSTANDING THE TEXT

1. Identify to whom the **narrator** of this **poem** is speaking. Explain whether there is any ambiguity about who is being addressed.

2. Explain what the narrator means by the term "normal borders" in line 6. In your notebook, write a paragraph explaining whether borders are ever "normal."

3. Select one visual **image** from this poem and explain why you think it is or is not well chosen.

4. Describe the **mood** of this poem. Explain how the poet has used language, imagery, and a story line to create the mood.

EXPLORING IDEAS AND IMPLICATIONS

5. Write a few paragraphs explaining a possible relationship between the opening quotation from "T'ai Chi Variations" and the poem. Compare your observations with a partner. Be prepared to share both your views with the class.

6. Conduct research about areas of the world where herds of wild horses still exist, including the wild horses of Sable Island in Canada. Prepare an oral **report** to present to the class about the lives of these horses. Consider using technology and/or visual aids in your presentation.

MAKING CONNECTIONS

7. Listen to the music called "Appalachian Spring" by Aaron Copland. Listen for the violins playing over the oboe. Read about the music and what Copland said it was about. Write a report explaining the relationship between this poem and the music. ■

The Skater

CHARLES G.D. ROBERTS

BEFORE READING

Remember a time when you were completely alone. Recall how this isolation made you feel. Make a brief statement of those feelings in your notes.

My glad feet shod with the glittering steel
I was the god of the winged heel.

The hills in the far white sky were lost;
The world lay still in the wide white frost;

And the woods hung hushed in their long white dream   5
By the ghostly, glimmering, ice-blue stream.

Here was a pathway, smooth like glass,
Where I and the wandering wind might pass

To the far-off palaces, drifted deep,
Where Winter's retinue rests in sleep.   10

I followed the lure, I fled like a bird,
Till the startled hollows awoke and heard

A spinning whisper, a sibilant twang,
As the stroke of the steel on the tense ice rang;

And the wandering wind was left behind   15
As faster, faster I followed my mind;

Till the blood sang high in my eager brain,
And the joy of my flight was almost pain.

Then I stayed the rush of my eager speed
And silently went as a drifting seed,—   20

Slowly, furtively, till my eyes
Grew big with the awe of dim surmise,

And the hair on my neck began to creep
At hearing the wilderness talk in sleep.

Shapes in the fir-gloom drifted near.   25
In the deep of my heart I heard my fear;

And I turned and fled, like a soul pursued,
From the white, inviolate solitude.

after READING

1. Reread the **poem**, paying special attention to the **mood**. Write a description of the poet's mood at the beginning and the end of the poem and include details from the poem that illustrate his moods.

2. Compare the poet's feelings in the poem with those you recalled in the "Before Reading" activity. In a few sentences, make an observation about how different individuals feel when faced with isolation in nature.

3. Write a brief **definition** of "retinue," "sibilant," "furtively," and "inviolate" as they are used in the **context** of the poem. Check your definitions with those of another student, and use a dictionary to verify or amend your definitions where necessary. With your partner, discuss the importance of these words in the poem, and make notes on your discussion.

EXPLORING IDEAS AND IMPLICATIONS

4. This poem is written in rhyming couplets. With a partner, discuss why this poetic form is appropriate for a poem about skating. Make notes on your ideas and be prepared to share them with the rest of the class.

5. Locate at least three examples each of **metaphor**, **simile**, and alliteration in the poem. (See The Reference Shelf, page 425.) Record them in your notebook and make a statement about the effectiveness of each of these literary devices as they are used in this poem.

MAKING CONNECTIONS

6. Read "Erosion" (page 5). Discuss with a partner the similarities/differences between the relationships of human beings to nature in the two poems. Record your ideas in point-form notes. ■

The Agony Behind the Ecstasy of the Dance

JANICE MAWHINNEY

"You must smile brilliantly while
performing in intense pain."

BEFORE READING

In a group of three, discuss the qualities of a good dancer. What is your perception of students who seem devoted to becoming the best they can be in dance, drama, or sports? Be prepared to present your ideas to the class.

You are a dancer.

You live in an insular, mirrored world full of physical pain and exhaustion. "Pain is never absent," says a member of the National Ballet of Canada's artistic staff and long-time dancer.

You are constantly measured against perfection, and told after every rehearsal and performance the ways in which you failed to achieve that perfection. Your professional feedback is even officially called "corrections."

Sure, you're beautiful. But you're never beautiful enough. The rooms you work in are lined with mirrors to remind you of this. Keep looking. Keep trying.

Your body is routinely expected to do physically impossible things. No matter how fine your mind may be, your brain is treated as an accessory to your body. When you are creating new work with a choreographer, you are likely to be left completely in the dark about what character or emotion you are dancing.

Your coaches, teachers, directors and choreographers constantly refer to you as "boys" and "girls," never as the men and women you actually are. It's a clear message about your status, and you do take the message in: Within a dance company, you often refer to each other with babyish nicknames that would be unthinkable and considered demeaning in any other workplace.

To dance seriously, you sacrifice your time for family and friends. You probably hardly know your family members, and have few if any friends outside dance.

It is necessary to get to know your body and the way it works more intimately and profoundly than anyone in any other job ever has to, and then to ignore the messages of pain and fatigue it sends you.

You must smile brilliantly while performing in intense pain. You must communicate all the emotional complexities and subtleties of your role while performing feats that would cause other athletes to shudder.

Your art is ephemeral. It doesn't get published or recorded or framed and hung, and is rarely filmed. You go out there and drive yourself to the brink, enjoy the three minutes of applause, then put your feet in a bucket of ice and hope some of the people touched by your performance will remember.

The only people whose feedback really counts to you are the three or four individuals professionally critiquing you, and sometimes your colleagues. No one else understands. No one else matters.

The odds of your rising to the top are poor, and the process of learning that for yourself is full of anguish. Is your neck long enough? Is your foot arched enough? Is the dancer beside you going to get the role you desperately wanted, for reasons you will never know?

Income for everyone who doesn't rise to the top is meagre. You'll be sharing

digs for years. Luckily you have to keep your weight down, so you won't have big food bills.

Casting can be hurtful and frustrating. You learn about the roles you tried for and didn't get by standing in front of a call board and searching until you see that your name isn't there.

Relationships are complex and intense and may be difficult. These other dancers are people who touch every part of your body and see you in almost every physical extreme you reach. Some of them are your rivals. Some of them you don't like. Sometimes you feel isolated and disconnected amid this enforced intimacy.

Sometimes you feel terribly vulnerable. You *are* vulnerable.

You have to do your stretching every day. It hurts, but you must do it. Your body is different from other people's and you have to work constantly to keep it that way.

Even if you turn out to be one of the few who rise to the top, you're ready for the dancer dumpster at an age when your elementary school classmates are just settling into the prime of their careers. There's no pension. There's no easy second career to jump into. There's often no time to think about it, especially if dancing comes to an end because of injury or an unexpectedly terminated contract.

You're left scrambling to discover the world outside dance; to fit into a society you've never had the time or energy to get comfortable with; to figure out how you're going to feed and clothe and house yourself from now on because all your training has prepared you for only one thing—the thing you can't do any more.

You have to sleep on a special mattress because your years in dance have left you with a bad back. Your feet are in rough shape, forever.

But somehow, it all has a magic that never leaves you. You couldn't have done it if you didn't have a passion for this art form. Your natural love of moving your body, pushing it as far as you can, has given you great joy.

You're a performer. It nourished you, being on stage, dancing in front of an audience. You communicated powerful things with your body. You moved people in your audiences.

In your heart you will always be a dancer. You'll always be drawn to the theatre when dance events are on. Something deep inside you will still be in full makeup and costume, up on stage with the others, moving your body splendidly and meaningfully.

Above all else, you are a dancer.

after READING

1. After reading this **essay**, write a letter answering a friend who has told you that he or she is considering becoming a professional dancer. Use information from this essay to explain why you do or do not support such a move.

2. a) A number of different jobs that must be performed in a dance company are mentioned in this essay. List the jobs and beside each explain what the person who does that job is responsible for. Add any other jobs that would be generated by a dance company.

   b) Create a newspaper advertisement for one of the jobs. Read the posted jobs created by other members of your class and apply for one of them.

   c) As a class, discuss which advertisement received the most job applications. Why?

3. In your notebook, copy sentences from this essay that illustrate the following: a simple sentence, a complex sentence, a compound sentence, and a compound-complex sentence. In each case, explain why the sentence you chose is an example of the kind of sentence structure. (See The Reference Shelf, page 410.)

EXPLORING IDEAS AND IMPLICATIONS

4. In a small group, write a short **dramatization** based on one of the aspects of a dancer's life described in this essay. Rehearse and perform the dramatization.

5. **Debate** the following resolution: Be It Resolved That More Physical Demands Are Made of Ballet Dancers Than Other Athletes. (See The Reference Shelf, pages 455–458.) You may need to do research to help you prepare your arguments.

6. Go to a dance performance or watch one on television. (Your school or local library may have videos of dance performances.) Then write a **review** for your classmates of what you saw and heard.

MAKING CONNECTIONS

7. With a partner, find and read the **poem** "Among School Children" by W.B. Yeats. Explain to the class what you think is the relationship between the poem and this essay. ■

The Story of Nil

GABRIELLE ROY

TRANSLATED BY ALAN BROWN

"Let him sing and there's not a heart but is lightened."

BEFORE READING

In your notebook write about the importance of music in your life.

Quite often I asked my small pupils to sing together. One day, in the midst of their rather colourless voices, I could make out one that was clear, vibrant and astonishingly accurate. I had the group stop and let Nil go on alone. What a ravishing voice, and how precious to me, who had never had much of an ear for music!

From then on I would ask: "Nil, will you give the note?"

He would do so without coaxing and without pride—a child born to sing as others are born to pout.

The rest, my flight of sparrows, took off in his wake, soon following rather well; for besides his rare talent, Nil seemed able to pass it on to the others. We listened to him and believed we too could sing.

My music hour was the envy of the teachers in neighbouring classrooms.

"What's going on? We're getting a concert from your room every day now!"

They couldn't believe it, for I had never before shone as a singing teacher.

Our old inspector was stupefied when he came around.

"What's this? Your children are singing a thousand times better than other years!"

Then he stopped staring suspiciously at me, and asked to have them sing once more; the first thing I knew he was off in a happy reverie in which he seemed not even to remember that he was a school inspector.

Shortly after this visit I had another from our principal, who said in a faintly sarcastic way:

"I understand your children are such fine singers this year. I'm very curious to hear these little angels. Would you ask them to perform for me?"

Our principal was a little man made somewhat taller by his crest of blond hair, combed up in the middle like the picture of Monsieur Thiers in the dictionary. His dress, which was that of our teaching brothers at the time, was also very impressive: a black frock-coat and a white, starched dickey.

I had the pupils come close in a compact group, with Nil, one of the smallest, almost hidden in the middle. I made a little sign to him. He gave the starting tone just loudly enough to be heard by those around him. A wire vibrating harmoniously somewhere near! And the choir took off with such zest and in such perfect unison that I thought: Even the principal must be dazzled by this!

At any rate the mocking smile vanished quickly from his face. In its place appeared, to my amazement, the same expression of happy reverie, as if he had forgotten that he was a manager always busy running his school.

Hands behind his back, he wagged his head gently in rhythm with the tune and even when the song was ended kept on listening to it in his mind a moment longer.

But he had spotted the captivating voice. He brought Nil out of the group, looked long and attentively at him, and patted him on the cheek.

As I accompanied him to the door, he said:

"Well, with your thirty-eight sparrows you've caught a meadowlark this year. Do you know the lark? Let him sing and there's not a heart but is lightened!"

I suppose I was too young myself to know what a lightened heart was. But I soon had some idea of it.

That day had started very badly, under a driving autumn rain. The children arrived at school wet, sniffling and ill-humoured, with enormous muddy feet that soon turned my schoolroom, which I loved to see sparkling clean, into a kind of stable. As soon as I went to pick up a still-intact clod of black earth, two or three children would make a point of crushing others with their toes, scattering them in the aisles, watching me slyly all the while. I hardly recognized my pupils in these little rebels who would have risen against me at the drop of a hat, and perhaps they didn't recognize in me their beloved school mistress of yesterday. What had happened to turn us into something resembling enemies?

Some of our most experienced colleagues blamed the moments before the storm, the children's delicate nerves being strained by the atmospheric tension; and some said it was the long school days following weekends or holidays. After that taste of freedom the return to school was like going back to jail; and they grew quite disobedient, and all the more excitable, fidgety and impossible because they felt in their bones, poor things, that their revolt against the adult world had not the slightest chance of ultimate success.

It was my turn to have one of those dreadful days when the teacher seems to be there to do nothing but scold, and the children to comply, and all the sadness in the world settles into this place which can be so happy at other times.

As the bad weather kept up, instead of working off this excess nervousness in the open air we had to go to the gym in the basement, where shoes were loud on the hard floor. The children fought about nothing. I had to treat split lips and bloody noses.

Afterwards, fresh from a visit to the toilets, the children left their desks one after the other to ask permission to go down again. Impossible to continue with my lesson in that traffic! One would leave, another would just be coming back, the door would open, a draught would blow scribblers to the floor and they'd be picked up covered with dirt, and the door would slam: another child was going out. Suddenly I could take no more. "No! That will do! There's a limit after all."

Now it happened that without thinking, but as if I had done it on purpose, my "no" fell on little Charlie, a gentle child, quite guileless, whom his mother purged two or three times a year with a mixture of sulphur and molasses. Relegated to his desk, Charlie couldn't hold in very long. The odour gave him away to his neighbours, little monsters who pretended to be shocked, and shouted from where they sat, as if it wasn't obvious enough: "Charlie did it in his pants." In haste I had to write a note to his mother whom I knew to be vindictive, while Charlie stood at my desk, his legs apart, whimpering with shame.

I hadn't long to wait for the consequences. Charlie had been gone a half-hour when the principal showed his head in the high glass of the door and gestured that he wanted to speak to me. It was a serious business when he called us out to the corridor. Charlie's mother, he told me, had phoned. She was so furious that he had trouble persuading her not to sue me. Laugh if you please, there was such a thing as parents suing a teacher for less

than that, and I was accused of having obliged Charlie's mother to re-wash his underwear, which she had done only yesterday.

I tried to present the facts from my point of view, but the principal remarked with some severity that it was better to let the whole class go to the toilet for nothing than to prevent one child in real need.

Perhaps because I was ashamed of myself, I tried to make the children ashamed at having shown their worst possible side all day. They weren't in the least contrite; quite the contrary—they seemed very pleased with themselves indeed, for the most part.

I went and sat down, completely discouraged. And the future descended on me, making all my years to come resemble this one day. I could see myself in twenty, thirty years, still in the same place, worn down by my task, the very image of the "oldest" of my present colleagues whom I found so pitiful; and thinking of them, my pity turned on myself. It goes without saying that the children took advantage of my dejection to chase each other up and down the aisles and add to the tumult. My glance fell on little Nil. While almost all the children were running amok, he was at his desk, trying to concentrate on his drawing. Apart from singing, what interested him most was to draw a cabin, always the same cabin, surrounded by curious animals, with chickens as tall as his cows.

I called to him, I think as if for help: "Nil, come here a second."

He came running. He was a funny little manikin and always oddly dressed.

On this day a pair of men's braces, barely shortened, held up pants that were too big, their crotch hanging to his knees. His boots must have been just as oversized, for I heard them clatter as he ran up. With his mop of tow-coloured hair and his square head, flat on the top, he looked like a good little kulak determined to get an education. In fact, when he wasn't singing he was the last one in the class that you'd take for a meadowlark.

He leaned toward me affectionately.

"What do you want?"

"To talk to you. Tell me, who taught you to sing so well?"

"My mother."

I had glimpsed her once when the report cards were given out: a gentle, embarrassed smile, high cheekbones like Nil's, fine, penetrating eyes under her snow-white kerchief, a timid shadow who left as she had come, in silence. Did she know more than a few words apart from her own Ukrainian tongue?

"So she teaches you in Ukrainian?"

"Why, sure!"

"Do you know many Ukrainian songs?"

"Hundreds!"

"So many?"

"Well, at least ten ... or twelve."

"Would you sing us one?"

"Which one?"

"Any one you like."

He took a firm stand as if to resist the wind, his feet wide apart, his head thrown back, his eyes already shining, in a trans-formation more radical than I had ever seen—the first time he had sung at school in his mother's language: a little rustic turned into one possessed by music. His body swayed to a catchy rhythm, his shoulders went up, his eyes flamed, and a smile from time to time parted his slightly fleshy lips. With raised hand he seemed to point with a graceful gesture at some pretty scene in the distance, and you couldn't help following the gesture to see what it was he found so pleasing. I couldn't tell which was better: listening to him with my eyes closed, to enjoy that splendid voice without distraction; or watching him sing, so lively, so playful, as if he were ready to rise from the earth.

When this delightful song was ended we were in another world. The children had gradually gone back to their seats. I was no longer in despair about my future. Nil's singing had turned my heart inside out like a glove. Now I was confident about life.

I asked Nil: "Have you any idea what the song's about?"

"Sure I have!"

"Could you explain it to us?"

He launched into the story:

"There's a tree. It's a cherry tree in bloom. In the country my mother comes from there's lots of them. This cherry tree, it's in the middle of a field. Some young girls are dancing around it. They're waiting for the boys that are in love with them."

"What a lovely story!"

"Yes, but it's going to be sad," said Nil, "for one of the boys was killed in war."

"Oh, that's too bad!"

"No, because that gives a chance to another fellow who was secretly in love with her, and he's the good guy."

"Oh! Fine! But where did your mother learn these songs?"

"In that country, before they left, when she was a little girl. Now she says that's all we have left from the Ukraine."

"And she's hurrying to get all that into your little head so it's your turn to keep it?"

He looked at me gravely to be very sure of what I had said, then he smiled affectionately.

"I won't lose a one," he said. And then, "Would you like me to sing another one?"

My mother had broken a hip about three months before. She had been immobilized in a plaster corset for a long time. The doctor had finally removed it and asserted that she would be able to walk if she persevered. She made a great effort every day, but couldn't manage to move her bad leg. I had seen her losing hope during the last week or two. I would catch her sitting in her armchair by the window looking at the outdoors with an expression of heart-rending regret. I would scold her so that she wouldn't think I was worried about her. Lively, active and independent as she was, what would her life be if she spent the rest of it a cripple? The horror I had felt one day at the thought of being chained for a lifetime to my teacher's desk gave me a glimpse of her feelings at the prospect of never leaving her prisoner's lookout at the window.

One day I had the notion of bringing Nil home to entertain her, for she found the days "deathly long."

"Would you like to come home, Nil, and sing for *my* mother? She's lost all her songs!"

He had a way of saying yes without a word, placing his little hands in mine as if to tell me: You know very well I'd go to the world's end with you. And it went straight to my heart.

On the way I explained to him that my mother was much older than his, and that it was hard at her age to get back her lost confidence. I still don't know what possessed me to get into explanations of that kind with a child of six and a half. But he listened, deadly serious, trying with all his might to fathom what I expected of him.

When my mother, who had just had a nap, opened her eyes and saw beside her this manikin in his wide braces, she must have thought he was one of the poor kids I had so often brought home so that she could make them a coat or alter one to their size. She said a little bitterly, but more in sadness, I think, at no longer being able to help:

"What's this? You know I can't sew anymore, except little things I can do by hand."

"No, no, it's not that. It's a surprise. Listen."

I made a sign to Nil. He planted himself in front of my mother as if to resist a strong wind, and launched into the happy song of the cherry tree. His body swayed, his eyes sparkled, a smile came to his lips, his little hand rose up to point, far beyond this sickroom, to what? A highway? A plain? Some open landscape, anyway, that he made you want to see.

When he had finished he looked at my mother, who said not a word, hiding her gaze from him. He suggested:

"D'you want to hear another one of my songs?"

My mother, as if from a distance, nodded her head, without showing her face, which stayed hidden behind her hand.

Nil sang another song, and this time my mother held her head high, watching the smiling child; and with his help she too was away, taking flight far above life, on the wings of a dream.

That evening she asked me to bring her a strong kitchen chair with a high back and help her stand up behind it, using it as a support.

I suggested that the chair could slip and pull her forward, so she had me lay a heavy dictionary on it.

With this strange "walker" of her own invention my mother resumed her exercises. Weeks passed and I could see no change. I was growing completely discouraged. My mother too, no doubt, for she seemed to have given up. What I didn't know was that, having realized she was on the point of succeeding, she had decided to go on with her exercises in secret so as to give me a surprise. A surprise it was! I was in the blackest despondency that evening when I heard her shout from her room:

"I'm walking! I can walk!"

I ran to her. My mother, pushing the chair in front of her, was progressing with tiny mechanical steps, like those of a wind-up doll, and she kept up her cry of triumph:

"I can walk! I can walk!"

Of course I don't claim that Nil performed a miracle. But perhaps he gave a little puff at just the right time to the flickering faith of my mother.

However that may be, this experiment gave me the urge to try another.

The previous year I had gone along with one of my colleagues and a group of her pupils who were putting on a little play for the old people in a home in our town.

Of all the prisons that human beings forge for themselves or are forced to suffer, not one, even today, seems as intolerable as the one in which we are confined by age. I had sworn never again to set foot in that home; it had upset me so. Maybe during the year I had made some progress in compassion, for here I was thinking of taking Nil there. He seemed the only one likely to be able to comfort the old people I had seen immured in the institution.

I spoke to the principal who thought for a long time and then said the idea had its good points ... very good points, but first I'd have to get permission from the mother.

I set about writing a letter to Nil's mother, in which I said something to the effect that the songs she had brought from the Ukraine and passed on to her son seemed to be beneficial to the people here, as perhaps they had been to her own people ... helping them to live.... And would she please lend me Nil for an evening that might go on rather late?

I read it to Nil, asking him to get it firmly into his head because he would have to read it at home and give an exact translation to his mother. He listened attentively and as soon as I had finished asked if I'd like him to repeat it word for word, just to be sure that he had memorized it. I said that wouldn't be necessary, that I had faith in his memory.

Next day Nil brought me the reply on a piece of paper cut out from a brown paper bag. It was in telegraphic style:

"We lend Nil to the old people."

It was signed in letters that looked like embroidery:

Paraskovia Galaida.

"What a beautiful name your mother has!" I said to Nil, trying to read it properly.

And on hearing my odd pronunciation, he burst out laughing in my face.

The old people's home had its own little auditorium, with a platform two steps high lit by a row of weak footlights which isolated it from the audience.

Caught in a beam of golden light, Nil was charming to see with his straw-coloured hair and the Ukrainian blouse with its embroidered collar, which his mother had made him wear. For my own part I missed a little seeing my manikin with the wide braces. On his face with its high cheekbones you could already see the joy he felt at the idea of singing. From my hiding place, where if need be I could prompt him as to what to do, I could see the audience as well as the stage, and it was among them, you might have thought, that the real drama was being played—that of life saying its last word.

In the first row was an old man afflicted with a convulsive palsy, like an apple tree that someone had shaken, still trembling long after its last fruit had fallen. Some-where someone was breathing with a whistling sound like wind caught inside a hollow tree. Another old man tried to keep up with his lungs in a race with death. Near the middle of the room was one, half paralyzed, whose living eyes in his inert face had an unbearable lucidity. There was a poor woman, swollen to an enormous mass of flesh. And no doubt there were those who were still unscathed, if that happy chance consisted here of simply being worn, wrinkled, shrunken and eroded by some process of unimaginable ferocity. When is old age at its most atro-cious: when you are in it, like these people in the home?—or seen from afar, through the eyes of tender youth that could wish for death at the sight?

Then, in that day's end, the clear, radi-ant voice of Nil rose as if from the shining morning of life. He sang of the flowering cherry tree, of the girls in love dancing their round on the plain, of the expecta-tions of youthful hearts. With a gesture that was charmingly at ease he would raise his hand and point to a distant road to be followed ... or a far horizon which, from his shining eyes, you imagined must be luminous. At one moment his lips parted in a smile that was so contagious it leapt over the footlights and appeared in all its fresh sweetness on the aged faces. He sang about Petrushka's adventure, and how he was caught by his own trickery. He sang a song that I had never heard, a gentle, melancholy song about the Dnieper River running on and on, bearing laughter and sighs, hopes and regrets, down toward the sea, until at the end everything melts into the eternal waves.

I didn't know the old people; they had changed so. In the dark evening of their lives this ray of morning had broken through to them. The palsied man suc-ceeded in holding still a moment so as to hear more clearly. The eye of the paralytic no longer wandered, searching, calling for help, but turned and fixed upon Nil so as to see him as well as possible. The man who had been chasing his own breathing seemed to be holding his breath with his two hands clasped across his chest in a marvellous respite from his affliction. They all looked happy now, hanging on the next notes from Nil. And the tragic spectacle of the audience ended in a kind of parody, with old men excited as children, some on the verge of laughter, others of tears, because they were rediscovering so vividly in themselves the traces of what was lost.

Then I said to myself that this was, after all, too cruel, and I would never again bring Nil here to sing and reawaken hope.

How the renown of my little healer of the ills of life began to spread, I have no idea, but soon I was getting requests from all sides.

One day, through the high glass door-panel, the principal made a sign that he wanted to talk to me.

"This time," he said, "it's a psychiatric hospital that's asking for our little Ukrainian lark. This is a serious question, and we must think it over."

Yes, it was serious, but once again, as if it were beyond my own will, my decision had been made. If Paraskovia Galaida gave her permission I would go with Nil to see the "madmen," as people called them then.

She agreed, with no trouble. I wonder now if she even worried about where we went. She seemed to have as much confidence in me as Nil did.

In the mental hospital also there was a little auditorium with a low platform, but without any bank of footlights or spots to separate this side from that. Everything was bathed in the same dull, uniform light. If the world of the aged in the home had made me think of tragedy's last act, here I had the impression of an epilogue mimed by shadows that had already passed on to a kind of death.

The patients were seated in docile ranks, most of them apathetic, their eyes bleak, twiddling their thumbs or biting at their lips.

Nil made his entrance on the narrow platform of the stage. There was a rustle of surprise in the audience. A few patients even grew excited at this marvellous apparition—a child, here! One of them, over-agitated, pointed his finger at him in a kind of joyous bewilderment, as if asking others to confirm what his eyes were seeing.

Nil took up his position, his feet apart, a lock of hair hanging over his forehead, his hands on his hips, for he was going to start with "Kalinka" which he had just learned from his mother. He caught its devilish rhythm with fiery charm.

From the very first notes there was a silence such as you would feel when the forest hushes to hear a birdsong somewhere on a distant branch.

Nil was swaying, filled with an irresistible liveliness, sometimes tracing a gentle curve with his hand, sometimes passionately clapping both hands together. The patients followed his movements in ecstasy. And always this silence, as if in adoration.

"Kalinka" ended. Nil explained in a few words, as I had taught him, the meaning of the next song. He did this with complete ease, no more nervous than if he had been in class among his companions.

Then he launched into his music again as if he would never grow tired of singing.

Now the patients were breathing together audibly, like a single, unhappy monster moving in the shadows, dreaming of its own release.

Nil went from one song to another, one sad, the next one gay. He no more saw the madmen than he had seen the aged, the sick, the sorrowful, with their torments of body and soul. He sang of the sweet, lost land of his mother which she had given him to keep, its prairies, its trees, a lone horseman crossing the distant plain. He ended with that gesture of his hand that I never tired of, pointing to a happy road, far away at the end of this world, and tapping the floor with his heel.

At once I was sure the patients were going to eat him alive. The nearest ones tried to reach him when he came down from the little platform. Those in the back pushed at the front ranks, trying to touch him too. A woman patient caught him by the arm and held him for a moment to her breast. Another pulled him away from her and kissed him. They all wanted to take possession of the wonder child, to take him alive, to prevent him at all costs from leaving them.

Nil, who had, without recognizing it, eased so much sadness, took fright at the terrible happiness he had unleashed. His eyes, filled with terror, called to me for help. A guard gently extricated him from the embrace of a sobbing patient:

"Dear child, little nightingale, stay here, stay here with us!"

Toward the back of the room another claimed possession of him, weeping:

"This is my little boy that they stole. Long ago. Give him back. Give me back my life."

He was all trembling when I got him in my arms.

"There, there, it's all finished! You made them too happy, that's all. Too happy!"

We had left the taxi, walking the rest of the way to Nil's house. He seemed to have forgotten the troublesome scene in the hospital, and his first care was to guide me, for as soon as we left the sidewalk I had no idea where I was going.

It was early May. It had rained hard for several days and the fields across which Nil was leading me were a sea of mud, with occasional clumps of low, thorny bushes that caught at my clothing. I could only guess at this strange landscape, for there were no street-lamps here. Not even what you could call a road. Just a vague path where trodden mud made the footing a little more firm than elsewhere. The path wound from one cabin to the next, and the feeble light from windows helped us somewhat. But Nil seemed not to need the light, for he jumped surefootedly from one fairly dry spot to the next. Then we stood on the edge of a stretch of soft mud that gave off water like a sponge. To cross it there was a walk of planks thrown zig-zag here and there. The gaps were always longer than a single step. Nil would leap across and turn around to give me his hand, encouraging me to spring. He was delighted to bring me to his home; there was not a hint of suspicion in this happy child that I might pity him for living in this zone of the disinherited. It was true that beneath that soaring sky filled with stars, these cabins with their backs to the city, looking out over the free prairie vastness, formed a strangely fascinating shantytown.

From time to time, a fetid smell wafted toward us in waves, spoiling the fresh spring air. I asked Nil where it came from, and at first he didn't know what I was talking about, I suppose because the smell was so familiar to him. Then he pointed behind us to a long, dark mass that blocked the horizon.

"The slaughterhouse," he said. "It must be the slaughterhouse that stinks."

Now we had crossed the muddy sea and I was fated that night to go from one surprise to the next, for the unpleasant smell suddenly gave way to the good, simple one of wet earth. Then the perfume of a flower reached me. We were coming close to Nil's house, and this was the powerful odour of a hyacinth in its pot outside near the door, struggling with a force almost equal to the last waves from the abattoir. Another few paces and the hyacinth had won. At the same time, from a nearby pond came a triumphant chorus of hylas.

Paraskovia Galaida must have been on the lookout for us. She came at a run out of their cabin which was itself, no doubt, made of old bits of plank and waste boards. In the light of a crescent moon filtering through the clouds it seemed to me amazingly pale, as clean and pleasant as if it had just been whitewashed. It stood in a fenced enclosure. A gate opened inward. So far as I could judge, it was made of nothing less than the foot of an iron bedstead mounted on hinges in the post. They squeaked as Paraskovia Galaida opened the gate and welcomed us into the perfumed dooryard. The strange light revealed that everything in the place was scrupulously clean.

Paraskovia took my hands and backed toward the house. In front was a rough wooden bench. She made me sit down between Nil and herself. At once the cat of the place left the shadows and leapt to the back of the bench, where he made his narrow bed, content to be one of us, his head between our shoulders, purring.

With Nil's help, I tried to express to Paraskovia Galaida something of the joy her small son's singing had brought to so many people; and she, with his help, tried to thank me for I wasn't quite sure what. Soon we had given up trying to pour out our feelings by means of words, listening instead to the night.

Then it seemed to me I caught a sign from Paraskovia Galaida to Nil. Her eyes closed, she gave him a starting note just as he gave it at school. A delicate musical throat vibration sounded. Their voices began together, one a little hesitant at first but quickly convinced by the stronger of the two. Then they flew upward, harmonizing as they rose in a strangely lovely song, one of life as it is lived and life as it is dreamed.

Under that immense sky it took your heart and turned it round and turned it over, as a hand might do, before leaving it an instant, with due gentleness, to the freedom of the air.

after READING

UNDERSTANDING THE TEXT

1. In your notebook, write a statement of the **theme** of this **story**. Below that statement, make a list of details from the story that led you to that conclusion. Discuss your findings with the class. Try to come to a common understanding of the meaning of "The Story of Nil."

2. Nil is a magical **character**. In a brief paragraph, explain what it is about the child that makes him magical.

3. Choose five words from the story that you did not know. In your notebook, record the word and write a **definition** for it. Underneath the definition explain the importance of knowing the meaning of the word in order to understand the story.

4. In a small group, discuss the significance of the following: the nightingale (page 308); the lark (page 301); the oxymoron, "terrible happiness"; and the repetition of the word or the idea of "prison." Bring your ideas to the class for discussion.

EXPLORING IDEAS AND IMPLICATIONS

5. With a partner, write a **thesis** for a **literary essay** about the simplicity of the story. Once you have written your thesis, individually write your essay to develop that thesis. Return to your partnership to review the points you have made in your essay, the organization of each paragraph, and the **diction**. Revise and edit your essay in preparation for publication.

MAKING CONNECTIONS

6. a) Find your favourite song or piece of music and record it on tape or CD. Analyze its effects on you, considering the lyrics, the instrumentation, beat, and **mood**. Present the music and your analysis of it to a small group of people with diverse musical tastes.
   b) As a listener in the group, make notes on the aspects of the presenter's music that you had not noticed previously. Make a list of questions for the presenter.

7. a) Find a popular self-help book on being happy. Examine the layout of the book, making notes on how the designer has made the book "user-friendly."
   b) Read at least one chapter of the book and critique the writer's advice. Post your critique with a photocopy or scanned copy of the cover of the book. ■

Sonnet 30

WILLIAM SHAKESPEARE

BEFORE READING

As a class, discuss the value of friendship in a person's life.

When to the sessions of sweet silent thought
I summon up remembrance of things past,
I sigh the lack of many a thing I sought,
And with old woes new wail my dear time's waste:
Then can I drown an eye, unused to flow,   5
For precious friends hid in death's dateless night,
And weep afresh love's long since cancell'd woe,
And moan the expense of many a vanish'd sight:
Then can I grieve at grievances foregone,
And heavily from woe to woe tell o'er   10
The sad account of fore-bemoaned moan,
Which I new pay as if not paid before.
    But if the while I think on thee, dear friend,
    All losses are restor'd and sorrows end.

after READING

UNDERSTANDING THE TEXT

1. In a single sentence, sum up the main idea in each of the quatrains and the closing rhyming couplet of this **poem**. (See The Reference Shelf, page 424.) In your notebook, explain whether you have ever experienced each of the ideas and the feelings that accompany them.

2. a) Identify the poetic device used in line 1. Explain whether it enhances the effectiveness of the line.

   b) Identify the **rhyme scheme** of this poem. Identify the stressed and unstressed syllables in the first quatrain of the poem. Identify the meter of the poem. (See The Reference Shelf, page 425.)

EXPLORING IDEAS AND IMPLICATIONS

3. With a partner, look up the characteristics of the sonnet in The Reference Shelf (page 423). Identify which characteristics of a sonnet this poem has and those it lacks. Identify the kind of sonnet this is and explain the reasons for your choice. Discuss what you think would be the hardest part of writing a sonnet. Be prepared to present your ideas to the class.

4. Select an effectively worded phrase from this poem and use it as the title for a poem of your own. With a partner, revise and edit your poem. Display the final version of your poem on a bulletin board for the rest of the class to read.

5. In your notebook, write a **personal essay** about the value of a "dear friend."

6. Look up the title *Remembrance of Things Past* in an encyclopedia of literature. Prepare a short oral **report** for the class on what you find. In your report, include some reasons why writers frequently make allusions to other works of literature.

MAKING CONNECTIONS

7. Read "To Keep the Memory of So Worthy a Friend" (pages 82–86). Give reasons why you do or do not think "Sonnet 30" might be about John Heminge or Henry Condell. ■

To His Coy Mistress

ANDREW MARVELL

BEFORE READING

One common form of argument uses the following formula: "If … then … but since … consequently." Here's an example: "If I had all the time in the world to study, then I would get great marks; but since I have to make money to go to university, consequently, I rarely study and am satisfied with mediocre marks." Create your own argument using the formula above. You can use any situation that comes to mind.

Had we but world enough, and time,
This coyness, lady, were no crime.
We would sit down, and think which way
To walk, and pass our long love's day.
Thou by the Indian Ganges' side   5
Should'st rubies find: I by the tide
Of Humber would complain. I would
Love you ten years before the Flood,
And you should, if you please, refuse
Till the conversion of the Jews.   10
My vegetable love should grow
Vaster than empires, and more slow.
An hundred years should go to praise
Thine eyes, and on thy forehead gaze:
Two hundred to adore each breast: 15
But thirty thousand to the rest.
An age at least to every part,
And the last age should show your heart.
For, lady, you deserve this state,
Nor would I love at lower rate.   20
    But at my back I always hear
Time's wingèd chariot hurrying near;
And yonder all before us lie
Deserts of vast eternity.
Thy beauty shall no more be found,   25
Nor, in thy marble vault shall sound
My echoing song; then worms shall try
That long preserved virginity,
And your quaint honor turn to dust,
And into ashes all my lust.   30
The grave's a fine and private place,
But none, I think, do there embrace.
    Now therefore, while the youthful hue
Sits on thy skin like morning dew,
And while thy willing soul transpires   35
At every pore with instant fires,
Now let us sport us while we may;
And now, like am'rous birds of prey,
Rather at once our time devour,
Than languish in his slow-chapt power,   40
Let us roll all our strength, and all
Our sweetness, up into one ball;
And tear our pleasures with rough strife
Thorough the iron gates of life.
Thus, though we cannot make our sun   45
Stand still, yet we will make him run.

after READING

UNDERSTANDING THE TEXT

1. With a partner, break down the **narrator**'s argument into the four parts discussed in "Before Reading."

2. Look up the meanings of the following words and trace the history of their meanings from their beginnings to modern times: coy, complain, quaint, sport, chapt (look up "chap"). For each word, explain how knowing more than a word's modern meaning broadens a reader's understanding of the poem.

3. **a)** In a small group choose one stanza and examine the **imagery**. For each image, write a detailed explanation of why that image works well in the **context** of the narrator's message to his love.

   b) In your group, decide whether or not the poet's use of hyperbole is effective or simply overdone. (See The Reference Shelf, page 419.)

4. In your notebook, describe the **rhyme scheme** and rhythm pattern in the poem. Explain how the rhyme and rhythm in the poem often dictate the **syntax** of the sentences. Refer specifically to at least two sentences in the poem. (See The Reference Shelf, page 425.)

EXPLORING IDEAS AND IMPLICATIONS

5. **Define** the expression "carpe diem." Using electronic and/or print resources, conduct an investigation into and write a **report** on why "carpe diem" would have been a popular subject in the 1600s for poets such as Marvell. Revise and edit your own work.

MAKING CONNECTIONS

6. Read "Fern Hill" (page 288). Both Thomas and Marvell are writing about time. Identify what point each makes about time. In a response to the two poems, write about which one you like better and why. Consider both **style** and meaning in your response. ■

If I Can Stop One Heart From Breaking

EMILY DICKINSON

BEFORE READING

In your notebook, explain one accomplishment that you feel makes your life meaningful.

If I can stop one Heart from breaking
I shall not live in vain
If I can ease one Life from Aching
Or cool one Pain

Or help one fainting Robin   5
Unto his Nest again
I shall not live in Vain.

after READING

1. With a partner, discuss what the main idea in this **poem** tells the reader about the **narrator**'s life. Be prepared to present your ideas to the class.

2. Punctuate this poem according to standard punctuation rules. Write a short explanation indicating which version of the poem you prefer.

EXPLORING IDEAS AND IMPLICATIONS

3. **a)** Write your own poem that ends with the line "I shall not live in vain." After the first draft, work with a partner to revise and edit the poem.

   b) As a class, collect the final drafts of all the poems to create a class **anthology**.

MAKING CONNECTIONS

4. Read the **essay** "What I Have Lived For" (page 21). Explain whether or not the central idea in Emily Dickinson's poem fits into one of the categories in Bertrand Russell's essay. ■

There Are Delicacies

EARLE BIRNEY

BEFORE READING

Recall **stories** or **plays** that deal with the idea of love, and discuss briefly with a small group the importance of time to those who are in love. In your notebook, record the ideas from the discussion.

there are delicacies in you
    like the hearts of watches
there are wheels that turn
    on the tips of rubies
& tiny intricate locks   5

i need your help
    to contrive keys
there is so little time
    even for the finest
        of watches   10

after READING

UNDERSTANDING THE TEXT

1. Compare the ideas about time in this **poem** with those generated in the "Before Reading" discussion.

2. In your notebook, write a few sentences that outline the main idea of this poem. One of your sentences should be used to explain the meaning of the final three lines.

3. Discuss with a partner the **extended metaphor** used by the poet, and the importance of words such as "delicacies," "hearts," "rubies," "intricate," and "contrive." In your notebook, record the ideas from your discussion.

EXPLORING IDEAS AND IMPLICATIONS

4. In your notebook, rewrite the poem using standard capitalization, punctuation, and sentences, beginning a new line at the beginning of a new sentence or clause. With a partner, compare the rewritten version with the original, discussing the impact on the reader of each version.

MAKING CONNECTIONS

5. Read "To His Coy Mistress" (page 313). Using a Venn diagram or another form of **graphic organizer**, compare the ideas and the form of both poems.

6. As an independent study, use the Internet or reference books on Canadian literature to find out about the life and literary works of Earle Birney, including an assessment of his importance in Canadian literary history. Make notes for an oral presentation to the class. (See The Reference Shelf, pages 448–452.) ■

Excerpt From Act 1 of
Leaving Home

DAVID FRENCH

"Just seventeen… and already the burdens of a man on his t'in little shoulders."

BEFORE READING

With a partner, make a list of the things young people should know about or should have done before they consider leaving home.

Background to the play

The first of David French's Mercer family plays, *Leaving Home* is written in the regional speech patterns of Newfoundland. The language is smooth and songlike in parts, and crashing and violent in others. The play is both tragic and comic; it chronicles the breakup of a family, the loss of two sons on one day, yet it contains comic details of everyday family life.

Jacob, the father, is the focus of the play. The first line refers to him, and before he sets foot on stage there is plenty of talk about Jacob, comparing him to others, anticipating his mood. This sets up the conflict between Jacob, his wife, and two sons, Ben and Bill. "The t'ree of you against the one of me." Competition for Mary's favour and attention is also apparent. Mary treats her husband and

sons as if they were all children, and Jacob complains about his sons: "I've never counted. Not since the day they was born." Ben, the oldest son, is too aware of the tension in the household, and says to his mother: "It's always been him and us." At the end of the play, the pattern of lying, withholding, hiding, pretending has finally been broken. And although Jacob really believes that "all we got in this world is the family," he is incapable of holding the family together.

French plots his drama at converging life events for the sons in the family: Ben has just graduated from high school, and Bill is about to marry his sixteen-year-old pregnant girlfriend. Even Mary, who is accustomed to protecting Jacob from the truth, is unable to block the sequence of events. In the end, however, she remains loyal to Jacob while supporting her sons in the choices they have made.

The past is as important as the present in *Leaving Home*. Jacob constantly refers to his own experience, measuring the worth and value of what is before him by the standards of his own upbringing. Jacob often reminisces about his youth and how he courted Mary. His realm of experience is limited to love and marriage, work and family. He is bewildered by Ben's graduation, and feels left out, not only because Ben didn't think Jacob would want to attend his graduation ceremony, but because Jacob himself didn't get past Grade 3.

French continues the battle between father and sons in *Of the Fields, Lately*, returns to the past of Jacob and Mary's courtship in *Salt-Water Moon*, and then recounts the newly transplanted lives of the extended Mercer family living in Toronto as Newfoundland joins Confederation in *1949*.

Cast of Characters

Mary Mercer   Bill Mercer
Ben Mercer   Jacob Mercer

SCENE

The play is set in Toronto on an early November day in the late fifties.

ACT ONE

The lights come up on a working-class house in Toronto. The stage is divided into three playing areas: kitchen, dining room and living room. In addition there is a hallway leading into the living room. Two bedroom doors lead off the hallway, as well as the front door which is offstage.

The kitchen contains a fridge, a stove, cupboards over the sink for everyday dishes, and a small drop-leaf table with two wooden chairs, one at either end. A plastic garbage receptacle stands beside the stove. A hockey calendar hangs on a wall, and a kitchen prayer.

The dining room is furnished simply with an oak table and chairs. There is an oak cabinet containing the good dishes and silverware. Perhaps a family portrait hangs on the wall—a photo taken when the sons were much younger.

The living room contains a chesterfield and an armchair, a TV, a record player and a fireplace. On the mantle rests a photo album and a silver-framed photo of the two sons—then small boys—astride a pinto pony. On one wall hangs a mirror. On another, a seascape. There is also a small table with a telephone on it.

It is around five-thirty on a Friday afternoon, and Mary Mercer, *aged fifty, stands before the mirror in the living room, admiring her brand new dress and fixed hair. As she preens, the front door opens and in walk her two sons,* Ben, *eighteen, and* Bill, *seventeen. Each carries a box from a formal rental shop and schoolbooks.*

Mary: Did you bump into your father?
Ben: No, we just missed him, Mom. He's already picked up his tux. He's probably at the Oakwood. (*He opens the fridge and helps himself to a beer.*)

Mary: Get your big nose out of the fridge. And put down that beer. You'll spoil your appetite.

Ben: No, I won't. (*He searches for a bottle opener in a drawer.*)

Mary: And don't contradict me. What other bad habits you learned lately?

Ben: (*teasing*) Don't be such a grouch. You sound like Dad. (*He sits at the table and opens his beer.*)

Mary: Yes, well just because you're in university now, don't t'ink you can raid the fridge any time you likes.

(BILL *crosses the kitchen and throws his black binder and books in the garbage receptacle.*)

Mary: What's that for? (BILL *exits into his bedroom and she calls after him.*) It's not the end of the world, my son. (*pause*) Tell you the truth, Ben. We always figured you'd be the one to land in trouble, if anyone did. I don't mean that as an insult. You're more . . . I don't know . . . like your father.

Ben: I am?

(*Music from* BILL'S *room.*)

Mary: (*calling, exasperated*) Billy, do you have to have that so loud? (BILL *turns down his record player. To* BEN) I'm glad your graduation went okay last night. How was Billy? Was he glad he went?

Ben: Well, he wasn't upset, if that's what you mean.

Mary: (*slight pause*) Ben, how come you not to ask your father?

Ben: What do you mean?

Bill: (*off*) Mom, will you pack my suitcase? I can't get everything in.

Mary: (*calling*) I can't now, Billy. Later.

Ben: I want to talk to you, Mom. It's important.

Mary: I want to talk to you, too.

Bill: (*Comes out of bedroom, crosses to kitchen.*) Mom, here's the deposit on my locker. I cleaned it out and threw away all my old gym clothes. (*He helps himself to an apple from the fridge.*)

Mary: Didn't you just hear me tell your brother to stay out of there? I might as well talk to the sink. Well, you can t'row away your old school clothes—that's your affair—but take those books out of the garbage. Go on. You never knows. They might come in handy sometime.

Bill: How? (*He takes the books out, then sits at the table with* BEN.)

Mary: Well, you can always go to night school and get your senior matric, once the baby arrives and Kathy's back to work. . . . Poor child. I talked to her on the phone this morning. She's still upset, and I don't blame her. I'd be hurt myself if my own mother was too drunk to show up to my shower.

Bill: (*a slight ray of hope*) Maybe she won't show up tonight.

Mary: (*Glances anxiously at the kitchen clock and turns to check the fish and potatoes.*) Look at the time. I just wish to goodness he had more t'ought, your father. The supper'll dry up if he don't hurry. He might pick up a phone and mention when he'll be home. Not a grain of t'ought in his head. And I wouldn't put it past him to forget his tux in the beer parlour. (*Finally she turns and looks at her two sons, disappointed.*) And look at the two of you. Too busy with your mouths to give your mother a second glance. I could stand here till my legs dropped off before either of you would notice my dress.

Ben: It's beautiful, Mom.

Mary: That the truth?

Bill: Would we lie to you, Mom?

Mary: Just so long as I don't look foolish next to Minnie. She can afford to dress up—Willard left her well off when he died.

Ben: Don't worry about the money. Dad won't mind.

Mary: Well, it's not every day your own son gets married, is it? (*to* BILL *as she puts on large apron*) It's just that I don't want Minnie Jackson looking all decked out like the Queen Mary and me the tug that dragged her in. You understands, don't you, Ben?

Ben: Sure.

Bill: I understand too, Mom.

Mary: I know you do, Billy. I know you do. (*She opens a tin of peaches and fills five dessert dishes.*) Minnie used to go with your father. Did you know that, Billy? Years and years ago.

Bill: No kidding?

Ben: (*at the same time*) Really?

Mary: True as God is in Heaven. Minnie was awful sweet on Dad, too. She t'ought the world of him.

Bill: (*incredulously*) Dad?

Mary: Don't act so surprised. Your father was quite a one with the girls.

Ben: No kidding?

Mary: He could have had his pick of any number of girls. (*to Bill*) You ask Minnie sometime. Of course, in those days I was going with Jeremy McKenzie, who later became a Queen's Counsel in St. John's. I must have mentioned him.

The boys exchange smiles.

Ben: I think you have, Mom.

Bill: A hundred times.

Mary: (*gently indignant — to* BILL) And that I haven't!

Bill: She has too. Hasn't she, Ben?

Mary: Never you mind, Ben. (*to* BILL) And instead of sitting around gabbing so much you'd better go change your clothes. Kathy'll soon be here. (*as* BILL *crosses to his bedroom*) Is the rehearsal still at eight?

Bill: We're supposed to meet Father Douglas at the church at five to. I just hope Dad's not too drunk. (*He exits.*)

Mary: (*Studies* BEN *a moment.*) Look at yourself. A cigarette in one hand, a bottle of beer in the other, at your age! You didn't learn any of your bad habits from me, I can tell you. (*pause*) Ben, don't be in such a hurry to grow up. (*She sits across from him.*) Whatever you do, don't be in such a hurry. Look at your poor young brother. His whole life ruined. Oh, I could weep a belly-ful when I t'inks of it. Just seventeen, not old enough to sprout whiskers on his chin, and already the burdens of a man on his t'in little shoulders. Your poor father hasn't slept a full night since this happened. Did you know that? He had such high hopes for Billy. He wanted you both to go to college and not have to work as hard as he's had to all his life. And now look. You have more sense than that, Ben. Don't let life trap you. (*BILL enters. He has changed his pants and is buttoning a clean white shirt.* MARY *goes into the dining room and begins to remove the tablecloth from the dining room table.*)

Bill: Mom, what about Dad? He won't start picking on the priest, will he? You know how he likes to argue.

Mary: He won't say a word, my son. You needn't worry. Worry more about Minnie showing up.

Bill: What if he's drunk?

Mary: He won't be. Your father knows better than to sound off in church. Oh, and another t'ing—he wants you to polish his shoes for tonight. They're in the bedroom. The polish is on your dresser. You needn't be too fussy.

Ben: I'll do his shoes, Mom. Billy's all dressed.

Mary: No, no, Ben, that's all right. He asked Billy to.

Bill: What did Ben do this time?

Mary: He didn't do anyt'ing.

Bill: He must have.

Mary: Is it too much trouble to polish your father's shoes, after all he does for you? If you won't do it, I'll do it myself.

Bill: (*indignantly*) How come when Dad's mad at Ben, I get all the dirty jobs? Jeez! Will I be glad to get out of here! (*Rolling up his shirt sleeves he exits into his bedroom.*)

(MARY *takes a clean white linen tablecloth from a drawer in the cabinet and covers the table. During the following scene she sets five places with her good glasses, silverware and plates.*)

Ben: (*slight pause*) Billy's right, isn't he? What'd I do, Mom?

Mary: Take it up with your father. I'm tired of being the middle man.

Ben: Is it because of last night? (*slight pause*) It is, isn't it?

Mary: He t'inks you didn't want him there, Ben. He t'inks you're ashamed of him.

Ben: He wouldn't have gone, Mom. That's the only reason I never invited him.

Mary: He would have went, last night.

Ben: (*angrily*) He's never even been to one

lousy Parents' Night in thirteen years. Not one! And he calls *me* contrary!

Mary: You listen to me. Your father never got past Grade T'ree. He was yanked out of school and made to work. In those days, back home, he was lucky to get that much and don't kid yourself.

Ben: Yeah? So?

Mary: So? So he's afraid to. He's afraid of sticking out. Is that so hard to understand? Is it?

Ben: What're you getting angry about? All I said was—

Mary: You say he don't take an interest, but he was proud enough to show off your report cards all those years. I suppose with you that don't count for much.

Ben: All right. But he never goes anywhere without you, Mom, and last night you were here at the shower.

Mary: Last night was different, Ben, and you ought to know that. It was your high school graduation. He would have went with me or without me. If you'd only asked him. (*A truck horn blasts twice.*) There he is now in the driveway. Whatever happens, don't fall for his old tricks. He'll be looking for a fight, and doing his best to find any excuse. (*calling*) Billy, you hear that? Don't complain about the shoes, once your father comes!

Ben: (*urgently*) Mom, there's something I want to tell you before Dad comes in.

Mary: Sure, my son. Go ahead. I'm listening. What's on your mind?

Ben: Well . . .

Mary: (*smiling*) Come on. It can't be that bad.

Ben: (*slight pause*) I want to move out, Mom.

Mary: (*almost inaudibly*). . . What?

Ben: I said I want to move out.

Mary: (*softly, as she sets the cutlery*) I heard you. (*pause*) What for?

Ben: I just think it's time. I'll be nineteen soon. (*pause*) I'm moving in with Billy and Kathy and help pay the rent. (*pause*) I won't be far away. I'll see you on weekends. (*Mary nods.*) Mom?

Mary: (*absently*) What?

Ben: Will you tell Dad? (*slight pause*) Mom? Did you hear me?

Mary: I heard you. He'll be upset, I can tell you. By rights you ought to tell him yourself.

Ben: If I do, we'll just get in a big fight and you know it. He'll take it better, coming from you.

(*The front door opens and* JACOB MERCER *enters whistling 'I's the b'y.' He is fifty, though he looks older. He is dressed in a peaked cap, carpenter's overalls, thick-soled workboots, and a lumberjack shirt over a T-shirt. Under one arm he carries his black lunchpail.*)

Mary: Your suit! I knowed it!

Jacob: Don't get in an uproar, now. I left it sitting on the front seat of the truck. (*He looks at* BEN, *then back to* MARY.) Is Billy home?

Mary: He's in the bedroom, polishing your shoes.

Jacob: (*Crosses to the bedroom door.*) Billy, my son, come out a moment.

(BILL *enters, carrying a shoe brush.*)

Put down the brush and go out in my truck and bring me back the tux on the seat.

Bill: What's wrong with Ben? He's not doing anything.

Jacob: Don't ask questions. That's a good boy. I'd ask your brother, but he always has a good excuse.

Ben: I'll go get it. (*He starts for the front door.*)

Jacob: (*calling after* BEN) Oh, it's too late to make up now. The damage is done.

Mary: Don't talk nonsense, Jacob.

Jacob: (*a last thrust*) And aside from that—I wouldn't want you dirtying your nice clean hands in your father's dirty old truck!

(*The front door closes on his last words.* BILL *returns to his room.* JACOB *sets his lunchpail and his cap on the dining room table.*)

Jacob: Did he get his diploma?

Mary: Yes. It's in the bedroom.

Jacob: (*Breaks into a smile and lifts his cap.*) And will you gaze on Mary over there. When I stepped in the door, I thought the Queen had dropped in for tea.

Mary: You didn't even notice.

Jacob: Come here, my dear, and give Jacob a kiss.

Mary: (*She darts behind the table, laughing.*) I'll give Jacob a swift boot in the rear end with my pointed toe.

(JACOB *grabs her, rubs his rough cheek against hers.*)

You'll take the skin off! Jake! You're far too rough! And watch my new dress! Don't rip it.

(JACOB *releases her and breaks into a little jig as he sings.*)

I's the b'y that builds the boat
And I's the b'y that sails her,
I's the b'y that catches the fish
And takes 'em home to Lizer.

after READING

UNDERSTANDING THE TEXT

1. Take the role of one of Bill, Ben, Mary, or Jacob and write a journal explaining what it's like being a member of your family.

2. Mary's speech is different from her children's. Using a graphic organizer, show how Mary's speech differs from her children's. In a well-constructed paragraph, explain the importance of these differences between Mary and her two sons.

3. With a partner, create an overhead diagram of the stage from the descriptions given in the excerpt. Make point-form notes on what the audience learns about this family from the set.

EXPLORING IDEAS AND IMPLICATIONS

4. a) In a group of four, prepare a presentation of this scene. Start the presentation with a tableau and create a second tableau somewhere during the scene. Be prepared to answer questions from the class in the role you are playing while you are in the second tableau. In your same group, prepare at least six questions for members of other groups to be asked during their presentations.

   b) As a class prepare an evaluation sheet for the presentation. Have at least one group give feedback for each presentation.

5. With a partner, make some predictions about what will happen to each of the characters in this play. Write an additional scene that could take place later in the play based on one of your predictions. You can add a new character (Kathy or Minnie). Be sure the events and the characters are logical extensions of those you have already read about.

MAKING CONNECTIONS

6. a) Read "The Story of Nil" (pages 300–310). Answer the following questions for that story:
   What is the theme of the story?
   What is the philosophy that Nil's mother subscribes to?

   b) Explain how the families in *Leaving Home* and "The Story of Nil" differ. What could the Mercer family learn from Nil's family?

   c) Write a letter from Nil or his mother to one of the Mercers or to the whole family in which the writer tries to explain how the Mercers could live a more satisfying life. ■

Excerpt From
Fugitive Pieces

ANNE MICHAELS

"We were Russian dolls. I inside Athos, Bella inside me."

BEFORE READING

With your classmates, take turns reading this novel excerpt aloud. If you are reading the story at home, read it aloud with a family member or friend.

The main character in Fugitive Pieces *is Jakob Beer, a Holocaust survivor who moves to Canada after World War II. In this excerpt, from the opening chapter, Jakob recounts the story of his rescue, by an unlikely hero, from the horrors of his Polish town.*

Time is a blind guide.

Bog-boy, I surfaced into the miry streets of the drowned city. For over a thousand years, only fish wandered Biskupin's wooden sidewalks. Houses, built to face the sun, were flooded by the silty gloom of the Gasawka River. Gardens grew luxurious in subaqueous silence; lilies, rushes, stinkweed.

No one is born just once. If you're lucky, you'll emerge again in someone's arms; or unlucky, wake when the long tail of terror brushes the inside of your skull.

I squirmed from the marshy ground like Tollund Man, Grauballe Man, like the boy they uprooted in the middle of Franz Josef Street while they were repairing the road, six hundred cockleshell beads around his neck, a helmet of mud. Dripping with the prune-coloured juices of the peat-sweating bog. Afterbirth of earth.

I saw a man kneeling in the acid-steeped ground. He was digging. My sudden appearance unnerved him. For a moment he thought I was one of Biskupin's lost souls, or perhaps the boy in the story, who digs a hole so deep he emerges on the other side of the world.

Biskupin had been carefully excavated for almost a decade. Archaeologists gently continued to remove Stone and Iron Age relics from soft brown pockets of peat. The pure oak causeway that once connected Biskupin to the mainland had been reconstructed, as well as the ingenious nail-less wooden houses, ramparts, and the high-towered city gates. Wooden streets, crowded twenty-five centuries before with traders and craftsmen, were being raised from the swampy lake bottom. When the soldiers arrived they examined the perfectly preserved clay bowls; they held the glass beads, the bronze and amber bracelets, before smashing them on the floor. With delighted strides, they roamed the magnificent timber city, once home to a hundred families. Then the soldiers buried Biskupin in sand.

My sister had long outgrown the hiding place. Bella was fifteen and even I admitted she was beautiful, with heavy brows and magnificent hair like black syrup, thick and luxurious, a muscle down her back. "A work of art," our mother said, brushing it for her while Bella sat in a chair. I was still small enough to vanish behind the wallpaper in the cupboard, cramming my head sideways between choking plaster and beams, eyelashes scraping.

Since those minutes inside the wall, I've imagined that the dead lose every sense except hearing.

The burst door. Wood ripped from hinges, cracking like ice under the shouts. Noises never heard before, torn from my father's mouth. Then silence. My mother had been sewing a button on my shirt. She kept her buttons in a chipped saucer. I heard the rim of the saucer in circles on the floor. I heard the spray of buttons, little white teeth.

Blackness filled me, spread from the back of my head into my eyes as if my brain

had been punctured. Spread from stomach to legs. I gulped and gulped, swallowing it whole. The wall filled with smoke. I struggled out and stared while the air caught fire.

I wanted to go to my parents, to touch them. But I couldn't, unless I stepped on their blood.

The soul leaves the body instantly, as if it can hardly wait to be free: my mother's face was not her own. My father was twisted with falling. Two shapes in the flesh-heap, his hands.

I ran and fell, ran and fell. Then the river: so cold it felt sharp.

The river was the same blackness that was inside me; only the thin membrane of my skin kept me floating.

From the other bank, I watched darkness turn to purple-orange light above the town; the colour of flesh transforming to spirit. They flew up. The dead passed above me, weird haloes and arcs smothered the stars. The trees bent under their weight. I'd never been alone in the night forest, the wild bare branches were frozen snakes. The ground tilted and I didn't hold on. I strained to join them, to rise with them, to peel from the ground like paper ungluing at its edges. I know why we bury our dead and mark the place with stone, with the heaviest, most permanent thing we can think of: because the dead are everywhere but the ground. I stayed where I was. Clammy with cold, stuck to the ground. I begged: If I can't rise, then let me sink, sink into the forest floor like a seal into wax.

Then—as if she'd pushed the hair from my forehead, as if I'd heard her voice—I knew suddenly my mother was inside me. Moving along sinews, under my skin the way she used to move through the house at night, putting things away, putting things in order. She was stopping to say goodbye and was caught, in such pain, wanting to rise, wanting to stay. It was my responsibility to release her, a sin to keep her from ascending. I tore at my clothes, my hair. She was gone. My own fast breath around my head.

I ran from the sound of the river into the woods, dark as the inside of a box. I ran until the first light wrung the last greyness out of the stars, dripping dirty light between the trees. I knew what to do. I took a stick and dug. I planted myself like a turnip and hid my face with leaves.

My head between the branches, bristling points like my father's beard. I was safely buried, my wet clothes cold as armour. Panting like a dog. My arms tight against my chest, my neck stretched back, tears crawling like insects into my ears. I had no choice but to look straight up. The dawn sky was milky with new spirits. Soon I couldn't avoid the absurdity of daylight even by closing my eyes. It poked down, pinned me like the broken branches, like my father's beard.

Then I felt the worst shame of my life: I was pierced with hunger. And suddenly I realized, my throat aching without sound— Bella.

I had my duties. Walk at night. In the morning dig my bed. Eat anything.

My days in the ground were a delirium of sleep and attention. I dreamed someone found my missing button and came looking for me. In a glade of burst pods leaking their white stuffing, I dreamed of bread; when I woke, my jaw was sore from chewing the air. I woke terrified of animals, more terrified of men.

In this day-sleep, I remembered my sister weeping at the end of novels she loved; my father's only indulgence— Romain Rolland or Jack London. She wore the characters in her face as she read, one finger rubbing the edge of the page. Before I learned to read, angry to be left out, I strangled her with my arms, leaning over with my cheek against hers, as if somehow to see in the tiny black letters the world Bella saw. She shrugged me off or, big-hearted, she stopped, turned the book over in her lap, and explained the plot ... the drunken father lurching home ... the betrayed lover waiting vainly under the stairs ... the terror of wolves howling in the Arctic dark, making my own skeleton rattle in my clothes. Sometimes at night, I sat on the edge of Bella's bed and she tested my spelling, writing on my back with her finger and, when I'd learned the word, gently erasing it with a stroke of her smooth hand.

I couldn't keep out the sounds: the door breaking open, the spit of buttons. My mother, my father. But worse than those sounds was that I couldn't remember hearing Bella at all. Filled with her silence, I had no choice but to imagine her face.

The night forest is incomprehensible: repulsive and endless, jutting bones and sticky hair, slime and jellied smells, shallow roots like ropy veins.

Draping slugs splash like tar across the ferns; black icicles of flesh.

During the day I have time to notice lichen like gold dust over the rocks.

A rabbit, sensing me, stops close to my head and tries to hide behind a blade of grass.

The sun is jagged through the trees, so bright the spangles turn dark and float, burnt paper, in my eyes.

The white nibs of grass get caught in my teeth like pliable little fishbones. I chew fronds into a bitter, stringy mash that turns my spit green.

Once, I risk digging my bed close to pasture, for the breeze, for relief from the dense damp of the forest. Buried, I feel the shuddering dark shapes of cattle thudding across the field. In the distance, their thrusting heads make them look as if they're swimming. They gallop to a stop a few feet from the fence then drift towards me, their heads swinging like slow church bells with every glory step of their heavy flanks. The slender calves quiver behind, fear twitching their ears. I'm also afraid—that the herd will bring everyone from miles away to where I'm hiding—as they gather to rest their massive heads on the fence and stare down at me with rolling eyes.

I fill my pockets and my hands with stones and walk into the river until only my mouth and nose, pink lilies, skim the air. Muck dissolves from my skin and hair, and it's satisfying to see floating like foam on the surface the fat scum of lice from my clothes. I stand on the bottom, my boots sucked down by the mud, the current flowing around me, a cloak in a liquid wind. I don't stay under long. Not only because of the cold, but because with my ears under the surface, I can't hear. This is more frightening to me than darkness, and when I can't stand the silence any longer, I slip out of my wet skin, into sound.

Someone is watching from behind a tree. I stare from my hiding place without moving, until my eyeballs harden, until I'm no longer sure he's seen me. What's he waiting for? In the last possible moment before I have to run, light coming fast, I discover I've been held prisoner half the night by a tree, its dead, dense bole carved by moonlight.

Even in daylight, in the cold drizzle, the tree's faint expression is familiar. The face above a uniform.

The forest floor is speckled bronze, sugar caramelized in the leaves. The branches look painted onto the onion-white sky. One morning I watch a finger of light move its way deliberately towards me across the ground.

I know, suddenly, my sister is dead. At this precise moment, Bella becomes flooded ground. A body of water pulling under the moon.

A grey fall day. At the end of strength, at the place where faith is most like despair, I leaped from the streets of Biskupin; from underground into air.

I limped towards him, stiff as a golem, clay tight behind my knees. I stopped a few yards from where he was digging—

later he told me it was as if I'd hit a glass door, an inarguable surface of pure air— "and your mud mask cracked with tears and I knew you were human, just a child. Crying with the abandonment of your age."

He said he spoke to me. But I was wild with deafness. My peat-clogged ears.

So hungry. I screamed into the silence the only phrase I knew in more than one language, I screamed it in Polish and German and Yiddish, thumping my fists on my own chest: dirty Jew, dirty Jew, dirty Jew.

The man excavating in the mud at Biskupin, the man I came to know as Athos, wore me under his clothes. My limbs bone-shadows on his strong legs and arms, my head buried in his neck, both of us beneath a heavy coat. I was suffocating but I couldn't get warm. Inside Athos's coat, cold air streaming in from the edge of the car door. The drone of engine and wheels, once in a while the sound of a passing lorry. In our strange coupling, Athos's voice burrowed into my brain. I didn't understand so I made it up myself: It's right, it's necessary to run....

For miles through darkness in the back seat of the car, I had no idea where we were or where we were going. Another man drove and when we were signalled to stop, Athos pulled a blanket over us. In Greek-stained but competent German, Athos complained that he was ill. He didn't just complain. He whimpered, he moaned. He insisted on describing his symptoms and treatments in detail. Until, disgusted and annoyed, they waved us on. Each time we stopped, I was numb against his solid body, a blister tight with fear.

My head ached with fever, I smelled my hair burning. Through days and nights I sped from my father and my mother. From long afternoons with my best friend, Mones, by the river. They were yanked right through my scalp.

But Bella clung. We were Russian dolls. I inside Athos, Bella inside me.

I don't know how long we travelled this way. Once, I woke and saw signs in a fluid script that from a distance looked like Hebrew. Then Athos said we were home, in Greece. When we got closer I saw the words were strange; I'd never seen Greek letters before. It was night, but the square houses were white even in the darkness and the air was soft. I was dim with hunger and from lying so long in the car.

Athos said: "I will be your koumbaros, your godfather, the marriage sponsor for you and your sons...."

Athos said: "We must carry each other. If we don't have this, what are we...."

On the island of Zakynthos, Athos— scientist, scholar, middling master of languages—performed his most astounding feat. From out of his trousers he plucked the seven-year-old refugee Jakob Beer.

after READING

UNDERSTANDING THE TEXT

1. In your notebook, write a response to this first chapter of the novel *Fugitive Pieces*, focusing on the elements of it that would encourage or discourage you from reading the rest of the novel.

2. In your notebook, retell the story of Jakob Beer in this excerpt.

3. a) With the class, discuss the advantages of reading this excerpt aloud with others.
   b) Discuss what sets this introductory chapter apart from others you have read.

4. With a partner, make a list of the functions of a first chapter in a novel. Examine how Michaels' first chapter fulfills some or all of these functions. Decide which functions are the most important.

5. In a small group, explore the way Anne Michaels links each of the following literary devices to the subject of her first chapter:
   - repeated references to sound or lack of sound
   - unconventional use of sentence fragments in paragraph 8
   - symbolic use of time of day and time of year
   - the **character** of Bella

EXPLORING IDEAS AND IMPLICATIONS

6. In an atlas, locate Biskupin and the Gasawka River and the Island of Zakynthos. Explain why knowing where these places are enhances your understanding and appreciation of the excerpt.

7. Research references to Tollund Man and Grauballe Man. Explain why Jakob compares himself to them.

MAKING CONNECTIONS

8. Read "What Do I Remember of the Evacuation?" on pages 44–45. Compare Jakob's experiences with being torn from his home with those of the **narrator** in Kogawa's **poem**. Be prepared to discuss your observations with a partner. ■

unit

1
2
3
4

Media
Studies

Cartoon

In your notebook, describe types of commercials you distrust. Consider the products, messages, and actors. Discuss your descriptions with the class to compare reactions.

"NEVER TRUST A COMMERCIAL SHOWING A SMILING BOY EATING A PLATE OF VEGETABLES."

after READING

UNDERSTANDING THE TEXT

1. Who is the **audience** for this cartoon? Explain how you arrived at your choice. Is this cartoon effective for that audience?

2. Explain how the artist has made the cartoon humorous. Focus on both the visual and the printed words.

3. Using the following headings, describe how the cartoonist created an effective visual for the cartoon: central focus, use of angles in the drawing, movement of the television character, unity of the drawing.

EXPLORING IDEAS AND IMPLICATIONS

4. a) With a partner, create a television or radio commercial for a product that might be difficult to sell. Brainstorm ideas before selecting one. Write a shooting or audio script for the chosen idea and exchange it with another pair for feedback. The feedback should focus on the use of selling techniques, the appropriateness of the commercial for the purpose and audience, and the **implicit** and **explicit meanings** given. Revise and edit your commercial based on the feedback you receive.

   b) Tape or display the shooting script of your commercial so your peers can critique it.

MAKING CONNECTIONS

5. Choose one specific advertisement that you dislike. Deconstruct the ad to understand why you dislike it. Consider visuals (print or TV ad), sound, script, **characters**, selling techniques, implicit and explicit meanings, and **bias**. Write a critique of the ad based on your findings. (See The Reference Shelf, pages 443–444.)

6. a) In a small group, discuss the question of whether or not young children can tell reality from fantasy. As a result of your discussion, create five rules you think advertising companies should adhere to when creating ads for children. Check how your rules compare with those presented in "Children's International Television Charter" (page 336–337).

   b) Present your rules to the rest of the class. ■

Children's International Television Charter

THE CONSULTATIVE GROUP ON EARLY
CHILDHOOD CARE AND DEVELOPMENT

"... we accept our obligation to entertain, inform,
engage and enlighten young people ..."

BEFORE READING

As a class, discuss advertising on children's television programming. Consider the kind
of products advertised, the way the products are presented, and the ways these advertisements are constructed in order to appeal to children. At the end of the discussion,
decide whether there need to be rules and guidelines in Canada for advertisers using
the public airways to sell products to children.

A Children's Television Charter was developed and presented at the World Summit
on Television and Children, held in
Australia in March, 1995. At the Summit
the Charter was discussed in depth by
delegates from over 70 countries. It was
then revised by a representative group of
Summit delegates.

The Charter is conceived as a worldwide television industry commitment
to principles embodied in the United
Nations Convention on the Rights of the
Child which has been ratified by over
90% of the world's governments.

The Charter will be circulated for
endorsement to children's television

industry leaders worldwide, including all
637 Summit delegates. The Charter will
be made public to ensure that viewers have
a standard against which to judge provi-
sion for their children. Telecasters and
producers will be urged to heed its seven
points when making decisions concerning
programme production, acquisition and
distribution. Advocacy groups, researchers
and festivals will be encouraged to adopt
the Charter as the standard for evaluating
service to young people.

Governments, advertisers and funding
organizations are called on to recognize
the need for stable, adequate support for
domestic children's television. Those

companies that endorse the Charter will be asked to report annually on their own performance vis-a-vis the Charter's standards. "This report will be a valuable strategic tool for those companies that take it seriously," said Anna Home, President of the European Broadcasting Union Working Group on Children's and Youth Programming, and the author of the first draft of the Charter.

THE CHILDREN'S TELEVISION CHARTER

As stated in the United Nations Convention on the Rights of the Child, which has been ratified by more than 170 countries, broadcasters should recognize children's rights in the production of children's television programmes. As those responsible for the world's most powerful and widespread medium, and its services to children, we accept our obligation to entertain, inform, engage and enlighten young people in accord with these principles. Specifically:

1. Children should have programmes of high quality which are made specifically for them, and which do not exploit them. These programmes, in addition to entertaining, should allow children to develop physically, mentally and socially to their fullest potential.

2. Children should hear, see and express themselves, their culture, their languages and their life experiences, through television programmes which affirm their sense of self, community and place.

3. Children's programmes should promote an awareness and appreciation of other cultures in parallel with the child's own cultural background.

4. Children's programmes should be wide-ranging in genre and content, but should not include gratuitous scenes of violence and sex.

5. Children's programmes should be aired in regular slots at times when children are available to view, and/or distributed via other widely accessible media or technologies.

6. Sufficient funds must be made available to make these programmes to the highest possible standards.

7. Governments and production, distribution and funding organisations should recognize both the importance and vulnerability of indigenous children's television, and take steps to support and protect it.

May 29, 1995

after READING

UNDERSTANDING THE TEXT

1. In a small group, discuss programs that are currently popular with young people. Consider the degree to which they meet the obligation to "entertain, inform, engage and enlighten." Be prepared to present your ideas to the class.

2. In your notebook, explain which of the principles in the Children's International Television Charter should apply to television programming aimed at teenagers.

EXPLORING IDEAS AND IMPLICATIONS

3. With a partner, analyze and assess a currently popular children's television program in terms of the Children's International Television Charter. Prepare a written **report** on your conclusions.

4. Conduct an Internet search to find out what advocacy groups exist in Canada that are concerned with children's television programming. Share and discuss your findings with the class.

5. Write an **essay** explaining whether it is more important to have a television charter such as the one described here for children or one for adults. Include reasons and examples to support your position. Revise your essay, focusing on effectiveness of support, organization, and **tone**.

6. **Debate** the following resolution: Be It Resolved That Making Producers of Programs for Young Audiences Follow the Principles in the Children's International Television Charter Conflicts with Their Freedom of Speech. (See The Reference Shelf, pages 455–458.) Research may be necessary to help you prepare your arguments.

MAKING CONNECTIONS

7. Identify your favourite television program when you were a child. Assess whether it met the principles of the Children's International Television Charter. Write an essay expressing whatever praise, reservations, or condemnation you now feel the program deserves. ■

One's a Heifer

SINCLAIR ROSS

BEFORE READING

In a group of four students, discuss a **story** or novel that you had *first* read and *then* seen in a movie or television **adaptation**. (You may also have seen a film or television presentation first, and then read the book or story.) Discuss the differences between the two versions. Explain which version you prefer and why.

My uncle was laid up that winter with sciatica, so when the blizzard stopped and still two of the yearlings hadn't come home with the other cattle, Aunt Ellen said I'd better saddle Tim and start out looking for them.

"Then maybe I'll not be back tonight," I told her firmly. "Likely they've drifted as far as the sandhills. There's no use coming home without them."

I was thirteen, and had never been away like that all night before, but, busy with the breakfast, Aunt Ellen said yes, that sounded sensible enough, and while I ate, hunted up a dollar in silver for my meals.

"Most people wouldn't take it from a lad, but they're strangers up towards the hills. Bring it out independent-like, but don't insist too much. They're more likely to grudge you a feed of oats for Tim."

After breakfast I had to undress again, and put on two suits of underwear and two pairs of thick, home-knitted stockings. It was a clear, bitter morning. After the storm the drifts lay clean and unbroken to the horizon. Distant farm-buildings stood out distinct against the prairie as if the thin sharp atmosphere were a magnifying glass. As I started off Aunt Ellen peered cautiously out of the door a moment through a cloud of steam, and waved a red and white checkered dish-towel. I didn't wave back, but conscious of her uneasiness rode erect, as jaunty as the sheepskin and two suits of underwear would permit.

We took the road straight south about three miles. The calves, I reasoned, would have by this time found their way home if the blizzard hadn't carried them at least that far. Then we started catercornering across fields, riding over to straw-stacks where we could see cattle sheltering, calling at farmhouses to ask had they seen any strays. "Yearlings," I said each time politely. "Red with white spots and faces. The same almost except that one's a heifer and the other isn't."

Nobody had seen them. There was a crust on the snow not quite hard enough to carry Tim, and despite the cold his flanks and shoulders soon were steaming. He walked with his head down, and sometimes, taking my sympathy for granted, drew up a minute for breath.

My spirits, too, began to flag. The deadly cold and the flat white silent miles of prairie asserted themselves like a disapproving presence. The cattle round the straw-stacks stared when we rode up as if we were intruders. The fields stared, and the sky stared. People shivered in their doorways, and said they'd seen no strays.

At about one o'clock we stopped at a farmhouse for dinner. It was a single oat sheaf half thistles for Tim, and fried eggs and bread and tea for me. Crops had been poor that year, they apologized, and though they shook their heads when I brought out my money I saw the woman's eyes light greedily a second as if her instincts of hospitality were struggling hard against some urgent need. We too, I said, had had poor crops lately. That was why it was so important that I find the calves.

We rested an hour, then went on again. "Yearlings," I kept on describing them. "Red with white spots and faces. The same except that one's a heifer and the other isn't."

Still no one had seen them, still it was cold, still Tim protested what a fool I was.

The country began to roll a little. A few miles ahead I could see the first low line of sandhills. "They'll be there for sure," I said aloud, more to encourage myself than Tim. "Keeping straight to the road it won't take a quarter as long to get home again."

But home now seemed a long way off. A thin white sheet of cloud spread across the sky, and though there had been no warmth in the sun the fields looked colder and bleaker without the glitter on the snow. Straw-stacks were fewer here, as if the land were poor, and every house we stopped at seemed more dilapidated than the one before.

A nagging wind rose as the afternoon wore on. Dogs yelped and bayed at us, and sometimes from the hills, like the signal of our approach, there was a thin, wavering howl of a coyote. I began to dread the miles home again almost as much as those still ahead. There were so many cattle straggling across the fields, so many yearlings just like ours. I saw them for sure a dozen times, and as often choked my disappointment down and clicked Tim on again.

2

And at last I really saw them. It was nearly dusk, and along with fifteen or twenty other cattle they were making their way towards some buildings that lay huddled at the foot of the sandhills. They passed in single file less than fifty yards away, but when I pricked Tim forward to turn them back he floundered in a snowed-in water-cut. By the time we were out they were a little distance ahead, and on account of the drifts it was impossible to put on a spurt of speed and pass them. All we could do was take our place at the end of the file, and proceed at their pace towards the buildings.

It was about half a mile. As we drew near I debated with Tim whether we should ask to spend the night or start off right away for home. We were hungry and tired, but it was a poor, shiftless-looking place. The yard was littered with old wagons and machinery; the house was scarcely distinguishable from the stables. Darkness was beginning to close in, but there was no light in the windows.

Then as we crossed the yard we heard a shout, "Stay where you are," and a man came running towards us from the stable. He was tall and ungainly, and, instead of the short sheepskin that most farmers wear, had on a long black overcoat nearly to his feet. He seized Tim's bridle when he reached us, and glared for a minute as if he were going to pull me out of the saddle. "I told you to stay out," he said in a harsh, excited voice. "You heard me, didn't you? What do you want coming round here anyway?"

I steeled myself and said, "Our two calves."

The muscles of his face were drawn together threateningly, but close to him like this and looking straight into his eyes I felt that for all their fierce look there was something about them wavering and uneasy. "The two red ones with the white faces," I continued. "They've just gone into the shed over there with yours. If you'll give me a hand getting them out again I'll start for home now right away."

He peered at me a minute, let go the bridle, then clutched it again. "They're all mine," he countered. "I was over by the gate. I watched them coming in."

His voice was harsh and thick. The strange wavering look in his eyes steadied itself for a minute to a dare. I forced myself to meet it and insisted, "I saw them back a piece in the field. They're ours all right. Let me go over a minute and I'll show you."

With a crafty tilt of his head he leered, "You didn't see any calves. And now, if you know what's good for you, you'll be on your way."

"You're trying to steal them," I flared rashly. "I'll go home and get my uncle and the police after you—then you'll see whether they're our calves or not."

My threat seemed to impress him a little. With a shifty glance in the direction of the stable he said, "All right, come along and look them over. Then maybe you'll be satisfied." But all the way across the yard he kept his hand on Tim's bridle, and at the shed made me wait a few minutes while he went inside.

The cattle shed was a lean-to on the horse stable. It was plain enough: he was hiding the calves before letting me inside to look around. While waiting for him, however, I had time to realize that he was a lot bigger and stronger than I was, and that it might be prudent just to keep my eyes open, and not give him too much insolence.

He reappeared carrying a smoky lantern. "All right," he said pleasantly enough, "Come in and look around. Will your horse stand, or do you want to tie him?"

We put Tim in an empty stall in the horse stable, then went through a narrow doorway with a bar across it to the cattle shed. Just as I expected, our calves weren't there. There were two red ones with white markings that he tried to make me believe were the ones I had seen, but, positive I hadn't been mistaken, I shook my head and glanced at the doorway we had just come through. It was narrow, but not too narrow. He read my expression and said, "You think they're in there. Come on, then, look around."

The horse stable consisted of two rows of open stalls with a passage down the centre like an aisle. At the far end were two box-stalls, one with a sick colt in it, the other closed. They were both boarded up to the ceiling, so that you could see inside them only through the doors. Again he read my expression, and with a nod towards the closed one said, "It's just a kind of harness room now. Up till a year ago I kept a stallion."

But he spoke furtively, and seemed anxious to get me away from that end of the stable. His smoky lantern threw great swaying shadows over us; and the deep clefts and triangles of shadow on his face sent a little chill through me, and made me think what a dark and evil face it was.

I was afraid, but not too afraid. "If it's just a harness room," I said recklessly, "why not let me see inside? Then I'll be satisfied and believe you."

He wheeled at my question, and sidled over swiftly to the stall. He stood in front of the door, crouched down a little, the lantern in front of him like a shield. There was a sudden stillness through the stable as we faced each other. Behind the light from his lantern the darkness hovered vast and sinister. It seemed to hold its breath, to watch and listen. I felt a clutch of fear now at my throat, but I didn't move. My eyes were fixed on him so intently that he seemed to lose substance, to loom up close a moment, then recede. At last he disappeared completely, and there was only the lantern like a hard hypnotic eye.

It held me. It held me rooted, against my will. I wanted to run from the stable, but I wanted even more to see inside the stall. And yet I was afraid to see inside the stall. So afraid that it was a relief when at last he gave a shame-faced laugh and said, "There's a hole in the floor—that's why I keep the door closed. If you didn't know, you might step into it—twist your foot. That's what happened to one of my horses a while ago."

I nodded as if I believed him, and went back tractably to Tim. But regaining control of myself as I tried the saddle girths, beginning to feel that my fear had been unwarranted, I looked up and said, "It's ten miles home, and we've been riding hard all day. If we could stay a while—have something to eat, and then get started—"

The wavering light came into his eyes again. He held the lantern up to see me better, such a long, intent scrutiny that it seemed he must discover my designs. But he gave a nod finally, as if reassured, brought oats and hay for Tim, and suggested, companionably, "After supper we can have a game of checkers."

Then, as if I were a grown-up, he put out his hand and said, "My name is Arthur Vickers."

3

Inside the house, rid of his hat and coat, he looked less forbidding. He had a white nervous face, thin lips, a large straight nose, and deep uneasy eyes. When the lamp was lit I fancied I could still see the wavering expression in them, and decided it was what you called a guilty look.

"You won't think much of it," he said apologetically, following my glance around the room. "I ought to be getting things cleaned up again. Come over to the stove. Supper won't take long."

It was a large, low-ceilinged room that for the first moment or two struck me more like a shed or granary than a house. The table in the centre was littered with tools and harness. On a rusty cook-stove were two big steaming pots of bran. Next to the stove stood a grindstone, then a white iron bed covered with coats and horse blankets. At the end opposite the bed, weasel and coyote skins were drying. There were guns and traps on the wall, a horse collar, a pair of rubber boots. The floor was bare and grimy. Ashes were littered around the stove. In a corner squatted a live owl with a broken wing.

He walked back and forth a few times looking helplessly at the disorder, then cleared off the table and lifted the pots of bran to the back of the stove. "I've been mending harness," he explained. "You get careless, living alone like this. It takes a woman anyway."

My presence, apparently, was making him take stock of the room. He picked up a broom and swept for a minute, made an ineffective attempt to straighten the blankets on the bed, brought another lamp out of a cupboard and lit it. There was an ungainly haste to all his movements. He started unbuckling my sheepskin for me, then turned away suddenly to take off his own coat. "Now we'll have supper," he said with an effort at self-possession. "Coffee and beans is all I can give you—maybe a little molasses."

I replied diplomatically that that sounded pretty good. It didn't seem right, accepting hospitality this way from a man who was trying to steal your calves, but theft, I reflected, surely justified deceit. I held my hands out to the warmth, and asked if I could help.

There was a kettle of plain navy beans already cooked. He dipped out enough for our supper into a frying pan, and on top laid rashers of fat salt pork. While I watched that they didn't burn he rinsed off a few dishes. Then he set out sugar and canned milk, butter, molasses, and dark heavy biscuits that he had baked himself the day before. He kept glancing at me so apologetically all the while that I leaned over and sniffed the beans, and said at home I ate a lot of them.

"It takes a woman," he repeated as we sat down to the table. "I don't often have anyone here to eat with. If I'd known, I'd have cleaned things up a little."

I was too intent on my plateful of beans to answer. All through the meal he sat watching me, but made no further attempts at conversation. Hungry as I was, I noticed that the wavering, easy look was still in his eyes. A guilty look, I told myself again, and wondered what I was going to do to get the calves away. I finished my coffee and he continued:

"It's worse even than this in the summer. No time for meals—and the heat and flies. Last summer I had a girl cooking for a few weeks, but it didn't last. Just a cow she was—just a big stupid cow—and she wanted to stay on. There's a family of them back in the hills. I had to send her home."

I wondered should I suggest starting now, or ask to spend the night. Maybe when he's asleep, I thought, I can slip out of the house and get away with the calves. He went on, "You don't know how bad it is sometimes. Weeks on end and no one to talk to. You're not yourself—you're not sure what you're going to say or do."

I remembered hearing my uncle talk about a man who had gone crazy living alone. And this fellow Vickers had queer eyes all right. And there was the live owl over in the corner, and the grindstone standing right beside the bed. "Maybe I'd better go now," I decided aloud. "Tim'll be rested, and it's ten miles home."

But he said no, it was colder now, with the wind getting stronger, and seemed so kindly and concerned that I half forgot my fears. "Likely he's just starting to go crazy," I told myself, "And it's only by staying that I'll have a chance to get the calves away."

When the table was cleared and the dishes washed he said he would go out and bed down the stable for the night. I picked up my sheepskin to go with him, but he told me sharply to stay inside. Just for a minute he looked crafty and forbidding as when I first rode up on Tim, and to allay his suspicions I nodded compliantly

and put my sheepskin down again. It was better like that anyway, I decided. In a few minutes I could follow him, and perhaps, taking advantage of the shadows and his smoky lantern, make my way to the box-stall unobserved.

But when I reached the stable he had closed the door after him and hooked it from the inside. I walked round a while, tried to slip in by way of the cattle shed, and then had to go back to the house. I went with a vague feeling of relief again. There was still time, I told myself, and it would be safer anyway when he was sleeping.

So that it would be easier to keep from falling asleep myself I planned to suggest coffee again just before we went to bed. I knew that the guest didn't ordinarily suggest such things, but it was no time to remember manners when there was some-one trying to steal your calves.

4

When he came in from the stable we played checkers. I was no match for him, but to encourage me he repeatedly let me win. "It's a long time now since I've had a chance to play," he kept on saying, trying to convince me that his short-sighted moves weren't intentional. "Sometimes I used to ask her to play, but I had to tell her every move to make. If she didn't win she'd upset the board and go off and sulk."

"My aunt is a little like that too," I said. "She cheats sometimes when we're playing cribbage—and, when I catch her, says her eyes aren't good."

"Women talk too much ever to make good checker players. It takes concentration.

This one, though, couldn't even talk like anybody else."

After my long day in the cold I was starting to yawn already. He noticed it, and spoke in a rapid, earnest voice, as if afraid I might lose interest soon and want to go to bed. It was important for me too to stay awake, so I crowned a king and said, "Why don't you get someone, then, to stay with you?"

"Too many of them want to do that." His face darkened a little, almost as if warning me. "Too many of the kind you'll never get rid of again. She did, last summer when she was here. I had to put her out."

There was silence for a minute, his eyes flashing, and wanting to placate him I suggested, "She liked you, maybe."

He laughed a moment, harshly. "She liked me all right. Just two weeks ago she came back—walked over with an old suitcase and said she was going to stay. It was cold at home, and she had to work too hard, and she didn't mind even if I couldn't pay her wages."

I was getting sleepier. To keep awake I sat on the edge of the chair where it was uncomfortable and said, "Hadn't you asked her to come?"

His eyes narrowed. "I'd had trouble enough getting rid of her the first time. There were six of them at home, and she said her father thought it time that someone married her."

"Then she must be a funny one," I said. "Everyone knows that the man's supposed to ask the girl."

My remark seemed to please him. "I told you, didn't I?" he said, straightening a little, jumping two of my men. "She was so stupid that at checkers she'd forget whether she was black or red."

We stopped playing now. I glanced at the owl in the corner and the ashes littered on the floor, and thought that keeping her would maybe have been a good idea after all. He read it in my face and said, "I used to think that too sometimes. I used to look at her and think nobody knew now anyway and that she'd maybe do. You need a woman on a farm all right. And night after night she'd be sitting there where you are—right there where you are, looking at me, not even trying to play—"

The fire was low, and we could hear the wind. "But then I'd go up in the hills, away from her for a while, and start thinking back the way things used to be, and it wasn't right even for the sake of your meals ready and your house kept clean. When she came back I tried to tell her that, but all the family are the same, and I realized it wasn't any use. There's nothing you can do when you're up against that sort of thing. The mother talks just like a child of ten. When she sees you coming she runs and hides. There are six of them, and it's come out in every one."

It was getting cold, but I couldn't bring myself to go over to the stove. There was the same stillness now as when he was standing at the box-stall door. And I felt the same illogical fear, the same powerlessness to move. It was the way his voice had lowered, the glassy, cold look in his eyes. The rest of his face disappeared; all I could see were his eyes. And they held me as the lantern had held me, held me intent, rigid, even as they filled me with vague and overpowering dread. My voice gone a whisper on me I asked, "And when you wouldn't marry her—what happened then?"

He remained motionless a moment, as if answering silently; then with an unexpected laugh like a breaking dish said, "Why, nothing happened. I just told her she couldn't stay. I went to town for a few days—and when I came back she was gone."

"Has she been back to bother you since?" I asked.

He made a little silo of checkers. "No—she took her suitcase with her."

To remind him that the fire was going down I went over to the stove and stood warming myself. He raked the coals with the lifter and put in poplar, two split pieces for a base and a thick round log on top. I yawned again. He said maybe I'd like to go to bed now, and I shivered and asked him could I have a drink of coffee first. While it boiled he stood stirring the two big pots of bran. The trouble with coffee, I realized, was that it would keep him from getting sleepy too.

I undressed finally and got into bed, but he blew out only one of the lamps, and sat on playing checkers with himself. I dozed a while, then sat up with a start, afraid it was morning already and that I'd lost my chance to get the calves away. He came over and looked at me a minute, then gently pushed my shoulders back on the pillow. "Why don't you come to bed too?" I asked and he said, "Later I will—I don't feel sleepy yet."

It was like that all night. I kept dozing on and off, wakening in a fright each time to find him still there sitting at his checker board. He would raise his head sharply when I stirred, then tiptoe over to the bed and stand close to me listening till satisfied again I was asleep. The owl kept wakening too. It was down in the corner still where the lamplight scarcely reached, and I could see its eyes go on and off like yellow bulbs. The wind whistled drearily around the house. The blankets smelled like an old granary. He suspected what I was planning to do, evidently, and was staying awake to make sure I didn't get outside.

Each time I dozed I dreamed I was on Tim again. The calves were in sight, but far ahead of us, and with the drifts so deep we couldn't overtake them. Then instead of Tim it was the grindstone I was straddling, and that was the reason, not the drifts, that we weren't making better progress.

I wondered what would happen to the calves if I didn't get away with them. My uncle had sciatica, and it would be least a day before I could be home and back again with some of the neighbors. By then Vickers might have butchered the calves, or driven them up to a hiding place in the hills where we'd never find them. There was the possibility, too, that Aunt Ellen and the neighbors wouldn't believe me. I dozed and woke—dozed and woke—always he was sitting at the checker board. I could hear the dry tinny ticking of an alarm clock, but from where I was lying couldn't see it. He seemed to be listening to it too. The wind would sometimes creak the house, and then he would give a start and sit rigid a moment with his eyes fixed on the window. It was the window, as if there was nothing he was afraid of that could reach him by the door.

Most of the time he played checkers with himself, moving his lips, muttering words I couldn't hear, but once I woke to find him staring fixedly across the table as if he had a partner sitting there. His hands were clenched in front of him, there was a sharp, metallic glitter in his eyes. I lay transfixed, unbreathing. His eyes as I watched seemed to dilate, to brighten, to harden like a bird's. For a long time he sat contracted, motionless, as if gathering himself to strike, then furtively he slid his hand an inch or two along the table towards some checkers that were piled beside the board. It was as if he were reaching for a weapon, as if his invisible partner were an enemy. He clutched the checkers, slipped slowly from his chair and straightened. His movements were sure, stealthy, silent like a cat's. His face had taken on a desperate, contorted look. As he raised his hand the tension was unbearable.

It was a long time—a long time watching him the way you watch a finger tightening slowly on the trigger of a gun—and then suddenly wrenching himself to action he hurled the checkers with such vicious fury that they struck the wall in front of him and clattered back across the room.

And then everything was quiet again. I started a little, mumbled to myself as if half-awakened, lay quite still. But he seemed to have forgotten me, and after standing limp and dazed a minute got down on his knees and started looking for the checkers. When he had them all, he put more wood in the stove, then returned quietly to the table and sat down. We were alone again; everything was exactly as before. I relaxed gradually, telling myself that he'd just been seeing things.

The next time I woke he was sitting with his head sunk forward on the table. It looked as if he had fallen asleep at last, and huddling alert among the bed-clothes I decided to watch a minute to make sure, then dress and try to slip out to the stable.

While I watched, I planned exactly every movement I was going to make. Rehearsing it in my mind as carefully as if I were actually doing it, I climbed out of bed, put on my clothes, tiptoed stealthily to the door and slipped outside. By this time, though, I was getting drowsy, and relaxing among the blankets I decided that for safety's sake I should rehearse it still again. I rehearsed it four times altogether, and the fourth time dreamed that I hurried on successfully to the stable.

I fumbled with the door a while, then went inside and felt my way through the darkness to the box-stall. There was a bright light suddenly and the owl was sitting over the door with his yellow eyes like a pair of lanterns. The calves, he told me, were in the other stall with the sick colt. I looked and they were there all right, but Tim came up and said it might be better not to start for home till morning. He reminded me that I hadn't paid for his feed or my own supper yet, and that if I slipped off this way it would mean that I was stealing too. I agreed, realizing now that it wasn't the calves I was looking for after all, and that I still had to see inside the stall that was guarded by the owl. "Wait here," Tim said, "I'll tell you if he flies away," and without further questioning I lay down in the straw and went to sleep again.... When I woke coffee and beans were on the stove already, and though the lamp was still lit I could tell by the window that it was nearly morning.

5

We were silent during breakfast. Two or three times I caught him watching me, and it seemed his eyes were shiftier than before. After his sleepless night he looked tired and haggard. He left the table while I was still eating and fed raw rabbit to the owl, then came back and drank another cup of coffee. He had been friendly and communicative the night before, but now, just as when he first came running out of the stable in his long black coat, his expression was sullen and resentful. I began to feel that he was in a hurry to be rid of me.

I took my time, however, racking my brains to outwit him still and get the calves away. It looked pretty hopeless now, his eyes on me so suspiciously, my imagination at low ebb. Even if I did get inside the box-stall to see the calves—was he going to stand back then and let me start off home with them? Might it not more likely frighten him, make him do something desperate, so that I couldn't reach my uncle or the police? There was the owl over in the corner, the grindstone by the bed. And with such a queer fellow you could never tell. You could never tell, and you had to think about your own skin too. So I said politely, "Thank you, Mr. Vickers, for letting me stay all night," and

remembering what Tim had told me took out my dollar's worth of silver.

He gave a short dry laugh and wouldn't take it. "Maybe you'll come back," he said, "and next time stay longer. We'll go shooting up in the hills if you like—and I'll make a trip to town for things so that we can have better meals. You need company sometimes for a change. There's been no one here now quite a while."

His face softened again as he spoke. There was an expression in his eyes as if he wished that I could stay on now. It puzzled me. I wanted to be indignant, and it was impossible. He held my sheepskin for me while I put it on, and tied the scarf around the collar with a solicitude and determination equal to Aunt Ellen's. And then he gave his short dry laugh again, and hoped I'd find my calves all right.

He had been out to the stable before I was awake, and Tim was ready for me, fed and saddled. But I delayed a few minutes, pretending to be interested in his horses and the sick colt. It would be worth something after all, I realized, to get just a glimpse of the calves. Aunt Ellen was going to be sceptical enough of my story as it was. It could only confirm her doubts to hear me say I hadn't seen the calves in the box-stall, and was pretty sure that they were there.

So I went from stall to stall, stroking the horses and making comparisons with the ones we had at home. The door, I noticed, he had left wide open, ready for me to lead out Tim. He was walking up and down the aisle, telling me which horses were quiet, which to be careful of. I came to a nervous chestnut mare, and realized she was my only chance.

She brushed her hips against the side of the stall as I slipped up to her manger, almost pinning me, then gave her head a toss and pulled back hard on the halter shank. The shank, I noticed, was tied with an easy slip-knot that the right twist and a sharp tug would undo in half a second. And the door was wide open, ready for me to lead out Tim—and standing as she was with her body across the stall diagonally, I was for the moment screened from sight.

It happened quickly. There wasn't time to think of consequences. I just pulled the knot, in the same instant struck the mare across the nose. With a snort she threw herself backwards, almost trampling Vickers, then flung up her head to keep from tripping on the shank and plunged outside.

It worked as I hoped it would. "Quick," Vickers yelled to me, "the gate's open—try and head her off"—but instead I just waited till he himself was gone, then fairly flew to the box-stall.

The door was fastened with two tight-fitting slide-bolts, one so high that I could scarcely reach it standing on my toes. It wouldn't yield. There was a piece of broken whiffle-tree beside the other box-stall door. I snatched it up and started hammering on the pin. Still it wouldn't yield. The head of the pin was small and round, and the whiffle-tree kept glancing off. I was too terrified to pause a moment and take careful aim.

Terrified of the stall though, not of Vickers. Terrified of the stall, yet compelled by a frantic need to get inside. For the moment I had forgotten Vickers, forgotten even the danger of his catching me. I worked blindly, helplessly, as if I were confined and smothering. For a moment I yielded to panic, dropped the piece of whiffle-tree and started kicking at the door. Then, collected again, I forced back the lower bolt, and picking up the whiffle-tree tried to pry the door out a little at the bottom. But I had wasted too much time. Just as I dropped to my knees to peer through the opening Vickers seized me. I struggled to my feet and fought a moment, but it was such a hard, strangling clutch at my throat that I felt myself go limp and blind. In desperation then I kicked him, and with a blow like a reflex he sent me staggering to the floor.

But it wasn't the blow that frightened me. It was the fierce, wild light in his eyes.

Stunned as I was, I looked up and saw him watching me, and, sick with terror, made a bolt for Tim. I untied him with hands that moved incredibly, galvanized for escape. I knew now for sure that Vickers was crazy. He followed me outside, and just as I mounted, seized Tim again by the bridle. For a second or two it made me crazy too. Gathering up the free ends of the reins I lashed him across the face. He let go of the bridle, and, frightened and excited too now, Tim made a dash across the yard and out of the gate. Deep as the snow was, I kept him galloping for half a mile, pommelling him with my fists, kicking my heels against his sides. Then of his own accord he drew up short for breath, and I looked around to see whether Vickers was following. He wasn't— there was only the snow and the hills, his buildings a lonely little smudge against the whiteness—and the relief was like a stick pulled out that's been holding up tomato vines or peas. I slumped across the saddle weakly, and till Tim started on again lay there whimpering like a baby.

6

We were home by noon. We didn't have to cross fields or stop at houses now, and there had been teams on the road packing down the snow so that Tim could trot part of the way and even canter. I put him in the stable without taking time to tie or unbridle him, and ran to the house to tell Aunt Ellen. But I was still frightened, cold and a little hysterical, and it was a while before she could understand how everything had happened. She was silent a minute, indulgent, then helping me off with my sheepskin said kindly, "You'd better forget about it now, and come over and get warm. The calves came home themselves yesterday. Just about an hour after you set out."

I looked up at her. "But the stall, then— just because I wanted to look inside he knocked me down—and if it wasn't the calves in there—"

She didn't answer. She was busy building up the fire and looking at the stew.

One's a Heifer

ADAPTED FOR TELEVISION BY RUDI DORN

Characters: The Boy, the Man, the Uncle

L.S. = long shot, *M.S.* = medium shot, *C.U.* = close up, *Ext.* = exterior, *Int.* = interior, *V.O.* = voiceover, or voice off

SCENE 1
Farmhouse. Ext. Day. Blizzard.
(Special effects.)

The front of a barn. Snow is drifting past the screen in violent white waves. The door of the barn opens wide. Out of the blackness a boy emerges, leading a sturdy horse by bridle. The horse, upset by the blizzard, rears and tries to back into the safety of the barn. After a short struggle, the boy manages to mount the horse and they are off, into the storm.

SCENE 2
Farm. Ext. Day. Blizzard.

The horse and rider are in the midst of the blizzard. Fences are broken or half covered by snow. Various shots.

SCENE 3
Farm. Ext. Day. Blizzard.

Another area close by to facilitate special effects. Another angle of the rider bracing the elements. Passing a half-buried cart or some broken field equipment to show the devastation.

Sound: Howling storm, rattling shingles. The boy's voice urging on the horse, muffled by the storm.

Various shots (M.S., C.U.) to establish a sense of motion and thrust against the elements.

SCENE 4
Open country. Snow. Day.

Possibly another angle of the same area. (Still needs some special effects, blizzard.)

There is a gust of wind. Eddies of snow whirling through the air. Slowly the camera pans into the open field. (L.S.)

Some distance away the horse and rider are crossing the snow-covered ground, leaving deep tracks in the snow. The blizzard is slowly losing its strength.

The boy's face, close (C.U.) showing relief. His face is crusted over with snow. He has trouble seeing the terrain ahead of him. His eyes are sore, his lips blue from the intense cold (Make-up). But the blizzard is over.

SCENE 5
Open country. Snow. Day.

The boy pulls the reins of the horse, looks about, then yells. Silence. There is no more sound. The blanket of snow is all around them. Slowly they continue what now obviously seems to be a search.

There are animal tracks in the snow. (C.U.) Note: *Animal tracks to be made by special effects or staging. The boy rides beside them, looking down and around. (C.U.) Then suddenly the tracks disappear in a snow-drift. Silence. Frustration in the boy's face.*

Suddenly he focuses his eyes. A long distance away there is a dark spot in the snow. He swings his horse around. As they are approaching the area the horse stops,

seemingly frightened, neighing softly. The boy jumps off the horse and pulling it by the bridle he moves closer. A dead calf is lying half buried in the snow. The boy leans over it, looks at it carefully, when suddenly the sounds from a herd of cattle are reaching him. He gets up startled, looks about. There is nothing at first. Quickly he remounts the horse and rides off in the direction of the sound.

Cut to:

SCENE 6
Farm area. Ext. Snow. Day.

A small herd of cattle is slowly moving toward a few dilapidated farm buildings. (Vickers' farm, also the barn area of Scene 1.)

When the boy sees the cattle he charges across the wide field trying to close in on them. At the last moment a wire fence stops him. Vainly he tries to intercept the herd of cattle by trying to get around the obstacle (fence).

Some of the calves in the herd seem to hold his attention. When he finally catches up with them, they have already entered the farm yard.

Cut to:

SCENE 7
Farmyard. Ext. Day.

Horse and rider are following the herd into the junky farmyard. Suddenly someone (the man) is shouting.
V.O.: *Stay where you are!*
A tall, ungainly-looking man moves toward them wearing a long black overcoat. He

grabs the bridle of the horse. For a moment he looks as if he wants to pull the boy out of the saddle.

Man: Didn't you hear what I said? Stay out!

Boy: (*steeling himself*) I want my two calves. One's a heifer. They are in there with your cattle.

Man: That's a lie.

Boy: The two red ones with the white faces. They are mine. They've got lost in the blizzard—they are mine. Listen, if you'll give me a hand getting them out again, I'll start for home right away.

Man: (*still clutching the bridle*) They are all mine, boy. All mine. I watched every one of them coming in.

Silence. Tension.

Boy: Just let me look. I'll prove it to you.

Man: (*with a crafty look, shaking his head*) You didn't see any calves of yours.

Boy: (*more upset now*) I know you're trying to steal them. All right, I'll go home and get the police after you, then we'll see whether they are our calves or not.

Man: (*with a shifty glance at the stable*) All right, look them over. Then maybe you'll be satisfied.

Crossing the yard he is still clutching the bridle. The boy gets off the horse, moves toward the door of the stable.

Man: (*intercepting him*) Wait here.

And disappears inside the stable. The shuffling of feet of the cows inside. The boy's face is cold and frustrated. The man reappears at the door and is more pleasant now.

Man: Will your horse stand or do you want to tie him?

Before the boy has time to answer, he takes the horse by the bridle and leads it into the horse stable (beside the cattle if possible). The

boy's look of mounting frustration as he follows the stranger.

Cut to:

SCENE 8
Int. Stable. Horse and cattle. Low key.

The man has tied up the horse, and motions the boy to follow him (through a low door separating the horse stable from the cattle).

Man: (*holding a kerosene stable lantern*) Watch where you are going—it's mighty dark in here. The blizzard has cut off all the power.

As soon as the boy has adjusted his eyes to the dark he goes straight toward two calves in a stall. He touches their heads, looking for their familiar marks. It's not them. The man watches him with a faint smile.

The boy turns and proceeds further into the darkness of the stable. There is a boarded-up area (or a low door, etc.). The boy stops in front of it, turns to face the stranger.

Boy: What's in there?

Man: Oh that. It's just a kind of harness room now. Until a year ago I kept a stallion.

He looks as if he is anxious to get the boy from that ominous area. For a brief moment his face looks dark and evil (Lighting).

Boy: Why don't you let me look inside?

Slowly the stranger is intercepting him, blocking the door. Sudden stillness. Only the breathing and shuffling of feet from the cattle.

The boy is managing not to show his sudden fear and looks squarely into the stranger's eyes. After what seems an eternity the stranger speaks.

Man: There is a hole in the floor—that's why I keep the door closed. If you didn't know, you might step into it, twist your foot. That's what happened to one of my horses.

The boy nods, as if believing him, and walks back toward his horse, followed by the man.

Boy: (*trying the saddle girths. His hands are still numb from the cold.*) You wouldn't have a cup of hot tea or something?

He stands very still, hoping the man doesn't discover his secret designs.

Man: (*after a moment of intense scrutiny*) After supper we can have a game of checkers. (*Suddenly he puts out his hand.*) My name is Arthur Vickers.

(*Smiles and exits.*)

Cut to:

SCENE 9
Int. Vickers' house. Night. Low key.

It is a large, low-ceilinged room, more like a shed or granary than a house. The table in the centre is littered with tools and a harness. On a cookstove are two steaming pots of bran and beans. Next to the stove is a grindstone, then a white iron bed covered with coats and horse blankets. Weasel and coyote skins are drying. There are guns and traps on the wall, a horse collar, rubber boots. The floor is bare and grimy. Ashes are littered around the stove.

The man walks about looking helplessly at the disorder, then tries to clear the mess.

Man: I've been mending harness. You get careless, living alone like this. It takes a woman anyway.

(*He is starting to unbuckle the boy's sheepskin, then takes off his own coat.*)

Beans, that's all I can give you. Maybe a little bacon.

The boy nods, feeling quite uneasy about having accepted the invitation. He warms his hands at the stove. He watches the man put some slices of bacon in a frying pan.

Man: (*while at the stove*) Yeah. It takes a woman. If I'd known I'd cleaned things up a little. (*Pan to boy.*) Some blizzard that was. But I got off cheap. Just lost a few shingles. It all needs fixing up anyway.

The boy looks around apprehensively when suddenly the man shoves a plate full of beans at his side.

Man: Here. That's yours. (*And goes to the table.*)

The boy grabs the plate and moves to the table, sits.

Man: (*follows with his own plate*) It's even worse in summer. The heat and the flies. Last summer I had a girl cooking for a few weeks, but it didn't last. Just a cow she was—a big stupid cow—and she wanted to stay on. I had to send her home.

His eyes are riveted on the boy trying to read his thoughts. Tension.

Man: You've heard about it?

Boy: What?

Man: Never mind. Eat. (*Silence. He swallows a spoonful, then fixes the boy.*) Whereabouts are you from?

Boy: Me? Oh, just from over that way. About ten, fifteen miles.

Man: (*quickly*) What does your father do?

Boy: I've got no father. My uncle farms— like you, that is.

Man: Eat. Don't talk so much.

Boy: I sure like this soup. I must be all frozen up inside.

Man: You are sure nobody told you to come here? (*beat*) What's your name, boy?

Boy: Richard, Richard Welland.

Man: Welland. Never heard of it. And you said your father was a farmer.

Boy: My uncle. I've *told* you my father was dead. (*silence*) That's very good bacon.

Man: Hmm?

Boy: The bacon is very good.

The man looks about as if he were hearing something.

Boy: What is it?

Man: (*startled*) Nothing. (*nods, smiles*)

Boy: (*stops eating, growing uneasy*) Maybe I'd better go now. Tim'll be rested.

Man: (*suddenly alert*) Who's Tim?

Boy: My horse.

Man: (*grunting with relief*) Oh. (*beat*) Eat. I said (*friendlier*), eat—Richard.

Boy: Listen, Mr. Vickers. It's getting dark out. I've got at least ten miles to go.

The man puts down his spoon firmly and gets up, blocking the door.

Man: It's no use, boy. You're going to freeze to death out there. Yes, sir, you better stay right here.

Boy: (*trying to conceal his mounting uneasiness*) Thanks, Mr. Vickers, but I have to go. They are waiting for me back home.

Slowly he has tried to make it to the door.

Man: (*blocking his way with a smile*) You stay right here, okay? I'll look after your horse.

The man exits into the night. The boy alone, stands very still, listening. Then quickly putting on his sheepskin he follows the man outside.

Cut to:

SCENE 10
Ext. Barnyard, stable area. Dusk.

The boy moves quickly toward the stable door. The door is locked from the inside. He rattles the door in frustration. Then moves along the grimy row of windows outside trying to peek inside. It is very dark. But suddenly he sees the man.

Cut to:

SCENE 11
Int. Stable. Night.

The man is standing beside the boarded-up area, very still, almost as if listening to someone. Then he swings around quickly, instinctively feeling that he is being watched. He turns quickly and goes for the door.

Cut to:

SCENE 12
Ext. Stable. Dusk.

The boy races back to the house. The man follows him quickly.

Cut to:

SCENE 13
Int. House. Dusk.

The door swings open, letting in the cold. The man enters, breathing hard.

Man: (*very quickly*) You don't know how bad it is sometimes. Weeks on end. Nobody to talk to. You just wouldn't know, boy. You're not yourself. You're not sure what you're going to say—or do. (*There is a hint of madness in his speech.*) Do you want to play checkers? (*Without* *waiting for an answer, he rambles on, smiling, scowling, etc.*) Sometimes I used to ask her to play, but I had to tell her every move to make. If she didn't win she'd upset the board and go off and sulk. She was very stupid. Women talk too much ever to make good checker players. This one, though, couldn't even talk like anybody else. She was a real cow.

The boy is standing a long distance apart from him, almost hugging the stove.

Boy: (*quickly*) Then why don't you get someone else—another woman—to stay with you?

The man goes slowly toward the area where he has stored his game of checkers.

Man: (*laughingly*) Oh, too many of them want to do that. Too many of the kind you never get rid of again. (*He empties the checkers on the table.*) What do you want, red or black?

Boy: I don't care, Mr. Vickers. I do think—

Man: (*dividing the checker drafts with a heavy hand*) Red. You take the red ones.

Then he looks straight at the boy.

Boy: (*after a furtive look in the direction of the stable*) Okay. Just one game.

Man: Sit down. You know how to play it?

The boy nods. They are both sorting out the drafts. Silence.

Boy: Mr. Vickers?

Man: Yeah?

Boy: Whatever happened to that woman?

Man: Oh, her. I had to put her out.

Boy: (*quickly*) She liked you maybe?

Man: She liked me all right. Just two weeks ago she came back and said she was going to stay. She didn't mind even if I couldn't pay her wages. (*beat*) She said

her father thought it time that someone married her. (*beat*) Your move.

Boy: She is a funny one.

Man: (*startled*) Why? Did you know her?

Boy: Me? No.

Man: Then what's so funny?

Boy: Everyone knows that the man's supposed to ask the girl.

Man: Ask for what?

Boy: To marry her.

Man: (*pleased about the remark*) Oh yeah. I told you, didn't I? She was so stupid that at checkers she'd forget whether she was black or red.

Silence. He lowers his eyes on the game. The boy, very self-conscious now, moves one of his red checkers across the board. Silence. The boy feels powerless, sits very still. There is the heavy breathing of the stranger. It's his move. The black drafts are his.

Boy: And when you didn't marry her, what happened (*very slowly*) then?

Silence.

Man: (*gently*) Why, nothing happened. I just told her she couldn't stay.

Boy: What did she do?

Silence. Pause.

Man: I went to town for a few days. (*beat*) When I came back she was gone.

Their eyes meet. The boy cannot hold the stare. Silence.

A wind has started outside, rattling the loose shingles. Both of them look up, listening. Suddenly the man gets up, goes to the stove—raking the coals.

Man: (*his back to the boy*) Go to bed.

Boy: We haven't finished the game.

Man: Go to bed. (*then with a warm smile*) You need the sleep, boy. Sleep.

The boy gets up and walks towards the bed

and sits on the covers. *Trying to think of a way out of the situation. The man watches him.* Is there anything else you need? If you have to go to the can ...

The boy's eyes are reflecting a "hope for escape." He looks quickly at the door.

Man: (*smiling*) ... it's right in there.

Boy: (*dejectedly*) No. Not now.

The man turns, walks toward him—then pushes him gently back on the pillow and covers him with the furs.

Man: (*gently*) A growing boy like you needs a lot of sleep.

Boy: Aren't you going to bed? I can easily sleep somewhere else.

Man: No. You stay right here. Don't you worry about me.

Slowly the man withdraws from the bed and goes to the door. Locks it firmly. Then sits down in his chair by the table. The boy is watching it all, his face half covered by the furs.

The wind, the shingles are rattling. Otherwise there is not a sound. It is night. The boy turns in his bed, trying to find a more comfortable position. The face of the man. He reacts. From the corner of his eye he watches the boy. The boy, close, very ill at ease.

The window, a strange sound outside it.

Startled, the man looks towards the window. Then his face relaxes again into stoic stupor. Each moment seems to be suspended. There is no peace this night. The man sits very still, contracted, motionless, as if gathering himself to strike. Then his hands are furtively sliding toward some checkers on the table. The boy's face, watching. The man is reaching for the checkers as if they are an invisible weapon. The man clutches the checkers. Slips slowly from the chair and straightens. His movements are sure, stealthy,

and silent like a cat's. The boy is blinking his eyes, closing them, hoping it is a dream. The face of the stranger has taken on a desperate, contorted look. Then he raises his hand, slowly. The face of the boy, his eyes now wide open.

Suddenly wrenching himself into action the man hurls the checkers, with such vicious fury that they hit the wall in front of him and are clattering back across the room. The boy has shut his eyes, afraid. He is not sure whether he has really seen all this.

Silence. Dead silence. Only the faint howling of the storm.

The man is standing limp and dazed in the middle of the room. He turns slowly and goes toward the stove. He inserts another log into the fire. His face, close, the dancing flames. The boy is very sleepy now. The man is sitting in his chair, his head slumped forward as if asleep.

The boy, aware of the sudden lack of movement and tension, is opening his eyes. The man sits very still. The boy throws back the furs. He slides out of the bed and slowly picks up his coat and heads for the door. The man opens his eyes. He has never been asleep. The boy stands frozen, not knowing what to do.

Man: (*very friendly*) I told you it's in there, boy.

The boy swallows hard and crosses the large room, careful not to come too close to the stranger.

SCENE 13A

There is a window in a tiny little room, all frosted over. The boy's face appears. His hands are scratching away at the thin layer of ice. It is black outside. The howling storm. The face of the boy.

Man: (*V.O.*) Want a cup of tea, boy?

Boy: (*without moving*) Yes, sir.
Pan off the face into blackness.

Cut to:

SCENE 14
Farm. Ext. Day.

Blackness. Transition. The sound of morning. Animals kicking their stalls. The gentle mooing of the cows.

Pan into brightness. (L.S.) The farmhouse sitting peacefully in the snow. Faint smoke rising from a chimney.

The man is emerging from the stable wearing his huge black coat.
Man: (*jovially*) Did you finish your breakfast?
Boy: (*running up from the house all flustered*) Yes, sir. Thanks for letting me stay the night. (*reaches for his pocket*) And I do want to pay for all your *trouble*.
Man: Oh never mind. That's quite all right. It was a pleasure to have you. It gets quite lonely here.
The boy tries to enter the stable.
Man: (*filling the image of the door*) I've fed and saddled your horse. Wait! (*And turns.*)
Boy: Well, thanks. You shouldn't have bothered.
Man: (*still trying to block the entrance to the stable*) I'll get it for you.
As he enters the stable, the boy slips past him quickly, trying to get another look at the ominous area where his calves could be hidden.

Cut to:

SCENE 15
Int. Stable. Day.

The man staggers after him but is not able to catch up with the boy who walks swiftly through the stable.
Man: (*upset*) Now listen, boy. I do have a lot of chores to do. Maybe next time you come back and we'll go shooting some rabbits and I'll pick up some things in town so that we can have better meals. I'm a pretty good cook you know, if I set my heart at it.
The boy stops abruptly at a stall, walks into it, starts stroking a horse's nose.
Boy: (*pretending interest*) I like that one. A real nice animal. How much you want for her? My uncle is looking for a horse like that since—I don't know when.
Man: She ain't for sale. And better be careful. She ain't used to strangers.
Boy: (*trying to pry the horse's mouth open*) Easy. How old would she be?
Man: About six years, I'd say. Yeah. Six years, or a little less. Listen, I ain't got much time for gabbing—
Boy: I'd say she's ten years at least.
Man: Ten years! She is six and not a day older.
Boy: Ten. Do you know how I can tell?
Man: You're not telling me about horses, boy.
Boy: (*very tense*) Come here, I'll show you.
The man moves quickly into the stall on the other side of the horse.
Man: What are you talking about? She was born in that stall over there.
Suddenly the boy pulls a knot and slaps the horse on the face. The horse backs up, almost trampling the man, and plunges toward the low entrance. (Action to be staged.)
Man: (*shouting*) Quick! The gate's open! Try and head her off. (*And he runs after the horse.*)

Instead of helping the man, the boy dashes toward the boarded-up area and starts prying it open. For a moment he panics, dropping the whiffletree, and/or starts kicking at the door.

He forces back the lower bolt and/or picking up the whiffletree he again tries to pry out the door a little at the bottom.

But too late. Suddenly the stranger is upon him. The boy struggles to his feet and fights back desperately. The man has him firmly by the throat. For a moment the boy goes limp and blind. In desperation he kicks him hard. With a blow the man sends the boy staggering to the floor. The eyes of the stranger are wild and frightening. Quickly, the boy gets up and makes a run for his horse, unties it, manages to lead it into the open followed by the crazed stranger.

Cut to:

SCENE 16
Ext. Stable area. Day.

Frantically the boy swings himself into the saddle. The man grabs the horse by the reins, gathering up the ends of the reins. The boy lashes the man across the face. There is no reaction. He hits the man again and again, until finally he manages to break free and with a dash across the yard he is out of the gate.

Cut to:

SCENE 17
Open fields (near farm). Day.

Through the deep snow, he keeps galloping, pommelling the horse with his fists, kicking his heels against its side. Then he stops, turns around.

The farm is now a lonely little smudge against his whiteness. A long distance off. (L.S.)

The boy slumps against the saddle, weakly (out of breath), and lies there until the horse decides to start on again.

Cut to:

SCENE 18
Ext. Barn. Day. Boy's home.

Slowly the boy rides into the yard. The barn door is open. A man (his uncle) emerges, intent on some chores. It is a cold and quiet day.
Uncle: Where the hell have you been all night? Mother wanted to call the police but I told her you was all right. Where have you been? We've been looking all over the place for you.
Boy: (*stops his horse*) I didn't get the calves, Uncle, but I know where they are.
Uncle: The calves? What are you talking about? They came home by themselves last night. Now you better get inside and get warm. I'll look after Tim. (*to horse*) Easy, boy.
The boy's face close. He gets off the horse and turns slightly, as if looking back.
Boy: They came home? Then what ...?
The small houses of the stranger are but a smudge in the snow. Then the houses closer. Then the stable. Then the door. The stalls. And the forbidden area.

after READING

UNDERSTANDING THE TEXT

1. In your notebook, make a brief **summary** of each of the "scenes" from the original Sinclair Ross story, including details of **plot** development. Consider a new scene to begin whenever there is a change in the **setting** or **characters**.

2. Compare the first six scenes of Rudi Dorn's television script with Part 1 and the first two paragraphs of Part 2 of the **story**. Make notes on how each version introduces the main character, the initial problem, and the details of the setting. With a partner, discuss the advantages and disadvantages of the introductory section of each version. In your notebook, **summarize** your discussion.

3. Compare Scene 18 of the television script with Part 6 of the story. Make notes on the ending of each version, including the characters involved, **dialogue**, and the continuation of the mystery or **suspense**. With a partner, discuss the advantages and disadvantages of the conclusion of each version. Make brief notes summarizing your discussion.

EXPLORING IDEAS AND IMPLICATIONS

4. In a small group, discuss the changes in the story that occur as a result of the switch from Sinclair Ross's use of the first-person **point of view** to the television adaptation's use of an objective camera recording the events from outside the central character. Make notes on the ideas from your discussion. Select one member of the group to make an oral presentation of your ideas to the class.

5. Write a series of paragraphs explaining to an **audience** of students in a lower grade the effects of at least five shots and camera angles used in "One's a Heifer." With a partner, revise and edit your paragraphs. As a class, create a rubric to assess these paragraphs of explanation.

6. Write a **review** of this television adaptation of "One's a Heifer," or of another film or television adaptation of a story or novel, for publication in your school newspaper. With a partner, revise, edit, and format your review to prepare it for publication.

MAKING CONNECTIONS

7. Read another story from this textbook. Using Rudi Dorn's adaptation as a model, work with a partner to rewrite one or two scenes of the story for a television show. Be prepared to read your work aloud to the class. ■

Will I Still Be Addicted to Video Games?

CHRIS TAYLOR

"Here ... the universe truly does revolve around us."

BEFORE READING

In your notebook, write your ideas about the future of video games. Where are they heading? How will they change? Will they always be as popular as they are now?

Jeff Bridges got zapped into it in *Tron*. Keanu Reeves reached it by means of a red pill in *The Matrix*. In Neal Stephenson's novel *Snow Crash*—a cult classic in Silicon Valley—our hero, Hiro Protagonist, goes there wearing goggles and a pair of virtual-reality gloves. It's where I expect to be spending my evenings in the twilight of my life, without ever leaving the comfort of my sofa. And—who knows?—maybe I'll meet you there.

What is it? It's a clean, well-lighted universe of one's own, built by computer but experienced through as many senses as you can afford. It's a perfectly legal mind-blowing experience to rival Timothy Leary's best trips, and it makes today's PlayStations seem as primitive a pastime as bobbing for apples in a barrel.

You could call it a game, although that word will cease to have any real meaning when this alternative world is complex enough to contain its own baseball leagues and its own population of children playing hopscotch on the streets. The people we meet there will look and feel almost as real as the ones we encounter during our waking lives. If you've chosen a multi-player universe, they may even be those same working stiffs, except that they will probably inhabit designer bodies that are a lot more interesting than their own. Our quests, our goals will be of our choosing and will almost certainly not involve corporate mission statements or our boss's action-agenda items. Here, our presence is of primary importance, and the universe truly does revolve around us.

Impossible? No, inevitable. Three important trends are on a collision course: the growing power and wealth of the game industry (the 21st century's answer to

Hollywood), exponential advances in silicon and biotechnology, and a demographic shift that will put purchasing power in the hands of a generation that was brought up on video games and sees no point in putting them away. Already, the majority of people who play on PCs and video consoles are over 18. Tens of billions of dollars are being spent by the likes of Microsoft and Sony to ensure that they'll still be customers at 81. The odds are in the video-games makers' favor; even Big Tobacco doesn't have a product this addictive.

How will we travel to our alternative universes? The most exciting possibility is to use some form of biologically engineered computer wired directly into our heads—an exobrain programmed to provide a better, more mathematically intricate imagination. In David Cronenbeg's recent movie *eXistenZ*, squidgy pink packages called bioports plug directly into special jacks at the base of players' spines. The upshot is rather like what happens to your TV when you connect it to a VCR and press PLAY. Visual and aural information from the real world is overridden; your bioport provides all the sensory stimuli you need. Technically, it's just a question of getting the right hookups. If there's anything we already know from playing games, it's that our brains eagerly adapt our physical responses to the onscreen action. Next time your six-year-old plays Pokémon on his Game Boy or your teenagers blast away at their pals on Quake, watch what happens to their breathing and blink rate. One steadily increases; the other drops away to almost nothing. Their bodies are getting ready to fight.

Not that there's anything unusual about this; play is one of our most natural activities. Like dreaming, it helps us to prepare for situations we might be forced to face in real life. (The U.S. Army already uses a Quake-style battle simulator to increase the weapons-firing responsiveness of its troops.) Imagine how you—or your business—could use a universe that mimicked the real one down to the slightest detail. Worried about asking your boss for a raise? Plug in the bioport, and see how a character like him might react. Want to see how well you could defend your home against an armed intruder? Enter your specs and have a go. Wary of giving your teenager the car keys? Let him drive around a virtual version of your hometown first.

"More and more, games are going to be about the player telling a story," says Will Wright, creator of this year's hottest PC game, The Sims. "It's up to us, the designers, to give them rich, open-ended environments." The Sims is very much in that do-anything vein; your aim is to micromanage the happiness of a suburban household, right down to the color of the roof tiles and the frequency of the bathroom breaks. In the future you may simply drop yourself into the Sims' house and hang out with them for hours at a time—a life away from life, a home away from home. Urban dwellers will escape their cramped confines by building vast Sims mansions in the cybercountryside; rural folk will get over their city envy by constructing a city of their own, brick by virtual brick.

What will make or break this scenario is the level of artificial intelligence found in the Sims themselves. After all, our brains were built to enjoy levels of social interaction higher than simply killing our opponents. We want to talk to them, to gossip, scheme and plot. Building computer characters that can pass our personal Turing tests is no easy task—but if anyone has the money and the motivation to fund neural network research, it's the game industry. "True artificial intelligence will come out of games first," says veteran designer Peter Molyneux, who should know. His latest epic, titled Black and White—to be released later [in 2000]—features creatures so complex they can go out and build websites of their own free will.

Personally, I'm planning to get my bioport operation just as soon as someone designs a total sensory version of the classic empire-building game Civilization. The task of supervising the entire span of human development—from cracking the whip at the construction of the pyramids to spearheading the colonization of outer space—should be enough to keep me occupied long past my 81st birthday. As Molyneux puts it, "What we're talking about is the ultimate drug. If I can build a world where you can smell a rose and be a god, would you ever want to come back?" Not me. In my dotage, I'll happily resign myself to the 21st century equivalent of a crack den with a pink squidgy thing strapped to my spine. Move over, Jeff, Keanu and Hiro—I'm coming in.

—*Originally published June 19, 2000*

after READING

UNDERSTANDING THE TEXT

1. Create a main and supporting idea map for this **article**. Compare your map with that of at least one other person.

2. In your notebook, write your reaction to Chris Taylor's speculation about the future of video games.

3. In a small group, identify the **audience** Taylor is writing for. Determine the age, reading level, interests, gender, and socioeconomic group. Write a brief **report** using these subtitles as organizers. Be sure to refer directly to the article in your report.

4. "More and more, games are going to be about the player telling a story." Explain what the writer means by this statement.

EXPLORING IDEAS AND IMPLICATIONS

5. a) In a small group, design a panel discussion answering the following questions: Are video games, especially virtual reality, healthy for our society? Each person in your group should become an expert on some aspect of video/virtual reality games and be ready to speak to the class as one of the panel members.

   b) As an audience member, take notes as the panelists speak and be prepared to pose questions to them.

6. a) Create a print advertisement for the "pink squidgy thing" Taylor talks about in his article. Remember to consider your audience and appeal to that audience's needs and desires. (See The Reference Shelf, pages 465–466.) Post your ads where they can be seen by the class.

   b) Choose the two ads you think are most effective. Identify the **implicit** and **explicit meanings** in the two ads. Explain the social implications of the ad.

MAKING CONNECTIONS

7. Locate and read "The Veldt" by Ray Bradbury. Write a statement of the **theme** of "The Veldt" (note the publication date of the story). Explain how the two young people in the **story** are not unlike Chris Taylor.

8. Read "You Are What You Play" (pages 259–260). As a class, discuss video games in light of the findings in this article. ▪

Advertising's Glossy New Face

NICK KREWEN

"... magalogues are picking up steam."

BEFORE READING

With a partner, discuss the relationship between the content of a magazine and the advertisements in the same magazine. Be prepared to present your ideas to the class.

Asian recording artist CoCo Lee hasn't released a record in North America, but she's already making waves.

Not on the radio, at least not yet, and not in the record stores, where her debut English-language album *Just No Other Way* won't be available to the Canadian public until April 9 [2000].

No, Lee is creating a stir on magazine racks, where for the past three months she's adorned the spring 2000 cover of *Sony Style* quarterly. A pose under the captions "Hot CoCo" and "The Soulful CoCo Lee" invites the reader to a prominent six-page spread about the Hong Kong singer.

David A. Keeps, West Coast editor of *Details* and author of the piece, gushes on about Lee, a Céline Dion-flavoured stylist who, he hastily declares, "has brought a new style—the gutsy vocal gymnastics of

urban music—to the sometimes lightweight songs of Asian pop." He labels her an innovator with "a competitive edge in the global pop arena."

An honest opinion? An insightful piece of pop-music journalism?

We may never know. For Lee is a Sony recording artist, and Keeps was hired to write about her for *Sony Style*, a glossy, graphically bold, 118-page periodical that never veers its focus from new Sony products, be it radios, robotics, or in Lee's case, recording artists.

And that's exactly what Time Inc. Custom Publishing, a division of Time-Warner Publishing, had in mind when it created *Sony Style* in 1999 with Sony Electronics: the magalogue.

Although it's not a new phenomenon in the world of publishing, magalogues are picking up steam. Combinations of magazines and catalogs that offer soft editorial features alongside their own product advertisements, magalogues are the latest marketing craze for retailers and manufacturers looking to enhance their customer relationships.

"It all has to do with building community," says Patrick Walshe, vice-president of Harrison Young Pesonen & Newell Media Management, a Toronto media-buying firm that spends more than $300 million annually placing ads for clients.

"They want their relationship with their customer to be more than a transactional relationship. They want to be seen as being an integral part of the customer's lifestyle and more than just a store."

Magalogues have also proven to be profitable, whether used as an incentive to draw consumers into a store or as direct mail perks for loyal customers. "There's a healthy increase in sales when a book comes out," says Sally Scott, director of marketing for Holt Renfrew, who retired the clothing chain's *Point of View* magazine in September 1999 to launch a more frequently published customized "book" called *Holt's* …. It will be published eight times a year.

"We have a loyal customer base, and we want to speak with them often, telling them about the new and exciting events that are happening in our stores," says Scott. "We find the books are a very successful way of doing that."

Holt Renfrew and Sony aren't alone. In the past five years, designer brands have been popping up with astonishing regularity: the Liquor Control Board of Ontario's *Food & Drink*, Toronto clothier Harry Rosen's *Harry*, Internet auctioneer eBay's *eBay Magazine*, and in the last year, Starbucks' *Joe* and Swedish furniture-manufacturer IKEA's *IKEA Space* … the list seems endless.

These days, if you walk into a store and you *don't* see a complimentary copy of a magalogue staring you in the face from a basket or a counter, it's considered a rarity.

"It's definitely a growing trend," says Scott Mowbray, managing editor of Time Inc. Custom Publishing, which produces *Sony Style* and 20 other custom publications.

Since he vacated his editorial post of *Vancouver Magazine* for Custom Publishing's greener pastures, he's seen his New-York-based editorial department grow from a staff of four to 40.

"We're only four years old, but we think we're on our way to being the biggest, and certainly the best custom publishing company in the U.S.," he says. "There's a huge opportunity for growth in North America."

Mowbray says the appeal of custom publishing lies in being an effective alternative marketing tool for promoting brand awareness. "The 30-second advertising spot is not the only way in which to establish a connection with people," he explains. "Some people want to go more in-depth about products, and I think that's the attraction there."

He argues that customers are fanatically devoted to brands and manufacturers, citing *Sony Style* as the perfect example. It retails at $8.95 (Cdn.). "I'm convinced that people are buying the magazine *because* of the brand," says Mowbray.

"I'm absolutely convinced of that, because Sony has some of the highest brand-recognition and brand-loyalty ratings in the world. I think anybody who grew up with Sony remembers their first portable radio or TV or Walkman, that they have a fair amount of affection for this quirky, giant company."

Consumer adoration is dandy, but what happens when magalogue publishers prominently rack their products beside "legitimate" magazines such as *Rolling Stone* and *Cosmopolitan*? Is there a potential to confuse the advertorial of *Sony Style* with the editorial of *Loaded*?

"These things are absolutely crystal clear as to what they are," Mowbray replies.

Lynn Cunningham, director of Ryerson University's magazine program and a magazine writer of 20 years, doesn't agree. She feels magalogues do the industry a huge injustice. "My basic feeling about the magalogue is that it cheapens the magazine form.

"Obviously from the retailer's perspective it makes a lot of sense, because what they're doing is capitalizing on the legitimacy of real magazines. But it blurs the line between what is a bona-fide journalistic enterprise in the form of a magazine and retailing in the form of a magazine."

She worries that magalogue publishers are perpetuating several illusions, such as the perception that they're on the same financial playing field as typical magazines.

"Their purpose isn't to make money, although any additional revenues are welcome. Their purpose is to expand awareness of that particular brand or product. Consequently, the same kind of economic restrictions when you're actually publishing a real magazine, where you should have more money coming in than going out, don't apply."

Neither does the need for objectivity. "I would say if CoCo were being featured on the cover of *Rolling Stone*, it would have a little more legitimacy than on the cover of *Sony Style*. She's a Sony artist, I take it. That's advertising."

Cunningham also argues that the high-end magalogue production values furnished by deep-pocket corporations place unrealistic expectations on legitimate magazines. "It may be difficult for magazines operating in the real world of less than 10 per cent pre-tax profit levels to meet those new standards," she says. "The fact is, it is expensive to produce a glossy magazine with a lot of great colour and expensive stock."

Most damaging, however, is the siphoning of magazine-ad revenues by retailers who share a vested interest with their suppliers, she says. "Magalogues can be in the position of strong-arming advertisers into their publication by implied or overt suggestion."

"They have a community of interested advertisers," argues Harrison Young's Walshe. "Look at *Harry*. Where better for Hugo Boss or Giorgio Armani to advertise, than to people who are loyal customers of Harry Rosen?"

Mowbray says he doubts custom publishing will ever threaten regular publishing. "Custom publishing is never going to overwhelm regular publishing as the dominant form of communication. I don't think the customers are banging down the doors asking for another custom published magazine, but they like the good ones when they get them."

And how do writers feel? Cindy Waxer, a local freelancer who regularly contributes to Wisconsin-based *eBay Magazine*, says she never confuses her employers or the integrity of an assignment. "If I'm writing promotional copy for one company, I'm making sure I'm not interviewing them the next week for a newspaper. That is something you have to be careful about, and you do have to stay at arm's length."

However, Waxer has no qualms, ethical or moral, about writing promotional copy if she's hired to do so. "I wrote for Columbia House's magalogue," she says. "They paid me well, so what possible moral qualms could I have? I'd have to write a stunning paragraph about how wonderful and talented Bryan Adams is, and I couldn't care less for him, but that's not necessarily a moral qualm for me."

Mowbray doesn't believe there's any moral duplicity with custom publishing, as long as you're upfront. "Our policy at Time Inc., because it's a traditional magazine-making company, is that if you tell the readers what you're doing, what's the problem?

"It's where you don't tell the readers what you're doing where you start to deceive. We make sure, whether it's a magazine that's branded like *Sony Style* or one that isn't, that we are straightforward with the reader."

If they aren't? "You only screw around a consumer once," says Walshe. "If you put a magazine on the stands, and people don't like it, they'll never buy you again."

—Originally published March 26, 2000

after READING

UNDERSTANDING THE TEXT

1. In your own words, define the terms magazine, catalogue, and "magalogue."

2. If available, obtain and read a copy of one of the magalogues mentioned in this **article** and write a **review** of it for people who shop at the business that produces it.

3. In a small group, discuss whether this article is **biased** or fair in presenting information about magalogues. Be sure to support your opinion with evidence from the article.

EXPLORING IDEAS AND IMPLICATIONS

4. With a partner, design the concept for a magalogue for one of your favourite retailers or retail brands. Have another partnership assess the concept for its appeal to the retailer as well as the consumer. Be prepared to present your concept to the class.

5. Write an **opinion essay** explaining whether magalogues should be allowed to be sold alongside other magazines on the racks at stores. Ask a partner to help you revise and edit your essay, focusing on strength of arguments, organization, and use of transitions. (See The Reference Shelf, page 445.)

MAKING CONNECTIONS

6. Watch for advertising supplements in a newspaper or magazine that you read on a regular basis. Use a chart to compare and contrast an advertising supplement with a magalogue. Share and discuss your findings with the class. ■

The Seeds of Pop Stardom

ARIEL TEPLITSKY

"... preened, coiffed, revamped,
   positioned and promoted."

BEFORE READING

In small groups, discuss examples of the "marketing" of popular singers and musicians. In your notebook, make a list of the types of marketing strategies your group has identified in the discussion.

Without their big break, budding pop sensations Luke McMaster and Rob James know they probably would never have made it this far.

In all likelihood, they'd still be struggling to make a name for themselves in Winnipeg, belting out mostly cover tunes at coffee houses and lunch-hour high-school concerts.

But 18 months ago, the duo, who go by McMaster & James, hit the jackpot most aspiring musicians only dream of when they caught the ear of a major recording studio. The label decided to take a calculated chance on the pair, promising to do everything in its power to ensure that McMaster, 24, and James, 21, become the successors to the musical lineage of such sensations as Hanson, Backstreet Boys, Britney Spears, 'N Sync, The Moffats, Christina Aguilera and Sky.

Musically, that may be a dubious pedigree, but it's a very profitable one, and if the plan works, McMaster and James will be famous and wealthy and BMG Canada, the label in question, will have another lucrative hit to its credit.

So far, everything is working according to plan. The duo has scored some solid publicity and is riding the wave of a national hit single in "Love Wins Everytime."

But the real test comes next week with the release of their carefully produced, self-titled debut album, which will likely decide the fate of their careers—and determine the success or failure of BMG's costly efforts.

"It's all coming to this, it's all culminating in this one day," says James emphatically, as the two sip chamomile with honey in the lobby bar of their Toronto hotel.

"It's a scary thing, but it's going to be a relief to finally have our album out there," agrees McMaster.

It's been a long time coming. BMG has invested close to half a million dollars in the pair, and for the past seven months, it has deployed an arsenal of tactics to build an image and create some buzz for McMaster & James.

The duo has been preened, coiffed, revamped, positioned and promoted. They were matched up with big names, opening for such pop staples as Monica, 'N Sync and Christina Aguilera. They harmonized the national anthem at a Blue Jays game. They got a slick new Web site.

Even before their first single had garnered any airplay, their image was plastered across the country on 1.2 million boxes of Kellogg's Corn Pops.

All this came as some surprise to the pair, whose music suddenly seemed secondary to the fanfare.

"We didn't even know that half of these things were possible," says James of the promotional blitz. "The Corn Pops thing? It didn't even cross our minds. It wasn't even a twinkle in our eyes when we signed.

"You wouldn't believe how many people have come up to me and said, 'Hey, you're on a Corn Pops box, aren't you?'"

The industry calls it setup, or seeding. Like fast food and khakis, an album's success depends in part on "brand" recognition. In today's hot-selling yet saturated pop music market, talent is only half the battle. Marketing is the other.

Which is not to imply that McMaster and James have no talent. But with so much competition, good songwriting and performance alone are scarcely enough to register a blip on teen radar.

"Promotion is absolutely key, perhaps more important than the raw attributes of talent," says John Jones, senior music programmer at MuchMusic.

Equally important, he says, is the talent of their managers, producers, marketers, publicists, consultants and A&R team.

That's not new to McMaster & James' team.

"There's a thousand groups releasing CDs every week," says Keith Porteous, vice-president of artist and repertoire (A&R) at BMG Canada. "We have to build a story that will set them apart."

Both McMaster and James were struggling solo performers when they met at a Winnipeg recording studio in 1997. After joining forces, they played R&B, pop and Motown covers, as well as their own material, under the moniker 2Face, at local schools and clubs.

Their Winnipeg-based manager helped them put together a demo, which it shopped around to various record companies. Eventually, Porteous agreed to come from Toronto to see them perform.

A year later, in December 1998, 2Face had a deal, and they haven't looked back since.

"With a little money, a little time, a little direction," says Porteous, "these guys are the sh-t."

THE SOUND

Sun is gonna rise / so don't worry about tomorrow / Everybody hurts sometimes / Let up in your heart / where the world will surely follow / Baby love wins every time.

Most, if not all, of the tracks on the upcoming album are of the safe, catchy, love-song variety—the hallmarks of boy-band generica. The challenge for the label is to distance its protégés from the Backstreets and Boomtangs already dominating the charts while aiming them at the same teen and tween market.

"It's not a boy group that's been auditioned and we just find all the songs and the productions," explains Porteous. "What sets them apart is they're the writers, the artists."

When the pair signed the record deal with BMG, their band name was changed from 2Face to McMaster & James to highlight them as a songwriting duo whose music is "timeless, appealing to generations of music fans in the same way as the songwriting teams of Lennon/McCartney and Hall & Oates," as the Web site gushes.

The musicians were flown to top production companies. While they were courting BMG, their management helped book a deal with Banana Toons in Vancouver, of 98 Degrees fame, which produced four of the album's 10 tracks.

The label later set them up with the Euro Syndicate in New York, which produced the first two singles, among others, giving "Love Wins Everytime" a Latin-tinged horn section and fattening the sound on other tracks.

THE IMAGE

As their bittersweet "soul pop" was being tweaked and tinkered with, it was time to give them an image that would be "more palatable" to the Corn Pops demographic.

"I think they went with the wholesome, goody-two-shoes boys look," smiles the boyish James, arms folded in front of his nylon Buffalo vest.

"Which is pretty much how we are anyway," laughs the marginally scruffier McMaster.

While there was no radical change in their appearance—from clean-cut to even more clean-cut—the guys were styled, dressed, and taught to apply their own makeup.

Designers supplied them with a new wardrobe so they could wear different clothes at every show. They watched other performers' videos—George Michael, Prince, Janet Jackson—as they developed their synchronized swivel-hips, claps, spins and other choreography designed to elicit gleeful screams at live performances.

"The most important thing with imaging an artist is finding where they look best, where they feel comfortable," explains Susan Desmarais, director of artist development at ViK Recordings, BMG's label for domestic music.

Working with a designer, Desmarais developed a logo and packaging concept for use on promotional materials, settling on a "planes, trains and automobiles" theme. Photos of the two, and their video, depict them walking toward or away from cars and helicopters, which, says Desmarais, is meant to convey a sense of constant motion—"just like they're always on their way somewhere."

THE PROMOTION

Now that they had a look and a sound, they needed to be discovered. Release the marketing hounds.

BMG set the publicity gears in motion last August when it included "Love Wins Everytime" on its *Planet Pop 2000* compilation and accompanying TV commercials. The album went triple platinum, and the seeding began.

"This was our plan from the beginning, that we wanted to take a long time to create awareness of them," says Porteous of the seven months and two singles that have passed without an album. He adds that the lengthy setup is a common strategy with the label.

The reason is that teens and tweens tend to spend money on names they are familiar with. Seven months of exposure gives the seed plenty of time to grow.

"It's usually viewed as a market that's more easily reached, because they have less distractions, like marriage or buying a home," says Brian Robertson, president of the Canadian Recording Industry Association.

Also, he adds, "establishing loyalty in that market is an investment in the maturing of those individuals."

Beginning last summer, the record company distributed thousands of flyers at Backstreet Boys and Britney Spears concerts in a "grassroots promotion," hyping the band and, more recently, directing the teen audience to the Web site. The site, in turn, beckoned feedback from visitors with incentives like the "Win a Valentine's date with Luke and Rob contest."

Then along came Kellogg's, which last September plugged "pop sensations" McMaster and James, along with 'N Sync and Billy Crawford on its cereal boxes.

But it didn't end there. To ensure airplay for the single, the pair were brought to Montreal in the summer and later Toronto, where they performed their music while strumming acoustic guitars as a sneak preview for radio programmers.

"That trip to Montreal is what started the momentum in the market," says Desmarais.

Next came a long string of public events, from in-store promotions to the Blue Jays gig to performing at 'N Sync concerts. These were combined with preview spotlights in teen magazines and on YTV last year.

Meanwhile, their video was making the rounds at MuchMusic, and with even greater success, strangely, at its Quebec counterpart, MusiquePlus.

The tour schedule has intensified in the last month. The duo's T.O. stopover was preceded by a whirlwind of high school gigs and media junkets across Quebec. Before that, it was a week on the west coast. Next, they're joining bands Prozzak and Soul Decision on a national tour.

Which brings us to the present.

Last Saturday [February 2000], they opened for Boomtang Boys in a free concert at Nathan Phillips Square for Winterfest, crooning and dancing to pre-recorded rhythms.

At the core of about 150 onlookers stood a knot of screaming teens. Every time the performers swayed, or dropped to one knee to reach an emotional pitch, it only seemed to excite them all the more. Something seems to be working.

Expectations are high, as more than 25,000 copies of the debut album are to be distributed nationally in the first shipment beginning next week, says Desmarais. (Average for a new Canadian pop act is about 10,000.) The company expects the album to go gold (50,000 sales) within three to four months, she says.

But the hype doesn't end here. It's only the end of the beginning.

Beyond the national tours and an upcoming ad blitz, the band has been pegged by BMG International to go abroad—to Europe, Asia, Australia, Latin America and eventually the United States. And it's only their first album.

So, if you haven't yet heard "Thank You" or "Love Wins Everytime," don't worry. You will. There's even a Spanish version in the works.

With such a marketing juggernaut behind the band, the music itself seems more of an afterthought.

But in the end, argues University of Toronto professor Julian Tanner, success still comes down to what it always has: "good songs, well performed, by sexy performers."

Strip away the hype and promotion. What you're left with are two excited young guys on the brink of something. It may be a rise to stardom, or a slow fade from our sights. Either way, we're about to find out.

"Ultimately it's still about songs and connecting people with songs. That's still the core value of the business," says John Jones.

"But could Milli Vanilli have a hit today? Of course they could."

—*Originally published February 17, 2000*

after READING

UNDERSTANDING THE TEXT

1. Consult the list of marketing strategies you made in the "Before Reading" activity. Make additions or deletions based on information you learned from this **article**.

2. In a sentence, identify the "target market" for the music of McMaster & James. In your notebook, record four specific details from this article that prove your statement.

3. In a paragraph, explain the marketing industry's terms "setup" or "seeding." With a partner, discuss your explanation and revise your paragraph as necessary.

4. Make a list of specific technical language from the music industry or from marketing used in this article. With a partner, discuss and write **definitions** of the terms as used in **context**. Join with another partnership to explain and clarify your ideas.

EXPLORING IDEAS AND IMPLICATIONS

5. Write a letter that Luke McMaster or Rob James might have written to a friend in Winnipeg telling how he feels about all the "hype" and marketing of the two young men and their music. Working in a group, revise your letter to include specific information that reflects the content of this article, maintaining a consistent **voice**. Select the best letter from your group and read it aloud to the class.

6. **Debate** the following resolution: Be It Resolved That Marketing Strategies Are More Important Than Talent in the Making of Pop Stars. (See The Reference Shelf, pages 455–458.) Research may be necessary to help you prepare your arguments.

7. Visit the Internet Web site of McMaster & James (or of another rising musical group). In your notebook, make notes on the target **audience** for the Web site, any Marketing strategies or tie-ins that you observed, and the **style** of writing used.

MAKING CONNECTIONS

8. The article mentions that appearances and promotions were "combined with preview spotlights in teen magazines ...." Read articles from two or three different teen magazines about the same up-and-coming musician, singer, or group. Make notes about any similarities in the information, language, or photographs. Discuss with a partner whether you can detect evidence of the magazines' use of publicity releases by the record company's marketing or public relations department. Be prepared to present your findings to the class. ■

The Branding of Learning: Excerpts From *No Logo*

NAOMI KLEIN

"They are fighting for their brands
to become ... the core curriculum."

BEFORE READING

Make a class list of places where advertisements appear that you no longer bother to notice.

[M]arketers and cool hunters have spent the better part of the decade hustling the brands back to high school and pouring them into the template of the teenage outlaw. Several of the most successful brands had even cast their corporate headquarters as private schools, referring to them as "campuses" and, at the Nike World Campus, nicknaming one edifice "the student union building." Even the cool hunters are going highbrow; by the late nineties, the rage in the industry was to recast oneself less as a trendy club-hopper than as a bookish grad student. In fact, some insist they aren't cool hunters at all but rather "urban anthropologists."...

[F]ast-food, athletic gear and computer companies ... carry with them an educational agenda of their own. As with all branding projects, it is never enough to tag the schools with a few logos. Having gained a foothold, the brand managers are now doing what they have done in music, sports and journalism outside the schools: trying to overwhelm their host, to grab the spotlight. They are fighting for their brands to become not the add-on but the subject of education, not an elective but the core curriculum.

Of course the companies crashing the school gate have nothing against education. Students should by all means learn, they say, but why don't they read about our company, write about our brand, research their own brand preferences or come up with a drawing for our next ad campaign? Teaching students and building brand awareness, these corporations seem to believe, can be two aspects of the same project. Which is where Channel One, owned by K-111 Communications, and its Canadian counterpart, the Youth News Network, come in, perhaps the best-known example of in-school branding.

At the beginning of the decade, these self-styled in-school broadcasters approached North American school boards with a proposition. They asked them to open their classrooms to two minutes of television advertising a day, sandwiched between twelve minutes of teenybopper current affairs programming. Many schools consented, and the broadcasts soon aired. Turning off the cheerful ad patter is not an option. Not only is the programming mandatory viewing for students, but teachers are unable to adjust the volume of the broadcast, especially during commercials. In exchange, the schools do not receive direct revenue from the stations but they can use the much-coveted audiovisual equipment for other lessons and, in some cases, receive "free" computers.

Channel One, meanwhile, charges advertisers top dollar for accessing its pipeline to classrooms—twice as much as regular TV stations because, with mandatory attendance and no channel-changing or volume control, it can boast something no other broadcaster can: "No audience erosion." The station now boasts a presence in 12,000 schools, reaching an estimated eight million students.

When those students aren't watching Channel One or surfing with ZapMe!, an in-school Internet browser first offered free to American schools in 1998, they may turn their attention to their textbooks— and those too may be sending out more messages to "Just Do It" or "CK Be." The Cover Concepts company sells slick ads that wrap around books to 30,000 U.S.

schools, where teachers use them instead of plastic or tinfoil as protective jackets. And when lunchtime arrives, more ads are literally on the menu at many schools. In 1997, Twentieth Century–Fox managed to get cafeteria menu items named after characters from its film *Anastasia* in forty U.S. elementary schools. Students could dine on "Rasputin Rib-B-Cue on Bartok Bun" and "Dimitri's Peanut Butter Fudge." Disney and Kellogg's have engaged in similar lunch-menu promotions through School Marketing, a company that describes itself as a "school-lunch ad agency."[1]

Competing with the menu sponsors are the fast-food chains themselves, chains that go head-to-head with cafeterias in 13 percent of U.S. schools. In an arrangement that was unheard of in the eighties, companies like McDonald's and Burger King now set up kiosks in lunchrooms, which they advertise around the school. Subway supplies 767 schools with sandwiches; Pizza Hut corners the market in approximately 4,000 schools; and a staggering 20,000 schools participate in Taco Bell's "frozen burrito product line." A Subway sandwich guide about how to access the in-school market advises franchisees to pitch their brand-name food to school boards as a way to keep students from sneaking out at lunch hour and getting into trouble. "Look for situations where the local school board has a closed campus policy for lunch. If they do, a strong case can be made for branded product to keep the students on campus."[2] The argument works for administrators such as Bob Hanson, the director

---

1. *Wall Street Journal.* 24 November 1998.
2. "A La Carte Service in the School Lunch Program," fact sheet prepared for Subway by Giuffrida Associates, Washington D.C.

©1995 Tribune Media Services, Inc. All Rights Reserved.

Mixed Media

ADVERTISEMENTS MOVE INTO SCHOOL CLASSROOMS
- NEWS ITEM

Vocabulary Words
1. Mc Muffin
2. Pop-Tart
3. Cocoa Puffs
4. Gatorade
5. Whopper
6. Reebok
7. Nike
8. Nintendo

of nutritional services for the Portland, Oregon, school district. "Kids come to us with brand preferences," he explains.[3]...

Students may also find that brand wars are being waged over the pop machine outside the gym. In Canada and the U.S., many school boards have given exclusive vending rights to the Pepsi-Cola Company in exchange for generally undisclosed lump sums. What Pepsi negotiates in return varies from district to district. In Toronto, it gets to fill the 560 public schools with its vending machines, to block the sales of Coke and other competitors, and to distribute "Pepsi Achievement Awards" and other goodies emblazoned with its logo. In communities like Cayuga, a rural Ontario tobacco-farming town, Pepsi buys the right to brand entire schools. "Pepsi—Official Soft Drink of Cayuga Secondary School" reads the giant sign beside the road. At South Fork High School in Florida, there is a blunt, hard-sell arrangement: the school has a clause in its Pepsi contract committing the school to "make its best effort to maximize all sales opportunities for Pepsi-Cola products."[4]...

Not surprisingly, in the U.S. and Canada the fiercest scholastic marketing battles are fought over high-school gym class and university athletics. The top high-school basketball teams have sponsorship deals with Nike and Adidas, which deck out teenagers in swoosh- and stripe-festooned shoes, warm-ups and gym bags. At the university level, Nike has sponsorship deals with more than two hundred campus athletics departments in the U.S. and twelve in Canada. As anyone familiar with college ball well knows, the standard arrangement gives the company the right to stamp the swoosh on uniforms, sports, gear, official university merchandise and apparel, on stadium seats and, most important, on ad banners in full view of the cameras that televise high-profile games. Since student players can't get paid in amateur athletics, it is the coaches who receive the corporate money to dress their teams in the right logos, and the amounts at stake are huge. Nike pays individual coaches as much as $1.5 million in sponsorship fees at top sports universities like Duke and North Carolina, sums that make the coaches' salaries look like tokens of appreciation.

As educational institutions surrender to the manic march of branding, a new

---

3. *Wall Street Journal*, 15 September 1997.
4. The Center for Commercial-Free Public Education, Oakland, California, 9 October 1997 release.

language is emerging. Nike high schools and universities square off against their Adidas rivals: the teams may well have their own "official drink," either Coke or Pepsi. In its daily broadcasts, Channel One makes frequent references to the goings-on at "Channel One schools." William Hoynes, a sociologist at Vassar College who conducted a study on the broadcaster, says the practice is "part of a broader marketing approach to develop a 'brand name' consciousness of the network, including the promotion of the 'Channel One school' identity."[5]

As several critics have pointed out, Channel One isn't just hawking its advertisers' sneakers and candy to school kids, it is also selling the idea that its own programming is an invaluable educational aid, one that modernizes such arid, outmoded educational resources as books and teachers. In the model advanced by these broadcasters, the process of learning is little more than the transferring of "stuff" to a student's brain. Whether that stuff happens to be about a new blockbuster from Disney or the Pythagorean theorem, the net effect, according to this theory, is the same: more stuff stuffed. So Fox's attempts to flog *Anastasia* in schools didn't stop with lunch-menu ads; it also provided teachers with an *Anastasia* study guide." Jeffrey Godsick, Fox senior vice president of publicity and promotion, explained that Fox was providing a service to the schools, not the other way around. "Public school

teachers are desperate for materials that will excite the kids," he said.[6]

It's impossible to know which teachers use these branded materials in class and which ones toss them away, but a report published by the U.S. Consumers Union in 1995 "found that thousands of corporations were targeting school children or their teachers with marketing activities ranging from teaching videos, to guidebooks, and posters to contests, product giveaways, and coupons."[7]

It will come as no surprise that it is the folks at the Nike World Campus who have devised the most advanced hybrid of in-class advertisement, public relations exercise and faux teaching aid: the "Air-to-Earth" lesson kit. During the 1997–98 academic year, elementary school students in more than eight hundred classrooms across the U.S. sat down at their desks to find that today's lesson was building a Nike sneaker, complete with a swoosh and an endorsement from an NBA star. Called a "despicable use of classroom time" by the National Education Association and "the warping of education" by the Consumers Union, the make-your-own-Nike exercise purports to raise awareness about the company's environmentally sensitive production process. Nike's claim to greenness relies heavily on the fact that the company recycles old sneakers to re-cover community center basketball courts, which, in a postmodern marketing spiral, it then brands with the Nike swoosh.[8]

---

5. *Extra! The Magazine of Fairness and Accuracy in Reporting,* May/June 1997 10, no. 3.
6. *Wall Street Journal.* 24 November 1998, B1.
7. "Captive Kids: Commercial Pressures on Kids at School," Consumers Union paper, 1995.
8. Josh Feit, "Nike in the Classroom: Nike's effort to teach kids about treading lightly on Mother Nature meets with skepticism from educators and consumer watchdogs," *Willamette Week,* 15 April 1998

after READING

UNDERSTANDING THE TEXT

1. With a partner, identify the **thesis** of this excerpt and create an outline to demonstrate the organization of the points within it. Record your work on chart paper for comparison with the class.

2. **a)** Describe the **tone** of this excerpt. In your notebook, make point-form notes on how Klein has created that tone. Consider use of emotive language, level of language, and sentence structures and lengths.
   b) Evaluate the effectiveness of the tone for the purpose of the excerpts.

3. Examine each paragraph in the excerpts. For each paragraph, label the type of development Naomi Klein has used. Assess the variety of development included in the excerpt.

EXPLORING IDEAS AND IMPLICATIONS

4. Using electronic and/or print resources, conduct research into Naomi Klein's background. Write a brief explanation for an incoming Grade 11 student of why you think Klein is either a credible resource or a resource to be avoided when doing research on advertising.

5. **a)** As a class, using information from the excerpt, make a list of places where advertisements often appear in schools.
   b) Individually, look around your school for ads or for product endorsements. Keep a list of what they are and where you find them to bring back to the class for discussion.

6. **a)** In a small group, use electronic access to Canadian newspapers and news magazines to inform yourself about the controversies surrounding "Youth News Network." Bring your information back to the group.
   b) Using the information gathered by the group, write a group **essay** arguing for or against the use of Youth News Network or any other form of nonvoluntary advertising in Canadian classrooms. Be prepared to exchange essays for revision and editing.

MAKING CONNECTIONS

7. With a partner, imagine a time before television and radio. Plan an advertising campaign for a product using the advertising vehicles of the time. Plan a multifaceted approach to getting your product known. Be prepared to share your campaign and discuss your approach with the class. ■

As You Can See From My Brand-Name Clothing, I Am NOT Poor

M. LUCAS

"... $220 Fubu jacket and
$95 Tommy Hilfiger sweatshirt,
I could not possibly be poor."

BEFORE READING

As a class, make a list of "in" brand names for clothing, shoes, purses, backpacks, and accessories. Count the number of students in the class who own something with these brand names.

Just because I happen to live with my four brothers and sisters in my mom's two-bedroom South Side apartment, work at Taco Bell, and don't have a car, some ignorant types assume that I don't have much money. But, as you can clearly see from my $220 Fubu jacket and $95 Tommy Hilfiger sweatshirt, I could not possibly be poor.

Sure, I make $8.90 an hour at Taco Bell, but that couldn't possibly be my only source of income, could it? If my total weekly take-home pay were only $245, why in the world would I spend practically that much on a Nautica sweater and pair of Timberlands? That would mean I'd have spent 40 hours slinging Chalupas just for that one shopping trip to the mall. That'd just be plain stupid. So, obviously, I must be rolling in dough. And I am. You can tell by my special non-poor-people clothing.

Yes, it's obvious that I'm not like all those other losers who are working at Taco Bell and living with their moms. No, I'm a player. Take, for example, my socks. If I didn't have money to burn, I certainly wouldn't spend $22 for a pair of basic white athletic socks with a teeny-tiny Calvin Klein "CK" on them, would I? Of course not. I'd need to save my cash to get my telephone reconnected, or to pay off my loitering fine. But, luckily, I'm not in that situation, and everyone knows it just by looking at my clothes.

I'll admit it: A lot of people here on the South Side are poor. In fact, most of my relatives are poor, including my mother and all my siblings. But just look at these Lugz boots. And look at this Sean John baseball cap. They prove that I'm in an entirely different social class from my relatives, as well as from all those suckers who ride the bus with me every day.

Except for Angela, that is. I met her Monday on the Dundas streetcar. She clearly belongs to a higher class of people like myself. I could tell because she was decked out from head to toe in expensive gear: Fubu jersey, Pepe jeans, and Fila shoes, not to mention a big gold chain around her neck. Angela was holding her two-year-old son, but he obviously isn't placing much of a financial strain on her, as he was wearing a complete matching Abercrombie & Fitch outfit, which must have cost around $140. Recognizing how much Angela and I had in common, I asked her out on the spot. We went to dinner at Fran's that very same night.

after READING

UNDERSTANDING THE TEXT

1. In your notebook, write a response to this **essay**. With the class, discuss your responses.

2. Define **satire**. Explain how this essay fits the **definition** of satire. In a brief paragraph, assess its effectiveness as a satirical piece.

3. Make a list of stereotypes about poor people mentioned by the writer in the essay. Discuss whether an essay like this perpetuates the stereotypes or subtly undermines them.

4. With a partner, determine the **audience** for this essay by looking at the language and **diction** the writer has chosen. Support your choice with specific references to the text.

5. State the purpose of the following devices:
   - the writer's repeated use of questions throughout the article
   - the writer's use of a sentence fragment at the beginning of the last paragraph

EXPLORING IDEAS AND IMPLICATIONS

6. **a)** In a group of four, develop a resolution for a **debate** based on the topic of brand names. When you have had your topic approved, research and prepare for the debate. (See The Reference Shelf, pages 455–458.)

   b) As a class, develop an assessment form for a debate and assess the members of the groups as they present their debates.

7. Using this essay as a model, write your own satirical essay on a **topic** of your choice. Exchange your work with a partner and examine the writing for the elements of satire and a strong voice aimed at a specific audience.

MAKING CONNECTIONS

8. Examine Dan Piraro's cartoon about shoes (page 42). Create your own cartoon based on this essay. Make your cartoon a single frame satirizing our modern need to buy brand-name goods. Be sure to do a series of thumbnail sketches before choosing the best idea. Have a partner give you feedback on both your idea and your execution. Create a book of *Brand Name Cartoons* using the work of your classmates. ■

M&M's Plain Candies Are Switching to the Sweet Sound of Milk Chocolate

COURTNEY KANE

"Dull, bland, simple, ordinary, boring?"

BEFORE READING

As a class, nominate current television commercials for the title of "Most Entertaining." Discuss also whether these advertisements could be considered "Most Effective."

What does the word "plain" convey? Dull, bland, simple, ordinary, boring?

That's how the marketing executives at M&M/Mars see it, anyway. So, after 46 years, the company has decided to change the name of its Plain variety of M&M's candy—you know, the one without the peanuts—to what's considered a more appetizing moniker: Milk Chocolate.

"The name change is a long time coming," said Michael Tolkowsky, vice-president for marketing and licensing at the M&M/Mars division of Mars Inc. in Hackettstown, N.J.

"For all this time," he added, "we've always internally sort of felt like, 'Hey, that's not nearly the best way to refer to it. M&M's milk chocolate is too good to be called Plain.' "

To spread the word about the name change, M&M/Mars is introducing an ambitious multimedia campaign worth $10 million (U.S.), or about $15 million (Canadian). BBDO New York created the theme: "Same great chocolate. Much better name."

The campaign takes the tongue-in-cheek tone that has recently become a staple of ads for M&M's, which are centred on animated, anthropomorphic confectionery characters with contemporary personas infused with such attributes as sarcastic humour and sassy tongues. Animated M&M's characters have been around since 1954, but they had pleasant, passive personalities, all but begging consumers to eat them.

That went the way of the 5-cent candy bar in 1995 when BBDO New York, part of the BBDO Worldwide unit of the Omnicom Group, won the M&M's account.

"When we got the business, the characters were very appealing, but they were somewhat two-dimensional," said Charlie Miesmer, vice-chairman and senior executive creative director at BBDO New York. He oversees the M&M's creative effort along with Susan Credle, a copywriter, and Steve Rutter, an art director. "We've made them somewhat irreverent kind of characters that are human."

"So when the need comes five years later to announce a product change," he added, "you can do it in the context of that background."

One aspect of the campaign is to lampoon the seeming preoccupation with politically correct speech. In one spot that mimics a public-service announcement, to be shown on television and in movie theatres, people describe their jobs with such euphemisms as "administrative assistant" for secretary and "domestic care giver" for baby sitter. They are followed by the Red M&M's character, which declares, "I am not a Plain M&M. I am a Milk Chocolate M&M."

Another commercial features Patrick Warburton, the actor best known for his role as Elaine's boyfriend, Puddy, in *Seinfeld*. Warburton, who has appeared in three other spots for M&M's, is seen with Red looking up synonyms for "plain" in a thesaurus.

As Warburton rattles off several unflattering synonyms, Red asks: "So you think 'plain' is a bad word?"

With restrained contempt, Warburton looks at Red and says, "Let's look up 'stupid.' "

"His delivery is marvellous," Miesmer said. "He has this wonderful, restrained, laconic kind of humour."

A print ad features Red, with an unusually enlarged head, growling to his fellow character Yellow: "Whaddya mean this name change has gone to my head?"

The ad will appear through early fall in publications including *Cosmopolitan*, *GQ*, *People*, *Rolling Stone* and *Sports Illustrated*.

Other elements of the campaign will include a satellite "media tour" featuring the Red character and promotional tie-ins at the Nascar Independence Race in Daytona, Fla.

The name change takes the Plain variety back to its original designation at the candy's debut in 1941: The name was switched from Milk Chocolate to Plain when the Peanut variety was introduced in 1954.

Other changes have taken place, such as updating the logo and adding pictures of M&M candy pieces, but the familiar brown and white colour scheme remains the same. M&M/Mars conducted research among consumers to determine whether the name change would be deemed confusing, Tolkowsky said, and found it would not be.

Not everyone, though, agrees it's a good idea.

"I think it's just a bad case of what I call tinkering," said Jack Trout, president of Trout & Partners, a marketing strategy company in Greenwich, Conn.

"People's habits change so slowly," he added, "And if that has been called Plain, then it's Plain. I don't care what you call it."

—Originally published July 3, 2000

after READING

UNDERSTANDING THE TEXT

1. **Summarize** the history of the use of the word "Plain" to describe M&M's candies during the time they have been in existence.

2. Make a list of new or unfamiliar words in this **article** and look them up in a dictionary. Record **definitions** for these words in your notebook.

3. In a paragraph, explain why the "multimedia campaign" introduced to "spread the word about the name change" is described as "ambitious" in the fifth paragraph. In a second paragraph, indicate your suggestions for making the campaign even more "ambitious."

4. "That went the way of the 5-cent candy bar in 1995 when BBDO New York, part of the BBDO Worldwide unit of the Omnicom Group, won the M&M's account" (page 383). Analyze the above sentence with a partner. Consider the following questions:
   - What does "That" refer to?
   - What is meant by "the way of the 5-cent candy bar"?
   - What is the subject of the verb "won" in this sentence?
   - What is the relationship between BBDO New York, BBDO Worldwide, and the Omnicom Group?
   - Could the ideas in this sentence be stated more clearly?

   Be prepared to present ideas from your discussion with the class.

EXPLORING IDEAS AND IMPLICATIONS

5. Make a list of words in advertisements that could be replaced with ordinary words. Turn your list into a **glossary** by providing the "real" meaning behind the "hype."

6. Write an **opinion essay** explaining the importance of humour in advertising that targets a teenage **audience**. Revise and edit your essay in preparation for submission.

7. Draw your own "animated, anthropomorphic confectionery character" for one of your favourite snacks. Decide on an audience for your **character** and outline the reasons for the looks, clothing (if clothed), and colours used in the character's design. Have a partner evaluate its suitability for an advertising campaign.

MAKING CONNECTIONS

8. With a partner, select a current advertisement and identify the message(s) it is intended to convey. Assess the effectiveness of the advertising techniques used to convey the message(s). Be prepared to present your observations to the class. ■

Hey, It's Not as if I'm a Serial Killer

DAVID ISRAELSON

"... my role is not that complicated."

BEFORE READING

With a partner, discuss your understanding of the activities of public-relations persons or "spin doctors," as they are sometimes called. How have they been portrayed in recent films, television shows, or magazine **articles**? **Summarize** your discussion in point-form notes.

Please allow me to introduce myself—I am some people's worst nightmare. I am what is commonly known as a spin doctor, a practitioner of the so-called art of public relations.

A monster, according to some people. Silly people, I say.

It's true that a lot of folks consider my line of work as bordering on the satanic. Spin doctors manipulate, they say.

They're vermin. They lie, and when they can't do that, they twist the truth, for a hefty fee.

Actually, I think what I do is rather nice.

I think PR is a helping profession.

I also think I can say this with a bit of authority, since I have been both a producer and a receiver of public relations material over many years. For a long time,

I was a reporter (at this newspaper, in fact), and part of my job was to sift through mounds of public-relations material and decide which ones would be worth my writing about.

Then I joined a public-relations agency.

I'll concede that as a journalist, receiving a lot of that PR material was a chore. A recent survey of Canadian business journalists by the Angus Reid Group found that reporters typically receive 30 press releases per day, plus one media kit.

That's more than 8,000 pieces of promotional material every year. No one could possibly pay proper attention to all that. You have to pick out the good from the bad.

But that doesn't make public relations a bad thing. The supermarket is full of food you like as well as food you don't like, but no one calls supermarkets evil.

It seems to me that the people who criticize public-relations activities tend to become all hot and bothered without really analyzing what they're concerned about. In some cases, they're not even clear about what we do. So let me help.

The criticism tends to fall into several predictable, tiresome categories. The complainers say PR is deliberate deception, it's a tool only for the rich and powerful, it somehow taints your news and it's irritating.

I say to these people: Just chill, will you?

Let's analyze what it is PR people like me actually do, and let's answer the critics' contention that we are the scum of the Earth.

As a public-relations person, my role is not that complicated. I try to help my clients communicate to all of you, through vehicles like this newspaper, or through TV or, lately, the Internet.

Sometimes, my clients have important, worthwhile things to convey. Sometimes they don't, but they want to tell you anyway. Sometimes they have useful information to get across, but they're not very good at doing this.

In any case, I try to help them talk to you. If I do a good job, you'll probably listen, but nobody is forcing you to do so. Now, let's look at these boring criticisms:

→ Is PR deceptive? Well, it can be, in the sense that dressing up something to make it look better is a form of deception. But have you ever put on fine clothes for a job interview? Said something polite in a social situation? Is it really such a terrible crime to help someone be more presentable? By the way, I haven't had to tell any lies. Most good reporters would see through lies quite easily anyway.

→ Is PR just a tool for the rich? Get real.

Yes, powerful corporations and politicians hire spin doctors to manipulate their images, and they pay good money. But so do charities, environmental groups, non-profit arts groups—not exactly rich folks.

On the corporate side, clients these days tend to be small-business people, or geeky brainiacs who need help explaining what their New Economy company does.

→ Does PR taint your news? Well, certainly your publicist would love to spin the story right into the newspaper or onto TV. But that rarely happens. Both reporters and the public are smart enough to distinguish image-building from reality.

Look at the recent examples. Is a well-known airline in Canada getting across its message that it's a caring, efficient operation? Has the Canadian Alliance persuaded you that it offers a new type of politics, free of cheesy backroom tricks? In the U.S., did Microsoft's intense PR convince that country's justice department that it's just a hard-working company, not a monopoly?

Doesn't sound that tainted to me.

→ Finally, is public relations really that irritating? I suppose it is if you're easily irritated by things like colourful displays, movie promotions, talking to people, throwing parties, having fun.

But if you're like that, I think you're going to need a lot of public-relations help.

after READING

UNDERSTANDING THE TEXT

1. In your notebook, make a list of the things a public-relations person actually does, according to the writer of this article. Compare your list with the ideas generated in the "Before Reading" discussion.

2. Reread this article paying close attention to the vocabulary, level of language, and writing **style**. Make a two-column chart in your notebook. In the first column, record four examples of "Formal Expression." In the second column, record five or six examples of "Informal or Colloquial Language." (See The Reference Shelf, page 403.) Write a short paragraph explaining the effect on the reader of the writing style used in this article.

3. Locate in this article examples of "public relations" (written without a hyphen) and "public-relations" (written with a hyphen), and observe the grammatical function of each form. Write a few sentences in your notebook accounting for the use of both forms and explaining the use of the hyphen.

EXPLORING IDEAS AND IMPLICATIONS

4. In the article, Israelson suggests that the role of a public-relations person is "to try to help ... clients communicate to all of you," by "dressing up something to make it look better" and "to help someone be more presentable." In a small group, identify the techniques used by Israelson in the article to perform his public-relations role on behalf of the public-relations business.

MAKING CONNECTIONS

5. Visit the Web sites of agencies, businesses, or organizations on both sides of a controversial issue such as environmental pollution or biotechnology to see whether you can detect where the techniques of public-relations persons have been used to present a particular **bias** or one-sided **point of view**. Be prepared to present your findings to the class.

6. Contact by telephone (or e-mail) the public-relations department of a large corporation in your community, or an officer in a public-relations firm, and ask for more specific information about the role of public-relations persons. (If possible, you might invite a public-relations person to come to your class.) As part of your inquiry, ask which postsecondary courses are possible preparation for a career in public relations, and what skills in writing and oral presentation are required in public relations. Make a list of these skills and compare them with your own current skills in writing and oral communication. ■

Sports Logos an Insult to Aboriginals

NOAH AUGUSTINE

"Who said it was okay for professional
teams ... to adopt our cultural icons
and images for mass ridicule?"

BEFORE READING

1. a) In a small group, discuss the **images** or stereotypes that are associated with terms such as "Eskimos," "Indians," "Redskins," or "Braves."

   b) Discuss whether you have ever felt that you have been stereotyped in any way.

Last Thursday evening, I watched rather helplessly as nine Indians were thrashed and battered about by just as many men in blue and white uniforms. Normally, I would have done something about it—called for backup, at least. Instead, I cheered with each stinging tag and swinging blow delivered by this bunch of big-bat-swinging bullies.

They were the Toronto Blue Jays, of course, beating up on the celebrated Cleveland Indians. And, although I am an Indian (Mi'kmaq, I prefer) hailing from the Maritimes, I remain a big fan of the Indian-swatting Jays. One might assume that because Cleveland proudly displays an image of some misshapen Indian that all people of Indian descent

must be Cleveland fans. Not true. In fact, the use of this imagery is insulting to most aboriginal people.

The issue of professional sports teams using Indian symbols is one that may not concern most Canadians, although it can be argued that Canadians have less tolerance for racism—and are less blatant in its exercise—than our neighbours in the U.S. We are, as they say, politically correct, at most times.

Nonetheless, for me, as an aboriginal person, the use of these religious symbols and caricatures of Indian chiefs or spiritual leaders as sports logos is as offensive to my cultural heritage as it would be for an African Canadian to observe the "Boston Blacks"—or for religious people to see the image of a rabbi, an archbishop or the Dalai Lama stitched into the shoulder patches of professional sports teams.

If a television image of thousands of baseball fans screaming "war chants" and waving fake tomahawks in support of the Atlanta Braves is baffling me and my understanding of society, I can only wonder how such acceptance of less-than-subtle racism is affecting our younger generations. Who said it was okay for professional sports teams—and their millions of adoring fans—to adopt our cultural icons and images for mass ridicule?

One American youth, in a 1997 Grade 8 writing assignment on his school's use of an Indian symbol, explained it this way: "We simply chose an Indian as the emblem. We could have just as easily chosen any uncivilized animal." Is the education system the most effective tool we have in our fight against racism? I sometimes wonder.

With baseball's Atlanta Braves and Cleveland Indians, football's Kansas City Chiefs and Washington Redskins, and hockey's Chicago Blackhawks, professional sports organizations are turning a blind eye to racism in professional sports.

Professional athletes within these organizations serve as role models for all youth, including aboriginal youth. With this comes a certain responsibility.

Like so many Canadian kids, it is the dream of many aboriginal youth to someday lace up a pair of skates and face off against hockey's best. When Everett Sanipass, a Mi'kmaq from Big Cove First Nation, was drafted by the Chicago Blackhawks in the 1986 NHL draft, almost every aboriginal youth in Atlantic Canada proudly displayed the team logo—an Indian face with war paint—on everything from jerseys to lunch pails. Sanipass was the Wayne Gretzky of aboriginal hockey. It didn't matter which team he played for; what mattered was that he played in the big league. And if Sanipass said it was good, then it was great. The logo he wore could have just as easily been any "uncivilized animal." Kids do not recognize such symbols of racism but do become victims of the assault.

With dreams and aspirations comes sacrifice. It is admirable for sacrifice to be recognized as hard work and dedication, but let it not be admirable to accept tolerance of racism as just one more sacrifice. Many feel that aboriginal people should be honoured that Indian imagery is the logo of some sports communities. But what honour lies in ridicule and mockery? Take, for example, a 1998 *Washington Post* sports headline, referring to a Dallas football victory over Washington, which read: "Cowboys finish off Redskins."

At the root of this issue is the trademark business. It's a multi-million-dollar industry. However, change is in the air. Last year, the Washington Redskins had seven trademarks, including their logo, cancelled for federal registration based on a complaint from several tribes. The Trademark Trial and Appeal Board found "Redskins" to be "disparaging" to native Americans. The ruling is under appeal.

Even though, as it is said, money makes the world go 'round, court actions can change that. Perhaps, someday, respect will have a greater value than the almighty dollar.

—*Originally published July 11, 2000*

after READING

UNDERSTANDING THE TEXT

1. a) In your notebook, **summarize** Augustine's arguments in this **essay**.
 b) Make a list from the essay of the negative stereotypes of First Nations people contained in team names, logos, or fan behaviour.

2. In your notebook, explain why the opening paragraph of Augustine's essay is effective.

EXPLORING IDEAS AND IMPLICATIONS

3. a) Write a newspaper editorial or a letter to the Canadian Football League arguing that the city of Edmonton should change the name of its football team, the Edmonton Eskimos.
 b) After your first draft, revise and edit your editorial or letter with a partner.

MAKING CONNECTIONS

4. Watch television shows and commercials and make notes on how certain groups (for example, teenagers, lawyers, and the elderly) or races of people are depicted. Be prepared to share your findings with the class.

5. In small groups, read "Lament for the Dorsets" (page 188). Discuss whether Al Purdy's portrayal of the Dorset people could be considered stereotyping. Make a chart of specific details from the **poem** to support arguments on both sides of the issue.

6. Read "Stereotypes Are for 'Others'" (pages 164–165). Based on your understanding of this and Augustine's essay, create a poster, targeted at a young **audience**, that teaches the harmfulness of stereotyping people. ■

unit

1
2
3
4

The Reference Shelf

The English Language

Note: For a more detailed discussion of grammar, punctuation, research, and writing, and for additional examples and exercises, students and teachers should refer to *The Harcourt Writer's Handbook* (Toronto: Harcourt Canada, 1999).

THE DEVELOPMENT OF THE ENGLISH LANGUAGE

All languages change, and therefore they have histories. The history of a language is the description of how it has changed over time. During the past 1500 years, English has developed from a dialect of a Teutonic or Germanic language spoken by a few thousand people to one of the world's principal languages. There are now more than 350 million native speakers of English, and it is the worldwide language of technology and communication.

The history of the English language is normally divided into four periods:

Old English	A.D. 450–1100 (approximately)
Middle English	A.D. 1100–1500 (approximately)
Early Modern English	A.D. 1500–1800 (approximately)
Present-Day English	1800–today (approximately)

The dates used to mark changes in the language correspond fairly closely with the dates of important political and social events in British history: the Anglo-Saxon Invasion, 449; the Norman Conquest, 1066; the effects of the Renaissance and the introduction of printing in England, around 1500; and modern developments in transportation, communication, and language after 1800.

The Old English Period (450–1100)

Early in the fifth century, the Romans, who had conquered and occupied Britain three and a half centuries earlier, withdrew their armies, and the native Britons or Celts were left defenceless. The Jutes, Angles, and Saxons from what is now Denmark and the North Sea coast of Germany invaded Britain and overwhelmed the Britons.

	Withdrawal of Romans from Britain	Anglo-Saxon Invasion
ROMANS OCCUPY BRITAIN	A.D. 410	449 c.450

These invading peoples spoke dialects of a Teutonic or Germanic language. The Angles called their new country *Angle-land* (England) and their language *Englisc*.

Characteristics of Old English

Old English, like German or Latin, contained many **inflections** (word endings or additions for verbs, nouns, and adjectives that indicated grammatical relationships such as tense, person, number, or case). The pronunciation of vowels and consonants was very different from modern English. When people began to write the language, they borrowed the Roman alphabet and spelled words phonetically, as they were sounded. Learning to read and understand Old English requires the same type of study as does learning to read and understand a new or different language.

Literature in Old English

During the Old English period, Latin was most commonly used for writing in monasteries. However, some Old English texts have survived. The Anglo-Saxon ruler, King Alfred the Great, who reigned from 871 to 901, wrote in the West Saxon dialect and had many Latin texts translated into English. The best-known poem in Old English is the anonymous heroic epic *Beowulf*. It is over 3000 lines in length and tells the story of the hero Beowulf's victories over the monster Grendl and the even-more-terrifying Grendl's Mother, of his battle with a dragon, and of his death and burial.

Vocabulary from Old English

Many words have come into our modern language from Old English, including some of the simplest and most basic words in our vocabulary:

Words for house/home	Words for people and animals	Words for parts of the body	Words for time or the universe	Words for abstract ideas
house	man	head	day	good
wall	woman	feet	night	evil
stone	child	arm	sun	death
roof	wife	teeth	moon	life
door	sheep	ear	stars	holy
ground	cow	tongue		

***Beowulf* written**

8th century

OLD ENGLISH PERIOD

1. In small groups, use a comprehensive etymological dictionary to research additional words that have come from Old English. Make a list on chart paper for display in the classroom.

2. Using print and/or electronic sources, locate and read excerpts from Old English texts such as *Beowulf* or the work of Alfred the Great. Be prepared to report your findings and experiences to the class.

3. As a class, discuss reasons for the survival of the commonplace or simple words from Old English.

The Middle English Period (1100–1500)

When the Normans, from what is now Normandy in France, conquered England in 1066, they brought with them a language and culture very different from that of the Anglo-Saxon people. For about a century after the Norman Conquest, two distinct languages were spoken in England—the Norman French of the new ruling class and the Old English of the native people. French, which had originally developed from Latin, was the language of the court, government, art, culture, and literature. Old English continued as the language of the lower classes, of labour, and of farming. As the two languages and cultures blended together over the years, the new combined language became what we now call Middle English.

Characteristics of Middle English

While Old English relied on inflections, Middle English used word order to convey meaning and the relationship between words. The word order in the poetry of Chaucer is quite similar to modern English usage.

Literature in Middle English

There is a fairly large quantity of surviving literature in Middle English, particularly after 1250. Poetry that is still read and studied today includes *The Canterbury Tales* of Geoffrey Chaucer (see "The Clerk of Oxenford," page 58), *Piers Plowman*, and

Reign of King Alfred the Great		Surviving manuscript of *Beowulf*	Norman Conquest of England
871–910	OLD ENGLISH CONT'D	c.1000	1066 Old English co-exist

Sir Gawain and the Green Knight. Also studied and performed today are the Middle English mystery and morality plays, including the famous *Everyman.*

Vocabulary in the Middle English Period

After the Norman Conquest, both the conquerors and conquered people had different words for similar ideas and things. As a result, English is very rich in synonyms, which provide subtle connotations or shades of meaning. In general, the more commonplace words survived from Old English, while words associated with rank, position, luxury, or leisure are French in origin. Thus we have pairs of words such as *work* and *labour, speed* and *velocity, house* and *mansion, stir* and *agitate, hide* and *conceal, hut* and *cottage.*

New words that entered our language at that time were associated with polite society, government, feudalism, the church, and leisure activities. These words included *law, judge, parliament, armour, chivalry, penance,* and *archery. Baker* and *bread* are English in origin, while *confectioner* and *pastry* are French. In Sir Walter Scott's novel *Ivanhoe,* one of the characters, a swineherd, complains bitterly to a court jester that the animals that are tended by Saxon servants have English names such as *swine, sheep, ox,* and *calf,* but when they are served at the tables of the Norman masters, they have French names such as *pork, mutton, beef,* and *veal.*

The Old English words *king* and *queen* were retained, but the titles of French nobility were adopted into English—*prince, baron, marquis, earl, viscount,* and *duke.* Many words associated with the arts are from Norman French: *painter, design, music, dance, literature, poetry, verse, ballad, comedy, tragedy.*

 ACTIVITIES

1. In a small group, use an etymological dictionary to research additional words that have come from Norman French during the Middle English period. Make a list on chart paper for display in the classroom.

2. Using print and/or electronic sources, locate and read excerpts from Middle English texts such as Thomas Malory's *Le Morte d'Arthur* or Geoffrey Chaucer's *The Canterbury Tales.* Report to the class on your findings and experiences.

Chaucer's
Canterbury Tales

with Norman French until c.1150   MIDDLE ENGLISH PERIOD   1387

The Early Modern English Period (1500–1800)

In 1476, William Caxton imported and operated the first printing press in England. The impact of printing on the English language was immediate and brought about many of the changes that distinguish Early Modern English from late Middle English. Printing established linguistic norms, helped to standardize spelling, and created a much larger body of literate people than was possible when all texts were in manuscript.

The Problems of English Spelling

One of the major effects of printing was that it was largely responsible for standardizing English spelling. Before printing, and even after printing had been introduced, writers spelled more or less phonetically. In texts from Elizabethan times we can find words such as *where* and *guest* spelled many different ways: *whair, wher, whear, wheare*; *ghest, gheste, gueste, gest, geste*. Likewise *been, bin*, and *beene* seem to have been used interchangeably, and the *-ly* suffix also appears as *-lye* and *-lie*. As printing became more and more common, spelling became more standardized.

Changes in Pronunciation

When a language is spelled phonetically, there are no silent letters. Some of the confusion in Modern English is due to the fact that pronunciation was changing as spelling was becoming fixed. In the sixteenth and seventeenth centuries many words were spelled with sounds that have changed or disappeared in present-day pronunciation. In Middle English, the vowel sound in words like *head* and *bread* was pronounced as *ee*; this pronunciation has been retained in our current pronunciation of *eat, feat*, and *read*. In Shakespeare's time, people pronounced many letters that have since become silent—for example, the *w, g*, and *k* in *wrong, gnaw, knee*, and *know*; and the *t* sound in *Christmas, whistle*, and *castle*. The sound of *gh* was lost in many words such as *fought, caught*, and *night*; in other words it changed to an *f* sound, as in *tough, laugh, cough*, and *enough*.

Additions to Vocabulary in the Early Modern English Period

When the influences of the Renaissance—the rebirth of interest in the arts and literature of classical civilizations—reached England in the 1500s, a huge influx of words from Latin and Greek occurred. Borrowings from classical Greek during that

	Gutenberg invents printing from movable type in Germany	Wm. Caxton sets up first printing press in England		
MIDDLE ENGLISH CONT'D	1450	1476	c.1500	Influence of the Renaissance on English

time include *skeleton, autograph, enthusiasm, athlete,* and *daffodil.* Among the borrowings from Latin came *excursion, adapt, dexterity, expectation,* and *indirect.*

World exploration and trade, along with the coming of machines and industrialization, added many new words to the language:

From Italian	From Spanish	From Dutch	From Arabic
soprano	alligator	sloop	algebra
stanza	mosquito	yacht	sugar
opera	armada	yawl	tapestry
violin	cigar	skipper	zero
solo	cargo	skate	assassin
From Chinese	**From Persia**	**From India**	**From North America**
silk	bazaar	calico	toboggan
tea	shawl	thug	moose
cash	sofa	veranda	moccasin
tycoon	caravan	bungalow	skunk
		polo	tobacco

The Influences of Shakespeare and The King James Bible

The popularity of the plays and poems of William Shakespeare had a significant impact on the language. (See "Sonnet 30," page 311, and "To Keep the Memory of So Worthy a Friend," pages 82–86.) Shakespeare's writing contained the largest vocabulary of any writer of the time, and he was innovative in borrowing words from other languages and in coining new words. Today, many people use language and expressions, such as a *foregone conclusion,* that have come directly from Shakespeare without actually being aware of their source.

The Protestant Reformation led to new translations of the Bible, culminating in the King James Bible in 1611. It used plain, simple language, mainly of native English origin. It was widely distributed and read in homes throughout England. As a result, its style and prose rhythms had a great influence on the literary language, and even on the spoken language, for centuries.

King James Bible		Jonathan Swift's *Gulliver's Travels*	Samuel Johnson's *A Dictionary of the English Language*
1611	EARLY MODERN ENGLISH PERIOD	1726	1755

Attempts to Standardize the English Language

The Early Modern English Period is marked by great literature, and by a growing awareness of the rapid changes that were taking place in the language. Between 1660 and 1715, many English scholars, including Daniel Defoe, Joseph Addison, and Jonathan Swift (see "The Grand Academy of Lagado," pages 91–93), suggested the establishment of a national academy that would serve as a governing body to set standards for English spelling and usage and to develop rules for English grammar.

After seven years' work, Samuel Johnson published *A Dictionary of the English Language* (in two volumes) in 1755. When he began his work, Johnson announced that his purpose was to refine and fix the language, but by the time he finished his dictionary, he had come to realize that language change was inevitable and that no living language could ever be "fixed" or frozen. However, the 40 000 entries in Johnson's dictionary encouraged standardized spelling, hastened the adoption and use of many new Latinate words, and established "The Dictionary" as an authority to be consulted by readers and writers.

✸ ACTIVITIES

1. In a small group, examine the listed words (page 399) that came into English from other languages during this period. Discuss why you think that so many of these words are nouns.

2. If there are members of the class who speak another language, identify words in English that are almost identical to words in the other language. Use an etymological dictionary to find out how these words came into English.

3. Read the Introductions in a number of comprehensive dictionaries. Assess the purposes stated in these introductions and compare them with the purposes of the dictionary-makers of the Early Modern English Period.

Present-Day English (1800–Today)

By the early 1800s, most of Britain's exploration and worldwide colonization were complete. In Queen Victoria's time it was said that "the sun never set" on the British

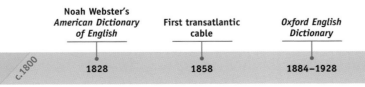

	Noah Webster's *American Dictionary of English*	First transatlantic cable	*Oxford English Dictionary*	
c.1800	1828	1858	1884–1928	PRESENT-DAY ENGLISH

Empire. The century after the American Revolution (1776) marked the division of English into national dialects that developed fairly independently and set their own standards. However, except for minor differences in vocabulary and spelling, the language has retained an astonishing worldwide uniformity. By the early stages of the period, English was universally accepted as a language of scholarship and literature. Major influences on the language in this period came from the rapid increase in science, technology, and international communication; from universal education and literacy; and from the work of modern authors, scholars, and lexicographers.

Spelling Reform and Dictionary-Making

The nineteenth century saw further attempts at spelling reform in England and North America. One of the best-known American spelling reformers was Noah Webster. When he published his dictionary in 1828, he included spellings that today distinguish British English from American English. For example, *-re* endings became *-er* (*theater* instead of *theatre*); *-our* endings became *-or* (*labor* instead of *labour*), and *-que* endings became *-ck* (*check* instead of *cheque*).

Webster's two-volume *American Dictionary of English* contained 70 000 entries and was the largest dictionary in English. Webster's *New Third International Dictionary*, most recently published in 2000, contains 450 000 entries, which include 100 000 new entries.

In 1857, the *Oxford English Dictionary (OED)* project began in England. It was designed to include every word that had appeared in English since the year 1150. The dictionary contained 15 487 pages and 1.8 million words and their contexts. During the 1970s and 1980s, a four-volume supplement was added to the original 13 volumes and was eventually integrated with the original material to form a second edition of the *Oxford English Dictionary*.

Additions to the Vocabulary of Present-Day English

The growing number of inventions and technological advances created an influx of new words into the language. In the 1800s, *railway, locomotive, photography, camera, airplane*, and *aircraft* came into use. The early 1900s gave us *air raid, newsreel, broadcast, close-up*, and *microphone*. In the 1940s and 1950s, *foxhole, paratrooper, jeep, blockbuster*, and *telecast* appeared. Discoveries in science and medicine during the nineteenth and twentieth centuries have added *vaccination, penicillin, immunology, orthodontics*, and *plutonium* to the language. We have also formed many new words by adding prefixes

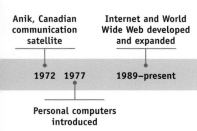

Anik, Canadian communication satellite

Internet and World Wide Web developed and expanded

1972 1977   1989–present

Personal computers introduced

and suffixes to existing words: *transoceanic, postgraduate, preschool, subtitle, gangster, receptionist, hospitalize*. The recent worldwide expansion of satellites, telecommunication, digital telephones, and computer technology has added hundreds of new terms to the English language: *software, laser, fibre optics, digital, fax, e-mail, Internet*.

English: The International Language?

English has become the most widely used language in the world today. It is the international language of air traffic controllers, and the worldwide language of communication technology. It has been estimated that English is used for four-fifths of the information stored in computers in all parts of the world. Scholars and scientists from every nation publish in English to reach the widest possible audience. The world's contact with English has been increased by the film and television industries. The major U.S.-based Cable News Network (CNN) has viewers in about 150 countries and territories. Through modern developments in telephones, satellite broadcasting, international film distribution, and computer e-mail and voice communication, speakers of English in every corner of the world have become familiar with the sounds and vocabulary of other varieties of English. The effects of such exposure include the uniting of English speakers, the slowing of differences between various dialects, and the development of a world standard for English.

 ACTIVITIES

1. Read the English passages from 1623 in "To Keep the Memory of So Worthy a Friend," pages 82–86, and from 1726 in "The Grand Academy of Lagado," pages 91–93. Locate the words that have changed in spelling since the Early Modern English period. Identify the patterns or groupings that these changes fall into. In a group, discuss the significance of these changes in the development of present-day English.

2. In a small group, compile a list of English words that have recently come to be used in the area of computers and electronic communication. Be prepared to present your list to the class.

LEVELS OF LANGUAGE

Slang is the informal and usually short-lived vocabulary used by particular groups or in special, informal contexts; it is usually not appropriate to use slang in formal written work, but it is often used in fiction to show character and create mood.

A **colloquialism** is also an informal, conversational expression that is often inappropriate to use in formal written work. Many dictionaries will tell you whether an expression is considered slang or colloquial.

Jargon is the specialized language used by a profession, trade, or group. Jargon must be used carefully in oral and written work because it may mislead or exclude nonspecialists, or obscure meaning.

Good writing uses simple, clear language—called plain English—and avoids the use of slang, colloquialisms, and jargon.

Dialect is a local version of language, with its own vocabulary and sentence structure.

We use **Standard Canadian English** in our schools. This is the oral and written English used by a broad range of Canadian society (including government, medicine, law, science, business, and the media). Standard Canadian English follows accepted rules and practices of grammar, usage, spelling, and punctuation.

Formal and Informal Language and Style

Language is like clothing: often it is fine to speak casually. At other times you need to "dress up" your language to fit the occasion. It is important to know when and how to use **formal** and **informal language**.

PARTS OF SPEECH

A **noun** names a person, place, or thing. Nouns are commonly classed as **common** (book, pen), **proper** (Canada, Mary), **collective** (class, team), **concrete** (desk, chair), and **abstract** (love, honesty).

A **pronoun** takes the place of a noun. Pronouns agree with their antecedents (the words to which pronouns refer) in number and gender but take the case of the role they play in a sentence. Pronouns can be classed as **possessive** (my, her, your) or **relative** (who, whom, whose, which, that).

A **reflexive pronoun** directs the action of the verb back to the subject. Example:

Manuel bought *himself* a bicycle helmet.

A **relative pronoun** is used to introduce a subordinate clause and relate the clause to another word in the sentence. The most common relative pronouns are *who, whom, whose, which,* and *that.* The word to which a relative pronoun refers is called its antecedent. Example:

Janice, *whom* I have known for years, is my lab partner in Biology this year.

An **adjective** describes a noun or pronoun. Adjectives can be **positive** (good, fast, beautiful), **comparative** (better, faster, more beautiful), or **superlative** (best, fastest, most beautiful).

A **verb** expresses an action or a mode of being. Verbs can be classed as transitive, intransitive, and linking or copula.

Transitive verbs express an action toward an object (person or thing). Example:

Our teacher *brought* some new books to class. (The action "brought" is directed toward "books.")

Intransitive verbs express action or tell something about the subject without directing the action toward a receiver (object). Example:

The children *laughed*. (The action of "laughed" is not directed toward an object or receiver.)

Copula verbs link or connect the subject with a noun, pronoun, or adjective in the predicate of a sentence. They express a state of being or becoming rather than an action. Examples:

Mr. Johnson is a systems analyst. (Mr. Johnson = systems analyst)

Shakespeare's plays remain popular centuries after his era. (plays = popular)

The **verb tense** tells when the action occurs. The three most commonly used tenses in English are **present**, **past**, and **future**. Do not change needlessly from one tense to another. When writing about events that take place in the present, use verbs in the present tense. Similarly, when writing about events that occurred in the past, use verbs in the past tense.

Verb voice can be active or passive. **Active voice** expresses an action that is done *by* its subject. Example:

James *wrote* the letter. (The subject "James" performs the action "wrote.")

Passive voice expresses an action that is done *to* its subject. Example:

The letter *was written* by James. (The subject "letter" receives the action "was written.")

The passive voice is also used when the doer of the action is unknown or not important to the context. Example:

An announcement *was made* over the PA system. (You don't know who made the announcement—the doer of the action is unknown.)

The active voice tends to be more direct, hard-hitting, and forceful; however, the passive voice is used to create clarity in reports, manuals, and scholarly essays.

Proofread carefully for **subject–verb agreement** when the subject and verb are separated in a sentence.

✴ ACTIVITY

Identify the correct verb in the following sentences:

The decline in political leadership in the country is reflected in the oversimplifications that characterizes/characterize political debate today.

The criteria on which an essay is evaluated in this class is/are clear to all the students.

An **adverb** describes the how, when, or where of a verb, or other adverb. In English, adverbs frequently end in *ly*.

Some Specific Verb Forms

An **infinitive** is a verb form preceded by the preposition "to." It can be used as a noun, adjective, or adverb. Examples:

To count your blessings is *to show* your gratitude. (Both "to count" and "to show" are infinitives. As nouns, they act respectively as subject and subjective completion of the copula verb "is." As verbs, they express action and have as objects "your blessings" and "your gratitude.")

The car *to buy* is the red convertible. ("To buy" is an infinitive. As an adjective it modifies the noun "car.")

The convict ran *to hide*. ("To hide" is an infinitive. As an adverb it modifies the verb "ran.")

A **gerund** is a verb form usually ending in "ing." Gerunds are verb forms used as nouns. Like other nouns, they can be modified by an adjective. Like other verbs, they can also be modified by adverbs. Example:

Swimming is good exercise. ("Swimming" is a gerund. As a noun, it is the subject of the predicate verb "is"; as a verb, it shows action.)

A **participle** is a verb form. It can be in the present tense (ending in "ing") or in the past tense (often ending in "d" or "ed"). Participles are used as adjectives. Like other adjectives and verbs, they can be modified by an adverb. Examples:

Blushing, the star athlete admitted that he was embarrassed when he dropped the trophy. ("Blushing" is a present participle. As an adjective, it modifies the noun/subject of the sentence, "athlete"; as a verb, it shows action.)

Roasted chestnuts taste delicious. ("Roasted" is a past participle. As an adjective, it modifies the noun "chestnuts"; as a verb, it shows the action of roasting, which has already been completed.)

Note: Since both gerunds and participles are verb forms that can end in "ing," they are distinguished by the way they are used in the sentence, i.e., as a noun or adjective.

Infinitive phrases include the infinitive form of a verb and its object or modifier. They can be used as nouns, adjectives, or adverbs. Examples:

To express your ideas clearly is important. (In this sentence, "To express your ideas clearly" acts as the noun subject of the verb "is." Within the infinitive phrase, "To express" has an object "ideas" and is modified by the adverb "clearly.")

Pink is the colour *to wear in the new year*. (Here, "to wear in the new year" acts as an adjective modifying the noun "colour." Within the infinitive phrase, the prepositional adverb phrase "in the new year" modifies the infinitive "to wear.")

Three years ago, I left home *to find myself a job*. (Here, the infinitive phrase "to find myself a job" is used as an adverb modifying the verb "left." Within the infinitive phrase, the infinitive "to find" has both a direct object "job" and an indirect object "myself.")

Gerund phrases include the gerund form of a verb and its object or modifier and are used as nouns. Examples:

The loud singing was as annoying as the man who sang it. (The gerund phrase "The loud singing" acts as a noun because it is the subject of the verb "was." Within the gerund phrase, "loud" is an adjective modifying the noun part of the gerund "singing.")

Skiing downhill is exhilarating. (The gerund phrase "Skiing downhill" acts as a noun because it is the subject of the verb "is." Within the gerund phrase, "downhill" is an adverb modifying the verb part of the gerund "skiing.")

Participial phrases include the participle form of a verb (ending in "ing") and its object or modifier. They are used as adjectives. Example:

Hearing footsteps, the woman turned around. (The participial phrase "Hearing footsteps" acts as an adjective modifying the noun subject of the sentence "woman." Within the participial phrase, "footsteps" acts as an object of the verb part of the participle "Hearing.")

Conjunctions

A **conjunction** is a word that joins words or groups of words used in the same way. Common conjunctions are *and, but, or, so, for, when*. A conjunction can also be a group of words: *as though, except that, in order that, so that, not only ... but also*.

Conjunctions can be divided into two classes: coordinating and subordinating.

A **coordinating conjunction** (*and, but, nor, so, or, for, yet*) combines words or groups of words used in the same way (e.g., principal clauses). Example:

She wrote down the number *but* she lost it.

A **subordinating conjunction** (e.g., *although, if, when, provided, that, whenever, because, unless, while, though*) combines a main idea (principal clause) and a secondary or less important idea (subordinate clause). Example:

Though they didn't win the match, the team was happy to have made it to the finals.

Other parts of speech

A **preposition** relates a noun or pronoun to some other words in the sentence. Examples include *at, behind, by, in, into, near, of, on, to, through, under, with*.

An **interjection** is a word or words that express emotion or thought but are not essential to the sentence. Examples include *alas, hey, oh dear, oops, ouch, well, wow*.

PARTS OF SENTENCES

Sentences come in a variety of forms. Some sentences are simple; some are complex. All sentences have a subject and a predicate. Sentences may also include such elements as an object, a subjective completion, prepositional and participial phrases, and principal and subordinate clauses.

A **subject** indicates who or what performs the action of the predicate. Example:

John broke the window. His *mother* was not amused.

A **predicate** indicates what is said about the subject; the key word in the predicate is the verb. Example:

Raj *wrote* the letter.

An **object** receives the action of a transitive verb. Example:

The barking of the dog woke *Ian*.

A **subjective completion** describes the subject after a linking or copula verb. Example:

My father is an *architect*.

A **prepositional phrase** begins with a preposition followed by a noun or pronoun (the object of the preposition), and any adjectives modifying that object. Example:

The raccoon *in the cage* has rabies.

Prepositional phrases have two types: prepositional adjective phrase and prepositional adverb phrase.

A **prepositional adjective phrase** modifies a noun or pronoun. Examples:

The members *of the orchestra* went on strike. (The adjective phrase "of the orchestra" modifies the noun "members.")

All *of us* disliked the movie. (The adjective phrase "of us" modifies the pronoun "all.")

A **prepositional adverb phrase** modifies a verb, adjective, or adverb. Examples:

They stopped *for lunch*. (The adverb phrase "for lunch" modifies the verb "stopped.")

Kelly is good *at Science*, but better *at Math*. (The adverb phrase "at Science" modifies the adjective "good," and the adverb phrase "at Math" modifies the comparative adjective "better.")

Is the weather warm enough *for tennis*? (The adjective phrase "for tennis" modifies the adverb "enough.")

A **clause** is a part of a sentence that consists of a subject and a verb. A **principal (independent) clause** refers to the main idea and makes sense on its own. Example:

He did not watch television.

A **subordinate (dependent) clause** refers to the secondary idea and does not make sense on its own. Example:

He did not watch television *because he had to do his homework*.

A **restrictive (essential) clause** is necessary to the meaning of the sentence. Commas are not used around restrictive clauses. Example:

The girl *who just phoned me* is my best friend.

A **non-restrictive (non-essential) clause** contains information that is not needed to understand the main idea in the sentence. Commas are used to set these clauses off from the rest of the sentence. Example:

Shakespeare, *who wrote poetry as well as plays*, was voted by many people as the Person of the Second Millennium.

Types of Subordinate Clauses

Adjective clauses are subordinate clauses used to modify a noun or pronoun. Examples:

This is the restaurant *that serves my favourite food*. ("That serves my favourite food" is an adjective clause modifying the noun "restaurant.")

Jeremy, *who is my nephew*, is a professional wrestler. ("Who is my nephew" is an adjective clause modifying "Jeremy.")

Adverb clauses are subordinate clauses used to modify a verb, adjective, or adverb. Examples:

After I read the letter, I tore it up. ("After I read the letter" is an adverb clause modifying the verb "tore.")

His pitching arm is stronger today *than it ever was*. ("Than it ever was" is an adverb clause modifying the adjective "stronger.")

Noun clauses are subordinate clauses used as nouns. Examples:

Everyone agreed *that the action was bad for the team*. ("That the action was bad for the team" is a noun clause acting as the object of the verb "agreed.")

Whoever broke the vase will face the consequences. ("Whoever broke the vase" is a noun clause and the subject of the sentence.)

SENTENCE VARIETY

In order to create variety in your writing, you need to know about different sentence types and orders.

Types of Sentence by Purpose

An **assertive** sentence makes a statement. Example:

Management will make a decision today.

An **interrogative sentence** asks a question. Example:

Who ate my cake?

An **imperative sentence** makes a command. Example:

Come here.

An **exclamatory sentence** expresses an emphatic or emotional utterance. Example:

Oh, you hateful person!

Types of Sentence by Structure

A **simple sentence** has one principal clause with a subject and predicate. Example:

My son is the best player.

A **compound sentence** has two or more principal clauses that need connecting words. Example:

Michael felt sad, but Joan was happy to be leaving the country.

A **complex sentence** has one principal clause and one or more subordinate clauses. A connecting word is used to relate the subordinate clause(s) to the principal clause. Example:

I was late because I missed the bus and had to wait 30 minutes for the next one.

A **compound-complex** sentence contains two principal clauses and at least one subordinate clause. This is the most difficult sentence structure to use correctly. However, the ability to combine some ideas and to subordinate others demonstrates a sophisticated control of language and ideas. Example:

When Bill left, he locked the door, but he forgot to turn off the lights. ("He locked the door" and "he forgot to turn off the lights" are both principal clauses; "When Bill left" is a subordinate clause.)

Sentence Order

A **natural order** places the subject before the predicate. Example:

The customer was angry.

An **inverted order** places the predicate before the subject. Example:

Behind the social persona lurked an evil mind.

A **split order** places part of the predicate before the subject (or between the subject and the verb) for emphasis or effect. Example:

Maria, when she won the award, shed tears of joy.

Using Unconventional Grammar

Occasionally a poet or advertising copywriter will use incorrect grammar intentionally to grab the reader's attention or create a memorable phrase. A novelist, story writer, or dramatist may also have a character use incorrect or unconventional grammar to create an impression of, or to reveal information about, that character.

 ACTIVITY

Identify the grammatical error in each of the following sentences and assess whether the error enhances or detracts from the idea being expressed.

Totally recyclable. Socially conscious. And here to stay. (from an advertisement by the Aluminum Marketing Council)

Drive careful.

With one small stone are made. (from "Grandmother," page 14)

SPELLING

Using Prefixes, Suffixes, and Root Words to Help You Spell Correctly

When you understand root words, prefixes, and suffixes, you will find that you start to spell words correctly more often.

A **prefix** is added to the beginning of a word in order to change or add to the meaning of the word. Examples: *sub-, counter-, dis-, un-, mis-*.

A **suffix** is added to the end of the word to change its meaning or form a new word. Examples: *-able, -ly, -ful, -ism, -ion*.

The **root** of a word is the part of the word to which prefixes and suffixes are added. Many root words in English have Greek or Latin origins.

 ACTIVITY

Identify the meaning of the prefixes, suffixes, and roots in the following words. Use a dictionary as required.

prenatal	homophone	dictatorship	beautifully
postmortem	atheist	trainee	

Understanding Frequently Confused Words, Including Homophones

When proofreading for spelling, be especially vigilant about words that sound the same or have similar sounds, but different meanings.

If you are not sure of the difference in meaning of the following frequently confused words, look them up in a dictionary. Following are some words, including homophones (words that have the same pronunciation), that are often misspelled:

- *advice, advise*
- *allusion, illusion*
- *affect, effect*
- *seize, seas, sees*
- *stationary, stationery*
- *there, their, they're*

Spelling Words Ending in *-cede*, *-ceed*, and *-sede*

Verbs ending in *-cede* include the following: *accede, concede, recede, antecede, secede, cede, intercede,* and *precede.*

The only common verbs ending in *-ceed* are *succeed, proceed,* and *exceed.*

The only verb ending in *-sede* is *supersede.*

PUNCTUATION

End stops such as the **period** (.), the **question mark** (?), and the **exclamation mark** (!) are used to end a sentence. Other punctuation marks (**commas, dashes,** and so on) perform different functions.

A **comma** (,) is used after an introductory word, phrase, or clause; to separate items in a list; after the introduction to direct speech; and to make the meaning of the sentence clear.

A **dash** (—) is used before or around a definition or clarification of a word, phrase, or idea. For example:

In a democracy, a premise of jurisprudence—science or philosophy of law—is that everyone is equal before the law.

A **colon** (:) is used to introduce a list, an example, a quotation, or an explanation. The colon is also used in dramatic dialogue to indicate that a character begins speaking.

A **semicolon** (;) is used to join principal or independent clauses in a sentence. This use is sometimes referred to as a "soft" period. It is used in this way with some transitional words and phrases. For example:

Patty likes to act; her sister gets stage fright. (The semicolon here replaces a period because the two ideas are very closely connected.)

Rajiiv felt shy; however, he soon made some new friends. (There are several transitional words and phrases like "however" that usually require a semicolon when used.)

The semicolon is also used between items in a series when the items themselves contain commas. For example:

My painting class will meet on Monday, October 16; Tuesday, October 24; Monday, October 30; and Friday, November 3.

Alana, Eric, and Tina voted for Kelly; Claude, Francine, and Alison voted for Helga. (The use of commas in the two principal clauses makes the semicolon useful for clarity.)

A **hyphen** is used to combine words or parts of words to form an expression that needs to be seen as one word. Examples:

ex-ballplayer, run-on sentence

Quotation marks are used to indicate direct speech and the titles of short poems, stories, and articles. **Direct speech** requires quotation marks; **indirect speech** does not. Examples:

Direct: "Do you have a loonie?" Dad asked. "I need one for the parking meter."

Indirect: My dad asked me for a loonie for the parking meter.

Italics or **underlining** are used to indicate the titles of books, full-length plays, newspapers, and magazines. Example:

We read an article called "Getting Carried Away with Shoes" from *Reader's Digest*.

Parentheses are used around a word, phrase, or idea that could be left out without destroying the sense of the writing. These words, phrases, or ideas are sometimes called "parenthetical." They are also used around references and notes inserted into a text. Examples:

My favourite drink is chocolate milk (real chocolate, real milk).

Many British novelists have dealt with the theme of social inequities (see Austen, Dickens).

Points of ellipsis (…) are used by writers to show that part of a quotation has been left out or to indicate a pause in dialogue. Examples:

The prime minister, who was in China at the time, said the report was nonsense.

with ellipses becomes

The prime minister … said the report was nonsense.

Reading and Researching

READING STRATEGIES

Backgrounds of Readers and Writers Influence the Interpretation of Texts

With some texts (e.g., a bus schedule), every reader will get the same information and understanding. With most texts, however, readers will not get exactly the same meaning because of differences in personal experiences and prior knowledge. For instance, a student who has experienced being stereotyped will understand "Stereotypes Are for Others" by Maria Coletta McLean (page 164) in a different way than a student without that experience. Readers' personal experiences and prior knowledge affect their understanding of and preferences for texts. Because class and group discussions of texts draw on a wide range of experience and knowledge, they can help to refine your comprehension of what you have read.

Similarly, each writer writes from his or her own personal experience and knowledge. Chaucer could not have written about automobiles because they were not part of his experience. An author's view of people, emotions, and values will reflect his or her own experience and knowledge. For this reason, it is always important that you read critically in order to evaluate the information and ideas in a text. In some cases, you may alter your ideas in light of new information in a text; in other cases, you may disagree with a text because it does not seem valid in light of your experience.

Using Prior Experiences and Knowledge

You can bring prior experiences and knowledge from your own life, from personal reading, and from your previous studies to help create both interest in and understanding of what you read. You might bring previous knowledge about
- the subject of the piece
- the issues in the piece
- the author
- the author's style and themes
- the setting (time, place, and historical period)
- subject-specific information (science, mathematics, history, geography, another language, technology, art, music, drama)
- vocabulary

Predicting

Predicting is a skill that makes you think ahead before you read. Whether or not your predictions are correct doesn't matter as much as the interaction you are having with the text. Once again, this kind of activity can increase your interest in what might, at first, seem to be a boring text.

Before Reading

- Use the title to predict the content of the text and its purpose.
- Look at any illustrations or graphical elements to establish possible events (fiction) or points the writer is making (non-fiction).
- Read a summary or cover blurb to predict what might happen, who is involved (fiction), or the writer's point of view (non-fiction).
- Use the vocabulary in the first few lines to predict the author's style, the time in which the piece is set, the difficulty of the piece (fiction and non-fiction), or the specific subject matter to be discussed (non-fiction).
- Read the first one or two paragraphs to predict the narrator's tone, the initial problem in the story, something about the characters (fiction), the audience for whom it was written (fiction and non-fiction), the thesis or point of view (non-fiction).

During Reading

- Predict what decisions the characters will make (fiction).
- Forecast how the setting might change and the effect this could have on the action (fiction).
- Try to foresee changes in the direction of the plot (fiction).
- Predict what arguments or details a writer might use to support important points (non-fiction).

After Reading

Questioning can help you create and maintain interest in what you are reading. Wondering on paper (which is really what questions are) also helps you decide what you need and want to know. You can use questions at any time before, during, or after your reading to help you predict.

Questions are useful to help you recall, restate, reflect on, and analyze what you have read.

Questions to help you recall might include the 5Ws and 1H: who, what, where, when, why, and how (the same questions that are used for creating a news report).

To restate, try using one of the following to start your question:
How could I
- rephrase?
- reword?
- explain?
- illustrate?

To help you reflect, think about some of the following question starters:
- What would happen if ...?
- What would I have done ...?
- What else could have happened ...?
- If I could choose one part that makes me feel ... what would it be?
- Which character do I most identify with?
- I wonder if the writer ...?
- How is this like ...?

You could use some of the following questions to help you analyze:
- What evidence do I have that ...?
- What conclusions can I draw ...?
- What reasons are there for ...?
- What can I infer from ...?
- What arguments can I select ...?
- How do I know that ...?
- What proofs do I have that ...?
- What do I need to find out about ...?

READING FOR UNDERSTANDING

Close Reading of a Text

The demand for analytic reading of texts increases as you progress through your schooling. It is important that you know how to read a text closely in order to discover details in it that you might miss in a cursory reading. The student essay on Pratt's poem "Erosion" (page 5) demonstrates how much can be learned from close reading and analysis.

When reading literature, one of the most important concepts to establish is the theme of the piece. A theme is different from a subject. The subject is what the piece is about; the theme is what the author is saying about the subject. There may be more than one theme in a piece of writing.

You can use heuristics (sets of questions) such as the following to help you establish the theme:
- What is the piece of writing about?
- What is the author saying about that subject?

OR
- Who wins?
- Who loses?

- What is won?
- What is lost?
- Whose side is the author on?

Examining the answers to these questions may help you discover the meanings and ideas the author is conveying through his or her work.

Creating a Theme Statement

When creating your theme statement, put your ideas about the theme in one or more sentences. A single word can often capture the subject of a piece of writing, but not the theme. Try starting your sentence with "The author is saying that…."

 ACTIVITY

As a class, read one drama, poem, or short story in this textbook. Using one set of questions above, come to an understanding of what the author is saying to his or her audience. In a small group, discuss your ideas about the theme and come to a consensus. Present your theme (and any differing opinions) to the class. Discuss the similarities between the themes that various groups have identified.

Elements for Emphasizing or Developing Themes

Certain elements appear in all types of literature. Much like the elements of design in visual arts, these elements are tools the author uses in his or her writing to emphasize or develop the theme. Below is a list of these elements.

Figures of speech: including simile, metaphor, alliteration, and onomatopoeia

Rhetoric: imagery, word choice, sentence structure, and diction

Structure: the way the writing is put together
Prose
- chapters
- divisions within chapters
- sequence of events
Poetry
- stanzas
- typographical layout
- line divisions
- groups of stanzas (sometimes called "chapters" or "books," or simply given numbers)

Drama
- acts
- scenes
- prologues, epilogues

Setting: includes both time and space
Time
- era
- time of year
- time of day

Space
- real or fantasy world
- country, city, rural, or urban
- dark or light
- enclosed or open space

Character:
- what the character does, says, says about him- or herself and others
- what others say about him or her
- how the character reacts to others and to a variety of situations
- what the author or narrator says about him or her
- his or her physical features and psychological makeup
- what motivates him or her

Perspective: the type of narration (in novels, short stories, and poems) and the way we see the action (in drama)

Create your own set of questions by asking yourself this question: How does any one or a combination of design elements help emphasize or develop the theme?

 ACTIVITY

In a small group, choose a piece of literature from this textbook that you have not previously studied. Answer the following questions:
- Which one or two elements are the most evident in the author's work?
- How do these elements develop and change throughout the work?
- What pattern(s), if any, emerge(s)?
- How does each of these elements support or emphasize the theme of the writer's work?

Write a thesis about the work based on the theme and the elements you have identified.

Understanding Strategies Used in Writing Prose and Poetry

Writers are often asked, "Did you mean to ...?" Yes, writers do think of symbols, image patterns, metaphors, irony, contrasts, and a host of other things when they write. Some start their work with an image or symbol at the core; others bring it in as they draft and redraft their work.

For readers to draw out the greatest meaning from a text, it is important that they be aware of how writers use the tools of their trade and notice the writers' techniques and how their writing has been crafted.

The following are some tools that writers use for both prose and poetry:

- **Syntax** is the structure of a sentence or the way a sentence is put together.
- An **allusion** is a reference to a well-known character, place, or story or to another literary work. For example, "The young player threw the baseball with Herculean strength." The allusion is to the great strength of the Greek hero Heracles. (Note: Hercules is the Roman name for Heracles.)
- An **oxymoron** juxtaposes (places side by side) two opposites to create a vivid image. Examples: "crashing silence," "loving hate," "bittersweet."
- **Contrast** is used to show how two characters, objects, or ideas are different.
- **Hyperbole** is a fancy name for exaggeration. It can be used seriously to create in a reader's mind a picture "larger than life," or it can be used comically to make a reader laugh.
- **Understatement** is the opposite of hyperbole. It shows something as much less important than it is. The effect of understatement is often ironic or sarcastic.
- Three types of **irony** are verbal irony, dramatic irony, and situational irony. **Verbal irony** occurs when the real or intended meaning of a word, phrase, or sentence is different than what the speaker of that word, phrase, or sentence intended. A different kind of irony occurring in fiction and drama is **dramatic irony**. This takes place when the reader or viewer shares knowledge with the writer that a character does not have. The character will then say or do something that foreshadows what the audience knows will happen, but that the character has no idea about. The character speaks more truly than he or she can possibly know. **Situational irony** occurs when what actually happens is different from what is expected by the reader or viewer.
- A **symbol** is an object, person, or action that is used to represent some other idea, principle, object, theme, or character. A country's flag is the symbol of that country; each hockey team has its symbol on its jersey. Many names are symbolic. Many of those names are also allusions to famous people.

Reading Prose

Plot

Plot does not always drive a piece of fiction. A story may be character driven or thematically driven. No matter what drives a story, there is always some kind of plot, however thin.

Jack Hodgins, a famous Canadian novelist, identifies six things a plot-driven story must have:[1]

- a main character (protagonist) we care about or are interested in
- knowledge that this character has a goal and a strong reason for achieving it
- obstacles that stand in the way of the character's goal
- a sense that each event is somehow the cause of the event that follows
- conflicts that intensify to the point where something has to break, which then causes the main character's life to turn a corner
- a resolution that allows the reader to feel the story has come to a satisfying end

The ways writers approach writing a story are as varied as the number of writers themselves. A writer may outline the whole story before it is written, or a writer may develop a story from an idea about a character, a theme, or a situation.

Setting versus Scene

The word **setting** is most often used by students to mean the place or time in which a story is set. Writers, however, often use the word to describe a writing technique, that is, "telling about" a story. The word **scene** means "showing" the story. Most writers agree that "showing" is more effective than "telling."

To "show" a story
- use description
- appeal to the five senses
- include dialogue
- include action

Example 1

Once there was a boy named Arthur. He lived a long time ago. He had a magic birth that he didn't know about, and he was raised by a kind old man. Arthur was responsible for his stepbrother's horse, sword, and lance. One day, right before a competition, Arthur forgot his stepbrother's sword. He didn't have time to go back home before his brother's event, but he had seen a sword sticking out of a stone,

---

1. Jack Hodgins, "Specialized Tool: Fiction," *A Passion for Narrative* (Toronto: McClelland and Stewart Inc., 1993), p. 126.

so he ran over and pulled it out. After that he became king because the person who could pull the sword from the stone was destined to become king.

Example 2

"Where is my sword, little brother?"

Arthur felt a great weight growing in his stomach. He thought quickly. "I must have left it on my horse, sir." But he knew he hadn't. He sighed loudly. Ever since he was a child, Arthur had been forgetful. His stepfather would always pat him on the back, smile, and say, "That's all right, Wart. Someday you'll remember all right."

But today, Arthur knew even his stepfather wouldn't be so kind. This was, after all, his stepbrother's one chance to prove his skills as a young knight. Arthur forced a smile and swallowed the lump in his throat. He felt his face flame; he tasted the biting acid of fear.

His brother spoke before Arthur could think any more. "I'm going to make sure my name is on the contestants' list, Arthur. When you have my sword, bring it to me in front of the striped tent," he pointed, "over there."

As he watched his brother lead his horse toward the tent, Arthur remembered where he had seen a sword. Maybe he could borrow it just for the afternoon. He raced into the woods overlooking the fairgrounds. The sword was resting in a stone. Its hilt reflected the shafts of light shining through the trees. Arthur could smell success. He wiped the sweat from his palms, spat into them, and wrapped his small hands around the handle. He pulled, but the sword stuck. He tried again and thought he felt some movement. On the third try, the sword came out of the stone, so hard that Arthur landed—thwap!—on his rear.

 ACTIVITY

Decide which of the examples develops the setting more effectively. Give a reason for your choice.

Characters

As readers, we learn about character in the following ways:
- the author or narrator tells us
- the main character tells us herself or himself
- other characters tell us
- the character's own behaviour tells us

Characters differ from each other in these ways:
- appearance
- speech (level of language, dialect, speech rhythms, pet words)
- action (physical reactions to things; body language; facial expressions; habits such as coughing, throat clearing, giggling, talking constantly when nervous)
- thoughts and opinions

Narrative Point of View

A writer can use five main **points of view**:

1. **First-person involved**. The narrator is the main character in the story. This a very personal type of narration that makes the reader feel involved with the character who is telling the story. As well, the reader
   - should be clear about the amount of time that has passed between the events and the telling of them
   - should be able to decide whether the narrator has changed or developed since the events took place
   - must decide over the course of the story whether the narrator is reliable (whether everything he or she is saying is the truth)

2. **First-person observer**. The narrator may be a minor character in the story and have some role to play in the plot, or he or she may be observing the action from a distance, unknown to the characters in the story. In this point of view
   - the writer creates some distance between the reader and the events
   - the reader must question whether this narrator is telling the truth about the events as he or she saw them or was involved in them

3. **Third-person omniscient**. The narrator knows all, sees all, and tells all. This type of narrator is the most reliable since he or she can see inside and tell us, the readers, about every character's thoughts. The readers, however, may not feel very involved in the story.

4. **Third-person limited**. The narrator tells the story from the perspective of one or two main characters, but does not tell the thoughts of anyone else. This narrator has the same effect as the first-person narrator since the reader feels very close to the character whose story is being told. At times, the reader feels as though he or she is inside that character's head, but the narrator can also step back from the character or action. As well, this narrator is less reliable as a source of total information than the omniscient narrator.

5. **Third-person reporter**. The narrator tells the facts, without going into any of the characters' heads. In this point of view
   - the reader feels very distanced from the narrator as he or she cannot get into the heads of any of the characters and the reader can only hear what is being reported. This limits the reader's understanding of motivations and emotions, but engages the reader in trying to figure them out.
   - the narrator is only as reliable as his or her observations. Remember, he or she cannot be in every place at one time, so the reader might be missing some details.

Reading Poetry

Types of Poetry

A **narrative** poem
- tells a story
- may take the form of a ballad
- is generally organized in stanzas with a regular rhythm and rhyme scheme

A **lyric** poem
- conveys strong emotions and impressions

Although words to songs are called lyrics, lyric poetry is not necessarily set to music.

Blank verse, used frequently by Shakespeare,
- has a regular metrical pattern
- does not have a regular rhyme scheme

A **free-verse** poem
- has very few restrictions
- has no set rhyme, rhythm pattern, or line length

A **sonnet**
- is 14 lines of iambic pentameter verse
- is either Petrarchan, Shakespearean, or modern

Petrarchan (or Italian) sonnets
- consist of an octave (eight lines of regular rhyme scheme) followed by a sestet (six lines of regular rhyme scheme, ending in a rhyming couplet)
- the idea or mood is usually developed in the octave and changed or commented upon in the sestet
- typical rhyme scheme is *abba, abba, cde, cde*

Shakespearean (or English) sonnets
- consist of three quatrains (four-line stanzas with a regular rhyme scheme) followed by a rhyming couplet
- the idea or mood is usually developed through the quatrains and changed or summarized in the rhyming couplet
- typical rhyme scheme is *abab, cdcd, efef, gg*

A **modern sonnet** may adapt and change the traditional structures or rhyme schemes.

A **dramatic monologue** is a poem in which a narrator reveals him- or herself through his or her own speech. Dramatic monologues are frequently written in blank verse.

An **elegy** is a formal poem lamenting the death of an individual or a group of people.

An **epic poem** is a narrative poem that relates the mighty deeds or adventures of heroes in a lofty or majestic style.

The **haiku** and the **tanka** are two types of traditional Japanese poetry. Both have very specific forms, and both revolve around a strong image.

The haiku
- consists of three unrhymed lines: five syllables in the first, seven syllables in the second, and five in the third
- has a final line that resonates with more than one level of meaning
- is often about nature and the passage of time

The tanka
- consists of five unrhymed lines with a total of 31 syllables
- has the following format: lines 1 and 3 have five syllables each; lines 2, 4, and 5 have seven syllables each
- is often about love

Concrete poetry is arranged in a shape that enhances or reflects the topic.

Imagistic poetry
- tends to be fairly short
- focuses on one or two central images

Haiku is a type of imagistic poetry (although it was invented long before the imagist writers popularized imagistic poetry).

Sound

Authors use many devices to manipulate sounds in their writing. Here are some devices you should know. (Note: These are all elements of rhetoric; they are tools you can use not only when analyzing reading but also when you are doing your own writing.)

- Imitating an **accent** from a different culture can be an effective way to distinguish one character from another or to denote a feeling, mood, or culture. Be careful. Overuse can make a character laughable or can perpetuate stereotypes.
- **Alliteration** is the repetition of the initial sound in a series of words (*luscious lying lips*). The words do not have to be in sequence but should be relatively close to each other to sustain an effect.
- **Assonance** is the internal rhyming of vowel sounds. ("When shall we three meet again?" William Shakespeare)
- **Cacophony** is the mixture of harsh, discordant, or dissonant sounds. ("All day cars mooed and shrieked/Hollered and bellowed and wept" James Reaney)
- Like assonance, **consonance** is internal rhyme or repetition, except using consonants, not vowels. ("The blood-dimmed tide is loosed" William Butler Yeats)
- **Dialect**, such as a patois, is an effective tool for characterization but, like accents, must be used sparingly to avoid stereotyping.
- When a line of poetry continues on to the next line without any end marks, it is called **enjambment**:

   And no one will know of the war, not one
   Will care at last when it is done.
      Sara Teasdale

- **Euphony** is a blending of sounds to make a musical, lyrical sound.
- When words make or represent a sound, they are examples of **onomatopoeia** (e.g., *boom, boff, bang, clang*).
- An echo effect can be set up with the **repetition** of a word or series of words. If an entire stanza is repeated, it is called a **refrain** or **chorus**. (Watch that you don't overuse repetition as it can become tiresome and trite.)
- **Rhyme** is an obvious way of drawing attention to sound. End rhyme and internal rhyme are both effective ways to echo sounds.

Rhythm

Rhythm is the beat of the words and lines. Even prose lines have rhythm. That's why writing a series of simple, natural-order sentences becomes very monotonous; their rhythms are all the same.

Meter

In poetry, we usually talk about meter when we talk about rhythm. Meter comes from the combination of stressed (´) and unstressed (˘) syllables in words.

Here is an example.

David divides into two syllables: Dá vĭd. We stress the first syllable, not the second. Say David's name aloud with the accent on the second syllable. How does it sound? Does it sound a little more French? That's because many French names have the accent on the second syllable.

Foot

Poets use a variety of recognizable rhythm patterns. These patterns make up a **foot** in a line of poetry. A foot contains one stressed syllable and one or two unstressed syllables. Although there are many types, here are a few that you should know and that will give you a good start:

- **Trochaic** (/˘) is also called "running meter" (lightness, gaiety).
- **Iambic** (˘/) is also called the "walking meter" (thoughtful, dignified, exalted).

To remember these two common patterns, simply remember the nursery rhyme:

Márў hád ă líttlĕ lamb. (trochaic)
Ĭts fleéce wăs whíte aš snów. (iambic)

Iambic feet are most like English speech, and, because of that, Shakespeare used iambic feet most often in his writing.

Here are three others you should know:

- **Anapestic** (˘˘/) is also called "galloping meter" (movement, change, boldness, confidence).

  Shĕ căn kíll wĭth ă smíle
  Shĕ căn woúnd wĭth hĕr eyés
      Billy Joel

- **Dactylic** (/˘˘) creates an effect of movement, turbulence.

  Júst fŏr ă / hándfŭl ŏf / sílvĕr hĕ / léft ŭs,
     Júst fŏr ă / rĭband tŏ / stíck ĭn hĭs / cóat —
  Foúnd thĕ óne / gíft ŏf whĭch / fórtŭnĕ bĕ/réft ŭs,
     Lóst all thĕ / óthĕrs shĕ / léts ŭs / dévŏte.
     Robert Browning

- **Spondaic** (//) is a less common pattern that appears at the ends of lines and gives a slow or solemn effect to a line. (*Só sád.*)

Once you have broken a line of poetry into a set of patterns, you can count the feet in the line. Let's go back to

Márў / hád ă / líttlĕ / lamb. (This line has four feet.)
Ĭts fleéce / wăs white / aš snów. (This line has three feet.)

The first line would be called a trochaic tetrameter. The second line would be called an iambic trimeter. (Note: one foot per line = monometer, two = dimeter, three = trimeter, four = tetrameter, five = pentameter, six = hexameter, seven = heptameter, eight = octameter.)

Metrical Variation

Here are some **metrical variations** that you should be aware of:
- A short line often causes a person to read slowly or to pause in order to give the line as much time as the one before it. The result is that it makes the reader dwell on the idea, information, or imagery in this line.
- A long line often causes the reader to read rapidly in order to fit the line into an established pattern. This rapid reading results in a sense of lightness, speed, or vigorous activity.
- Changing a foot from the basic or overall pattern emphasizes the word that receives the change.
- Two or more stressed syllables in succession emphasize the thought of each word and its relation to the others.
- Great irregularity in any one line (especially several stressed one-syllable words) often expresses strong emotions.

Other metrical variations are
- blank verse, which is a poem that has a regular rhythm pattern but no rhyme
- free verse, which is a poem that has neither a regular rhythm pattern nor a rhyme scheme

Line Divisions

There are many reasons for dividing lines other than rhythm and rhyme. When you are reading or writing a poem, consider these reasons for grouping words into a line:
- to contain a complete thought
- to set off a strong image
- to emphasize a word or phrase
- to complete a thought started in a previous line
- to use to advantage a grammatical structure (phrase or clause)
- to create irony or a reversal of expectation

The Good, the Bad, and the Misinformed

How to Find "Useful" Information

Find	Assess	Toss	Record

Find

Find the locations of possible information:
- Make a list of things you want to find out.
- Start with very general resources such as dictionaries, encyclopedias, atlases, indexes (any or all of these could be electronic sources, depending on your library), then move to more specific sources such as books, magazines, periodicals, newspapers, CD-ROMs, the Internet, non-print resources (videotapes, audio tapes, artwork, etc.), and other electronic resources.
- If using books, skim tables of contents and indexes to find out whether your topic is listed.
- Scan articles for titles, illustrations, subtitles, and captions that include references to your topic.
- Search the Internet for relevant sites.
- Skim read to establish the amount and usefulness of the information.
- Save resources that look as if they will have the information you need.

Assess

Assess the resources you have saved:
- Look for information that is verified in several sources. Assessing is particularly important for information that comes from the Internet.
- Decide whether the information is useful, given the topic you've chosen.
- Ask yourself whether the resource presents a complete view or a one-sided view of your topic.

- Search out information that is clear, understandable, and at a level appropriate for you.
- Check whether the information is up-to-date.

Toss

Begin to weed and toss out information:
- Discard information that can be found in only one source and for which you cannot find support anywhere else.
- If the author is not reliable, do not use his or her information. (Ask a librarian, teacher, or other experts if you don't know.)
- Do not include anything that suggests racism, sexism, homophobia, or other forms of prejudice and bias.
- Discard information from old research or outdated sources.
- Do not include vague or over-generalized information.
- Avoid personal opinion pieces that don't contain facts.

Record

Begin to record information:
- Record information in an organized way (cue cards, special notebook, electronic file).
- Keep accurate records (including page numbers) for quotations you have used or ideas you have paraphrased.
- Put ideas in your own words to guarantee you understand them but be sure you document their source. AVOID PLAGIARISM!!! (See pages 431–433.)

CONDUCTING AN INDEPENDENT STUDY PROJECT

When you do an independent study project, you will individually pursue an area of personal interest. You are responsible for choosing a topic, organizing the necessary reading and research, and completing an oral and/or written assignment. Your teacher will consult with you on a regular basis on the progress of your independent study.

You should keep extensive notes in a **log** of all the work done as you work on this project and become an expert on your topic. Your log will include notes on your reading, reports on conferences with the teacher, records of time spent reading and researching, decisions taken regarding the focus of your written and oral presentations. Your rough work for both the written and oral presentations should be kept with your log. You will also write a **self-evaluation** as a final log entry describing what you learned about your topic, your work habits, and your research, writing, and presentation skills.

Objectives of an Independent Study Project

The objectives of independent study projects are
- to encourage broad reading in a special interest (i.e., a specific author, an era, a specific topic, a genre, or a theme)
- to encourage initiative, organization of study time, and self-discipline
- to develop further
  - research and notemaking skills
  - essay-writing skills
  - reporting (oral presentation) skills

Procedure for an Independent Study Project

Independent study projects usually follow a procedure that will help guide you through to successful completion. A typical procedure may be as follows:

1. **Conference 1**. Select an author or a subject and discuss it with your teacher. Formulate a prospective bibliography using the resources available in the library (school or public). Discuss this bibliography at your first conference.

2. Follow this conference by:
   a) **Reading**. Begin reading the books (novels, plays, poems, biographies, secondary sources, etc.) that you have chosen. Make careful notes. All notes should be handed in with the logs or essay.
   b) **Logs**. Keep log sheets up-to-date. Record the date and the work accomplished and books perused or read each day that you work on the project.
   c) **Research**. Focus your notes on your topic by highlighting pertinent data. Enrich your research by investigating other primary and some secondary sources (writings, audio-visual, media-related, and human resources).
   d) **Thesis creation**. Arrive at a thesis (a strong argument/opinion), which will become the backbone of your entire study.

3. **Conference 2** (about two weeks into the project). Bring along all notes neatly organized, logs and records of time spent and of reading progress, and the outline of your essay. This will help you determine whether new directions in your research are required.

4. Follow up this conference by:
   a) **Research**. Continue to read and explore a variety of resources to enrich your study.
   b) **Writing**. Begin the rough draft of your essay. The aid of a proofreader (a parent, adviser, peer) is suggested. Have this person initial your rough draft

after reading it and make suggestions for clarity of ideas, reorganization, examples required, deletion of redundant information, and so on.

c) **Presentation**. Prepare your oral presentation with the class in mind. This should be an introduction of your topic for a general audience. You might explain why you chose your topic, your successes and frustrations with your research, what you learned that you think the class would be interested in knowing, what you chose as the thesis of your essay, and anything else that would broaden the knowledge and understanding of your topic by your classmates.

d) **Essay**. Before you submit a formal academic research essay, complete with cover page, footnotes, and bibliography, work with a peer to correct spelling and mechanical errors.

e) **Logs**. Hand in the complete record of your study including all notes, drafts, self-evaluation, and the like.

f) **Evaluation**. You will be evaluated based on your presentation, essay, notes and logs of the process, and self-evaluation of the learning experience.

RESEARCH DOCUMENTATION

Plagiarism involves using someone else's work in your writing and claiming it as your own. It is a criminal offence of which every student should be aware. The University of British Columbia calls it the "most serious academic offence." Most schools, colleges, and universities have policies regarding plagiarism. The University of Toronto, for instance, outlines its plagiarism policies in its "Code of Behaviour," which students are expected to know. Consequences for a student who plagiarizes could be as severe as a zero grade and/or expulsion. To avoid charges of plagiarism, it is necessary to cite the sources of information and ideas in your work.

If you summarize or paraphrase someone else's ideas in your writing, do not use quotation marks around the reference, but do indicate the source of the idea in a parenthetical note following the reference or in a footnote or endnote.

If you use a direct quotation from someone else in your writing, integrate it into your text with an introductory sentence or phrase, and use quotation marks around the exact words of the person you are quoting. For example:

The Canadian Encyclopedia reports that Margaret Laurence was born in ...

We see Calpurnia's fear for Caesar's safety when she says, "You shall not stir out of your house today." (II, ii, 9)

The Canadian Human Rights Act "gives each of us an equal opportunity to work and live without discrimination."

If you need to change the punctuation of the original to suit the context in your own writing, put square brackets around any changes you make. For example:

Caesar responds that any harm that might come his way will dissipate "when they shall see [t]he face of Caesar." (The square brackets flag that the "t" on "the" was a capital in the original because it started a new line of poetry.)

In general, quotations should be kept short and relevant. In a case where your quotation goes on for several sentences, the quotation is best double-indented (from both margins) and single-spaced. For example:

The exact language of the report in this section reads:

> The mayor's task force found that residents wanted frequent and reliable garbage pickup at least twice a week in the summer and once in the winter. The additional summer service was requested due to concerns about odours and animals.

If there was a grammar or spelling error in the original, the word (sic) in parentheses indicates that you are aware of the error but have left the original intact. For example:

The witness was quoted as saying, "I never seen (sic) the man before."

At the end of a research report, it is necessary to provide your reader with all the sources you consulted in preparing the report. Sources are listed on a final page titled Bibliography, Works Cited, or References. Here is the format for a few typical sources. (Note: If you don't have a computer or are handwriting your work, you must underline all book titles and magazine or newspaper names that you might otherwise put in italics.)

Books

Author's last name, First name. *Title*. City of publication: Publisher,
    Year of publication.

Klein, Naomi. *No Logo*. Toronto: Alfred A. Knopf Canada, 2000.

Newspaper Articles

Author's last name, First name. "Title of article." *Name of Newspaper*
    Full date:Page(s) of article.

Drakes, Shellene. "Many Canadians Are Made to Feel Like Strangers in Their Homeland." *The Toronto Star* 29 January 2000:H6.

Magazine Articles

Author's last name, First name. "Title of article." *Name of Magazine.*
    Full date:Page(s) of article.

Leiper-Jefferson, Esther. "Esther's Comment." *Writer's Journal.* November/December
1999:59–61.

Encyclopedia Entries

Author's last name, First name. "Title of entry." *Name of Encyclopedia.*
    Year of publication.

Randall, Mary. "The Ozone Layer." *New Encyclopaedia Britannica.* 2000.

The Internet

Author's last name, First name. "Title of Work." Year or full date (if applicable) of
publication. <Internet address> (Date of retrieval).

Shirley Serafini, "The Governance Challenge in Canada: A Think Tank for Leaders." 11
September 2000. <http://www.inac.gc.ca/nr/spch/2000/ttk_e.html> (16 Oct. 2001).

or

Name of organization. "Title of Work." Year or full date (if applicable) of publication. <Internet address> (Date of retrieval).

Indian and Northern Affairs Canada. "Aboriginal Self-Government." November 1997.
<http://www.inac.gc.ca/pr/info/info105_e.html> (16 Oct. 2001).

Writing

WRITING FOR UNIVERSITY

Many students believe that writing is limited to English and the social sciences. On the contrary, most university courses demand some sort of writing. Look at the chart below. It is not exhaustive, nor does it represent every type of writing you might be required to do in university. It does, however, give you some insight into what might be required by the university you will be attending. For more information about writing at the universities you wish to apply to, go to their Web sites and look for a writing workshop or writing lab or information on specific courses. You could also phone the registrar's office and ask to speak to someone who will know the writing requirements of the courses in which you are interested.

Types of Writing	Social Sciences	English	Arts	Business	Math and Sciences
Abstract	✓	✓	✓	✓	✓
Academic proposal	✓	✓	✓	✓	✓
Admissions letter	✓	✓	✓	✓	✓
Annotated bibliography	✓	✓	✓	✓	✓
Application/résumé	✓	✓	✓	✓	✓
Arguments for a methodology	✓				✓
Case study	✓			✓	
Critiques of current research	✓	✓	✓	✓	✓
Description		✓	✓		

continued

Types of Writing	Social Sciences	English	Arts	Business	Math and Sciences
Essay	✓	✓	✓	✓	
Essay exams	✓	✓	✓	✓	
Lab report	✓				✓
Literature review	✓	✓	✓	✓	✓
Outline	✓	✓	✓	✓	✓
Précis	✓	✓	✓	✓	
"Real-world" documents	✓	✓	✓	✓	✓
Short report	✓	✓	✓	✓	✓
Summary	✓	✓	✓	✓	
Writing about literature		✓			

TONE AND PURPOSE

Language will change with the purpose and audience of your writing. The language you choose for a piece of writing helps create the **tone** or attitude, also known as **voice**, in your written work. Your language can range from very **formal** to **informal**.

The table below shows the characteristics of three levels of language: formal, moderate, and informal.

Levels of Language	Formal	Moderate	Informal
Vocabulary	• longer, less common words • few colloquialisms, popular phrases • little slang • few or no contractions	• long and short words • more popular language • some contractions	• shorter, simpler, everyday words • some slang, more popular words and phrases • contractions

continued

Levels of Language	Formal	Moderate	Informal
Vocabulary cont'd	• avoids the use of the pronouns *you* and *I*	• occasional use of the pronouns *you* and *I*	• frequent use of the pronouns *you* and *I*
Sentence and paragraph structure	• longer and more complex sentences and paragraphs	• combination of simple, compound, and complex sentences; average-length sentences and paragraphs	• shorter, simpler sentences and paragraphs
Tone	• academic and impersonal, often instructional	• varies, depending on purpose and audience	• conversational and casual—sounds like everyday speech

Depending on the purpose of your work, you may choose the form and the level of language that is most suitable. The following table shows some forms, their purposes, and the appropriate level of language used.

Forms of Writing	Purpose	Level of Language
Personal Writing: • diaries • journals • logs • lists • letters/notes	• communicate to self and others • record personal thoughts • reflect on activities, events, or experiences	• informal; short, simple, everyday words • may use colloquial language or slang • may use contractions • may use pronouns *I* and *you* • shorter and simpler sentences and paragraphs; unity and coherence may not always be present

continued

Forms of Writing	Purpose	Level of Language
Imaginative Writing: • autobiographies • letters • lyrics • monologues • poetry • scripts • stories	• used for self or others • amuse, entertain, evoke emotions, and provoke thought and reflection	• may range from informal to formal, depending on the tone the writer wants to achieve • verbs are generally more vivid and vigorous (less use of the verb *to be*) • nouns are more concrete and specific • the number and variety of modifiers (adjectives and adverbs) increases • figures of speech and other literary devices may be used
Informational and Academic Writing: • analyses • biographies • business letters • charts • editorials • essays • instructions • lab reports • news articles • plans • reports • reviews • summaries • surveys • textbooks • travelogues	• ask questions to gather information • record information • summarize information • inform • describe how to assemble or create • record and report observations, research, and analysis • interpret information, sometimes using graphics • argue and persuade	• may range from informal to formal depending on the purpose and audience • sentences and paragraphs are generally moderate in complexity • some subject-specific language, but mostly familiar vocabulary • some of this writing may be in point form

While you will be reviewing five different ways to develop individual paragraphs and essays, it is important for you to understand that no matter which method you use, you must provide details. Details add credibility and substance to your writing and are essential to creating convincing expositions, narratives, and descriptions. As well, you should remember you may use different types of paragraph development within your exposition.

Development by Cause and Effect

Cause and effect tells why something happens. Some questions for cause and effect are listed below.

- What has caused it?
- Where has it come from?
- Where is it going?
- What will happen to it?
- What is it used for?
- How does it fit into the larger scheme of things?
- What would happen if it didn't exist?
- Why does it exist?
- Could it be changed?

When organizing your cause-and-effect paragraphs, you can

- Start with a cause and show or try to predict its effect. (e.g., If handgun owner-ship is not regulated, more hand-gun-related deaths will occur.)
- Start with an effect and try to explain its cause. (e.g., Fewer secondary schools offer auto mechanics because of the expense of the program.)

CAUTION! Just because one event follows another, the first event is not necessarily the cause of the second. Examples:

I wore my red socks when I won my first tennis match.

Wearing those red socks did not necessarily cause my win.

I wrote two exams with the same pen and got over 80 percent on both exams.

Using that pen did not cause my success.

Development by Classification

Classification is used to show how something fits into a category or how it differs from a category. Some questions you might ask yourself are
- What other things are like it?
- What kinds of it are there?
- What is it part of?
- What goes along with it?
- How does it differ from others like it?
- What connects it to all the other things in the category?

If you are developing a paragraph or essay using classification,
- Be sure you have an adequate and accurate definition of the category.
- Ask yourself why it is important to look at the issue/idea as part of a category.
- Include both similarities to and differences from the category to create more interest.
- Make sure a connection exists between your subject and the categories that you create.
- If the category is a literary genre, you must research that genre for accurate information.

Development by Definition

Developing an essay by definition is the process of explaining what is meant by a term, an idea, or an object. When developing a definition, start with a general statement: "A hero performs an act or acts that put the welfare of others before himself or herself."

If you were writing a short essay on Anne Michaels' Athos as hero, you would need to find examples of his heroism that fit your definition (e.g., taking Jakob into his care). Having found the example, you would have to explain how the example fits your definition.

With each new example, start a new paragraph.

 ACTIVITY

Choose a character from one of the stories you have read in this textbook, and using definition, write a paragraph to prove that he or she is one of the following: dependent, a victim, a hero, courageous, ignorant.

Development by Chronology

Chronology is the order in which a series of events takes place. For example, a personal essay might focus on the series of events leading up to an election or the outbreak of war.

CAUTION! Using a chronological approach when writing about literature may lead to retelling the story instead of examining the various literary aspects of the story.

 ACTIVITY

For one of the stories or novel excerpts in this textbook, write a newspaper report in which at least one paragraph is developed by means of chronological order.

Development by Problem/Solution

Many writers use problem/solution as a method of organizing. This type of organization is particularly effective when you are writing a persuasive essay about a problem that may have a solution (e.g., shortage of summer jobs for students; young children finding inappropriate sites on the Internet; violence on television).

Similar to cause-and-effect organization, the problem is posed, its history or background is discussed, and a solution is proposed. When several solutions are offered, an explanation of the benefits and drawbacks of each should be discussed.

When offering possible solutions, a writer must mention a solution's negative points since readers will often have already considered what the writer is proposing and will know the strengths and weaknesses of the arguments beforehand. The writer loses credibility if he or she does not acknowledge these weaknesses. It is up to the writer, then, to prove that the strengths far outnumber the drawbacks.

 ACTIVITY

With a partner, research and discuss the pros and cons of genetically modified foods. Choose one of the major problems surrounding this issue (e.g., consumers unaware of the benefits of these new foods; businesses unconcerned about the long-term effects these foods might have). Write a persuasive essay on the problem and the solutions you have found.

To persuade an audience in any speech or piece of writing, you will have to appeal to logic, fact, and emotion.

Logic

If you are using **deductive reasoning**, base your argument on a sound **premise** (an assumption that is considered true because it can be proven).

The major form of deductive reasoning follows this order:
Major premise: All humans need water to survive.
Minor premise: A teenager is a human.
Conclusion: Therefore, a teenager needs water to survive.

If one of your premises is inaccurate, then your conclusion will be inaccurate.
Major premise: All humans need spring water to survive.
Minor premise: A teenager is a human.
Conclusion: Therefore, a teenager needs spring water to survive.

The major premise is incorrect because humans don't necessarily need spring water; any source of clean water will do just fine.

If you are using **inductive reasoning**, make sure you have enough facts and reasons to support your generalization. Inductive reasoning looks like this:
Generalization: Brand X is an exceptional product.
Proofs:
- Many studies have been conducted that show that the product does what it claims to do.
- I have used the product for 10 years and have been satisfied with its performance.
- I have used other products that claim to do the same thing, but they have not performed as well.
- A survey was conducted of 10 000 people who compared Brand X with Brand Y. Of those people, 9998 thought Brand X was better.

Poor inductive reasoning could look like this:
Generalization: Graduates from Confederation Secondary School are exceptional English students.
Proof: Last year I taught two students from that school in my university English class and both achieved A's.

There are too many unknowns in this proof. Were the two young people typical of students from Confederation S.S.? How did other students from that high school do in university English? Did any other students from Confederation S.S. take university English? What is the achievement in university English of students graduating in other years from that high school?

Fact

As you can see from the example of poor reasoning, it is important to have facts to support your points. Research is the only way you will be able to gather those facts. (See pages 432–437 for research pointers.) Remember, facts must be used properly.
- Use numbers and statistics the way they were meant to be used.
- Quote in context. Taking a quotation out of context may distort its original intent.
- Use full quotations. Leaving out a part of a quotation can change its whole meaning.
- Don't conveniently leave out some of the facts and include only those that support your argument.
- Be specific. Use details.

Emotion

You can appeal to your audience's emotions by using emotive language, vivid words, evocative words, and figures of speech. But it is unfair if you use techniques in hopes that your audience will stop thinking about *what* you say. We call these propaganda techniques. Below are some techniques that you should be careful about when using.

Testimonial

A celebrity says that a product or an idea is great.
- What qualifications does that person have to make him or her an expert?
- Does he or she have a bias?
- How much money is he or she receiving for the endorsement?

Bandwagon Appeal

Bandwagoning sounds like this: "Everybody is doing it!" You may have used this technique with your parents when you wanted to do something with your friends. When you hear this line, think:
- Who is "everybody"?
- Does "everybody" have your best interests at heart?
- Do you want to be part of that crowd?

Plain Folks

When a speaker says, "Just like you, I ...," pay attention. A speaker or writer might pretend to be "just like us" to try to convince us to go along with his or her ideas.

Name Calling

Speakers can negatively label people who think differently than they do in order to persuade an audience to go against that opposing point of view.
- Listen closely for labelling. Words like "spoiled brat," "whiner," "flaming liberal," and "cheap" all carry negative connotations.
- What is the purpose of calling the opposition that name?
- What emotion is the speaker trying to appeal to?
- Has the speaker any proof that the name is appropriate?

Glittering Generalities

Abstract words and expressions can be defined in many different ways by many people. That's why slogans for products often depend on glittering generalities. One example of using glittering generalities in an ad campaign is one presented some years ago: "Coke is it." What is "it"? People think of "it" in many different ways: the most refreshing, the best tasting, the least expensive, the most popular, the oldest, the greatest. When you hear a glittering generality, ask yourself, what exactly *does* that mean?

WRITING THE CRITIQUE

Unlike an essay, a critique does not start with a thesis, although you may arrive at a thesis by the end of the critique. Its form can vary from that of a report to that of an essay. The form you choose will depend on your purpose or on what your teacher wants. Following are steps to writing a critique.

1. Describe

The first step in a critique is to describe the piece of writing or media work. This step slows you down, makes you reread the writing carefully. In this step,
- Be objective.
- Do not extend your description outside what is on the page.
- Do not interpret. If the writing or media work has more than one meaning, keep your interpretation on the most literal level.

2. Analyze

After you have described the writing or media work, you should apply your close reading or viewing skills. Examine the writing for the elements of design (figures of speech, rhetoric, structure, setting, character, and perspective). (See pages 422–423.) To enhance your analysis, you may want to research the period in which the piece was written. A particular historical event may have had an influence on the writer. Biographical research is also a possibility.

CAUTION! Biographical research can lead to false assumptions about the work. Do not assume that the writing stems from the writer's personal experience. Consider the writings of Stephen King. If King had experienced everything in his books, he would have had a particularly odd and horrific life!

3. Interpret

Looking at the elements the writer has used and the description of the story, you can determine what the writer is saying through his or her work. Not all interpretations are "correct." Just because you think something is true does not necessarily mean it is true. Any interpretation must be supported with evidence based on the analysis you have done on the piece.

4. Evaluate

This part of the critique is your chance to assess or evaluate the success of the author's work. When you state your opinion, you will have to back it up with specific references to the work itself and to the analysis you have done.

 ACTIVITY

Read "Wild Horse Shakes Her Mane" on page 291. With a partner, work through the four steps of writing a critique. When you have completed your critique, compare it with the work of another partnership. As a class, discuss the differences and similarities of the critiques completed in the class.

Using Transitions

In order for your writing to flow logically from one sentence to the next, you need to include **transitions**. Transitions connect your ideas, helping your readers follow the logic of your argument. Transitions can be used between sentences in the same paragraph or as a logical bridge between paragraphs. Transitions come in many forms.

Using Repetition

Repetition of a word or phrase from one sentence or paragraph to the next will signal a continuation of the same topic. Example:

Grade 11 students sometimes find *writing essays* difficult. *Essay writing* challenges students' ability to think and write logically.

CAUTION! Overuse of this technique can result in a repetitive or monotonous voice.

Using Substitution (Pronouns, Synonyms)

Substituting a pronoun or a synonym for the subject in your previous sentence connects the two ideas. Example:

Doing science is more exciting than just *reading* about science. *The former* shows students how scientific principles work; *the latter* tells students how the scientific principles work.

CAUTION! Be sure the antecedent of the pronoun is clear. (For example: "Students like doing science, not just reading about science. *It* is exciting." What does the word "it" refer to, the doing or the reading?)

Using Transitional Words or Connectives

Transitional words or **connectives** show relationships between ideas. Here are examples of relationships and the kinds of transitional words that are used in each:
- to add ideas: *and, moreover, furthermore, further, similarly, too, likewise, again, in the same way, besides*
- to show cause and effect: *accordingly, therefore, as a result, consequently, hence, thus, for this reason, it follows that*
- to compare: *similarly, likewise*
- to contrast or introduce a limiting thought: *but, nevertheless, otherwise, on the other hand, conversely, on the contrary, however, yet, still*

- to introduce examples: *for example, for instance, such as*
- to indicate order: *next, in the second place, to begin with, first* (not *firstly*), *second, in conclusion*
- to show a relationship of time: *then, now, currently, at present, somewhat later, thereupon, thereafter, eventually, at the same time, meanwhile*
- to show a spatial relationship: *to the right, in the distance, straight ahead, at the left, above, below, in between*

Example

Many students love to study French; *furthermore*, they understand the value of learning to speak and write a second language.

Using Parallel Structures

Parallel structure (the same grammatical structure for all items that have the same function) is used in speeches, poetry, and other forms of writing for rhetorical effect. The repetition of words and phrasing reinforces parallelism and balance, emphasizing ideas and creating a persuasive case for them. For example, Sojourner Truth, in her speech "Ain't I a Woman?" repeats certain words and phrases to deliver her point and persuade her audience:

Ain't I a woman? Look at me! Look at my arm! I have ploughed *and* planted, *and* gathered into barns, *and* no man could head me! *And ain't I a woman?* I could work *as much* and eat *as much* as a man—when I could get it—*and* bear the lash as well! *And ain't I a woman?*

In instructions or manuals, parallel structure may be used to help the reader understand and follow a series of directions. For example, in a printer manual, the following instructions may be found:

1. Unpack the printer.
2. Put on the paper support.
3. Install the ink cartridges.
4. Load the paper.
5. Connect the printer.

Note that all sentences are imperative, each beginning with a verb and ending with a noun. These sentences use a parallel structure to clearly tell the user how to set up the printer.

Using Spellcheck in a Word-Processing Program

The spellcheck function in a word-processing program is very helpful and should always be used to check the spelling of a word-processed document. However, you still need to proofread your work very carefully. The spellchecker will not necessarily identify every spelling error or typo in your document and will identify some correctly spelled words as spelling errors.

A spellchecker only matches the words you have typed against a list in its memory. As a result, if you have typed "bit" for "bite," it will not indicate a spelling error since both of these words are correctly spelled; however, the words are not interchangeable in English usage and one may be a spelling error in your document. If a word is not in the spellcheck program's memory, it will be identified as a possible spelling error. Proper names are frequently flagged as spelling errors even when they are spelled correctly.

Oral Communication Skills

GOOD LISTENING SKILLS

Good listening skills are essential to oral communication. Your success at communicating depends on how well you listen to others and receive their messages. Below are some do's and don'ts of listening.

Do	Don't
• make eye contact with the speaker • review what the speaker has said • concentrate • try to recall facts and ideas • take notes • record instructions • ask questions • tune out outside noises • avoid distracting behaviours • use mnemonics (memory devices) • pay attention to non-verbal communication • pick up on message reinforcers such as charts, diagrams, photos, slides	• judge a person by appearance or delivery • fake attention • bring your prejudices to the presentation • avoid difficult ideas/concepts • tune out or let your mind wander • interrupt the speaker • use selective listening • make side comments to others or listen to or pay attention to the behaviour of others and their side comments

ORAL PRESENTATIONS

Just as it is important to listen while someone else speaks, whether in a formal or an informal group setting, so it is important that you speak well to convey your message effectively. As a student, you require good speaking skills for your various oral activities, including

- debates
- demonstrations
- dramatic reading
- group work
- independent study presentations
- performances—role-plays, readings, storytelling
- choral reading
- interviews
- meetings
- reports
- seminars
- speeches
- video presentations
- sales talks
- symposia

A formal oral presentation is one of the most common activities that you will be involved in. Here are some suggestions to help you plan an effective oral presentation.

Planning Your Oral Presentation[1]

Know Your Purpose

What is the purpose of your oral presentation?
- to inform
- to persuade
- to motivate
- to entertain

Know Your Audience

Consider their
- age
- interest in your topic
- reason for attending your presentation

Planning Your Content

Know Your Subject

- read—books, articles, electronic information
- talk—personal or phone interviews, discussions
- view—movies, documentaries, interviews
- record—on tape, on cue cards, in your notebook, on your computer

---

1. Based on S. Carlile Clark and Dana V. Hensley, *38 Basic Speech Experiences* (Topeka, KS: Clark Publishing, Inc., 1999).

- organize
  - Delete information that is not adding to your presentation.
  - Add information where you find you have gaps.
  - Substitute information that might be weak with stronger points.
  - Order your information in the most logical order, starting with a hook to get your audience interested and ending with a powerful conclusion.
  - Think of ways to get your audience involved.

Some General Tips for Presenting

- Get the audience's attention.
- Make them want to hear what you have to say.
- Make it clear to the audience why the material is important to them.
- If appropriate, involve your audience.
- Ask your audience to take some action (further study, a comparison with something they already know).
- Appeal to their emotions and needs (love, wealth, self-preservation, nationalism, loyalty, religions, political beliefs, desire for recognition, desire for adventure).
- Be sincere and enthusiastic.
- Use humour (words, anecdotes, body language, gestures, props) where appropriate.
- Incorporate visuals such as board work, posters, overheads, slides, electronic devices, presentation software.

Avoiding Stress in Formal Presentations

Being nervous before speaking in public is not uncommon. The extra rush of adrenaline you get when you're nervous can work in your favour to keep your speaking energized and exciting.

Signs of Stage Fright

Those of you who have "stage fright" may experience these symptoms of stress:
- Your breathing becomes faster.
- Your heart rate speeds up.
- You perspire more.
- You feel fidgety or feel as if you have butterflies in your stomach.
- You may feel nauseous or light-headed.
- Your mouth gets dry.
- Your knees feel weak.

Getting Past Stage Fright

You can help to calm your nerves and get past your stage fright by doing the following things:

- Speak in front of an audience as often as possible: Start with small groups and move up to larger and larger audiences.
- Pick a topic that interests you: If you are doing a debate or a presentation, choose ideas that will hold your attention. If you're not enthusiastic about your topic, you will not feel confident since you might feel the audience will not be interested either.
- Prepare: Most students who get stage fright are afraid they won't do a good job. Research thoroughly, create an outline, write out your oral presentation or speech and try it out, first in front of the mirror or into a tape recorder, then in front of your family or friends. Say the speech as many times as possible. Of course, this means you can't be writing your speech the night before it is due! While you are rehearsing, visualize yourself in the room where you will be presenting, in front of your audience.
- Memorize: If you have to memorize your presentation, use mnemonics to help you remember the order of your points or key words in your presentation. Mnemonics are memory aids. One useful mnemonic is creating an acronym, a word in which each of the letters stands for another word. You probably already know some acronyms to help you remember. MRS VANDERTRAMP is an acronym for the irregular verbs in French. ROYGBIV is an acronym for the colours of the spectrum in science.
- Think of the audience: The speech isn't about you—it's about them! You are trying to persuade, entertain, or inform *other* people, not yourself. Focus on them. Some experts suggest imagining your audience in their underwear!
- Move: Facial expressions and some hand gestures keep you relaxed and use up some of that excess energy you feel. You can physically move around if it is appropriate to the type of oral presentation you are giving.
- Wear appropriate clothing: You don't want to be worried about the length of your skirt or the need for a tie. Think about your audience. Think about the formality of the occasion. Decide on your clothing ahead of time. Wear it while you are practising your speech at home.

ENGAGING THE AUDIENCE

When you speak in front of an audience, it is important to be aware that the way you are perceived by the audience will have an influence on the way your speech is received and believed. You must be a credible speaker for the audience to stay with you. So how do you increase your credibility?

Competence

- Know what you are talking about.
- Know more about your topic than the majority of your audience does.
- Draw your audience's attention to your knowledge. This could be done by simply presenting enough facts that the audience can see immediately that you know what you are talking about. You could cite personal experience to demonstrate your understanding of your topic. Someone else could introduce you and draw attention to something in your background that shows you know about the topic.

Trustworthiness/Friendliness

- Tell the truth without embellishments.
- Give both sides to a story (just make sure your side is stronger).
- Use fair persuasive techniques.
- Give all the facts.
- Smile.
- Be calm.
- Be warm.

Rapport

- Identify who your audience is.
- Match your topic, tone, vocabulary, and diction to your audience and to the purpose of your presentation.
- Dress for the occasion.

In school, you will be speaking and listening in a variety of situations. These range from informal groups to large, formal assemblies. Many of the oral communication experiences you have in high school are "real-world" experiences that prepare you for life after school. Some of these experiences include

- speeches of introduction
- impromptu speeches
- lectures
- interactive class presentations
- phone interviews

SPEECHES OF INTRODUCTION

If you are asked to introduce a guest speaker to the class or to the school, it is important to do research and keep the following in mind:

- Know the topic on which the speaker has been asked to speak.
- Know the occasion on which the speaker has been asked to come (e.g., Remembrance Day assembly, World AIDS day, Black History month).
- Contact the speaker or the speaker's assistant and ask for his or her curriculum vitae. From this, you can learn about the speaker's educational and job history. Basing a speech of introduction solely on this information is fine, but your introduction may miss the speaker's human qualities.
- Contact the speaker. Explain your role in the day and ask some questions that will help you humanize the speaker. Watch that you do not become too personal, but try to ask questions you know the audience would like to know the answers to.
- Contact someone who knows the speaker well. Sometimes teachers will ask a friend or colleague to speak to the class or school; therefore these teachers may be able to help you with your introduction.
- Write your speech, remembering that you are going to establish the credibility of this speaker for the audience. (See pages 451–452.) Remember, your speech should not be much longer than two or three minutes.
- Once your speech is written, you may wish to fax or e-mail it to the speaker, just so he or she can read it and correct any misinformation or misinterpretations.

 ACTIVITY

Work in pairs. Both of you are coming to speak to the students of your school on a topic of your choice. Write a speech of introduction for your partner. Pair up with another partnership and present your introductory speeches.

IMPROMPTU SPEECHES

You may be called upon to make an impromptu speech in class. Impromptu speeches range from giving a lengthy answer to a question in class, to presenting a group's findings from in-class work, to giving a rebuttal in a debate, to answering questions in an interview.

It is difficult to prepare for the content of impromptu speeches, but you can think about ways you can order your thoughts. Questions can be used to help you think about what you are going to say. The simplest questions are Who? What? Where? When? Why? and How? (See page 415.)

LECTURES

As you move up to the more senior grades, you may be asked to give a lecture on an independent study you have conducted. A lecture must be informative but not boring. You should not memorize it, but you should know it well enough that you are not constantly reading from your notes.

Here are the steps to presenting a lecture:

1. Choose your topic. You may be limited by topics suggested by your teacher. In that case, choose a topic you already know something about or one that interests you. If there is time, go to the library and look at what is available on the suggested topics.
2. Think about your audience. Ask yourself what would interest them about the topic.
3. Research. Use credible, recent sources. Take notes from these sources using an organizer to help you keep on track. An example of such an organizer is shown in the chart below

General Topic: Advertising in Schools

Bibliographic Information: Klein, Naomi. *No Logo: Taking Aim at the Brand Bullies.* Toronto: Alfred A. Knopf Canada, 2000.

Call #: HD2755.5 . K57 2000

Topic	Information	Relationship to the Audience
YNN	• 12 minutes of news directed at teenagers • 2 minutes of commercials mixed in with the news • teachers unable to adjust volume • turning off the set is not an option • schools receive AV equipment for other lessons	• discuss "freedom" of learning in the classroom • discuss the trade-offs in order to get equipment • talk about the effects of being bombarded with ads during a "lesson"
Comments		

4. Research all sides of the issue.
5. Organize your information using an outline.
6. Learn the information so that you can speak about each of your points.
7. If necessary, write out the lecture.
8. Rehearse by yourself, with a tape recorder, in front of a mirror, or with a friend or family member watching you.
9. Use an overhead transparency or chart paper to present an outline of your points.
10. Speak slowly so that students can make notes.

SEMINAR PRESENTATIONS

Seminar presentations are common types of oral presentations. They may be conducted individually or with a group. Here are some pointers for making your seminar presentation interesting as well as informative:
1. Know your material. "Show" never outweighs "substance." No one is fooled by glamour and glitz when there is little content.
2. If you are required to present a piece of literature (a poem or a story), work on a creative presentation of the piece (choral reading, dramatic reading, selective reading, dramatization).
3. Use audio-visual devices (overheads, chart paper, slides, tape recordings, videos) to enhance your presentation.
4. Invite a guest speaker to enhance your presentation.
5. Involve the audience: ask a probing question to start the discussion; after making a point, ask the group to find examples of your point in the work being discussed; ask questions throughout; ask participants to summarize; ask them to relate the information to other works you have studied in class.

DEBATING

Debate Procedure

The Chair introduces the topic, introduces the speakers, explains the time limits, and announces the judges' decisions. It is up to the Chair to maintain the tone of the debate.

The First Speaker for the Affirmative   **4 minutes**

Give a brief introduction to the topic, define any necessary terms, note any points agreed on by all debaters, note any issues to be excluded, state clearly and briefly all the affirmative points, and prove the point you have chosen to deal with.

The First Speaker for the Negative   **3 minutes**

State agreements and disagreements with the interpretation of the topic by the first speaker, state the arguments for the negative side, indicate who will prove each argument, refute briefly the arguments of the first speaker, and present your own arguments.

The Second Speaker for the Affirmative   **3 minutes**

Refute the arguments of the first speaker for the negative and state your own arguments and proof.

The Second Speaker for the Negative   **4 minutes**

Refute any arguments for the affirmative as yet unanswered, state your own arguments and proof, and sum up the arguments for the negative side.

The First Speaker for the Affirmative   **1 minute**

Do not introduce any new arguments; refute arguments already made and sum up the affirmative arguments.

Debate Terminology

refute: to prove a statement or argument to be wrong or false

point of order: a question to the Chair regarding proper following of rules

point of personal privilege: a question to the Chair regarding a misrepresentation of your argument

Organizing a Constructive Speech

In a debate, the resolution states what the debaters are arguing for or against. The resolution is generally a request for change. It is written this way: "Be it resolved that ..."
 • the government change the graduated licence system
 • the voting age be changed to 16
 • the school day be lengthened

The **affirmative** argues *for* the resolution. The **negative** argues *against* the resolution.
    A **constructive speech** is given by both the affirmative (pro) side and the negative (con) side in a debate. The constructive speech is a persuasive speech aimed at convincing the audience that they should agree with your point of view. The organization of your speech will have a major effect on the way your points are received by the audience. The following are two ways to organize your constructive speech.[2]

---

2. Based on S. Carlile Clark and Dana V. Hensley, *38 Basic Speech Experiences* (Topeka, KS: Clark Publishing, Inc., 1999).

Method 1 Note: Negative side is shown in parentheses.	**Method 2**
1. State the resolution. 2. Present a history of the issue and explain how this history brought you to the resolution. (In the negative position, you will show how the history has brought you to believe the opposite of the resolution.) 3. Show that the resolution is needed (or not needed): • Use strong logic and facts to support (refute) this need. 4. Show that the resolution is practical (or not practical): • Use strong facts and reasons to show that the resolution will work (will not work), that it's "do-able" (not "do-able"). 5. Show that the resolution is desirable (or not desirable): • Use strong facts and reasons to show that it will (will not) benefit the individual or society. 6. Finish your speech with a con-cluding statement and a request that the audience support (reject) the resolution.	1. Present the history of the issue: • Outline events leading up to the present time. • Explain the significance of the issue. 2. Discuss the present-day effects of the issue: • Present examples, illustrations, facts, and views from authorities of these effects. 3. Discuss the causes that brought on the effects you discussed in Step 2: • Present examples, illustrations, facts, and views from authorities of these causes. • Volume of proof and accuracy are essential. 4. List possible solutions to the issue but show they are not the best alternatives. 5. Give *your* solution to the issue: • Show why your solution is best. • Present facts and reasoning to show it is best. 6. Show how your solution will benefit the audience: • Remember that you are out to convince your audience to accept your arguments; therefore, you must show that your idea will benefit them.

The Rebuttals

The **rebuttals** come after all the constructive speeches have been presented. Because the rebuttals are based on what your opposition has said, it will be necessary for you to make notes during your opposition's constructive speech.

However, if you are clever, during your research you will read about most of the points the opposition will make. Jot them down and prepare arguments for them before the debate even begins. If the opposition brings up one of those points, you will be ready with a well-thought-out and planned argument.

Here are some ways to attack or rebut a point made by the opposing side.

Show that the argument is illogical:
- Point out errors or weaknesses in the other side's premise, arguments, or conclusion.

Acknowledge the strength of the opponents' argument, but
- Show that you have an even better idea.
- Show that the long-term results will not be good.
- Show that their idea will work only part of the time.
- Counter the point with statistics and facts that are just as valid.

Dismiss the argument as irrelevant.
- Show that in the scheme of things, the argument is not important to the issue.

If you cannot rebut the point because it is excellent, admit that it is a good point and hope that the overall impact of your reasons, facts, and arguments is better!

TELEPHONE COMMUNICATION

Whether you are requesting information or having an interview over the telephone, you need to be clear. You may have a "face that launched a thousand ships" but even the beauty of Helen of Troy would not be able to influence an unseen person on the other end of the telephone. No one can see your facial expressions or your gestures. Content is everything.

Asking for Information

Before Calling

1. Write down the information you want to know.
2. Record the names and telephone numbers of the places you think you can get the information.
3. Have paper and pencil ready to record information given to you.

1. Identify yourself (name, where you are calling from).
2. Explain the reason for your call.
3. Ask for the person most likely to be able to help you.
4. Once you are speaking to the most appropriate person, make sure you take down his or her name.
5. Identify yourself again and thank the person for taking time for your questions.
6. Ask your questions. Record the answers.
7. If necessary, ask the person to repeat any information you might have missed.
8. If the person cannot help you, ask whether he or she knows who might be able to.
9. Thank the person once again.

Interviewing over the Telephone

Sometimes when you call a company about a job, you might be asked to give a telephone interview on the spot.

Before Calling

1. Be prepared with your résumé.
2. Think about the questions that might be asked in an interview and prepare answers for them.

On the Telephone

1. Explain why you are calling and ask for the correct person if a name has been given to you.
2. If you do not know whom to speak to, explain why you are calling and ask for the name of the appropriate person. Jot it down.
3. Ask to speak to that person.
4. Introduce yourself and explain why you are calling.
5. Ask any questions you have.
6. If the person starts to ask you questions, put your best interviewing skills into play.
7. If you are not being interviewed, and if you are still interested in the job, ask whether there will be interviews and request an appointment.
8. Thank the person by name and assure him or her that you will be at the appointed place at the appointed time. (TIP: If you do not know the location of the interview, get directions.)

In a group of three, set up a situation in which information is needed or a job interview is being conducted on the telephone. Have two members of the group role-play the situation while the third person makes notes on how well the person seeking the information or the job is doing.

CHORAL READING[3]

Choral reading is a reading or recitation performed by two or more people. When the audience hears a choral reading, the depth and variety of meanings for the piece should be clear. Not all readers must speak at the same time, but the group should coordinate the speaking so that both individual and multiple voices are heard within the reading. Music can be selected and added as background to choral reading.

Ways to Perform a Choral Reading

- Reading in unison: All voices speak together. It takes practice to make the many voices sound as one, matching voice tones, speed, and modulation.
- Echoing: One speaker may start a line, which is then echoed by one or more voices. The echo may occur on a full line or only on a few words for emphasis.
- Solo: Only one voice is heard at a time.
- Solo and group: One voice speaks and the rest of the group joins in on lines like the refrain or the chorus.
- Alternate/antiphonal reading: One or several voices speak one line and another or several voices speak another line, alternating throughout the piece.
- Soundscapes: One or more voices speak while other voices create a verbal soundscape that complements the content.
- Arranging by voice quality: To create different effects, voices can be grouped into three voice types: light, medium, dark. Both males and females can have light, medium, and dark voices. During choral reading, groups can organize themselves according to voice type. Different types can then be used to create specific tone combinations, just like a choir.

---

3. Based on David Booth, *Literacy Techniques for Building Successful Readers and Writers* (Markham, ON: Pembroke Publishers, 1996), pp. 48–49.

Steps to Producing a Choral Reading[4]

1. **Appoint a leader.** This leader is like a conductor who cues the different parts when they are to speak. He or she keeps an annotated script of the choral piece so that all the parts are readily available.

2. **Analyze the meaning of the selection.**
   - Are there unfamiliar words? Look them up.
   - What does the selection mean?
   - What are the emotions in the piece?
   - What feeling is the writer conveying to the audience?

3. **Look at the piece for sound cues.**
   - Is there a natural rhythm to the selection? Does it dance, plod, swing, march, gallop?
   - How can a regular rhythm be read without a singsong effect?
   - What words need to be emphasized?
   - Where are the pauses?
   - Where should the readers breathe? What phrases should be read without taking a breath?
   - At what volume should different parts of the poem be read?
   - How could the various voices in the group capture the mood of the words, phrases, and lines?

4. **Decide on how the voices could be used**—how the different choral effects could be incorporated.

5. **Experiment.** Annotate the selection as you make decisions.

6. **Finalize and practise.**

7. **Tape your reading during a practice.** Taping a choral piece can help reduce the stress of performance.

---

4. Averett Tanner Fran, *Creative Communication: Projects in Acting, Speaking and Oral Reading* (Topeka, KS: Clark Publishing Inc., 1996), pp. 266–67.

The Media

ANALYZING VISUAL AND MEDIA WORKS

Elements of Visual Production: Television, Video, Film[1]

People who make television programs, videos, films, and other visual productions must deal with two main things: picture elements (what the production looks like) and sound elements (how the production will sound).

Picture Elements

- original live-action or dramatized footage
- stock footage: archival footage or footage from other films
- interviews
- re-enactments
- still photos
- documents, titles, headlines, cartoons, other graphics
- blue screen (for special effects)
- special effects

Sound Elements

- sound recorded at the same time as visuals (on-the-street interviews, live concerts)
- sound recorded on its own and dubbed onto the film/tape
- voice-over: voices or commentary recorded separately from filmed visuals and then dubbed onto the film or tape
- narration: scripted voice-over spoken by narrator, filmmaker, or participant
- sound effects
- music
- silence
- ambient noise (background noise)

---

1. Information based on Arlene Moscovitch, *Constructing Reality: Exploring Issues in Documentary* (Montreal: National Film Board of Canada, 1993).

Camera Terms

As you make storyboards and prepare for filming, you will find the following camera terms helpful. These terms should help you to be specific, so that others can understand exactly what you mean.

Camera Angle

- **high**: sometimes called the bird's-eye view. The camera is placed well above normal eye level. Viewers feel that they are looking down on the subject and may consequently feel superior to it. This technique may make the subject appear overwhelmed and/or alone.
- **low**: sometimes called the worm's-eye view. The camera is placed below eye level. Viewers feel that they are looking up at the subject. This may make the viewers feel that the subject is more powerful than they are or that the subject is in control.

Camera Movement

- **tilt up**: the camera moves upward (from low angle to high)
- **tilt down**: the camera moves downward (from high angle to low)
- **pan**: the camera moves from right to left or left to right across an imagined horizon or panorama
- **dolly**: the camera moves in toward (dolly in) or out from (dolly out) the subject in a straight line. In this case, the camera is mounted on a tripod with wheels or on a makeshift dolly. The camera can be hand-held.
- **truck**: the camera moves right or left in a straight line and is usually mounted
- **zoom in or out**: the camera lens focuses in on or back from the subject (from wide angle to close-up and vice versa)

Camera Distance

- **extreme close-up**: a detailed shot of a very small area
- **medium close-up**: a shot that might include the head and shoulders of the subject
- **close-up**: a shot taken a short distance from the subject
- **medium shot**: a shot midway between a close-up and a long shot
- **medium long shot**: a shot that would have the subject in full view
- **long shot**: a shot in which the camera is placed far away from the subject
- **extreme long shot**: a shot that would have the subject in the distant background

The meaning of the word "cartoon" has changed over time. Originally, the word "cartoon" meant a full-sized, colour, preparatory drawing or painting on heavy paper. The drawing may then have been turned into an oil painting, an egg tempera painting, a mural, a fresco, a stained-glass window, or even a tapestry. Today, a cartoon is a drawing or series of drawings in which content, not the style of execution, is most important. The word "comic" implies that the drawing will be humorous or satirical, whereas a cartoon may be humorous, satirical, serious, or instructional.

Cartoons require us to read both pictures and words. Understanding what makes the visual part of the cartoon effective can increase your understanding and enjoyment of what you are seeing.

Whether a cartoon consists of one panel or several, most of the same rules for reading them apply.

Central Focus

The artist draws your attention to one part of the drawing. Here is a set of questions to help you look at how the artist has accomplished this:

- How large is the central focus compared with those objects around it?
- Is the shape of the central focus different from other shapes in the frame?
- Is the detail on the central focus more or less complex than the other objects in the frame?
- How does the colour differ from that of other objects?
- Has the artist drawn attention to the central focus by strong lines leading toward it (someone pointing to it, the lines from other objects leading the eye to it)?
- Is the central focus near the centre?
- Is the central focus in isolation—off by itself?

Point of View

Cartoons are much like frames in a film. The artist draws the action from a specific point of view and distance. To help you understand a cartoonist's point of view, review the sections "Camera Angle" and "Camera Distance" (page 463).

Movement

A cartoon can suggest movement in many ways. The most obvious ways are the use of "speed lines" suggesting someone is running or the repetition of a character in sequential frames following through on an action. If all the objects and characters are static in the cartoon, the artist can still suggest movement. A gesture, such as an arm in the middle of a punch, a full figure in mid-step, or an eye movement, can let us know that a character is moving.

Unity

Unity within a cartoon causes you to focus on certain aspects the artist wants you to notice. Repetition within a frame or between frames draws the viewer's eye. The closeness of one shape or object to another also draws the eye. If an artist places one object so that a line or edge of one shape continues to another shape, the viewer's eye will be drawn along that line.

 ACTIVITY

Examine any of the cartoons in this textbook. Describe how the artist has drawn attention to the visual aspects of the cartoon and how the drawing enhances the written message.

THE PITCH: HOW ADVERTISERS DRAW ATTENTION TO THEIR PRODUCTS[2]

Advertisers know we will pay attention to the unusual, interesting, and unexpected. There are several ways they grab our attention.

Appealing to Our Senses

Advertisers may use some of the following elements to appeal to our senses:
- motion
- lighting
- music
- special effects
- colour
- sound
- visuals
- action

Appealing to Our Emotions

When appealing to our emotions, advertisers use associations with an emotional state such as happiness or sadness.

2. Adapted from Hugh Rank, *The Pitch* (Park Forest: IL: The Counter-Propaganda Press, 1982).

Appealing to Our Intellect

To appeal to our intellect, advertisers may use such elements as

- news
- claims
- advice
- questions
- demonstrations
- scientific evidence
- real-life stories or testimonials

Building Our Confidence

Advertisers attempt to instill confidence in their product by

- using brand names we know and trust
- using people we think we know and trust (movie stars, actors dressed like doctors, dentists, researchers, etc.)
- using cartoon figures, animals, and other friendly figures
- using words associated with trust

Stimulating Our Desire

The products advertised generally use one of these claims:

- They keep a good thing going.
- They help users to obtain something good.
- They help users to avoid a bad thing.
- They get rid of a bad thing.

Advertisers claim that their products will provide us with something. The following 12 product claims are the most common:

- the best
- the most
- the most effective
- the most beautiful
- the rarest
- the newest
- the most classic
- the most reliable
- the easiest
- the most practical
- the fastest
- the safest

In addition, advertisers often suggest "added value" with their products. The following four categories are the most common added values:

- basic needs (food, health, security, money, sex, comfort, activity)
- fitting in (religious acceptance, scientific research, being popular, being elite, being average)
- love and belonging
- growth (success, respect, creativity, curiosity)

In a small group, find an example of one print advertisement, one radio commercial, one television commercial, and one Internet advertisement. Determine the audience each is targeting. Using the information above, create a chart demonstrating how each advertisement makes that audience pay attention. Be prepared to present your advertisements and commercials and your analyses of each to the class.

GLOSSARY

adaptation: In literary terms, a work that has been modified or altered. For example, the television show, *One's a Heifer*, is an adaptation of Sinclair Ross's story.

analogy: A comparison that focuses on something similar between two things that are otherwise not the same. An analogy is often used to explain a complex idea in terms of a simpler one.

anthology: A published collection of literary material including poems, short stories, novels, non-fiction selections, or other material.

antithesis: A figure of speech in which words or ideas are set up in parallel structure or balance against each other to emphasize the contrast in their meaning. For example, "To err is human; to forgive, divine" (Alexander Pope).

archetype: A literary term used to describe an image, character type, or plot that occurs frequently in myths, religion, folklore, and literature. Some archetypes often found in literary works are the images of the seasons, of life, death, and rebirth; the characters of the hero-adventurer or the fatal woman; the plot or story of the quest or the purifying journey. The poem "Archetypes" refers to Penelope, who is the archetype of the faithful wife who waits for many years for her husband Ulysses to return from his odyssey.

argumentative essay: See **essay**.

article: See **essay** and **newspaper article**.

atmosphere (or **mood**): The prevailing feeling in a literary work created through word choice, descriptive details, and evocative imagery. The description of the natural world in "Fern Hill" evokes an atmosphere of nostalgia and loss.

audience: The group of people for whom a piece of writing, film, television program, and so on is intended.

autobiography: The story of a person's life written by that person.

bias: An underlying preference for or prejudice against a particular idea, value, or group of people.

biography: The story of a person's life written by someone other than the person.

brochure: A printed booklet, or pages that are folded into panels, used to advertise or give information about a business, product, place, and so on. A brochure often contains colourful graphics or pictures.

caption: A heading or subtitle that accompanies a photograph, drawing, or cartoon.

caricature: An exaggeration or distortion of a character's most prominent features in order to ridicule him or her.

character: Refers to (1) an individual in a story, narrative poem, or play, and (2) the qualities of the individual. The latter are usually revealed through dialogue, description, and action. In *Fugitive Pieces*, for example, Athos's strength of character is revealed through his action of saving and adopting Jakob as his own.

cliché: An over-used expression. For example, *"Tired but happy*, we came home."

conflict: A struggle between opposing characters, forces, or emotions, usually between the protagonist and someone or something else. The central conflict in "Leaving" is between Aloo, who wants to leave home to study in America, and his mother, who wants to keep him close to home.

connotation: The implications or unstated associations conveyed by a word beyond its basic meaning. Connotations may be held in common by almost all people, or may be personal and private based on an individual's life experiences. See also **denotation**. "Slaughtering Chickens" makes use of the connotation of various words to arouse emotions in the readers.

consensus: An agreement by members of a group that, although it takes into account individual points of view, focuses on what all members of the group can agree to in order to proceed with a task. For example, there has to be a consensus about the interpretation of a drama by all members of the cast and crew in order to put on a coherent production of the drama.

context: The situation or background information relevant to understand a word, idea, character, or incident in a text. It could refer to the surrounding event(s) or information in a text, the background of the writer, or the social situation in which the text was written. As well, the context the reader brings to a text affects how a piece of writing is received and experienced.

debate: A discussion or argument that presents both sides of a topic. A debate can be formal, such as a televised debate between politicians. Formal debates take place in public, are guided by rules, and are overseen by a moderator. (See also The Reference Shelf, pages 455–458.)

definition: A statement or explanation used to clarify the meaning of words or concepts.

denotation: The basic or specific meaning of a word without associated ideas or emotions. See also **connotation**.

dialogue: A conversation between two or more characters. Dialogue is often used to reveal character and conflict.

diction: The deliberate choice of words to create a specific style, atmosphere, or tone. Also, depending on purpose and audience, writers may use slang, colloquialisms, jargon, or formal or informal levels of language. (See also The Reference Shelf, pages 402–403.)

drama: A story written in the form of dialogue intended to be acted out in front of an audience. It consists of plot complication and resolution, character revelation, conflict, setting, and theme. *Leaving Home* is a drama.

dramatic monologue: See **monologue**.

editorial: a newspaper or magazine article giving the opinion of the editor, publisher, etc. regarding a subject.

essay/magazine article/supported opinion piece/personal essay/literary essay: Non-fiction prose that examines a single topic from a point of view. It requires an introductory paragraph stating the main or controlling ideas, several paragraphs developing the topic, and a concluding paragraph. The title often identifies the topic. Formal essays are usually serious and impersonal in tone. Personal or informal essays reveal the personality and feelings of the author and are conversational in tone. "What's In This Toothpaste?" and "What I Have Lived For" are examples of this type of non-fiction writing. Essays can be informational, persuasive, argumentative, or literary.

An **informational essay** provides information to the reader. It has supporting details and frequently involves some analysis of the information presented.

A **persuasive essay** uses supporting details and argumentation to persuade the reader to accept the writer's point of view.

An **argumentative essay** argues for or against a question or a position on a topic, issue, and so on.

A **literary essay** discusses and analyzes themes, characters, meanings, etc. of a work of literature. "Poetic Techniques and Themes in the Poem 'Erosion'" is a literary essay.

etymology: The historical origin and development of a word. Most dictionaries provide the etymologies of words. (See also The Reference Shelf, pages 400–402.)

eulogy: A speech or writing in praise of a person, action, etc.

explicit meaning: An idea or a message that is stated directly by the writer. For example, David Suzuki explicitly states in his essay that "[a]dding another three billion people [to the planet] will be disastrous unless we start reducing our impact now." See also **implicit meaning**.

exposition: A piece of writing that presents information, explains ideas, or presents an argument. It is a generic term for writing that is not drama, narration, or description. An example is "How Does a Word Get into the Dictionary?"

extended metaphor: See **metaphor**.

flashback: A device that shifts the narrative from the present to the past, usually to reveal a change in character or illustrate an important point. "To Everything There Is a Season" is presented almost entirely as a flashback in which an adult narrator looks back at a time when he was 11 and just on the verge of entering the adult world.

flyer: A printed notice used to advertise a product or service.

foreshadowing: Refers to clues that hint at what is going to happen later in the plot. Foreshadowing is used to arouse the reader's curiosity, build suspense, and help prepare the reader to accept events that occur later in the story. Some people may argue that the discussion of fugu poisoning, which caused the death of the narrator's mother, in "A Family Supper" is possibly a fore-shadowing of the fate of the family.

glossary: A list of special, technical, or difficult words with definitions or comments.

graphic organizer: A chart, graph, Venn diagram, or other visual aid used to record, organize, classify, analyze, and assess information.

image/imagery: A picture created by a writer using concrete details, adjectives, and figures of speech that gives readers a vivid impression of what or who is being described. The descriptions of the grandmother in "To Set Our House in Order" clearly convey an image of a woman who was icy, lacking in affection, and emotionally distant from the narrator. Similes, metaphors, personification, and symbols are all specific kinds of imagery.

implicit meaning: An idea or message that must be inferred by the reader. The theme of a short story or the qualities of the characters, for instance, are rarely stated directly, but can be inferred from details provided in the story. For example, we can infer from "Erosion" the awesome power of nature. See also **explicit meaning**.

informational essay: See **essay** and **exposition**.

interior monologue: See **monologue**.

interview: A recorded discussion, usually structured in a question–answer format. Examples of interviews are those between an employer and a job applicant, a reporter and a politician, an immigration officer and a new immigrant.

invective: Writing that denounces or is insulting to something or someone.

irony: A literary device that creates a contrast or discrepancy between what is said and what is meant, or between expectations and reality. For example, the reader is aware that Aloo in "Leaving" will never return home, despite his promise to do so. (See The Reference Shelf, page 419, for common types of irony.)

journal: A notebook that contains personal reflections and responses to writing, events, incidents, and people.

layout: A plan or design of a page of a book, advertisement, newspaper, or other printed material that shows the placement of the words and illustrations or photos. Layouts can be done by hand or by using computer software.

literary essay: See **essay**.

memoir: A form of autobiographical writing dealing with personal recollections of people or events. "Other Side of the Hyphen" is a memoir.

metaphor: A figure of speech that makes a comparison between two seemingly unlike things without using connective words such as *like* or *as*. An example is "lamb white days" in "Fern Hill," in which the narrator compares his days of youth with the pure whiteness of lambs, untainted by thoughts of age. See **simile**.

Sometimes writers use an **extended metaphor**—a metaphor that develops its comparison over several lines or paragraphs of a piece of writing or even throughout the entire piece. "99" has an extended metaphor of chess in which Wayne Gretzky is the wizard at the game.

monologue: A speech by one person telling a story, revealing character, or describing a humorous or dramatic situation.

A **dramatic monologue** is a form of poetry in which a character speaks to a definite but silent listener and thereby reveals his or her own character.

An **interior monologue** is a form of writing that reveals the inner thoughts of a character.

mood: See **atmosphere**.

narrative: Another word for story. Narratives have the following elements: plot, conflict, characters, setting, point of view, and theme. Narratives may be fictional or non-fictional, and include novels and (auto)biographies (or personal stories/narratives) as well as short stories and anecdotes.

narrator: The person or character who tells the story.

newspaper article/report/story: Non-fiction prose that informs readers about an event or issue. It has titles in the form of brief sentences (also known as headlines). The most important information appears first in a newspaper article so that the reader can stop reading once he or she has sufficient information on the topic.

obituary: An account of a person's life, character, or achievements published in a magazine or newspaper shortly after the person's death. "National Icon Was Larger Than Life" is an obituary of poet Al Purdy.

opinion essay: See **essay**.

paradox: An apparent contradiction that, upon deeper analysis, contains a degree of truth. The phrase "green and dying" in "Fern Hill" seems to be a contradiction. But on close analysis it contains some truth, since with each passing day, a person draws closer to his or her death— even at the height of youth.

parody: A humorous imitation of a piece of writing, film, or drama that mocks the original by exaggerating or distorting some of its salient features.

pathetic fallacy: A literary device in which nature or inanimate things are described in a way that is sympathetic or prophetic about events or the emotions of the characters. In "The Skater," the narrator's sense of fear and isolation is reflected in "the white, inviolate solitude" of the wilderness.

personal essay: See **essay**.

personal narrative: See **narrative**.

personification: A metaphor in which human attributes are given to inanimate objects. For example, the tattoo in "Tattooed" is made to come alive through the poet's description (e.g., "the rose writhe" and "the skull grin").

persuasive essay: See **essay**.

play: See **drama**.

plot: A series of events and the thoughtful interrelations of these events, their causes and effects, and so on; the main story in a narrative or drama. The main plot in "The Broken Globe" shows how a father and son drift apart because of their differing beliefs about the shape of the earth (science vs. religion). Years later, when the son's friend pays the father a visit, the father reveals his bitterness and continues to cling to his belief. (See also The Reference Shelf, page 420.)

poem/poetry: A unique form of writing about experiences, thoughts, and feelings, frequently divided into lines and stanzas, that uses compressed language, figures of speech, and imagery to appeal to readers' emotions and imagination. There are a variety of poetic structures with different requirements of length, rhyme, rhythm, stanza formation, and so on. (See also The Reference Shelf, pages 423–427, for types of poetry.)

point of view: The perspective from which a story is told. (See also The Reference Shelf, pages 422–423, for types of point of view.)

proposal: A plan, offer, or suggestion put forward for consideration. The information in a proposal is organized to support the proposed conclusion.

prose: Ordinary language or literary expression not marked by rhythm or rhyme is called prose. As Molière put it in *The Bourgeois Gentleman*, "All that is not prose is verse. All that is not verse is prose." The protagonist of the play is proud and pleased to find out that he has been speaking prose all his life and he didn't even realize it! This type of language is used in short stories, essays, and modern plays.

pun: A play on words. For example, in *Romeo and Juliet* (III, i), as Mercutio lays dying, he says, "Ask for me tomorrow and you shall find me a *grave* man." The word "grave" could mean both "serious" and "dead in the grave."

report: An oral or written account or opinion formally expressed, based on findings from investigation or inquiry.

research report: A form of non-fiction writing intended to inform an audience about a particular topic. It contains factual information that is carefully researched from authoritative sources. (See also The Reference Shelf, pages 429–433.)

résumé: A summary of a person's work experiences, skills, education, and interests.

review: A form of writing that discusses the good and bad points of a book, film, work of art, and so on. It usually provides a synopsis or description of the work and focuses on a few key aspects, using evidence to support arguments.

rhyme scheme: The pattern of end rhymes. A rhyme scheme is indicated by assigning each new end rhyme a different letter of the alphabet. For example, the rhyme scheme of the first stanza of Emily Dickinson's poem is *abab*. (See also The Reference Shelf, pages 423–425.)

role-playing: Assuming and acting the role of a character, fictitious or real, and using dialogue and/or gestures, appropriate to the individual, to present the character to an audience in an improvisation.

sarcasm: A cutting expression or remark.

satire: A literary work that ridicules human vices and follies, often with the purpose of teaching a lesson or encouraging change. "As You Can See from My Brand-Name Clothing, I Am Not Poor" takes a satirical look at society's consumerism.

setting: The place and time of a story, play, or poem. (See The Reference Shelf, pages 420–421.)

short story: A short fictional prose narrative having only one major character, plot, setting, and theme. The short story usually focuses on a single conflict, character, or emotional effect.

simile: A figure of speech that makes a comparison between two seemingly unlike things using a connective word such as *like* or *as*. An example is "there are delicacies in you/like the hearts of watches" in "There Are Delicacies." See **metaphor**.

speech: A public address, usually given in formal language, often to persuade an audience. William Faulkner's speech is delivered at the acceptance of his Nobel Prize.

stanza: A set number of lines grouped together to form units in poetry.

story: See **short story**.

storyboard: A series of panels with sketches and dialogue, representing the shots in an advertisement, film, or television program used, to plan a script for a film or video.

style: The particular way in which a writer expresses himself or herself in writing. It is the sum effect of the author's choice of voice, vocabulary, sentence structure, and use of devices such as imagery, onomatopoeia, and rhythm.

summary: A brief account giving the main points of a story or article.

suspense: The condition of being uncertain about an outcome, used by writers to create tension, excitement, or anxiety. In "Forbidden Clothes," readers are kept in suspense as to what Nasreen will decide: to keep the clothes or to return home to her parents.

symbol: A person, place, or thing that stands for both itself and for something beyond itself.

The broken globe in "The Broken Globe" symbolizes the conflict between the farmer's beliefs and those of the scientist.

syntax: The order or systematic arrangement of words in a sentence. In general, syntax makes the ideas expressed orally or in writing clear and easy to understand.

theme: A statement of the central idea of a work, usually implied rather than directly stated. One theme of "Snow White" is the cruelty of society toward people who are different.

thesis: A main or controlling idea or statement about a topic that a writer proposes and supports in an essay. The thesis in "Poetic Techniques and Theme in the Poem 'Erosion'" states that "Pratt emphasizes the power of the sea against nature and humanity through the use of parallel structure, repetition, and effective diction." See **topic**.

tone: The attitude a writer expresses toward his or her subject. The tone of writing may be formal or informal, personal or impersonal, angry or cheerful, bitter or hopeful, and so on. The tone of "Other Side of the Hyphen" is a mix of hopefulness, sadness, and regret.

topic: The subject that is being written or talked about. The subject of "Hey, It's Not as if I'm a Serial Killer" is the public relations profession. (Note: Topic and thesis are often confused: **topic** is the subject matter; **thesis** is the statement about the topic.)

topic sentence: A sentence that states the subject of a paragraph. The sentence "Students may also find that brand wars are being waged over the pop machine outside the gym" begins one of the paragraphs in "The Branding of Learning." The paragraph then continues to give evidence to support this statement.

typography: The arrangement, appearance, or style of printed words.

voice: This word has three different meanings in this textbook.

Verb voice refers to whether a verb is active or passive. The active voice is usually recommended since it tends to be more direct, hard-hitting, and forceful. The passive voice makes writing more formal and a little bit distant, and is most appropriate in formal, objective reports. (See also The Reference Shelf, page 404.)

Voice is also used in the context of oral presentations to discuss volume, clarity, etc., when speaking.

Voice also refers to the distinctive style or tone of an individual writer or speaker. "About Effie" has the distinctive voice of a young narrator who is worried and sad about the disappearance of the housemaid.

INDEX

Acknowledgements

Text

Other Side of the Hyphen by Lynn Teo, from *Duo-Tang Dynasty: The Chinese School Years* by Lynn Teo. Vancouver: Bonnie Day Press. **Erosion** by E.J. Pratt, reprinted from *Collected Poems* by E.J. Pratt, by permission of University of Toronto Press. Photograph of E.J. Pratt's notebook reproduced with permission from the E.J. Pratt Collection, Victoria University Library, Toronto. **What's in the Toothpaste?** by David Bodanis, from *The Secret House* by David Bodanis. © 1986 Simon & Schuster, New York. **Grandmother** by Pat Kertzman and **Esther's Comments** by Esther Leipper-Jefferson, from *Writers' Journal*, Vol. 20. No. 6. **What I Have Lived For** by Bertrand Russell, from *Autobiography of Bertrand Russell*, The Bertrand Russell Peace Foundation Ltd. **About Effie** by Timothy Findlay, from *Dinner Along the Amazon*, copyright © 1984 by Timothy Findlay. By permission of Penguin Books Canada Inc. **To Everything There is a Season** by Alistair MacLeod, from *Island: The Collected Short Stories of Alistair MacLeod* (Toronto: McClelland & Stewart, 2000). Used by permission of McClelland & Stewart, Ltd., The Canadian Publishers. **Getting Carried Away With Shoes!** by Alyse Frampton, *Smithsonian*, November 1999. Reprinted in *Reader's Digest*, July 2000. **Bizarro** cartoon by Dan Piraro. Reprinted by permission of Universal Press Syndicate. **What Do I Remember of the Evacuation?** by Joy Kogawa. Reprinted with permission of McClelland & Stewart Ltd., The Canadian Publishers. **My Canada** by Tomson Highway. Reprinted by permission of the author. **Green Grass, Running Water** by Thomas King, copyright © 1993 by Thomas King. All rights reserved. **How Does a Word Get into the Dictionary?** Copyright by Merriam-Webster Inc. Reprinted with permission from the publisher. For additional information visit Merriam-Webster OnLine at www.Merriam-Webster.com. **The Nobel Prize Speech** by William Faulkner, from *Essays, Speeches and Public Letters* by William Faulkner, edited by James B. Merriwether, copyright © 1965 by Random House, Inc. Used by permission of Random House, Inc. **Ultimate Discourse** by E.L. Doctorow, reprinted from *Esquire*, August 1986, by permission of *Esquire*. **Writers Don't Have to Explain** by Susan Swan. Originally presented as part of the Millennium Wisdom Symposium organized by the Robarts Centre for Canadian Studies at York University, Daniel Drache Director and Susan Swan Chair, 2000. **The Interview** by Uma Parameswaran, from *Contemporary Verse II* 13, 1. **Can the Inuit Keep Their Voice?** by Stephanie Nolen, from *The Globe and Mail*, July 25, 2000. Reprinted with permission from *The Globe and Mail*. **Those Anthropologists** by Lenore Keeshig-Tobias. Permission received from the author. First published in *Canadian Women Studies Journal*, 1983. **To Keep the Memory of So Worthy a Friend** by Ethel Wilson from *Mrs. Golightly and Other Stories*. Copyright © Ethel Wilson, 1961. Reprinted by permission of Macmillan Canada, an imprint of CDG Books Canada, Inc. **Costa Rica** by Michael Zack. Reprinted by permission of the author. **Chip** cartoon by Thach Bùi, *Toronto Star*, May 11, 2000. **And Baby Makes Six Billion** by David Suzuki. Reprinted by permission of the David Suzuki Foundation. **In Praise of the Printed Word** by Kiri Nesbitt, *The Toronto Star*, January 13, 2000. **Food** by Marcia Kaye from *Homemaker's*, October 2000. **Long Distance Calling** by Lenora Steele, from *Room of One's Own*, Vol. 22:3. **When I Heard the Learn'd Astronomer** by Walt Whitman, from *Leaves of Grass*. **Polaris** by Zoë Landale, *Room of One's Own*, Vol. 22:3. **Small Change Can Add Up to a Big Loss** by Ellen Roseman, *Toronto Star*, March 26, 2000. Reprinted with permission from The Toronto Star Syndicate. **Will We Plug Our Computers into Our Brains?** by William Gibson, *Time*, Vol. 155, no. 25, pp. 54, 56. **The Broken Globe** by Henry Kreisel, from *The Almost Meeting*. Reprinted by permission of NeWest Press. **To Set Our House in Order** by Margaret Laurence from *A Bird in the House* by Margaret Laurence. Used by permission of McClelland & Stewart, Ltd., The Canadian Publishers. **Unnatural Causes** by Lillian

Allen from *Wanna Do This Everyday*, Women's Press, Toronto, © 1993. Reprinted by permission of the author. **The 1st** by Lucille Clifton. From *Good Women: Poems and a Memoir 1969-1980* by Lucille Clifton. Copyright © 1987 by Lucille Clifton. Reprinted by permission of BOA Editions, Ltd. **Going Up (and Down) in the World** by Alex Sprintsen, *The Globe and Mail*, October 17, 1990. **Many Canadians Are Made to Feel Like Strangers in Their Homeland** by Shellene Drakes, *Toronto Star*, January 29, 2000. Reprinted with permission from The Toronto Star Syndicate. **Stereotypes Are For Others** by Maria Coletta McLean, *Toronto Star*, September 6, 1994. Maria Coletta McLean is the author of *My Father Came from Italy*, published by Raincoast Books. **Picture of Erick Off Baranof Island, Alaska** by Nancy Pagh, *Grain Magazine*, Vol. 28, no. 1. **A Small Place** Part One from *A Small Place* by Jamaica Kincaid. Copyright © 1988 by Jamaica Kincaid. Reprinted by permission of Farrar, Straus & Giroux, LLC. **Postcard** by Margaret Atwood from *Selected Poems 1966-1984*, copyright © Margaret Atwood 1990. Reprinted by permission of Oxford University Press Canada. Excerpt from **The Pearl** by John Steinbeck, copyright © 1945 by John Steinbeck, © renewed 1973 by Elaine Steinbeck, Thom Steinbeck and John Steinbeck IV. Used by permission of Viking Penguin, a division of Penguin Putnam Inc. **The Average** by W.H. Auden from *New Year Letter* by W.H. Auden, Faber & Faber, 1964. **Zits** cartoon reprinted by permission of King Features Syndicate. **National Icon Was Larger Than Life** by Val Ross, *Globe and Mail*, April 24, 2000. Reprinted with permission from The Globe and Mail. **Lament for the Dorsets** by Al Purdy from *Selected Poems*. Reprinted by permission. **Archetypes** by Suniti Namjoshi from *From the Bedside Book of Nightmares*. **Turning Points** by Susan Klauber, from *Face-Off at Center Ice* by Susan Klauber, Blue Light Press, Fairfield, Iowa. **99** by Mark Cochrane from *Boy Am I*. Reprinted by permission of Wolsak and Wynn. **Ex-Basketball Player** from *The Carpentered Hen and Other Tame Creatures* by John Updike. Copyright © 1982 by John Updike. Used by permission of Alfred A. Knopf, a division of Random House, Inc. **Tattooed** from *Collected Poems* by William Plomer published by Jonathan Cape. Used by permission of

The Random House Group Limited. **Barn Door Detail** by Rob Filgate, *The Fiddlehead*. Excerpt from **Murder on Location** by Howard Engel, Penguin Books Canada, 1986. **The Road Not Taken** by Robert Frost from *The Poetry of Robert Frost* edited by Edward Connery Lathem. Copyright © 1969, by Henry Holt & Co., LLC. Reprinted by permission of Henry Holt & Co., LLC. **Which Is Better: College or University?** by Ann Eby, *Toronto Star*, January 29, 2000. **Leaving** by M.G. Vassanji, from *Uhuru Street*. Used by permission of the Canadian Publishers, McClelland & Stewart, Toronto. **Gravity** by Alishya Schrauwen, *Toronto Star*, July 18, 2000, p. D1. **She, Plural** by Bibiana Tomasic. Used by permission of the author. **A Family Supper** by Kazuo Ishiguro. Copyright © 1982 by Kazuo Ishiguro. Reprinted by permission of the author and Rogers, Coleridge & White, Ltd., 20 Powis Mews, London W11 1JN. **A Visit of Charity** from *A Curtain of Green and Other Stories*, copyright © 1941 and renewed 1969 by Eudora Welty, reprinted by permission of Harcourt, Inc. **You Are What You Play** by Vincent Bozzi, *Psychology Today*, October 1989, p. 69. Reprinted with permission from *Psychology Today Magazine*. Copyright © 1989 Sussex Publishers, Ltd. **Forbidden Clothes** by Jamila Gavin. Copyright © 1992 by Jamila Gavin. Reprinted by permission of David Higham Associates. **Slaughtering Chickens** by Charles Finn, *Globe and Mail*, May 8, 2000, p. A16. Excerpt from **Fugitive Pieces** by Anne Michaels. Reprinted by permission of McClelland & Stewart. **Kate's Poem** from *Look Through My Window* by Jean Little. Text copyright © 1970 Jean Little. Reprinted by permission of HarperCollins Publishers, Ltd. **Fern Hill** from *Dylan Thomas: The Poems*. Reprinted by permission of David Higham Associates and the Trustees for the copyright of Dylan Thomas. **Wild Horse Shakes Her Mane** from *T'ai Chi Variations* by Sandy Shreve, *The Fiddlehead*, No. 203. **The Agony Behind the Ecstasy of the Dance** by Janice Mawhinney, *Toronto Star*, March 25, 2000, p. J3. Reprinted with permission – The Toronto Star Syndicate. **The Story of Nil** from *Children of My Heart* by Gabrielle Roy. Copyright © 1977 by Éditions Alain Stanké Ltée. Translation by Alan Brown copyright © 1979 McClelland & Stewart Ltd. Used by permission from McClelland & Stewart, Ltd., The Canadian Publishers. **There Are Delicacies** from *Selected Poems 1950-60*, reprinted by permission of McClelland & Stewart Ltd., The Canadian Publishers. Excerpt from **Leaving Home**, copyright © 1972 by David French. Reprinted by permission of Stoddart Publishing Co. Limited. **Lo Linkert** cartoon from *Reader's Digest*, May 2000. Reprinted by permission of the artist. **Children's International Television Charter** reprinted by permission of the Philippine Children's Television Foundation and Consultative Group on ECCD Website. **One's a Heifer** from *The Lamp at Noon and Other Stories* by Sinclair Ross. Used by permission of McClelland & Stewart Ltd., The Canadian Publishers. **One's a Heifer** Television Adaptation by Rudi Dorn of "One's a Heifer" from *The Lamp at Noon and Other Stories* by Sinclair Ross. Used by permission of The National Film Board of Canada. **Will I Still Be Addicted to Video Games?** by Chris Taylor, *Time*, Vol. 155, no. 25, June 19, 2000. © 2000 Time Inc. Reprinted by permission. **Advertising's Glossy New Face** by Nick Krewen, *Toronto Star*, March 26, 2000, p. E5. Reprinted by permission of the author. **The Seeds of Pop Stardom** by Ariel Teplitsky, *Toronto Star*, February 17, 2000, p. L3. Reprinted with permission – The Toronto Star Syndicate. **The Branding of Learning** from *No Logo* by Naomi Klein. Reprinted by permission of Random House. **Mixed Media** cartoon. © 1995 Tribune Media Services, Inc. All rights reserved. Reprinted with permission. **M&M's Plain Candies are Switching to the Sweet Sound of Milk Chocolate** by Courtney Kane, *Toronto Star*, July 3, 2000, p. C2. **Hey, It's Not as if I'm a Serial Killer** by David Israelson, *Toronto Star*, July 3, 2000, p. A13.

Every reasonable effort has been made to acquire permission for copyright material used in this text, and to acknowledge such indebtedness accurately. In particular, we would appreciate any information regarding the copyright holders of **Snow White** by Grace Hu and **As You Can See From My Brand-Name Clothing, I am Not Poor** by M. Lucas.

Illustrations

Paul Watson/3 in a Box: Activity Icons, 317; Thom Sevalrud/i2i art inc.: 89; Kevin Ghiglione/i2i art inc.: 114; Nicholas Vitacco: 122; Eric Colquhoun/3 in a Box: 155; Susan Leopold: 179, 289; Mark Gabriel: 197; Oleg Koulikov/3 in a Box: 241; Rose Zgodzinski/3 in a Box: 259; Laurie Lafrance/3 in a Box: 269.

Photographs

Joseph Sohm, ChromoSohm Inc/CORBIS: 52; T. Atherton/Ivy Images: 76; Al Purdy/International Festival of Authors (Frank O' Connor): 86; Super-Stock: 126; Mark Synder/Ivy Images: 216; H. Huntley Hersch: 297.